THE
MODERN
WOMAN'S
GUIDE TO
LIFE

THE
MODERN
WOMAN'S
GUIDE TO
LIFE

by
ELIZABETH CHAPMAN,
MAGGIE KASSNER,
KAREN KRIBERNEY
and a bunch of other babes

Illustrations by Elizabeth Chapman

PERENNIAL LIBRARY

Harper & Row, Publishers, New York
Cambridge, Philadelphia, San Francisco
London, Mexico City, São Paulo, Singapore, Sydney

FIRST EDITION

Library of Congress Cataloging-in-Publication Data

Chapman, Elizabeth, 1952–
    The modern woman's guide to life.

    Includes index
    1. Women—Life skills guides.   I. Kassner, Margaret
II. Kriberney, Karen.   III. Title.
HQ1221.C48   1988   640'.43'088042   88–45019
ISBN 0-06-055116-X
ISBN 0-06-096248-8 (pbk.)

93 RRD 10 9 8

*This book is dedicated to
our mothers:*

*Maxine Hood
Jean Jaszi
Marie Kassner*

CONTENTS

Introduction ix

CHAPTER 1: Women at Work 1

CHAPTER 2: Modern Moolah 31

CHAPTER 3: Solo Acts 47

CHAPTER 4: Modern P'S & Q's 55

CHAPTER 5: Modern Men 77

CHAPTER 6: Modern Merchandise 107

CHAPTER 7: The Vanities 119

CHAPTER 8: The Modern Mode 137

CHAPTER 9: Home Ec 153

CHAPTER 10: Modern Vegetation 237

CHAPTER 11: Modern Woman at Ease 261

CHAPTER 12: Modern Women in Distress 295

CHAPTER 13: The Medicine Cabinet 307

CHAPTER 14: Modern Run-Arounds 353

CHAPTER 15: Miss, Mrs. or Ms. Cellaneous 403

CHAPTER 16: The Modern Mom 419

Contributors 445

Index 453

THE MODERN WOMAN: Introduction

What's a Modern Woman to do?

How about the laundry, dropping off the kids, getting ready for work, shopping, cooking, cleaning and entertaining, just for starters? We're the busy gender, desperate for a moment's rest and usually getting none.

We thought it was interesting that *The Modern Man's Guide to Life*, our companion volume, was written after some modern men went out trying to buy tropical fish for an apartment aquarium and couldn't find any guys to give them good advice on the subject. What Modern Woman has time for that kind of stuff? Nobody we know.

In fact, the last words in this book are about tropical fish — which goes to show that if you really want to know something, ask a Modern Woman. And between here and there, you'll find thousands of other tips, hints, observations, opinions and a few good stories — all compiled with the aim of giving you a smoother passage through what is bound to be another busy day.

* * *

By the way, this isn't the only book on the market for women. Almost every week, *The New York Times Book Review* carries a lengthy notice about a book written by a woman — generally, a woman who teaches Women's Studies at some college — about Women.

Sometimes, the book is about Women and History. Sometimes, the book is about Women and Men. Occasionally, it's a book about Women and Art or Women and Politics or Women and Women. The review is almost always written by another woman who teaches Women's Studies at some other college — although from time to time, the *Book Review* allows a woman who has written a novel about women to carry the critical flashlight.

This goes on week after week (one recent streak ran eight weeks). But despite its title and intended audience, this book will not be reviewed in The New York Times Book Review. It has no pop-psychological patina, no historical revisions, no self-help theological theory, no rhapsodic rhetoric designed to take the edge off careful discourse, and it does not aspire to add to the academic accretion of women's books. This book will not help you explain why you do the crazy things you do. Instead, this book is intended to make getting through your day a little easier so that you'll have more time to *do* the crazy things you do.

Once, women like us were educated by mothers, grandmothers, aunts, older sisters and other assorted females on how to do practically everything — and how to look swell while doing it. No more — and more's the pity. After all, what does grandma know about hiring and firing office help?

But somebody out there knows. And they told us. And, sister, we're telling you.

* * *

Readers of *The Modern Man's Guide to Life* will be familiar with the method by which we have come to possess the information in this volume. We circulated a request for helpful hints on almost every aspect of modern life we could think of. Our assumption was that everybody's an expert at *something*. So we asked women — and men — to give us their take on some aspect of the daily grind that they had mastered. We sent our letters to friends and asked them to photocopy it and give it to other friends and so on. This, we thought, is a terrific way to write a book.

The replies we received were interesting and informative and sometimes entertaining and bizarre. But they were all useful to one degree or another. And while this book doesn't pretend to produce any scientific data, the people we heard from also provided us with a look at the stereotypical Modern Woman, many of whom are not pleased about living in a society that sends its children off to day-care centers and its parents off to old-age homes so everyone else can go skiing and buy BMWs. Modern Women are tired of situational ethics and living by political and social fashion. They expect no special treatment — just *fair* treatment.

* * *

If much of the information in this book seems commonplace and conventional, it is. After all, what a women needs to know about cars, clothes, careers and carpentry really hasn't changed that much. And if it seems we've neglected to provide every answer, we've at least tried to give you enough information to ask useful questions.

We want to know what we've missed. If you think of something that you think should be in a future edition of *The Modern Woman's Guide to Life*, say so. Send your material to

The Modern Woman
P.O. Box 4709
Hampden Station
Baltimore, MD 21211

We'll probably rewrite and edit what you have to say, and we can't give you anything more than a pat on the back and a promise to list your name in the book. But Modern Women everywhere will appreciate your contribution.

* * *

We owe heavy for this book. For acknowledgements and a list of contributors, please see our back pages. (EC, MK, KK)

A MODERN DISCLAIMER

This book costs a lot less than an hour of professional advice on almost any subject covered here. So it stands to reason that if you really want help solving some of life's more vexing problems, you ought to go out and get some expensive professional advice. You get what you pay for, as they say, and what you won't get in this book is a substitute for the care and advice of people who are paid to dispense such care and advice. The contents of this book are for information only.

Women at Work

Modern Women know that the best job is the one that pays the most money for the least amount of work.

In the best of all possible worlds, women would work to gain personal fulfillment or intellectual stimulation. But in the real world, most women work for one reason — to earn a living. After all, the prevailing economic climate has done more to make the workplace coed than all the social legislation put together.

So, for most women, holding down a job is not an option, it's a necessity. After all, what right-thinking person *wants* to spend most of her time turning a profit for somebody else? And as for personal fulfillment, the chances are you won't find it coming off an assembly line, and it sure didn't roll behind your desk.

The sad fact is, there are only a handful of jobs that can offer anything more than some walking-around money and a reasonable social atmosphere. If you're looking for the meaning of your life at work, you're looking in the wrong place.

Navigating the waters of the working world can be risky business. It's usually not enough just to be on time, do your job well, and go home. A lot of women have to work harder, longer and better to be respected — and maintain a homelife involving a husband and children on top of it. So what's a poor working girl to do?

Well, what a Modern Woman doesn't want to do is take it all like a man. The greater glory of the daily grind won't fool the Modern Woman.

C O N T E N T S

Chapter One: *WOMEN AT WORK*

**FAMILY FEUDS: Compromising — The Best Boss —
WHEEL OF FORTUNE: Getting in the Door —**
Tripping **— THE PLANET OF WORKING WOMEN:
Passports, Please — The Daily Diary — Best Behavior
—** Wrong Moves **— Woman's Burdens — Dumb Guys
— Fault Lines — Trust Yourself — Psyching Up — Do
Say So Yourself — Overtime — Sick or Tired —** Work
Injuries **— Das Love Boot — Sexual Harrassment —
POLITICS: One of the Boys — Self-Defense — Dealing
with Adversaries — Life Before Promotions — Raise
and Call — Uniforms — MINDING MEETINGS:
A Good Scout — A Minute's Worth — Tempus in a
Teapot — Plenary Lore — SPEAK EASY: Say What?
— Ahead of the Weather — LIFE AT THE TOP:
Executive Actions — Ready, Aim — The Size of
Resignation — The Terminatee — All the People —
I Love Ya, You Jerk — Reprimands — Incentive Plans
— Away in a Manager — NETWORK NEWS —
SMALL BUSINESS: How Much Money? — Control
Yourself— Open the Money Dam — Marketing
Surveys — House Work — The Home Office — Risky
Business — Type-A — Whoa, Pardner — Location,
Location, Location — But, Buy — Record Keeping —
Drive-Thru — KARD KRAZY: What Your Card
Should Look Like**

FAMILY FEUDS

For the single woman, the workplace often offers a support system and a ready-made family. You share a common goal and your efforts are recognized. But while your nine-to-five world may be just great and very rewarding, your emotional life away from work may be a total wreck.

COMPROMISING

First, a dash through the mother *versus* job question. Then to work.

A modern woman can't have it all unless she wants to trade the quantity of experience with the quality. To be a good mother means giving less to a career, but to fulfill career goals may mean marriage and family suffer. At different times different areas will need more attention. Compromise is survival. (NSc)

Unfortunately, most women must work outside the home just to contribute to the basic needs of the family. However, you must weigh the disadvantages against the advantages. For instance, realistically ascertain how much money you can make given your experience, educational background, and other factors, then figure out how much you will be paying for reliable and safe child-care. And don't forget, you'll also have to spend money on transportation, clothes and meals.

If you'll be paying more than 50 percent of your earnings to child-care, it's not worth the effort and the probable guilt you'll experience of leaving your child somewhere everyday. (BN) **See** *Day Care* **in** *CHAPTER SIXTEEN: THE MODERN MOM*. *Don't go to work* if you really don't have to. You'll do a lousy job and your life will be miserable. (KLi)

THE BEST BOSS

Working for someone else — a faceless CEO in Detroit or a computer or even someone you know and like — can never be as rewarding as working for yourself, your love interest, or especially your children. Going out to work can be wonderful, but no amount of money or perks or accolades can replace or compensate for a mutually loving relationship. Believe me, your boss and coworkers aren't going to empty out the pan you've been throwing up in, or go with you to your aunt's funeral, or cry with you when your cat gets personal with the tires of a passing Ford. (LK)

A dissent: It's very difficult to come home after work and deal with dating or even a live-in relationship. At work, a woman has a sense of belonging, respect and is taken seriously — much more than she could expect from a relationship or even a marriage. Some women choose work over love, marriage or children just for these reasons. I know where I stand at work, much more than I do with a man or even my friends. (GL)

WHEEL OF FORTUNE

Finding the right job can be a matter of luck as much as anything else. Still, there are ways to increase your control of your job search.

GETTING IN THE DOOR

Start with friends: When you're broke and you need a job, the situation has a touch of urgency that should eliminate any shyness on your part. Call all your friends — and acquaintances — and let them know you're looking for a job, ask if they have any leads. Walk right along the edge of presumption. Ask the people you know to do the things that you think you'd do for them if they were in your boat. Then don't forget who helps and who ducks out. (BP) If you're married, ask your husband to keep an ear open during his business day for any possible job openings. Run through the list of family members who might have a connection or two you can exploit. Learn to love your in-laws, especially if they can help you land an interview. (ED)

Get your résumé ready: It's a good idea to have your résumé written by a professional résumé writer. A pro résumé writer can make the job filing papers you had three years ago sound as if you quietly and single-handedly saved IBM from bankruptcy. (PL)

Read all about it: Check the Sunday classified ads only. Spend the week sending résumés and cover letters and phoning prospects for interviews. Most companies advertise only on Sunday to get the most for their money. (BD)

A dissent: If you're a professional looking for work, you'll *never* find one by looking in the classified ads. By the time professional jobs appear in the classifieds, they've already been filled. Often, employment laws make it necessary to advertise jobs — even when the company has already chosen its own candidate. Academic institutions are the biggest perpetrator here. *(Anon.)*

Be persistent! Try to get through to the head honcho, not just his secretary. This way, you can get a better feeling about the company and any chances you have of being employed there. (NA)

Join up: Want to get back into the work force? Join associations and clubs — anything from Toastmasters to the PTA (but *not* the PTL). After becoming acquainted with various people, you'll hear about job openings and you can just ask around. Once people know you socially, they'll be more likely to be on your side. (CR)

The first step: When you get to the interview stage of applying for a job, prepare for it as if it were a test by doing your homework. Do as much research as you can on the firm you're applying to. Try to be familiar with the product or service the company offers. Get any information you can on your possible employer and tailor your presentation to fit the company image. (AG)

Arrive early. Go into the restroom to comb your hair. Run hot water on your hands so

that they will feel human for the handshake. You want the blood to flow as if you were a living person, and you don't want your hands to be sweaty. You absolutely cannot fly from the street straight into the office of the interview. You *must* stop in the restroom first. If the building has no restroom, then you don't want to work there anyway. You need to be composed. (DL)

The minute you step into the building, be polite to every single person you see. Treat everyone graciously. Don't ruin your chances by being abrupt with the receptionist or anyone else. Besides, it is only right to treat everyone well, regardless of whether or not you think they can help you.(SI)

Be prepared: Come to the interview with all of your paperwork (résumé, references, permits, licenses, etc.) prepared and organized. Try to come up with some good reasons to explain why you want to join this particular firm and, more importantly, why they should want to hire you. During the interview, remember not to fidget. Sit quietly and try to appear calm and composed. Hold up your end of the conversation, but don't try to dominate the interview. (AH)

There is a whole list of standard interview questions. They seem so silly, but be prepared, because interviewers really ask them. Go to the library and find books on the subject of the job search. You'll find the list. Read it. (AJ)

Approach with a sense of adventure. You are walking into an office where you have never been to speak to a person you have never seen. It's exciting, even amazing. (RO)

Interview the interviewer in a *very* subtle way. After all, you are preparing to give hours and months and years to this job. It had better be the one that you want. Besides, interviewers want you to ask questions. It shows you've been thinking. But never dominate the show. Ease yourself in there with grace. (MF)

Eye-to-eye: Look the interviewer in the eye. Smile now and then. (TF)

Scaling the heights: It's really something the way interviewers always sit about one foot higher than the interviewee. They must do something to the cushions in the chairs. The interviewee always feels like a fourth grader come to see the principal. You know. Once you sit down, the interviewer's desk is about at your chin level. It's like going to court. (SL)

The interviewer is not God. Maybe the interviewer doesn't like interviewing. Maybe the interviewer is even nervous. Interviewers have to play a game, just like you, so approach the situation as one human being to another, with decency and respect, not like an awed subject before royalty. (PJ)

Brown's axiom: Less is more. Don't go on and on. The interviewer leads and you follow. It's a dance. Answer the questions. (MK) **See also** *The Simple Rule of Conversation* **in** *CHAPTER FOUR: MODERN P's & Q's.*

Be discreet: Never never never ever cut down your former employer or bitch about your last job. Don't gossip. Don't complain. You want to be as honorable as possible. People want to be able to trust you. You want to be a person who can be given secrets and be relied upon to keep them safe. (KM)

Don't be proud: When being interviewed for an entry-level position, ask the personnel manager if there is any other position similar to the one for which you've applied that might open in the company. Let the interviewer know that you're really in need of a job, that you are willing to start at the bottom and that you would give your all to the company. (RP)

Don't fidget: Stay where you are. If the interviewer leans *waaaay* back, don't lean forward to compensate. It's a power thing to lean *waaaay* back. Just stay as you are. Don't fold your arms in front of you. Sit straight, keep your arms relaxed, don't smoke, and look into the eyes of the interviewer. (AB) Remember your hands. Don't let them wiggle around or twitch. If you walk into the interview with a pencil or pen in your hand you'll end up playing with it. Some people still think pens and pencils are phallic symbols, and you don't want to give anyone the wrong idea. (TF)

The last word: After the interview, send a note of thanks. (EE)

THE PLANET OF WORKING WOMEN

Sometimes it seems we are strange visitors in a strange land.

PASSPORTS, PLEASE

Entering the business world, a traditional male territory, can be terrifying, especially for an older woman. But women have shown themselves to be more competent and honest in business because they've *always* had to be this way in their customary role. So have no fear — managing an office and dealing with clients and the eccentric personalities of coworkers is nothing compared to keeping a family running. (DL)

THE DAILY DIARY

Keeping track: Women entering the work force are often intimidated by the role models they have chosen. As much as one might like to emulate these paragons, it can be difficult when starting out to envision oneself enjoying such success. One way to deal with this feeling is to keep a daily journal. In the beginning, it can allow you to savor your small successes; as time goes by, it can give you a reliable measuring stick of your progress. (ANP)

BEST BEHAVIOR

Busting chops: Modern Women should understand the difference between assertive and aggressive behavior — in men's terms.

Be aware that while you may think you're conducting yourself in an eager-to-get-ahead way, some men will consider you a hard-assed, nickel-plated bitch and will probably spread stories that you're a dyke. This cannot be avoided, but it can be handled by ignoring it and getting on with business. But first make sure you *aren't* acting like a hard-assed, nickel-plated bitch. (LBY, MK)

WRONG MOVES

Undynamic entrance

Too many frills

Lack of eye contact

Large emotion

WOMAN'S BURDENS

Slack is something that often remains uncut for a Modern Woman at work. Men are often eager to misunderstand women's behavior. Don't make their job easy for them.

Don't ever cry at work. You'll put yourself into a second-class position. You'll be seen as a person who doesn't have what it takes to play the game. (LB)

Take it home: If you think you'll burst into tears any minute, think again. If you can't wait until you get home to let the tears flow, duck into a restroom. *(Anon.)*

One of the only emotions open to a man in the business world is anger. It does not mean as much as when a woman shows anger, and it is important for a woman to remember that. Think of tears. A man in tears in the office is a major event, while a woman in tears is only an unfortunate event. Anger in a man is just an unfortunate event. Don't let it blow you down. (LG)

Learn to take jokes, even though male humor can be aggressive and mean. Rough humor is a form of communication that is considered very acceptable between men in the business world. If you're going to be there, you'd better prepare for it and learn to make fast and humorous comebacks to these barely disguised attacks. (PJ)

Learn to love humor. In business, men are better at it than women. I've gone to a lot of interviews in my life, and the straightest, dullest ones are always given by women. They talk as if they have just finished reading the list of Fifty Most Asked Interview Questions. I want to burst out laughing: "Hey, are you seriously asking me with a straight face how I see myself five years from now? Did you just read that in your How To Interview book?" Maybe men ask the same questions, but they disguise them better, and they joke more. Sometimes I feel like I've just left a loony bin. But they learn what they need to learn, believe me. (BA)

DUMB GUYS

It's de rigueur for men to be stupid amongst themselves. Slaps on the back, a nasty joke or two, references to excrement and body parts are all part of the business world of men. When a woman comes on the scene, the men feel they can't loosen up in these old ways. We have to be lenient enough to allow them to feel at ease. But don't participate in this weird male camaraderie — it won't be appreciated. (FLi) As soon as a woman enters business meetings or dinners, it seems as though the men clam up, as if they can't be themselves. Women sort of represent a roadblock to them. (SMcP)

Women are competing with men for the same positions. Some employers will hire a woman over a man because they know they'll get superior work for a lot less money than they would have to pay a man. They know they're getting a great deal. Don't let them do it to you. (WK)

FAULT LINES

Oversights and mistakes happen. Men have a hard time coping with errors and tend to cover up their part in one. Women are so used to accepting the guilt of every situation that we are naturally more able to cope with a problem that really is our fault. So don't emulate the boys — cope with the problem. (TR) **See under** *Executive Actions*, **below.**

TRUST YOURSELF

Don't make every situation one in which you are compared to a man or your behavior to men's behavior. Women must learn to trust themselves when put in power positions. *There's no need to emulate men,* or act out some preconceived idea about handling situations as a man would handle them. That's a jerky idea. Use your natural instincts and forget all those preconceived notions. (BNo)

PSYCHING UP

Swat 'em on the fanny: In the business world, men often use sports metaphors in order to communicate with one another. If you are in a situation where this happens and you don't know what they are talking about, try to fake it, if you can. Ask a good friend later. Remember what you have learned for the future. (TB)

Learn team play. Remember, you don't have to like the people you are playing with to play with them. (FDD)

Face it: *you're never going to be one of the boys.* Unless you're a pro at softball, you're not going to want to play on the company team. You're not going to want to go out with the boys for drinks unless you want to give the impression that you're out there looking to pick someone up. You're not going to trade jokes in the locker room. You're not going to slap someone on the back unless you want to look like a dimwit. But you can get along and gain respect, anyway. Don't sulk about not making the softball team. Don't dwell on your hurt about being excluded. You know, doing a good job still means something out there. (LB)

Don't take competition in business life personally. If you do, it will kill you. (ED)

Don't expect praise for a job well done. You are supposed to do your job well, and if you do, you can expect to hear nothing. No news is good news. (CD)

But note: It's not good enough to just do a job well. You've got to make people *know* that you've done it. If you expect to sit back and be noticed just because you've done an excellent job, you're going to wait a long, long time. (SD)

Insecure people drive other people bananas. There is nothing more exhausting than trying to build up a person's ego time after time after time. It's not wrong for a person to be sensitive, but don't be so sensitive that other people see you as being on the verge of disintegration. It's just no fun to play with people like that. (CMu)

Avoid being compulsively thorough and sensitive and afraid of mistakes. Men see preoccupation with the details of a thing as an indication of insecurity. You have to get out there and barrel. (SL)

Don't forget that it's all a put-on. Don't be overwhelmed by the bluffing and big-boy strutting. Those big boys are worried about their hair falling out and what people think of them and how they're doing, just like every other human being. (AB)

A note to chronic victims: Men have worked their asses off for thousands of years. They suffer. They die early. Give 'em a break. They are not the enemy. (SC)

DO SAY SO YOURSELF

Although humility is a virtue, there are times when virtues can work against you. For instance, excessive modesty in the office can definitely stunt a promising career. If that project you worked on day and night for two weeks gets raves from your boss and you dismiss it by saying, "Oh, it was nothing," he might just believe you! If you invite others to belittle your abilities by leading the attack, don't be surprised when they follow your lead. (MK)

No doubt: If you have self-doubts, save them for your confidante or therapist. Don't discuss them at the office. (GS)

OVERTIME

Do not be afraid of extra work that may prove your ability to handle additional responsibilities. It is helpful if the extra work assigned or requested of you increases your visibility. If not, make your own opportunities — volunteer to help organize the employee picnic or the company Christmas party, for example. Keep in mind that it is wise to volunteer for activities that are favored by people higher on the ladder of success. Many times this can be an opportunity to show your organizational skills.(GS)

Overtime pay: If you are not specifically exempted from the overtime provisions stated in the Fair Labor Standards Act, you're losing money! You are due time and a half for any hour's work over a forty-hour work week unless you are an executive, administrative (this does *not* include secretaries) or professional employee. Certain other workers may also not be included, but such a circumstance will almost certainly be spelled out in your company's work rules. If you are due overtime pay, don't be reluctant to ask for it. It's your money and time, so know your rights. *(Anon.)*

SICK OR TIRED

No, I really **am** *sick:* Calling in sick is something even the most conscientious of us do every now and then. Whether it's some species of flu or just the need for a spontaneous day off, the challenge is to convince your boss that you really are sick. While we certainly don't condone lying, here are some tips to help you make your boss think of sending you a get-well card.

Be considerate. Call as soon as possible, preferably at the time you usually arrive. This shows that even though you may be dying, you're still a responsible individual.

Make sure you *talk directly to your boss* or supervisor. Messages left with secretaries or receptionists don't always make it to the top and could make it look as though you're being evasive.

Don't go overboard. If you spend ten minutes describing your symptoms in graphic

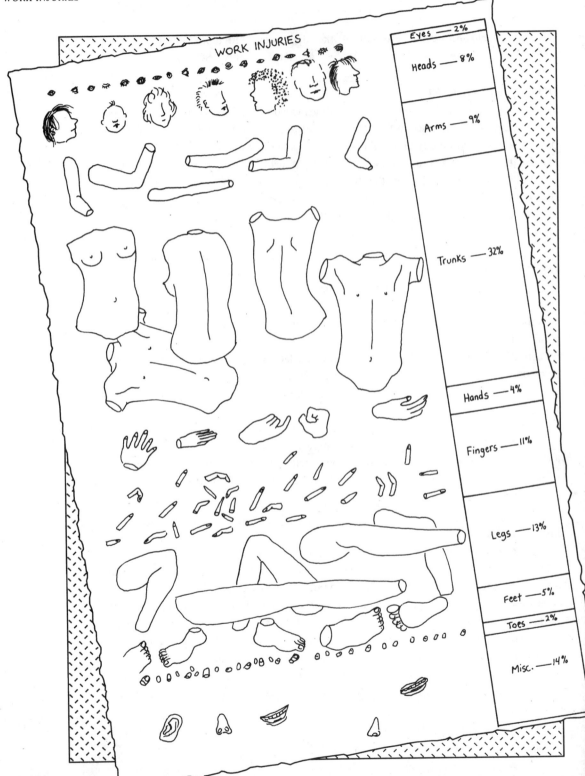

detail, it may be construed as overkill. Tell your boss what you think you have, when you think you'll be back to work, and how to handle any work you've left pending.

Finally, *don't push your luck.* Consider carefully — is this day off really necessary? Sometimes it's worth going to work with that annoying almost-cold just so that when you do call in sick, you'll be credible. (MK)

DAS LOVE BOOT

Dating a colleague is charting an unmarked course on the dangerous sea of love. If it doesn't work out, you'll both be drowning. Proceed only if you are willing to place the relationship over the job, because chances are you won't have the job for long. (GC) **See also under** *How to Meet a Lover* **in** *CHAPTER FIVE: MODERN MEN.*

SEXUAL HARASSMENT

Pure and simple: Sexual harassment is any activity defined by sex or sexual preference that creates a disadvantaged class. (GC)

Sexual harassment can be exhibited in many ways. If you're beginning to feel like you'd better get a quick sex change operation in order to do your job well, or keep the job, it's time to act.

• First, check around and see if other women on the job are getting the same treatment.

• Bounce your story off a friend. See if you're being too sensitive or somehow letting yourself open to the irritation.

• If the signals you're getting from Slimy Sam indeed do seem out of line, go to that person's superior, not as a woman in distress, but as a person whose function in the company is being diminished unfairly. You may even try to corner Sam by the water cooler and confront him with the situation to see what he has to say for himself. (GC, AD) **See** *JERK DEFENSE* **in** *CHAPTER FOUR: MODERN P's & Q's.*

Some women, just as some men, can be sexual antagonists. So what if you're a woman in power? Don't be an ass. (BNN) **See also under** *WORKING WONDERS* **in** *CHAPTER FOUR: MODERN P's & Q's.*

Don't abuse your power as a woman and claim sexual harassment as a strategy in some sort of personal vendetta against a man. There are plenty of women who really *are* victims, and their success in pursuing their cases can be hampered by eroding the credibility of the problem. Sexual harassment is a very serious charge. Make sure that sexual harassment is really what happened. *Once you're sure,* though, go get him. *(Anon.)*

POLITICS

Office politics share one thing in common with ordinary politics: it brings out the most despicable traits of our species. It creates corporate thugs out of dishonest people and dishonest people out of frightened ones.

The best way to handle a political issue at work is to duck it. *(Anon.)*

If you devote the time to polishing work skills that others devote to office politics, you will never have to worry about having or getting a job. (GC)

It's everywhere: The phrase *office politics* is really a misnomer since you don't need to work in an office to be confronted with the maneuvering and manipulation of the business world. In almost every job, from supermarket cashier to bank president, there's bound to be some competition for advancement, which generally provides fertile ground for backstabbing, dirty tricks and end runs.

You basically have *two ways to deal with office politics.* You can either try to ignore it and just do your job or you can roll up your sleeves and get down and dirty with the best of them. Each option has its own problems but the best way to deal with office politics is probably a combination of the two.

Pick your battles very carefully — try to avoid getting involved in conflicts that have only mediocre chances of getting you what you want. (PA, KK)

Be unpredictable. If your opponents aren't sure how you'll react or when, they'll have to be much more cautious about their own strategies, giving you more room to maneuver. (LK)

Silence is golden. Don't let anyone know your strategy for dealing with a situation. That way no one can jump the gun and head you off. (HG)

The throat: If you decide you must attack, don't use half measures — go straight for the kill. Being kind will only get you counterattacked by a wounded rival. (WK)

ONE OF THE BOYS

Here's the problem: You're in a work situation in which you could gain a lot by accepting invitations from co-workers for one of their frequent nights out. However, if you were to try to keep up the the boys you might end up with a perpetual hangover (not that you can't drink as much as they can, but proving it night after night can put a strain on even the best liquor tolerance). In addition, you may find that the company of your coworkers is not what you'd choose for the basis of your social life. But if you start declining invitations, you'll be looked at as an outsider and miss some important chances to make brownie points (unfortunate but necessary). So here are some ways to confront the problem and work your way around it:

• *Accept invitations* when you think doing so will do you some good. And make the most of the occasion — for example, if that position you've been angling for is suddenly open or things have been particularly tense around the office lately.

• *Suggest activities* that appeal to you and offer an alternative to an evening in a bar.

• *Tip off the waitress* or bartender to water your drinks.

• *Switch* to plain soda when you've had enough. After all, you have nothing to prove, right? (TK)

SELF-DEFENSE

War zone: Chances are someday you'll find yourself surrounded by the worst sort of co-workers, each of them armed with a knife and going for your flank. Here are some basic defense strategies:

Don't put it in writing. That way you can deny ever having had anything to do with it. Throw away your pens if you think a disaster is on its way. (MJ)

Along the watchtower: You've got to let people know that *you* know what is going on. And you need a large network of people on your side to help you know what you need to know. If you are aware of what is going to happen before it happens, you'll be prepared to deal with it. And people will be less apt to try and sneak up on you. They'll know there is no point. (LL)

There's always a snitch reporting everything to the boss. It's usually not particularly difficult to recognize this person. Try to be reasonably friendly to the snitch. There are many times when you will want to communicate something to your boss, but not in person. Let it drop to the snitch, and she will carry it to the boss. (SB)

A survivor speaks: It's pretty cutthroat where I work. People steal one another's ideas all the time. Now I keep a little journal going of who came up with what when, and who thought it was a swell idea and who didn't. That keeps things straight and makes it clear who's playing dirty. (EE)

Don't allow yourself to be intimidated by executives performing your same job. They're not performing on your fears. They're regular people, just like you. With time, you will be able to translate their thought patterns and language. This is really not what you want to do, but you can pretend with the best of them. (ND)

DEALING WITH ADVERSARIES

Be wary of new business relations who want to get into personal discussions. There are plenty of good reasons for letting time go by before making personal contact. A person expressing too much interest in your personal life may be looking for ammunition with which to shoot you down later on. (GC)

During your probationary period on a new job, concentrate on fulfilling the requirements of the job at the expense of creating personal relationships. (TRS)

LIFE BEFORE PROMOTIONS

Know your bosses: Understand their habits and schedules. Know when they are usually available and when they are unreachable. Know when a question on a quick memo will be simpler than an in-person question. Don't always go to your bosses with problems. You want to bring in good news from time to time so that you will not be dreaded. (LL)

At the beginning, do your job in a solid, satisfactory manner. Don't aim to shine like a star in heaven. Your boss will begin to feel that she hired the wrong person for the job. Do a decent job in the beginning. Shine a little later. (NNR)

Leapfrogging: Never take your concerns to your boss's boss. Going around your superior rarely pays. There is an order to these things, and if you step on someone's toes, you'll likely be sorry. (TT)

RAISE AND CALL

If you know, without a doubt, that you deserve a raise, ask for it. Don't just wander in one morning, flushed with new indignation, and demand more cash. Take your time and do your homework.

First, *do some research* to determine what others in your field and capacity are earning.

Schedule a meeting with your boss mid-week, preferably after lunch. With your usual camaraderie, *firmly state what you want* without being obnoxious or threatening.

Proudly *list your accomplishments* and contributions to the company. **See** *Do Say So Yourself,* **above.**

Don't discuss personal needs — you must make your superior feel she's gaining something, not making your house payment easier.

It's your job to *create an atmosphere of collaboration* not opposition.

Most of all, let your boss know you are true to your word and that everyone is going to benefit from your getting the raise. (LH)

One other thing: Be prepared to look for another job if your raise request is refused. Staying on is admitting you're not worth it. (HE)

UNIFORMS

You choose: No matter what, first you want to impress your boss; next, you want to make a good impression on your co-workers. And finally, you want to fit into the company's environment without sacrificing your individuality. But watch out if you have a flamboyant taste. Don't dress as if you were looking for confrontation; if your normal instinct is to dress to the nines, aim for someplace between four and five. *(Anon.)*

A dissent: This is America, after all. Wear whatever pleases you. Sure, if you're a woman climbing a ladder, wear pants, designer trousers, and if you're behind a soda fountain in Bakersfield, by all means, wear a skirt. But only if you want to. Try not to let your employer curb your tastes or inclinations unless it's a clear threat to the company's well-being. (KK) *See also CHAPTER TWO: MODERN MODES.*

MINDING MEETINGS

The best meetings are exceedingly brief and profoundly insightful. Hence, few have ever attended a good meeting. Worse, people who go to a lot of bad meetings eventually end up presiding over bad meetings of their own. Time to adjourn.

A GOOD SCOUT

Be prepared: Meetings usually fail because of a lack of preparation. Meetings should never just "happen." (JJ)

A MINUTE'S WORTH

Is this necessary? Ask yourself if the meeting is really worth having. Don't schedule a meeting simply because there has always been one on Thursday afternoons. Can you get the job done without it? Then don't have the meeting. Simple. (SS)

Calling endless meetings tells your staff that you place no value on their time. (BNo)

Send out an agenda a couple of days before the meeting. Let everyone have a chance to know what issues are going to be addressed. Ask for feedback before the meeting to be better prepared for potential boardroom violence. (RE)

Trench life: If you're calling a meeting between two factions, make sure beforehand that your faction agrees among itself so that you can present a united front. (BB)

Don't include every single soul in the meeting. Include only those who will be affected by it. You'll never come to any agreements if you involve everyone — except about the amount of time wasted. (HG)

Be seated: Take the head of the table. Give people a feeling that you are in control of things by having the agenda clearly printed on an easel. Look like you mean business. Appear calm and sit up straight. Remember what kids do to teachers who seem ill-prepared or nervous? They massacre them. (MM)

Listen up: Let other people give their opinions first; otherwise they may spend time agreeing with you. Rephrase contributions to be sure you understand clearly. Let people know you are really listening to them. Never criticize in a meeting. A lousy idea is a lousy idea. People will know it without anyone having to point it out. (FC)

Stick to the agenda: Don't let the discussion wander off the track, or you'll be there all day. However, if a valuable issue is raised, don't ignore it. Make a note of it, but get back to the agenda. (HH)

TEMPUS IN A TEAPOT

An hour is plenty for any meeting. When the hour is up, stop the proceedings unless there's a compelling reason to continue. Summarize the decisions that have been made before you end the meeting, and delegate responsibility to be sure decisions turn to action. (TE)

Timely advice: A great way to have employees arrive promptly for a meeting, and to keep it short and to the point is to schedule it at an odd time. For example, 11:40 A.M. or 4:20 P.M. (DD)

PLENARY LORE

An agenda agenda: Running a meeting is nobody's idea of fun, but if you have to do it, here are five simple rules to keep in mind:

1. Hire entertainment. (Just kidding!)

2. Keep your list of participants small – only those people who need to be there should be there.

3. Don't schedule too many topics. If you focus on just one or two issues, you'll get more done.

4. Try to look for workable solutions to problems instead of figuring out who was responsible for the problem in the first place.

5. Keep things as informal as possible. Parliamentary procedure is great for a political convention, but five people trying to figure out a great slogan don't need *Roberts' Rules of Order.* (MK)

SPEAK EASY

Modern Women know that style is sometimes a suitable substitute for substance — especially if the subject is something petty and you want to keep it that way. Besides, men are always listening for a shrill gaffe, so don't get your merds wixed up.

SAY WHAT?

Q & A: Try not to turn your statements into questions. Say, "He gave an excellent report." Don't say, "He gave an excellent report, didn't he?" Omit little phrases like "you know," "sort of," "well." Say what you have to say. (AL)

Women are more encouraging to a speaker than men are. Women tend to nod their heads and murmur in agreement and say "Is that so?" much more often than men do. When you are talking to men, don't become unnerved by their silence. Keep on truckin'. (GB)

Yeah, but. . . In a meeting, jump in and interrupt. Men interrupt one another all the time. If you sit there and wait politely for the speaker to finish, you will never get a chance, and everyone will think you have a vacant brain. (JMcE)

A dissent: Manners are manners. If a man interrupts, he's a boor. Same goes for a rude woman. (KK)

Altitude: First of all, you're shorter than everyone else. It is hard to be heard in a swarm of men six feet tall. You're going to have to make yourself heard *without* being shrill. Try folding your arms across the small of your back. That's what tall men do when speaking to children. Who knows? Maybe you can fool 'em! "Five foot two? Damn! All this time I had her figured at six-one!" *(Anon.)*

Wipe that smile: Consider your smiles. Smiles are often gestures of submission. They can indicate nervousness, apology, or can soften a negative message. They can be used to seek approval. They are more often used by women than by men. (CNC)

Don't blink: Woman gaze more than men gaze because they are usually in a position of less power and need to be ever-vigilant. The stare, on the other hand, is a sign of dominance. (KB)

Don't fidget when you talk. Don't use your hands. Sit on them. Don't tap your fingers or scratch your head. Don't shrug. Don't tilt your head. And while you're remembering all that, be natural at the same time. (LL)

AHEAD OF THE WEATHER

When I am expected to chit-chat I grow desperate. I sit in gatherings like a tombstone while a little tornado careens about inside my head. I feel it crashing against the walls of my skull. It is saying, "Oh my God, there *must* be something inside here that I can use." There never is. I *really* admire chit-chatters. Is it something in the genes? (EJ) **See also** *Talk Shoppe* **in** *CHAPTER FOUR: MODERN Ps AND Qs.*

LIFE AT THE TOP

So you finally made it to the upper echelon. Careful: It's not only lonely up there, it's also precarious.

EXECUTIVE ACTIONS

You're the Boss: Avoid hiring lots of people all at once. Try to take as much time as you can over as long a period as you can. Don't just hire the dazzlers. Fill most spots with plain, reliable types — a variety of plain, reliable types, for a variety of good ideas. (BL)

Hiring: Try to hire from within. It hurts morale when people inside a company see outsiders taking the jobs. If you do hire from outside, do it to fill the lower level jobs. If you fill the higher level jobs with outsiders, it will not reflect well on your past ability to make good choices. People will wonder why your own people lack the qualifications. (LL)

A dissent: Bring people in from the outside now and then to stir everyone up, get things cooking. (BB)

Oops! You've made a huge mistake. Admit it, and then analyze it. You want to avoid repeating your mistake, and you want to know how to improve. *Don't concentrate on what caused the problem.* Instead, figure out how it could have been avoided. (KLi)

Hire and higher: Looking to move up? The top dogs in your company will be reluctant to promote you unless you have prepared your department for the transition by already having someone on hand who can step into your place. How do you find that person?

Don't be afraid to delegate authority. You don't want a department that would collapse without you. Give people different kinds of responsibilities on different projects. See how well they cope.

Don't worry that your employee might do an even better job than you. After all, *you* hired the person. (DD)

A good hire shows insight on your part. Your superiors will recognize that quality and they'll also know that your department will run smoothly after your promotion. (KP)

Don't trust recommendations. A poor employee in a corporation is more likely to be shuffled here and there than fired. You'll have all kinds of departments calling you up trying to pawn the person off on you. They'll give you all kinds of fine recommendations. (PK)

Screening: Don't hire a person until she's been through at least three interviews with you and with other managers. Take prospective employees to lunch, too. See if they can survive it. (LM)

Steady on: Has the applicant had one job for years and years? This can make me just as wary as if that person had held ten jobs in ten years. It could indicate a lack of confidence. (BC)

Driven: Hire the way you drive — don't trust a soul out there. When you are given references, check them thoroughly. People will do everything they can to look their best during an interview, so, of course, it can be a time of complete dishonesty. Check the past. That is where the truth will be. (AW)

Whom do you love? I like to have both a male and a female on board for dealing with the public. Some clients don't deal well with women, and some don't deal well with men. So they have a choice. (JJ)

READY, AIM. . .

Fire: On the day that I have to fire someone, I vomit all morning before I leave for work. Having the power to change the course of someone else's life is not my cup of tea, but I have to keep my perspective. This one person is causing problems for ten other people. Do we all suffer? (PF)

The task of firing in a large corporation is extremely difficult. You are much more likely to face a lawsuit, because lawyers are much more likely to want to take a case against a huge company, particularly if the suit is filed on a contingency basis. So, before you fire, consider the courts of law. Do you have the evidence necessary to justify your action before a court? (MB)

Axe-wielding tyrants don't have productive employees, and neither do cowards. (SA)

Firing is a job. It is management's responsibility to see that everybody pulls her own load. When one person slacks off, everyone suffers. Initially, the others work harder because of it, but eventually their productivity falls, too. After all, why should they work their butts off if that one clown doesn't have to? (MB)

Gardening: You've got to weed out the bad, because bad employees are contagious. Because of them, everyone else will turn sour after a while. Bringing in new people now and then keeps the rest on their toes. (PK)

THE SIZE OF RESIGNATION

Style: This whole thing should happen with class. There are polite resignations and impolite resignations. An impolite resignation can ruin you for years and years. Believe me, everyone will hear about it. Your friends will hear about it. All those potential future employers out there will hear about it. Ten years later someone may *still* be hearing about it. You worked hard to make a good impression when you *arrived* at your job, didn't you? You'd better make a good impression as you *leave*, too.

Do it in person and with a letter. Tell your boss why you are leaving, suggest a termination date, and say something nice. Don't say the company has worms for brains. Don't say it is leading you to an early grave.

Be prepared to stay on at least two more weeks and maybe a month. *Don't leave them in a lurch.*

If you are job-hunting while still employed, keep it quiet. Interviewers at other companies will usually respect this and not call your current boss for information about you.

Leave as many good feelings behind as you can. *(Anon.)*

The best time to look for a job is while you have one. Everyone wants to hire a successful person. Nobody wants a desperate person. Never speak against the firm you are leaving — not to the people in the firm, and not to the people outside the firm. And, *especially* don't cut your old job down during your next interview.

Keep secrets to yourself. Spies are dirty. (PSD)

THE TERMINATEE

Getting fired is horrible, but you can make it easier on yourself. If you fly off the handle, it will only tell your employer that the decision to dump you was a pretty damn good decision, after all. And your recommendation will *really* reek. You may feel that you now hate your miserable boss with all your might, but treat that boss well. Not for his or her sake. Oh no, not for that. But for your sake. You can be nice for your own sake, can't you? (EC)

Problems? Be very sure you know just what the problems are. Be sensible. Maybe you deserve to be fired. This way you can learn from it and not repeat mistakes in the future. It takes a brave soul to take this without crying, but try to take it without crying.

Be sure you are aware of severance terms in the way of pay, benefits and so on. *(Anon.)*

What next? You'll need to know what this employer is going to tell a potential future employer. Ask what to expect.

If you feel that the firing was an act of discrimination, get your facts straight and your head clear. You will need good evidence. (LDB) **See under** *LAWYERS* **in** *CHAPTER TWELVE: WOMEN IN DISTRESS.*

ALL THE PEOPLE

If you're the boss, consider all the people involved in your company. That means the people working the lower level jobs. Take time to talk to everybody. Build relationships with the people in the typing pool and the mailroom and in maintenance. Each group is vital, so don't devote all your energy to the big boys and girls on the top floor. (FG)

Prove it: If you're the boss, you're going to have to prove yourself. It is assumed, until he proves otherwise, that a male boss knows what he is doing. It won't work that way for you, Cookie. (PJ)

I LOVE YA, YOU JERK

Giving constructive criticism is an art. Try to state the positive first. That way you get them all disarmed and receptive to the blow that's coming. (BA)

When you criticize, never attack the character of a person. Even where it's accurate and merited, the effect will be negated by bottom-line self-justification: "Well, that's just the way I am," they'll think. "I can't change the way I was born."

Besides, in most professional contexts, it's not only unnecessary, it's inappropriate to make personal jabs. (PO'C)

REPRIMANDS

Stress test: Telling a subordinate that the job she's doing is less than perfect can be stressful for both of you. You can make criticism easier for yourself and the recipient by understanding exactly what you want changed and improved. Offer your cooperation in sharing the problem, but be firm in your idea that the situation must be corrected. Avoid a personal attack. Once the problem is openly discussed, with possible solutions also discussed, acknowledge to the person that you're comfortable the problem can easily be corrected. Show faith! (MG)

Be specific: If something has been poorly done, be specific about what the problems are. Don't just say something's a mess and expect people to know what to do with it. (HH)

INCENTIVE PLANS

Make sure your employees have every chance to attend seminars and workshops that will help them out with their jobs. Give a lot of recognition for jobs well done. It's amazing how many bosses only open their mouths to criticize. (DL)

Give credit for an idea to the one who came up with it. Sounds simple, doesn't it? It greatly increases the number of great ideas. (PL)

Have parties—birthday parties, Halloween parties, project completion parties. Sounds corny, but it really creates a team feeling. Strengthening the social aspects of a place of employment makes people care about the whole unit, not just themselves. (JJ)

Treat them like adults. Don't make clucking noises or give reproving glances when someone arrives a few minutes late. Try not to treat your employees like truculent kids behind a fast-food counter. (FD)

Two ways: You can motivate through fear or through praise. It's pretty simple, isn't it? (FD)

A clue to appropriate conduct by a supervisor: Is she criticizing the work or the person? No one has to accept personally degrading, insulting or offensive behavior in the guise of "constructive criticism." When confronted by statements such as "How could you be so stupid?" or "You never get anything right!" demand that the person deal with the specifics of the job, not generalities or perceptions of personality. *Stay calm.* Don't lash back in the same manner as the buffoon who is acting childishly, but be firm in not submitting to intimidation. (SB1)

AWAY IN A MANAGER

*A **male boss*** can treat his employees like a crew of slaves, and folks will refer to him as "demanding." If a female treated her employees that way, there would be mutiny. (LO)

Yuk: I use a lot of humor. God, it really helps the world go round. The morale of my employees is crucial. (LL)

Sorry: If I am the one who needs to apologize, I go ahead and apologize. I *hate* to apologize, but when it must be done, it must be done. It can be the fastest and easiest way to solve a problem. (PK)

Name game: I know everyone's name. That means two hundred names. I spent hours and hours and hours learning them. It pays off. I learned this years ago when the owner of a store I frequently patronized remembered my name from the first day. Intellectually, I knew that his store was no better than the one down the street, but I was drawn to his every time. Even though I knew his remembering my name was just a tactic on his part, I could not resist shopping there. (KJ)

Vote on it: Ask advice from your managers before making a big decision. It's important to build a consensus. This is disturbing to some men who feel a boss should just charge ahead; they may think you're too soft. They are playing a risky game by not ensuring company support. (NC)

Home-grown: Develop managers who can run things — who can do more than simply follow orders. Keep a close eye on what's going on, but let the managers manage. Allow people to use their brains and you'll have people who enjoy their work and are more productive. (PH)

NETWORK NEWS

What you get from a network is information, one of the most precious commodities in a decision-maker's armory. Without good information, you are powerless.

Information has a wide range of ancillary perks, too. You can, for example, get referrals: Someone who doesn't know can give you the name of someone who does. It's horrible to be out in the cold, because you'll be the last to know anything. When you're on the inside, you'll hear it all. (CC)

Networking means using contacts to make your way in the world. It's a method of locating help and support just the way the Old Boys do. Just what do you suppose turns the world? Do you really think big people meet one another formally over a big boardroom table while obeying all the laws of God and government? They met over *dinner* first. Someone introduced someone to someone who knew something who shared it with someone else and they all went to dinner and had some drinks and remembered so and so whom they called afterwards and they made a few shortcuts through a little red tape, and *then* they went into the big boardroom. That's how it works. Get in on it. (AS) **See** *Getting in the Door,* **above.**

Cold cuts: This seems a little cold, but are you having lunch with the same old pals you've had lunch with for twenty years, or are you having lunch with new people who have jobs and expertise that could come in handy one day? (KPH)

Good contacts: Back in high school you probably said disdainfully, "Oh, she just got that job because her mom knows the manager!" — as if obtaining a job that way was practically a sin. Now that you are grown-up, you know that that *is* the way the world works. If it takes your mom knowing the manager, well, get on the phone, Mom! (LJ)

SMALL BUSINESS

As long as you have to work, you might as well work for somebody loved and respected by your friends and your family — even if it's somebody you really never thought of as a captain of industry.

HOW MUCH MONEY?

Small bucks: If you're looking to start your own business, a huge capital investment isn't always necessary. Start with something to market — a skill, special knowledge or an actual product — and build your business around that. Work with something you're good at and like to do. Start small — cater your friends' parties or baby—sit their kids for the weekend. Self—confidence, pride and ambition can be all you need to get started. (PSA)

A dissent: A new business will not make money the first year. You need enough cash to run it and live off of while you wait. There will always be unexpected expenses, and money will not arrive at the right times, so plan carefully. (MB)

It's a matter of money. You'll need it. Do you have it? The Small Business Administration has worksheets to help you plan potential income and planned expenses, although perhaps you're loaded with dough and the only reason you have for starting a business is the desire to fill up your soul. In that case, those worksheets will hardly matter. (RR)

Where does the money come from? Look into your savings account to see if anything is there. Then look about for those who love you. Can you borrow from them? You may be able to obtain some financing from a lending institution, but you'll have to provide them with a personal asset good enough to give them the necessary feeling of security they need in order to lend. Your integrity is an important personal asset and financial institutions will pay a lot of attention to it, but your house is more what they have in mind. (KJ) **See under** *Net Worth* **in** *CHAPTER TWO: MODERN MOOLAH.*

Walk softly: Don't approach a lending institution without a business plan. Complete one of the plans the SBA puts out. Go in there prepared to prove your competence. (JGu)

Study the bank. Is it a creaky old place? Are the employees cobwebby? You want a bank with a little energy, don't you? Will the bank be able to handle your needs? And remember, applying for a loan is like applying for a job. You'll want to sparkle and shine in a nice, calm way. (TR)

CONTROL YOURSELF

In the past, women haven't been at the controls. You can have control if you're willing to put out the effort and plan it right.

Don't feel you have to jump the credibility gap, like moving into an office you can't afford or advertising in fancy periodicals or trade magazines. Doing this too soon may deplete your ready cash reserve. Most successful businesses spent their first years in warehouses or inexpensive locations and depended a lot on word-of-mouth advertising and help from friends. (CGr, TR)

OPEN THE MONEY DAM

Chances are your expectations of yourself and the dreams you have of success are above what you can actually have in the early stages of starting up your own business. *The main objective is to get a constant cash flow started.* You can't charge for the amount of effort (CGr)

Doing a job "well enough" is not doing a mediocre job, it's doing the best you can do and it's what the client expects. (SV) Never give your all. They'll all expect it. You can *never* do it all. (CGr)

Don't underprice or overprice yourself. You must figure out what your services are going for. Figure out how much money you need to make each day. Cover it. Include hidden expenses like driving time and gas. (LC, LB) Double your ideal price for a job, because it will *always* take longer than you expect. (CGr)

Join associations in and outside your field. It's institutional advertising. (TR) You'll feel insecure at first but you will gain immediate credibility by just being there. You must be one of them or else you wouldn't be there. (CGr)

List yourself in the phone directory. Choose the category carefully. Try to visualize realistically where people would look in a directory for a business like yours. Be honest with yourself. Don't list your business someplace where you'd *like* to see it; list it where people will *look* and see it. People really do let their fingers do the walking for them. (TR)

MARKETING SURVEYS

One of the first things you need to do when you're thinking of starting your own business is to conduct a survey to determine if there's a market for your potential product or service. There's a whole slew of companies who will do this sort of thing for you, but if you're working on a low budget you can do your own survey for almost nothing. Here's what you do.

Make up a list of questions to which you'd like the answers. For example, if you're going to open a dating service you would want to ask people their marital status, if they have ever used a dating service, what they would like to see in a new service, and so forth. (There are plenty of books in the library to help you make a comprehensive list.)

Reach out: Get hold of a reverse phone book. This is a phone book that lists phone numbers by address instead of by name. Many libraries have a copy or you can ask your local phone company where you can get access to one. Call a sample of people in the areas you figure your business will service. Remember, the more people you call, the more accurate your results will be. Be polite and professional; be prepared for a fair amount of out and out rejection and some downright rudeness. When you reach someone who will talk to you, ask your questions and note the answers.

The final analysis: When you feel you've taken a large enough sampling, analyze your results for patterns of purchasing, interest in your product, and other salient factors. This information can guide you in planning how your business should run. It can also help you get financing by showing the market potential of your business. (MK)

ESP: Small business operators are clever enough to understand what customers want before they know it themselves. (KGG)

HOUSE WORK

The ideal situation for most women is to be able to find a paycheck parked right next to the hearth. And, in fact, working at home is possible — provided you plan clearly before you start.

If you have children, do you have a place to work where you will not be disturbed? Can you arrange your schedule around your family? If not, can you work in spite of them? Do you have the self-discipline to get going without someone else telling you to? Can you afford to begin a business that will probably bring you only expenses for many months? Can you work alone or are you a person who needs hustle and bustle to be happy? (AK)

Make sure that your friends know you've got a business. Tell them you can't chat during business hours. Get an answering machine. Have a designated work area that nobody messes with. Make two flags — one red, one green. When the red flag is up, nobody in your family should come near you except in a terrible emergency. (DD)

THE HOME OFFICE

If you're going to work out of your home, you must live fairly close to a metropolitan area. Busy clients will not drive very far to do business with you. For most people — especially those who have to commute every day — driving time is often a waste of time. (RL)

Working out of your home can save you money, but you have to consider a few things first to make it all work for you. Keep the area of your home that you're going to devote to business, tidy and clean, especially if clients come to you. (BLo) *Never cook food* — don't even start dinner in a Crockpot — if there's even a slim chance a client or potential customer may show up. (SM)

There's no way you can be productive at home if you have children under foot. You can set up a work pattern around their preschool or grade school hours, but never conduct business while they're at home. The same goes for talkative friends or neighbors! (TR)

Although it's the traditional role of the mother to give her children her undivided attention, trying to run a business with kids around just doesn't work. Arrange for a nanny or day care for your kids, and don't feel guilty about it! Make sure you feel absolutely secure about the center or person you're leaving your kids with — that's the only way you'll feel able to do a good job on your job. (SN) **See** *Day Care* **in** *CHAPTER SIXTEEN: THE MODERN MOM.*

RISKY BUSINESS

Ninety percent of small businesses fail due to poor management, but some reasons for failure are beyond anyone's control. The overall economy of the area may be rotten, the demand for the product may suddenly vanish, or the city may tear up the street in front of your building. (HL)

TYPE-A

It takes a certain personality type to start a small business. Consider carefully beforehand whether or not you are that type. You should be a self-starter, an organizer. You need a certain level of aggression and energy and the ability to bear it all, especially because small businesses rise and fall every single day. (PK)

WHOA, PARDNER

Are you going to be looking for a business partner to help you in the areas where you are not especially proficient? Watch out, this is terrible and tricky, this partner thing. (FDD)

Ask a lawyer for advice on partnerships, limited partnerships, corporations, etc. You'll need to see one anyway to get the papers prepared. (DC) **See under** *Lawyers* **in** *CHAPTER TWELVE: MODERN WOMEN IN DISTRESS.*

LOCATION, LOCATION, LOCATION

The chamber of commerce and city and state development agencies probably can help you with your questions concerning location. Find out about utilities, parking availability, taxes, rents, zoning regulations, number of competitive businesses in the area. (RR)

BUY, BUY

If you buy a business, you won't have to equip it and you'll gain the firm's old customers. Holding onto some of the previous personnel could also be very helpful. But watch out when you buy a business. If the former owner was the devil, maybe nobody will come for miles around. Why is he selling, anyway? Is all the equipment rotten? Is the building located over a sinkhole? (TD)

If you buy somebody else's headache, study the business records of the establishment. Try to go back at least five years — ten is better. Every business should have copies of income tax returns, at least. Watch out, though. Inaccurate tax returns may be specially prepared just for you, you lucky thing. Insist on accurate records. It won't help if they're bent on deception, but insist anyhow. (LL)

RECORD KEEPING

Records are crucial. Clean books make planning and decision-making easier and help provide you with information that can help you enormously. Scrimping in record keeping can cost you dearly. If you are not familiar with income tax records and accounting, hire someone. There are accountants and management consultants out there waiting for you. (PK)

DRIVE-THRU

Buying into a franchise is great. The business is already going. You will benefit from the franchisor's experience. It will require less money on your part. Your business will already be well known. The place works — it's already proven that it does. The lay-out, fixtures and so forth are all okay. You'll receive good training from the company, who will also help you with your advertising. What a deal. (HG)

A dissent: You're not the big boss when you buy into a franchise. You have to pay the franchisor a royalty on a percentage of gross sales. If your franchisor mismanages, you'll suffer also. You won't be free to make management decisions, and you've got to write them reports all the damn time. (HC)

The capper: Franchising has to do with fast food, isn't that it? Sad little managers running about bossing employees who are trained to smile, that's what it is. Everyone in a franchise, it seems, must wear a hat. (JN)

KARD KRAZY

When you drop off your business card, don't drop the ball.

WHAT YOUR CARD SHOULD LOOK LIKE

Hand-made art and lettering, fancy type and junky logos may look great to you, but to other people your card will come off looking messy and illegible, not to mention cheap and amateurish.(**See illustration.**)

Keep it simple, easy and common. If you don't have a good sense of professional design, pay a designer or typesetting establishment to design your card and make it ready to take to the printer. Talk over your ideas with the designer and let her advise you.

Don't be ambiguous. Design is not a theoretical exercise. Be specific when you talk about what you want your card to look like. Bring samples of other logos and corporate identities. Make sure you have a clear understanding with the designer about type style, ink and paper colors and the paper stock that will be used.

Be sure to sign an agreement regarding price and date of delivery.

Shout: If you really feel that your card should stand up and holler, consider embossing the logo or your name, or use an unusual color blend — but avoid rainbows and flourescent colors. The designer will have a big book of color swatches for ink color choices and lots of paper samples for you to choose from.

LESS IS MORE

Not so good.

Much better.

Before the artwork goes to the printer, check it *carefully* for typographical errors or other mistakes. Read the address and telephone number on the artwork out loud to a friend. Make absolutely certain that the card will contain accurate information.

Avoid extraneous messages. Don't put clutter around the message your card is supposed to deliver. (JCS, KK)

Modern Moolah

Money has a sensual significance. A sawbuck, for example, has a feel all its own, sort of like taffeta with a twist. And, while most of the money you can hear doesn't really count, the soft rustle of hundreds can be sweetly seductive.

But Modern Women know that when money talks, it's usually not worth listening. Besides, money stinks, you can't put it in your mouth, and you not only can't take it with you, you can't even take it seriously.

On the other hand, money does act as a wolf-repellant if carefully applied around the door, keeping you warm, the kids fed and the shirt on your back. So it pays — and sometimes pays well — to take care of the stuff.

C O N T E N T S

Chapter Two: *MODERN MOOLAH*

MONEY FOR SOMETHING: Net Worth — Income — Credit — Budgets — Ten Simple Ways to Save Money — RISKY BUSINESS: A Guide to Determining Risks in Investments — Retirement Planning — Women as Stock Investors — Savings — Three Investment Questions — Safest Investments — Passbook Savings — Money Market Funds — Stocks — Bonds — Money — PROPERTY: Buying a House — Closing the Sale — Condominiums — Condo – Co-Op Conundrum — How and When to Buy Property — Real Estate Investment — INSURANCE: Homeowner's Insurance — Term: Insurance — Whopper Insurance — Fine Print — Lifers — Disability Insurance — Group Plans — Health Insurance

MONEY FOR SOMETHING

In a world of games and gameplayers, the score is kept in account books and expressed in dollars.

NET WORTH

Worth her salt: Although every Modern Woman knows what she's worth as a person, occasionally she has to state her worth in more prosaic terms. Banks, insurance companies and credit bureaus usually want to see your net worth in terms they understand. So here's how to figure out what the world thinks you're worth:

• *Add together:*

Liquid assets: Cash, savings accounts, checking accounts, life insurance (cash value), investments (stocks, bonds, CDs, profit-sharing plans, etc.). What you're looking for here is the money that's more or less in your pocket.

Non-liquid assets: Real estate, furs jewelry, cars, that priceless oriental rug, your grandmother's brooch — in general, we're talking about stuff that's worth something, but only after a value has been established, a buyer found and the money received. Things like paintings and other collectibles must be appraised by a recognized expert — auction houses can sometimes help you here.

This gives you your total assets. Looks pretty good?

• *Well, now subtract:*

Short-term Liabilities: Credit card balances, installment loan balances, taxes due, insurance premiums, and all the other bad news that shows up in the mailbox.

Long-term Liabilities: Mortgage, car loan, student loans, and so on.

•*What you have left is your net worth.* With any luck you have a plus sign in front of the figure. If not, remember, you're still a beautiful human being. (MK)

INCOME

Always have more than one source of income. If you don't already have more than one, make developing a second source of income a sort of part-time job.

The most financially successful people who produce their own income know this simple fact: You are apt to be pulled into an area of economic interest if you have to depend upon it financially, so having more than one source of income is very prudent — as well as educationally broadening. (LCh)

CREDIT

Secure credit during times you don't and *won't* use it. The price of maintaining a line of credit based upon a charge card account is worth the convenience. When you do need credit, use what you have and don't let the lender know of your needs. (JGu)

BUDGETS

Here's an oddity — *a budget that actually works:*

• *Set aside 10 percent minimum* as part of a savings program. *Never* invade this. Forget that it's there. Pretend it's money you're sending into space.

• *Give over five percent* to a more risky program of investment. Stocks or real estate.

• *Allow no more than 25 percent* of your income to go for rent, although you can boost this up to 35 percent if it's for the purchase of living space.

• *Buy fewer, better quality clothes,* rather than more at cheaper prices. Quality means material, not style. **See under** *Don't Dress for Cartoons* **in** *CHAPTER EIGHT: THE MODERN MODE.*

• *Don't use tax withholding* to "save" money from your paycheck. Take the extra time to plan it so you come out even at the end of the year.

• *Stay on top of your expenses* by occasionally keeping a running record of all your expenses. If you can do this, you aren't the kind of person who is going to have financial trouble in the first place.

• *Pay your monthly bills* around your paydays, even if you are a few days early. Reserve money against less than monthly obligations (taxes, quarterly utilities, etc.).

• *Buy items before the need arises.* Hunger of any sort is a tyrant.

• *If you are single,* eat and shop single; if you are a couple, share. Either way, don't overindulge. If you do happen to overconsume at one meal, skip the next one or two. Fine yourself.

• *Shop used.* Buy items you know you can resell at a 50 to 100 percent mark-up. Bulletin boards at work aren't there for nothing. **See** *THRIFT SHOPPING* **in** *CHAPTER SIX: MODERN MERCHANDISE.*

• *Stay alert* to bargains. The best things in life may not be free, but they can be reasonable. (LCh)

TEN SIMPLE WAYS TO SAVE MONEY

1. Buy cheap soap. Often it is of better quality than more expensive soaps.

2. Eat first, then shop. Never buy groceries on an empty stomach.

3. Buy things before you need them.

4. Buy out of season. **See** *Season Ticket* **in** *CHAPTER SIX: MODERN MERCHANDISE.*

5. Quit smoking. This one isn't so easy. **See under** *How To Break Bad Habits* **in** *CHAPTER FOUR: MODERN P's & Q's.*

6. Use the pen instead of the phone. **See** *A WOMAN OF LETTERS* **in** *CHAPTER FOUR: MODERN P's & Q's.*

7. Substitute lighter meats for darker. Switch to fowl from red meat.

8. Snack on vegetables.

9. Bus instead of drive. Walk as much as you can.

10. Use the library as your source for magazines and newspapers. (KAL)

RISKY BUSINESS

The trouble with investing your money is that it only becomes interesting when it becomes frightening. In this, of course, investing resembles love. Alas.

A GUIDE TO DETERMINING RISKS IN INVESTMENTS

The only time-proven method is to assign a rating that is based solely on two factors:

1. The investor's degree of control over the investment.

2. The amount and quality of information the investor possesses about the investment.

Don't invest in your emotions. Don't play hunches — unless you've got money to waste — and don't let your good intentions wipe out your investment account. Investing without thinking is like driving without brakes. (CMu)

RETIREMENT PLANNING

Here are some guidelines for planning a retirement fund:

• Ten percent of your salary or active income should go into an Individual Retirement Account (IRA). It is the second best investment. (Education is first.)

• Remember: An IRA is an empty vehicle into which you can put a savings account, stocks, whatever is currently legal. Don't let the various financial institutions that sell stocks or savings accounts tell you that their product *is* an IRA. An IRA demands a certain conservative approach, but it can also be enhanced by a degree of flexibility and creative investing.

• IRA contribution limits change from time to time.

• If you started an IRA after you paid for your education, you'd be independent way before any currently recognized retirement age (sixty-two to sixty-five years old) and probably before the generally recognized early retirement age (fifty-five to fifty-nine).

• As of late 1987, you could contribute up to $2000 per year to an IRA and withdraw it at retirement, disability, death, or at age fifty-nine and six months (even if you aren't retired). (LCh)

WOMEN AS STOCK INVESTORS

American women are surprisingly passive as stock market investors. It is estimated that 95 percent of the transactions on the New York Stock Exchange (NYSE) are conducted by men.

When women invest, they are less likely to gamble or invest emotionally and more likely to make their investment based on fundamental information about the performance or potential of a company or product.

Women do better than men when both invest as individuals. (LCh)

SAVINGS

Women save more than men, even though they earn less. Economists say that one of the reasons the United States is behind Germany and Japan economically is because Americans save at a rate of about one-fourth the Japanese, and one-half the Germans.

In Japan, the women control the paychecks, the family budget, and the investing of "disposable" income. Japanese women account for 80 percent of the individual stock transactions in Japan, and their trading record has been phenomenal. The "Japanese Dow" is at 27,000 points, indexed to 1945 at 100. (LCh)

THREE INVESTMENT QUESTIONS

For any investment you make, ask yourself these three questions:

1. What rate of return are you looking for?

2. How large a risk is this investment?

3. How liquid is the investment — i.e., how easily can it be converted into cash? (LL)

SAFEST INVESTMENTS

The Federal Treasury guarantees *government bonds* and notes, and the Federal Deposit Insurance Corporation (FDIC) protects most *bank savings accounts,* so these are the safest investments.

PASSBOOK SAVINGS

Your passbook savings account is very safe, but the interest rates are very low. If you have between $500 and $100,000 to invest, certificates of deposit are a good plan. There is a penalty for early withdrawal, but the interest rates are the highest paid on any savings account. (LCh)

MONEY MARKET FUNDS

were established so that people with as little as $1000 could get higher rates by pooling their money with others in the fund. It is easily accessible, and there are no commissions on deposits or withdrawals. (KPH)

STOCKS

Corporations issue *common and preferred stocks.* Both represent ownership of a portion of a corporation's assets.

• The Board of Directors determines *dividends* paid on common stock.

• A stock's *value fluctuates,* depending on the company's anticipated earnings and on general economic conditions.

• *Capital growth* means an increase in the trading price of a stock and is one of the ways a stock can provide return. The other way is through dividends.

• *Dividends* are those 46¢ checks your roommate always used to receive in the mail from the stocks her grandfather bought in her name.

MONEY

Coin of Sidon

Coin of ancient Thrace

East Indian Money Tree

Isle of Man half penny

King George III

Coin of ancient Corinth

Roman Coin

Australian shilling

Italian five-lire

New Zealand florin

"Ant's nose" of China

Colonial Token

Estonian Kroon

Early Roman Coin

• *Income stocks* provide those steady little incomes. *Growth stocks,* on the other hand, aren't big on steady little dividends but do have potential for more of an increase in investment value. They are riskier and jazzier. Most stocks are actually not entirely one or the other. (KPH)

Go for more growth investments if you are young. Concentrate more on income-producing stocks if you are older. (JJ)

A mutual fund is an investment company that invests a pool of capital from many people. The management fee for most mutual funds is quite small. The fund takes responsibility for what to buy, when to buy, and when to sell. (FSR)

BONDS

Federal income *tax on interest* does not have to be paid on municipal bonds, which are bonds of cities, states, and other taxing districts. The interest rate is not as great as the rate on most corporate bonds. (TB)

The federal government guarantees U.S. savings bonds, which are a very safe investment. (PO'C) **See** *Safest Investments,* **above.**

A corporate bond is a loan to a company by a bondholder. The company promises to pay the holder a fixed rate of interest for a certain period of time. The bondholders are the first to be paid if the company's assets are liquidated. (PO'C)

PROPERTY

Property is a rewarding form of investment, if only because it's usually pretty big. You can invest fifty grand in gold and put the stuff in your closet. Or you can invest fifty grand in a vacant lot and dig for gold. In the long run, property is a pretty good deal. As has been pointed out a number of times, it is a rather fixed commodity.

BUYING A HOUSE

Make sure it won't fall over: Once you are serious about a house, first have an independent appraisal conducted by a professional. The sellers will have already done this to arrive at their price, but you can sometimes profit by doing the same thing. The appraisal will establish the value of the property based on a number of factors, such as the sale price of similar properties in the neighborhood and the added value of any improvements. If you have any questions about the structural soundness of the property, have a house inspector or engineer take a look at it. Friends can sometimes recommend an inspector, or look in the Yellow Pages. Check with the Better Business Bureau if you have any doubts about your choice.

Usually, it is fine to make an offer before calling in an inspector. It is usually written into the contract that purchase is contingent on the report of an inspection service. If it isn't written in, get it in.

Inspection: You can do a lot of checking on your own.

• Look for cracks, especially in newer houses, because this indicates poor construction.

• Do the floors squeak?

• When you are alone in a room, put a marble on the floor. If it rolls by itself to the other side of the room, you are in trouble.

• Do the windows stick?

• Is there insulation around the windows and in the attic and basement?

• Are there screens and storm windows available?

• Check each room for the number of electrical outlets.

• Turn on several faucets at the same time to see if water pressure stays the same.

• Check for mustiness and dampness in the basement.

• Find out what kind of pipes are used in the house. The best pipes are copper, bronze, or brass.

• Ask the owner to show you some fuel bills.

• Know whether the house is connected to a city sewer system or to a septic tank. How much does it cost to clean the tank?

• Don't assume that everything you see is part of the deal, or you may move in to discover no refrigerator and no stove. (BDe, CAFu)

Look for a house that costs no more than two and one-half times your annual income. If that means a $15,000 house, keep renting. (LL)

Have established credit before you go looking to purchase a house. Nobody likes a person who has always paid cash and has no debts.

This is how you can do it. Apply for a little loan of perhaps $1000 and repay it promptly in as short a time as is allowed. Or buy something on the installment plan at a store and pay for it promptly. Now you have the beginnings of a good credit history. You can gradually build your credit line. Don't try to run up too much credit too quickly; once credit companies start declining your applications, you're in trouble. (JDP)

A down payment is usually 10 to 30 percent of the purchase price of the house. Cash in stocks or savings bonds, if you have them. Lenders can be wary of loaning you great amounts to make the downpayment. They may question your ability to carry your mortgage and repay the loan at the same time. Try borrowing from a well-to-do relative if that is at all possible. *(Anon.)*

Try to make a down payment as small as you can. Keep some money for emergencies. You will have to pay higher monthly payments, but this will be made up in income tax deductions that you will be allowed. (SKo)

Check with the mortgage loan officer at your bank *before* you see the real estate agent. Ask the loan officer to help you decide what price range you can afford. Ask about the bank's interest rate and down-payment requirements. Know what you probably can and cannot do before you start house-hunting. (JDP)

Mortgages can be obtained from savings banks, savings and loan associations, pension funds, commercial banks, and insurance companies.

Prepayment of your mortgage is not necessarily advantageous. You may have to pay the interest anyway that you would have paid over the entire natural course of the loan. (BDe)

CLOSING THE SALE

You've found the house you want to have. You put a *binder* on it. This is an advance agreement between the buyer and the seller to purchase property subject to certain conditions. Usually this is accompanied by a relatively small sum of money known as *earnest money.*

The big day arrives a couple of months later when you are handed the keys to the house, but during those two months of waiting, your mortgage application will be reviewed and approved, the lender will appraise the house, and a title search will be made.

On closing day you will be expected to pay the *closing costs,* which are usually 5 to 8 percent of the purchase price of the house. These costs cover the mortgage application, the appraisal fee, the attorney's fee, the title search, the title insurance, and the survey and recording fees. Be sure you know beforehand what all the items are that you will be asked to pay for at time of settlement. (BDe)

CONDOMINIUMS

"Condo" sounds like safe housing. In fact, condos are real estate developments with common facilities administered by a community association that you are *required* to join. Be an active member unless it does not matter to you who controls your life.

Do not enter the condo world if you cannot get along with people. It is not *your* lawn out there. It is *everybody's* lawn. If you want to dig it up and plant vegetables, you have to call a meeting first. When the roof needs repairs, you may opt for the finest repair service, while the rest of the group wants to call the Econo-Trust-Us service. It is not entirely your life anymore. On the other hand, condos are usually more secure than apartments or private homes, and there is a closeness to your neighbors that may warm a lonely heart.

When buying a condo, check the reputation of the developer.

• Find out if any complaints have been filed against the developer with the real estate commission.

• Does the builder make good background checks before choosing buyers, or is a wad of bills all she wants?

• Will you be trapped into an unsuccessful development, or will your deposit money be refunded if a certain number of units remain unsold by a specific time?

• Don't believe what the developer tells you about maintenance costs. Ask for a breakdown and show it to a real estate professional.

• Ask to see the budget of a long-running condo. Does the association have reserves for unexpected emergencies?

  • Is there a membership fee to use the pool or tennis courts?

  • Check all the bylaws. Can you stand them?

  • Is parking free? How about for your guests?

  • What kind of insurance is involved concerning common grounds?

  • Attend a few condo meetings. Are the residents involved in condo wars?

  • Don't believe anything unless it is in writing. (BDe, CLC)

CONDO – CO-OP CONUNDRUM

In a condominium, buyers own their apartment units outright, plus a share in the common facilities.

In a cooperative, buyers purchase shares in a corporation that owns and holds the mortgage on a building. Shares vary according to the size of the unit and its purchase price. Tenant-shareholders have a proprietory lease that gives them the right to their units.

There are many advantages for the tenant-shareholder. You will not be faced with rising rents. You can make major changes on your unit and know that these changes belong to you and not your landlord. You will receive certain tax benefits. Chances are, because everyone in the building has a stake in it, the overall quality of life will be better than if it were a building of unrelated strangers with no real concern for the place. (DS)

In a co-op you will be tied with all your neighbors to a joint mortgage. This is fine if you like your neighbors. You will elect board members who will spend all year complaining about you while you spend the year complaining about them. You will have to obey the bylaws of the corporation. If, for example, the corporation votes out cats, you will have no choice but to send the cat somewhere else, whether she is 16 and ailing or not. (EC)

HOW AND WHEN TO BUY PROPERTY

Mini-Monopoly: Here are some rough rules to get you started thinking about property investment:

  • Try to buy a "second" property as an investment.

  • Buy during the low inflation, recessional side of a business cycle. Use the Commerce Department's index or the Consumer Price Index (CPI) as a rough guide, along with the quarterly Gross National Product (GNP) announcements.

  • Buy low, sell high, of course. Then

  • take your proceeds and invest in government bonds with maturities of at least four years.

  • Sell the bonds when interest rates drop, since the bonds will increase in price.

  • Bank the proceeds and wait for the next cycle.

  • Stay flexible. Do not tie up capital during boom times, no matter what rates are being offered. (LCh)

If you want to make a living buying, fixing up, and selling houses for a profit, *be prepared to do almost all of the fixing yourself* if you want to really make any money. **See** *FLOORS, THE WALLS, MS. FIX-IT and HOT AND WET* in *CHAPTER NINE: HOME EC*

Worst house, best neighborhood: Try purchasing a really ugly house that you know has good plumbing, heating, and electricity in a reasonable neighborhood. Then make it pretty. Wallpaper costs less than electrical overhauls, and you can do it yourself. (BDe)

When doing house renovation, check all the second-hand stores for things like shutters, mantels, etc. that can be incorporated into the house. (KGG)

Rent control is marvelous for the renter, but if you are the landlady it may not allow you to increase rates enough to cover your costs. (PPK)

Before you buy a multifamily dwelling, have a professional house inspection. Be sure that your purchase offer is contingent upon a good inspection, and also contingent upon the approval of the seller's federal income tax returns for the last two years. (PPK)

Consider investing in commercial property such as stores, factories, or warehouses. There will be no rent controls, leases are long, no one will call you in the middle of the night, and your tenants will probably be very reputable. (LHi)

Consider other uses for a building. Lawyers love to set up shop in Victorian houses. Railroad depots are turning into restaurants all over the place. (NCo)

REAL ESTATE INVESTMENT

If you are planning on investing, *consider location* first of all. Never trust a deal that seems too good. Invest in something close to home. You know your own town better than any other. (PPK)

INSURANCE

Want to bet you're going to die tomorrow? What about odds on your house and everything you own going up in smoke next week? This is the stuff of insurance companies, sort of elaborate casinos where you wager a set amount against the odds that something really dreadful will happen to you.

Some days you wonder how insurance companies survive.

HOMEOWNER'S INSURANCE

covers a number of different things. It covers the cost when your house burns down, but also when someone trips on your front porch or when your luggage is stolen far from home. It will not cover flood or earthquake, which is bad news for those who live on top of the San Andreas Fault (although they can obtain a special earthquake policy from the federal government). (RP)

There are four general areas covered by homeowners policies:

• *Damage to your home* or any structures on your property.

• *Expenses and legal awards* when a claim is filed against you for causing a person injury or damage to property.

• *Damage to your personal property.*

• *Expenses if your home becomes uninhabitable* and you must live elsewhere until it has been repaired. (KGG)

Most homeowner's policies cover lost credit cards. Without such coverage, you are liable for the first $50 on each card. (TO'C)

Insuring your house for 80 percent of its replacement cost is really all that you need. A home is hardly ever 100 percent destroyed, so the extra cost isn't worth the risk.*(Anon.)*

Know what's in your house. After the fire, you won't be paid for the things you can't remember. Take photos of your possessions and write detailed descriptions of everything. Store this information in a safety deposit box. Give a copy to your agent and another to your lawyer or a relative.

Every time your policy is renewed, be sure to have your house reappraised so that you do not underinsure it. Keep copies of all receipts and sales information on any valuables that you keep in your home and keep this information in your safety deposit box. (LL)

The insurance company considers several factors in determining how much coverage you will pay.

• Your premium will be lower if your home is brick or stone rather than wood.

• If the only fire department is miles and miles and miles away, you'll pay more.

• If there is a high crime rate in your area, your premiums will be higher — if you can get coverage at all.

If you are having trouble finding a company who will accept you, check with the state insurance department. (BA)

Check to see what discounts you may be eligible for. Rates may go down for people who have deadbolt locks, burglar alarms, smoke detectors, and the rest. (CAF)

If you are a renter, you can get coverage for the contents of your unit. The landlord must insure the building. (FL)

You must obtain **business insurance coverage** if you operate a business out of your home. (BA)

Be sure you know exactly when your policy expires, because there is usually no grace period. You may be only one day late to renew, but your house may burn to the ground on that day. (KY)

TERM: INSURANCE

Here's a glossary that will enable you to converse with insurance agents in a language they will understand:

• *Premium:* The amount you pay for your policy. The premium you pay for a group policy at work will be lower (or none at all if your employer pays for it) than an individual policy premium. Paying annually will cost you less than making smaller payments throughout the year.

- *Loss ratio:* Percentage of premiums paid out in benefits. The larger that figure, the better for you. Look for 65 or 70 percent.
- *Benefits:* This is the amount payable by the insurance company to you or your beneficiary. Read your policy very carefully, especially wherever you see phrases like *pre-existing conditions* or *exclusions and limitations.*
- *Deductibles:* Amounts you pay before the coverage takes over. The higher the deductible, the lower the premium.
- *Co-insurance:* A provision by which both the insured and the insurer share the covered loss in a specified ratio. You may pay 20 percent, and the insurer 80 percent, for example.
- *Pre-existing conditions:* A physical or mental condition that existed before the purchase of the policy.
- *Exclusions:* Specific conditions that the policy will not cover.
- *Waiting period:* How long you must wait from the date of employment or application for coverage to the time the insurance becomes effective.
- *Elimination period:* Period of time between disability and start of benefits during which no benefits are payable.
- *Family policy:* A policy providing coverage on all or some family members.
- *Reasonable and customary charge:* Charge for health care consistent with the going rate in your area for similar or identical services.
- *Lifetime stop-loss:* Puts a cap on all expenses you must pay after a certain amount has been reached.
- *Option:* Something you pay extra to have. *(Anon.)*

WHOPPER INSURANCE

Insurance companies want to make a profit, and the people who work for them are salespeople. Do not believe everything they tell you. Shop around. Check out many companies before making any choices. Constantly reevaluate your insurance needs to be sure that you are not buying more than you really require. To save the most on your total bill, take the maximum deductible you can afford. Buy insurance only from companies that your state has licensed. (KY)

Independent agents can work miracles with insurance. A good, reputable independent — a professional who sells policies from many different companies, and, theoretically, understands the industry's trends — will work hard to see that you get the best deal from a wide variety of offreings. And don't be afraid to shop around the quotes given to you by an independent agent; the chances are very good that you'll be satisfied with the price and the service. (BDe)

FINE PRINT

An insurance policy defines your rights and the rights of the company who insures you. Read the policy as soon as you get it no matter how horrible a task it is. Make a note of anything you do not understand and ask the agent to explain it to you. (PN)

LIFERS

You don't need life insurance if nobody depends on you. Life insurance is to protect individuals who rely upon the earnings of others. (JMcE)

To make a good choice in life insurance, go to several different agents. Present them with identical information and have each one draw up a proposal for you. Circulate the proposals among all the agents and ask them to give their judgements on each. Read what everyone has to say. Decide. (BA)

Give photocopies of your policy to your attorney and beneficiaries so that claims procedures are not held up because nobody knows how to get into your safety deposit box. (PAN)

Health, lifestyle and occupation are the standards looked at by the companies when deciding whether or not to insure you. An overweight man who smokes heavily, uses intravenous drugs, and works in a coal mine will have a more difficult time getting insurance than a slender nonsmoking woman who works in a flower shop. Look for a company that specializes in "rated" risks. You'll have to pay more, but you'll get coverage. (DWi)

DISABILITY INSURANCE

If you must make a choice between buying life insurance or disability insurance, buy disability insurance. The chances of you being disabled before age sixty-five are much greater than the chances of you dying. Disability insurance will provide you with a large portion of the money you would have earned had you not become disabled. (DWi)

GROUP PLANS

If your employer offers group disability insurance, take it.

Disability insurance will take one of two forms, *short- or long-term.*

• Short-term insurance provides income replacement for up to two years, while long-term continues for life.

• Group insurance is always cheaper than individual coverage, but with group insurance your benefits are taxable. Individual insurance benefits are not.

• You must give up your group insurance if you leave your job. (DWi)

HEALTH INSURANCE

The cost of medical care in this country is ludicrous. Once you come into contact with the medical industry, a relatively minor ailment can be financially crippling. Health insurance is essential; here are some questions to help you decide on an appropriate plan:

• Does your group health insurance cover all family members?

• What is the deductible?

• Do you have to use their doctors?

• Do they encourage second opinions before approving surgical procedures?

• Do they stress physician accountability?

• Are psychiatric costs covered?

• How long is the waiting period before you are eligible?

• When the policy uses the term *hospital,* does that cover clinics, drug treatment centers, stress counseling, etc?

• What if you leave your employer or retire? Can your policy be converted into an individual policy with no break in coverage?

Check around and compare answers before you choose.

Health insurance comes in two forms: *basic health* and *major medical.*

• *Basic health insurance* covers stays in the hospital up to about 120 days, X-rays, lab tests, drugs and medications, normal hospital nursing services, and so forth. Many basic policies don't cover doctor's visits and fees.

• *Major medical insurance* (also called *catastrophic coverage*) is designed to cover major illnesses or accidents where a long hospital stay is necessary. Many major medical policies will pick-up the doctor's fees. (LL)

A health maintenance organization — or HMO — is an insurance program in which a group of physicians have banded together to provide comprehensive health care. Rather than accepting health insurance payments, the doctors are paid out of a flat monthly fee that all the patients pay. So what you are doing is paying your health care costs before you incur them. You must use physicians or hospitals affiliated with your HMO. (LL)

Health insurance tips:

• Policies should allow you to change your mind within ten days of signing. All your money should be returned.

• If you are a heavy smoker, you may have trouble finding insurance unless you can convince the company that you have quit for good.

• Keep an emergency fund for medical bills that insurance does not cover. Keep it in a joint account so that someone else will be able to get to it if you cannot.

• Check under Medicare for nursing service coverage.

• Don't jump into a health plan without careful investigation first.

• Review your insurance every year to be sure it is still the best plan for you and your family.

• Keep a list of policy numbers and company names in case the original papers are lost.

• Some companies refuse to renew a policy on an individual basis. Watch out for them.

• Check with the state insurance department if you have any questions about whether or not a company is reputable. (AOp, CH)

Solo Acts

The modern world isn't very kind to women —
Modern or otherwise. It's a planet full of small
adventures that become bigger when you have to face
them alone. Still, we start out on our own, and even if
we don't stay alone, it never hurts to know what to do
with a little independence.

C O N T E N T S

Chapter Three: *SOLO ACTS*

TALKING TO OURSELVES: A Dozen Ways to Pass a Lonely Night — Stop and Smell the Fitness Center — Drinking Alone — How to Eat Alone — Lone Survivor — Pleasures of Living Alone — Not Missing Much, Anyway — Circles of Friends — Battlin' Buddies — Cling-Free — Boy Friends — Grim Groom — Friend or Acquaintance? — Pal Definitions

TALKING TO OURSELVES

Living alone requires a special sort of dialogue. Call it talking to yourself, if you want. But at least it's talking to someone who cares.

A DOZEN WAYS TO PASS A LONELY NIGHT

1. Rent a videotape. Men may be in short supply, but VCRs aren't. **See** *Happy Hooking* **in** *CHAPTER ELEVEN: MODERN WOMAN AT EASE.*

2. Call your mom and dad and chat for a long time.

3. Write long letters to people you love. **See** *A WOMAN OF LETTERS* **in** *CHAPTER FOUR: MODERN P's & Q's.*

4. Read.

5. Clean the whole house. It is good for the soul. Do the refrigerator, too. See *CHAPTER NINE: HOME EC* **for complete instructions.**

6. Paint a picture.

7. Take a drive to anyplace and check into a motel or hotel. It doesn't matter if the place is fancy or plain, but try to get a room where the neon signs flash against the drapes. It makes your loneliness romantic. **See under** *OFF-ROAD TRAVEL* **in** *CHAPTER FOURTEEN: MODERN RUN-AROUNDS* **for tips on traveling.**

8. If you have a big, big dog, take a lone, long walk in the dark. Everything is beautiful at night, but don't go unless you have a big dog.

9. Prepare a week's worth of dinners for the freezer. It is a horrible thing to do, but it is constructive, and you were just going to spend time being lonely anyway.

10. College libraries are often open until midnight. Go to one and browse and read until it closes. Then go to an all night diner for a pot of tea. Write a letter to someone as you sip your tea — writing is a good way to keep unwelcome strangers from approaching you. Then drive home and go to sleep.

11. Go to a movie. It's one of the few crowded places where humans get along well together. Besides, it's comforting to sit anonymously in a full room.

12. Go to sleep early and plan to record your dreams.

See also *BOREDOM* **in** *CHAPTER ELEVEN: MODERN WOMAN AT EASE.*

STOP AND SMELL THE FITNESS CENTER

It's a sure bet that if you go racing around all the time, doing what you have to do and wondering why you never meet people, the answer is that you never stop long enough to interact with them. Don't park it back at the house every day to do your unwinding. Go to a bar or coffee house. Or a gym. Or a park. But stop moving long enough to let something happen. For some reason, lonely people are terrified of standing still too long, I guess because they think someone might spot them as being lonely. Being busy is no substitute for good company, companionship or friends. (GSt) See *How To Meet a Lover* in *CHAPTER FIVE: MODERN MEN.*

DRINKING ALONE

There's nothing mysterious about casual nightlife as a single. The people you see are the same people who work in offices all day and who ride the bus just like you do.

Don't go into a cowboy bar to drink alone. Go into the bar of a restaurant you enjoy and just sit down and do it. (BV)

If a drink arrives at your table from a man at another table, smile, but don't accept more than one drink if you want to continue drinking alone. If he sends over a sandwich, smile, but don't accept more than one sandwich. Some men send over sandwiches, have you heard about that? (EJ)

Wear plain clothes. Dress the way you would to rake leaves on a brisk autumn day. Dress "cornflake." Dress as if you were preparing to appear on a cereal box. You want to avoid the "come hither" look. (EJ)

If someone asks to join you, tell him no pleasantly — unless you want the company, of course. It's not right to be rude. It's hard for men to do the things they do. (WP)

See also under *SAUCE STUPIDE* **in** *CHAPTER ELEVEN: MODERN WOMAN AT EASE* **for lots more info on this subject.**

HOW TO EAT ALONE

With a plate, cup, silverware, napkin.

Spread some printed material around you and hold a pen in your hand. You don't really have to write anything. Stare into space and look as if you are ruminating. Chew on your pen. People will assume you are preparing for an important meeting and leave you alone. (TB)

Breakfast and lunch are simple, but dinner is another thing. Walk in with confidence, but don't get huffy in your attempts to assert yourself. When you're gracious, they can't pin you with anything, and they'll look like slobs if they don't treat you as well as you are treating them. (RR)

LONE SURVIVOR

This may not be a very upbeat topic for the Modern Woman, but it, too, could eventually be seen as positive. What is involved in living alone, just me in a house or apartment? Can one ever get used to it after living with children, husbands, lovers? There are no recipes to make this condition palatable to all women who live alone, but sharing the process of adjusting to alone-ness can be interesting and revealing. (EK)

I think the most important thing for a Modern Woman to understand is that the expression *modern woman* does not mean anything at all. That is, in our world, there is no common understanding of this phrase to tell us what we are, no acceptable model given to us to copy, no finished image we can happily hold up as our ideal. There has never been a Modern Woman before, so we must search for what the phrase might possibly mean to us; we must seek to find out what we might be. It is difficult, but necessary, to look straight into the fact that, as Modern Women, I and you — "we" — perhaps do not yet exist. We do not know who we are. The task of finding out is, for all of us, truly a solo act for which the scenario has to be written by each alone, over and over, every day and in every way. (SB)

PLEASURES OF LIVING ALONE

Sometimes a person is tired of being touched. Tired of invaded nights and disrupted dreams. Tired of being clean and smooth and sweet-smelling. A person wants to throw on an old nightgown and heap the blankets into a mountain and forget to brush her teeth and just curl into the night. (NJo)

You can turn on the radio and sing down the halls at 5 A.M. You can wear no clothes and use the bathroom with the door wide open. You can eat cottage cheese with your hands. You can watch all the most mindless television shows and not have to justify yourself. (NAR)

When you live alone *you can walk through the door and find giant peace.* You don't have to cooperate or leave notes or call home if you are late. You can go with any friend to any place at any time. When you are home, you can vacuum the floors and then sit on the couch and look out the window as the sun sets. You don't have to worry about dinner because you can make oatmeal and salad. The only crumbs on your clean floor will be your crumbs. *(Anon.)*

You will not have to point to the shampoo, bath soap, clothes detergent, bleach, cleanser, tampons and aluminum foil, because nobody will ask you why there is still no food in the house if you just spent $25.00. (EL)

There is order. Everything is in control when you live alone. (AO)

When you live alone there will be *no hopeless conversations* to get into where everyone ends up feeling bad and nobody knows why. (GF)

No one will be angry with you over something you don't remember saying. (NC)

NOT MISSING MUCH, ANYWAY

Whether you're alone by choice or circumstance, chances are that sometime you're going to get that awful, empty, lonely feeling. While it doesn't always help, sometimes keeping in mind that nothing lasts forever can be soothing. There will come a time when the days will be too full, your schedule too hectic, and you'll long to be alone, even for just one night. Savor your time alone and save that feeling for when you need it. (JS) **See advice under** *Leaving a Lover* in *CHAPTER FIVE: MODERN MEN*.

I've picked this category because it's strangely foreign to me. I'm a loner — true loners are born, DNA factor, perhaps; it's a long and evolving morphology. Loners are not lonely people. They are individuals "edited out" because of nonadaptability to their environment.

"Let's all get together!" or "Togetherness is the only way to succeed!" We hear these statements crashing against our ears like drumbeats. So far I have not found a person who could enjoy "together" moments that are utterly simple. Someday I will, and when I find this "friend" I will no longer be a loner. (MWH)

CIRCLES OF FRIENDS

Look for women of like mind to form a communal sharing and support network. A meditation practice to act as a common practice for deepening spirit/soul growth and connection. I'm finding a wonderful sense of community in Buddhist practice. (CS)

A woman does need female friends and *lots* of them. Limiting yourself to too few friends can cause you to miss out on exciting adventures. I enjoy maintaining various circles of friends. Concentrating on one circle becomes boring. (KM)

It's impossible to find a friend after the age of twenty — because after that you have to deal with lovers and husbands and loud babies and political opinions and religious beliefs. When you are young you can find a friend in ten minutes. Now that we are all so set in our ways, it is like trying to find a way through an incredible maze to get to another person. (GT) See *180° Relationships* in *CHAPTER FIVE: MODERN MEN.*

So your dearest friend has two babies, right? But you still try and go over for a visit, and you are saying something really *major,* and there is your dearest friend with both her ears zeroed in to the sounds of her children. Sure, her eyes are sometimes on you, but her ears are always far away. So what do you do, come back in eight years? (AZ)

Your friend was always a sane person and now she is pregnant for the first time and she is acting like this sort of thing has never happened before in the history of the world. (SLe)

It's true, her little three-year-old daughter really is a doll. Bright. Cute. Enchanting, as a matter of fact. One of the few little children I really adore. Still, that's *all* she ever talks about. *(Anon.)*

Her first baby truly was remarkable. I know for a fact he was speaking in full sentences at the age of eleven months. I heard him. Then her second baby was born. He is still saying "mama" and "dada" and "doggy" at twenty months. You know, like a normal kid? I am secretly thrilled. *(Anon.)*

BATTLIN' BUDDIES

Two of your very best friends have had a fight. Not just a simple little disagreement, but one of those major rhubarbs where there really is no black or white point of view — although each of your friends thinks that her case is obvious. How can you avoid being put in the middle and possibly losing one or both of them?

Common sense says you should refuse to take sides. Don't be tempted to play judge; the friends it will cost you won't be worth the petty power you'll gain. You can't be put in the middle if you don't let yourself be put there. Explain to each of them that you think you can see both sides of the issue and therefore would prefer not to become involved.

This doesn't always work. Sometimes a friend will accuse you of not being her true friend unless you support her point of view. In this case, it is she who is not the true friend and you must resign yourself to the loss of the relationship. (MK)

THE WRONG BOYFRIEND

If you should meet your friend's boyfriend or husband and find that the two of you have mutual lust, remember that if you convince yourself you just couldn't help yourself, you're telling yourself a lie. You *can* help yourself, you must help yourself. There is no excuse for stealing a man. None! (MK) **See** *The Other Woman* **in** *CHAPTER FIVE: MODERN MEN.*

How do I get along with *my best friend's husband?* He's a jerk! I have never liked anything about him. Therefore, my best friend and I do things by ourselves. But I have never told her my feelings on the subject. There are some things one ought to keep to oneself. *(Anon.)*

I was in love with my best friend's lover. Nobody ever knew it. Nobody ever will. *(Anon.)*

Whenever I come over he always hems and haws and gets all clumsy and says, "Well, I guess I'll just leave you two gals to your girl-talk," and then he goes away. It all sounds terribly unmodern, but the guy is so big and awkward and dopey about the whole thing that my heart just goes out to him, even though I've only spent about ten minutes in the same room with him in my life. (JY)

I like him just fine, but she doesn't like him much at all. *(Anon.)*

When we were fourteen we swore we would never let something concerning a boy come between us. When we were twenty-two something concerning a boy came between us. (CD)

He was studying to be a pediatrician. He was also an alcoholic. One day he was very drunk. He asked me to come by. He wanted to talk about my best friend, the girl he loved. I was afraid he might hurt himself. I went. I listened to him for two hours. Then he asked me to get into bed with him. I said no. Then my best friend returned from work. She stood in the doorway and looked into my eyes. "What are you doing here?" she said. I walked out of the house. I knew our friendship was over. It just was. I shouldn't have gone over. I didn't do anything wrong, but I shouldn't have been there. It wasn't my business to stick my face into the most painful part of her life, no matter how dear we were to one another. When men get into the picture, nothing is the same anymore. It's like the end of childhood. *(Anon.)*

CLING-FREE

Friendships don't always last forever. People change and friends drift away, never to be heard from again. But that doesn't necessarily mean that they weren't really friends. It's a sad thing when a friendship ends on a bad note because it was forced to endure after it should have ended. If you allow friends to move on when the time comes, you'll be left with happy memories instead of bitterness. (JJ)

BOY FRIENDS

It is possible to have a platonic friendship with a man. If the two of you can deal with each other in an asexual way, as people instead of by gender, it's a great way to get an inside view of a man's world.

However, some men — and some women — are totally unable to forget stereotypical behavior and in that case, never the twain shall meet. *(Anon.)*

GRIM GROOM

If your friend is making a big mistake by dating or marrying a man you just know isn't right for her, don't decide *you* know best. It's her life and her mistake to make. And, after all, you could be wrong. Just wait and see — and be there to prop her up if you were right all along. (SB)

FRIEND OR ACQUAINTANCE?

Acquaintances are what you have lots of. The girl next to you in eighth grade history whom you liked but forgot the day the semester was over. The person at work who is nice to joke with. Your neighbors who collect your mail and always mention getting together for dinner sometime. Friends are what you have less of. The one who calls you long distance even when there is no big news. The one who holds back your hair when you are sick. The one who accidentally stumbled into the ugliest moment of your life and heard your mother scream at you, "What are you, anyway, a *whore*?" and she knew your mother didn't really mean it, and she forgave your mother. (LW)

PAL DEFINITIONS

What is a friend? A friend is somebody who sends us a long letter from which we take an excerpt that seems to offer a definition of friendship, then use the rest of the letter someplace else. That's what a friend is, and we've got a batch of them.

A friend is a husband who has spent five years not being able to breathe because of the cat you both got before anyone knew about any allergies. The cat is still there because you love it madly and because your husband loves you madly. (SEM)

A friend is someone who knows you don't feel right about an abortion but she goes ahead and tells you she is pregnant and might do that. She knows you will still love her. *(Anon.)*

A friend is someone you know had an abortion and it is something she never told you but you found out by accident and realize she never told you because she was afraid you might be angry and you realize how much it must have hurt her to keep that secret from you all these years. (EA)

A friend is someone who is a whiz at cards and all you can master is Crazy Eights and she says, "Look, I'm going to teach you Hearts. Even an *idiot* can master Hearts." And it turns out you can't even comprehend Hearts, and somehow she loves you anyway. (LM)

Modern P's and Q's

It's getting downright surly out there across the face of the deep. Rudeness is like a global pollution pattern , spreading ominously everywhere. Eskimos are rude. Africans are rude. There are rude Spaniards and rude Swedes. Right here, close to home, there are fifty states full of rude people.

This must stop. Modern Women know that one reason there's so damn few modern gentlemen is that there's a severe shortage of modern ladies.

So the next time a Modern Man stands when you approach a table, don't ask him where he's going. Just be thankful he's there.

C O N T E N T S

Chapter Four: *MODERN P's & Q's*

**CIVILITY: Why Worry About Manners? — There
Ought to Be a Distinction — What Manners Mean to
Women — Manners and Men — Teach Your Children
Well — Cover-Up — To Be or to Smoke — Taxicabs
— Applause — Engaging Etiquette — Wedding
Worries — How to Plan a Small Wedding — Toilet
Torture — Singing in the Pain — Gifts — Modern
Mortals — In Carpools — At the Table — Dining Out
— Bar Etiquette — One-Woman Show — Good Form
— Place Settings — Wine Time — After Dinner — The
Cocktail Party — Pool Parties — Entertaining on the
Earth — Hosting Weekend Guests — How to Be a
Guest — JERK DEFENSE — Getting Rid of a Jerk —
BAD HABITS: How to Break Bad Habits — Good Bad
Habits — Chart Your Progress — God Will Get You —
TALK SHOPPE: The Simple Rule of Conversation —
Silent Language — Small Steps to Small Talk — Tips
for Good Conversation — A WOMAN OF LETTERS**

CIVILITY

Good manners start at home. Once they're out the front door, though, anything can happen.

We received a lot of *questions* about etiquette, many of which we disregarded, since they could easily be answered by consulting the closest book on the subject. Other questions became the framework for our own discourse on etiquette. Where we addressed specific circumstances, we relied on what we thought was right; sometimes we consulted a cross-section of etiquette handbooks, but whenever we could we let contributors answer the question.

We also received a number of contributions either complaining about the lack of mannerly men or remarking on behavior that our mothers and grandmothers would have taken for granted.

One contributor — an *Anon.* — sent us what amounts to a précis of this section. We decided to reprint it entire, since it addressed our own concerns in a charming and much more disarming way than we could. Here it is:

WHY WORRY ABOUT MANNERS?

First of all, because we fear for our lives. Who is that person coming toward us on the street? Does someone in that window way up there have a gun? Is someone going to hurt us?

Manners are important because they comfort us by proving that chaos has not yet triumphed over all the earth. Isn't it less likely that we will be shot from an upper window in a world where people say "please" and "thank you" and hold open doors for one another? "Please" and "thank you" means our society has not yet totally disintegrated.

People still follow rules! I breathe a sigh of relief when I see folks standing back ten feet from the person making the automatic teller transaction. After all, there is no sign saying "Stand Back Ten Feet." But people are courteous. And what about in movie theaters? A mass of people can still come together in peace. How about in the ice cream parlors? People form lines. People wait. People say, "Excuse me." Sure, it doesn't *always* work out, but most of the time it still does.

Second of all, it's crowded out there. There are *millions* of us and we are all going in different directions. Without manners we would all fall over each other into confused heaps. We would bang into each other and get bruises or worse. Bigger people would always run through the doorways first, and smaller people would never make it through. Mothers pushing baby carriages would never leave their houses. There would be big fights at the supermarket check-out lines and in front of the pretzel machines. People would crowd into elevators and the elevators would all crash from the weight. Even *nice* people would begin to play their stereos all night long.

Third, we want to be liked. If we are good to other people, maybe they will like us more.

Manners are like grease, you see. They make our passage through life slipperier. Easier. And we will be less likely to die in elevator accidents.

Here are my suggestions for everyday rules:

1. If there are two women and one man walking together down the street, the man is not to walk in the middle. For one thing, he is usually taller and the women will not be able to see each other. Kind of like the centerpiece on the table. It's not supposed to be above the eye level of those seated. So the man walking is like the vase of flowers, in a way. Too tall. So don't put him in the middle. Also, he is supposed to pretend to be equally interested in both women, and it is easier for him to pretend this if he can see both of them at once.

2. The woman is supposed to precede the man unless in dangerous territory, and then the man goes first in order to aid the woman. I think this is pretty nice.

3. A woman sits to the right of a man. Sure, maybe this sort of thing doesn't make any sense, but if you can remember the way it's *supposed* to be, it just might make a future situation more simple.

4. On a crowded bus, do what seems decent and sensible. If someone appears to be more in need of a seat than you are, offer your's. Offer to the old, the weak, the very pregnant, the ones with piles of packages. No one seems to do this anymore. My father, who is seventy and walks with a cane, gave his seat to a woman in her ninth or tenth month of pregnancy because no one else gave her any thought, and then he stood for the next eight miles because no one gave *him* any.

5. Don't chew your gum like a cow.

6. If your son practices the drums, tell him to knock it off after ten at night. (**See** *Teach Your Children Well,* **below.**) The neighborhood will appreciate it. Always be aware of the noise you are creating. It is not fair to submit others to your blaring television, music, fights, etc. Your noise is your noise until it enters the ears of another.

7. Elbows are allowed on the table if you have to lean forward to talk to someone, but not while you are eating.

8. Dessert may be eaten with a spoon *or* a fork. That is a big relief to me, because I eat my ice cream with a fork.

9. Thank God, fingers are permitted when the bacon is crisp.

10. If you are choking to death, it is permissible to let someone know. *(Anon)*

THERE OUGHT TO BE A DISTINCTION

With so many etiquette columnists and authors around, we sort of thought the rules of behavior were overdocumented. Even our companion volume, *The Modern Man's Guide to Life,* which we think had the right attitude toward women (and which helped form our own list of what sort of behavior women have the right to expect from men), went on a little too long on the subject for our taste.

We do, however, embrace the notion that courtly manners — like many other aspects of our cultural environment — should celebrate gender distinctions. To advocate otherwise, we think, is silly, sort of like making fashion or hairstyles a political issue. Some things *ought* to make gender distinctions.

Readers who wish detailed information are urged to consult one of the many books available. The older titles are better than many of the recent ones, some of which seem to contain semisociological apologies for bad manners rather than helpful guidance and advice. Maybe good behavior has also become a situational sort of thing. We hope not.

So questions and observations about etiquette remain. If our advice about manners seems blunt, excuse us. We don't mean to be rude about it.

MANNERS AND MEN

Women should expect that every man has a reasonably thorough knowledge of mannerly behavior, and that if he violates the basic rules of etiquette, he is doing so on purpose. (KY)

What women should expect from men:

• A woman should expect to be able to walk down a street without hearing a chorus of whistles, shouts or animal noises.

• She should expect to be able to engage in conversation with a man without having him mistake her attention for flirtation. **See** *How To Flirt* **in** *CHAPTER FIVE: MODERN MEN.*

• She should expect that men will refrain from touching her in any familiar way.

• She should expect men to hold open doors for her.

• She should expect a man to offer to light her cigarette.

• She should expect a man to offer her his seat if there are no others available.

• She should expect men to stand when she approaches a table or when she is being introduced.

• She should expect men to wait to be seated until after she has taken her own seat.

• She should expect men to perform these courtesies without discussion or unnecessary comment.

Some comments from contributors:

If a man opens a door for you, simply thank him and smile. It isn't always easy for a man to do these polite things. (TP)

Boxing match: I went to pick something up from the industrial section of town. It was a very heavy box that I could have managed if I had to, but a big man with a cigar grabbed it before I had a chance. He said something about how a pretty little lady shouldn't have to lug around such a heavy thing.

I just loved it. It wasn't very liberated of me, but I don't care. That big, wonderful man dared to say and do all the things that he has been warned not to say and do for the last twenty years and it was great. (EP)

Once you've spent some time with a guy who opens doors for you, all the guys who don't seem like real clods. (BP) They are.

WHAT MANNERS MEAN TO WOMEN

Civil and courteous behavior is a matter of self-esteem as well as a compliment to those around you. (KV) Every social situation calls for an inner decision on how to act and react. Our responses to others are clear statements about our basic values, about our attitude toward other people, as well as all that stuff about how we were raised.

WORKING WONDERS

Don't expect the men at your firm to *always* pick up the lunch tab. Always pay for your own lunch bill. (TH)

In business etiquette, the rule is to treat everyone with the same consideration. Help anyone who seems to need it, excercise a logical give-and-take attitude. (CGr)

Address the women at your firm as "Ms." You can't possibly know what every woman's personal situation is and the term covers everything. Don't use it, of course, if the woman addresses herself as "Mrs. So-and-so." (TD)

Don't be a slob at the office. Leave your desk or room neat. Don't make yourself up in public areas or put your feet up on your desk. In other words, remember what your mother told you every day of your young life. (MH)

If you happen to be a woman in power, don't treat those who work for you like dogs. Treat them the way you want your superiors to treat you. (GY)

Never call a client or associate at home unless it's an emergency. When work is over, it's over. (TR)

When you want to give a gift to an associate or someone in the company, make it impersonal. These gifts could include theater tickets, a bonus or a bouquet of flowers. (RN)

If you must travel with a business associate who happens to be a man, buy your own drinks and don't expect him to foot the bill for your food or entertainment. (CGr)

Don't hang out in a hotel bar without your briefcase. (TR)

TEACH YOUR CHILDREN WELL

Manners are taught at home within the family structure through example, discipline and support. If we're disrespectful and obnoxious, we'll receive disrespect and be treated as morons. There's nothing old fashioned about knowing and showing kindness and caring.

A three-year-old doesn't have to know how to set a table for a formal dinner party, but she should be able to understand and respond to situations where a thoughtful "thank you," "please" and "pardon me" are in order. (IS)

Well-mannered children are happy children. People accept them because of their consideration and respect of others. (AKK)

COVER-UP

*Mr. or Ms?*When you are sending that anonymous person a letter and you haven't a clue if that person is a man or a woman, send a memo instead. After typing in your name, address and the date at the top of the letter, in the left-hand margin address the memo to the company and give the standard reference quotation. (GT)

These days some women are keeping their maiden names after they marry, and others are living with a man. How do you word an invitation or card?

• For the hyphenated woman, address the card with the man's name first and follow with the woman's name (including the "-" if that's what she normally uses).

• For live-together types you should simply include both names on the card or message, listing the woman's name first. (TL)

Homosexual couples, as well as live-togethers, must be invited as you would any other couple. Don't invite one and not the other. It's not gracious. (TR)

TO BE OR TO SMOKE

Hostesses need not supply cigarettes for a cocktail or dinner party, but make sure there are plenty of ashtrays about. (DW)

Never smoke while at table at a dinner party. Wait until dinner is over and either others light up, or wait until they congregate into another room where others are smoking. If you desperately need a cigarette or cigar, excuse yourself and step outdoors. (RGR)

A dissent: Take a cue from the host or hostess. If they smoke, you can feel free to do so. (DW)

Places not to smoke include hospitals, job interviews, business meetings, stores, elevators, homes with newborns, gyms, and homes where the people who live there don't smoke. (DK) **Also see** *In Carpools,* **below.**

When eating at a cafeteria or lunch counter, it's right to ask those sitting next to you if they mind if you smoke. Respect their answer. (TG)

TAXICABS

When entering a taxicab, the general rule of the gentleman opening the car door and allowing his companion to enter first is suspended these days. Instead, the gentleman will enter the cab first, presumably to ascertain that there are no evildoers lurking in the backseat or that the driver is not a homicidal maniac, but probably to absorb whatever gunk has been left on the seat. His companion will then enter and close her own door, while the gentleman gives their destination to the driver. (JWa)

A dissent: Taxicabs are part of the real world. In the real world, a gentleman holds open the door for a woman. If there are terrorists or cigar butts on the backseat, they'll be noticed by an attentive man. (GSt)

APPLAUSE

Have you wondered how people know when to applaud? How does it work? Well, sometimes it doesn't work.

You've heard it, you've been there: that terrible, non-zen sound of two hands clapping

— alone among *thousands* of hands. You look at your hands like they belong to a stranger.

At the ballet: Applaud when the conductor makes his first appearance. Applaud after a set if it will not spoil the mood or music. Applaud wildly but briefly after something that is particularly difficult and exceptional. Be sure to cut the applause short, as it can ruin the mood. If you have any doubts, sit on your hands.

In churches: Don't.

At competitions: Think about it. There you are at a chess competition. Suddenly white pulls a 5Q-R4 in the face of critical disapproval and manages to avoid a B-N2! And you're going to start slapping your hands together?

At concerts and recitals: Applaud the conductor and the soloists whenever they enter or exit. Do not applaud between movements of large works of music — even when you hear that little pause.

For the conductor: Applaud when the conductor takes the podium. He will bow towards you and then turn and face the music. That is when you stop.

For encores: Clap with all your heart if you wish. The performers will return for you. Don't worry for them, though, because when they decide to leave, they will leave. Your clapping won't keep them there forever.

For sacred music: Don't applaud.

For speakers: Applaud at the beginning and at the end — unless you're exercising censorship by rectitude, in which case you can whistle, cat-call, boo and clap throughout a speech by someone expressing a point of view with which you disagree.

At symphonies: Each time the conductor takes or leaves the podium, applaud. Applaud the soloists' first appearance, but wait until the entire work is finished before applauding the solo. Do not applaud individual movements of a symphony.

In the theater: Applaud the star's first entrance. Try not to interrupt the play with applause that will break the mood. (ALu)

ENGAGING ETIQUETTE

If you're a two-time bride, forget the engagement party. Have a private party with your second fiancé. (BK)

So, it didn't quite work out the way it should. Don't hawk that fab engagement ring. Give it back; it'd be dirty money. (OL)

Invitations to a wedding should be sent at least four weeks in advance, and certainly with an RSVP. (RK)

You must invite your family, their closest friends, your closest friends, and business associates to your wedding. You can, however, send announcements out to casual friends and to relatives that live far away or are far away from your heart. (TD)

If the wedding is suddenly called off — for any reason — call everyone on the guest list immediately, simply stating that the ceremony will not take place. Ignore snide comments. (FL)

WEDDING WORRIES

Thousand of words have been written in hundreds of books on how a wedding should be run.

There were once very strict rules that told you how many bridesmaids to have, when to announce an engagement, where to seat guests at the reception, and so on. While some people still treat these guidelines as gospel, things have loosened up a bit, and generally you can plan your wedding to suit yourself. Want to get married on the ferris wheel where he proposed to you? Go right ahead. Does City Hall seem like the right place to tie the knot? Feel free. Have the wedding of your dreams, whatever it happens to be. (LM)

What you have to pay for as a bridesmaid:
- Dress and accessories
- Transportation to and from the wedding site (if necessary)
- Contribution to the bride's gift from the bridesmaids
- A wedding gift to the bride and groom (ER)

If your parents cannot afford the wedding you've been dreaming of, be nice and plan a smaller, less expensive ceremony. Bigger doesn't mean better. Maybe you two, or the groom's parents can help pay for the sort of wedding everyone would adore and cherish. (TG)

When you're invited to a wedding and an RSVP is part of the invitation, respond immediately, indicating your acceptance or regrets. (TD)

Evening weddings seem more elegant and are certainly more romantic. (IS)

Writing your own ceremony is a really dopey thing to do. If you're going to go through with the traditional dress and are being married in a church, go all the way. It's very pretty. You have plenty of time to say those private vows to each other. (AC)

A dissent: A few words spoken to each other about your own feelings on your special day is perhaps more of a vow than the traditional weddings allow. (TD) **See also** *Sign Here* **in** *CHAPTER FIVE: MODERN MEN.*

Buy your fiancé a special little present. Give it to him at some private moment after the ceremony. It doesn't have to be fancy — it's a keepsake. (TR)

If you can't go to the wedding, you should send a gift to the bride's mother's home. Send it as soon as you know that you can't attend. (OT)

A gift of money is perfect for newlyweds. Enclose a card that says that you hope this gift can contribute to something they really need. (OT)

HOW TO PLAN A SMALL WEDDING

Since most small weddings are semi-formal or informal affairs, you can attend to most of the duties in a relaxed and leisurely fashion. The invitations, for example, can be hand-written, and the photographer can be a family friend. You can get by with a minimum amout of flowers at a smaller wedding — the bride's bouquet, the groom's boutennière and corsagesw and boutennières for parents and attendants are all that's really necessary. Likewise, music can be supplied by either a pianist, a small ensemble, or, if you're on a tight budget, you can use recorded music. Catering at the reception — if there is one — can be informal; a buffet is always pleasant, but if the wedding is small enough, a sit-down dinner might be the best arrangement.

Decide how small you want your small wedding to be. Once you have a fixed number of people in mind, it'll make it easier to cull your lists and decide which friends and relatives you most want to attend. Be sure you can explain to all those you will exclude why they weren't invited. Some sort of rule will help here: For example, by inviting only immediate family members and your best friend, you provide yourself with a built-in excuse. (ESR)

TOILET TORTURE

You're at a restaurant, bar, library, movie theater, racetrack or airline terminal when you decide to use the ladies room. You hang up your bag and your coat, put your tickets or books or carry-on luggage on the fold-down shelf, lift your skirt, lower your panties, and there you are, sitting in someone else's pee. It's demeaning and horrible and filthy to wipe strange urine off your bottom and the toilet seat before you can do what you desperately need to do. Let's all come to an agreement, please. Use the toilet seat covers or line the rim with toilet paper and just plunk yourself right down on the seat. I promise you, everything will be just fine. Think of it as an adventure. (KL)

SINGING IN THE PAIN

Don't sing in public even when your favorite song in the whole world comes on the jukebox. Chances are good that your voice won't sound as good to the people listening as it does to you. Of course, if you happen to be Roberta Peters, this does not apply. Group sing-alongs are also exceptions. If you simply can't help yourself, hum the tune under your breath. (MK)

A dissent: It's not impolite — in fact, it's fun — to bellow along with the radio or whatever, provided you're among close friends. (KO)

GIFTS

An anecdote: There it is, it's a necklace, I think. It's this huge rope with colored tassels like brooms. Beads, bright ones, like eggs. It's got bells on it, I swear to God. It's a necklace, or do you hang a plant from it? How could this happen? The only jewelry you've ever worn are necklaces that are almost invisible. A ring, maybe, with a small blue stone. A bracelet that barely glints in the sun. And now there he is, and there you are. And bells and eggs. Him smiling at you. (EA)

When you receive a gift that is really horrible you break into a sweat. Ignore the sweat, because if you mop your brow it will look suspicious. Smile, and say, "Oh, thank you so much." (DD)

Put it on the bottom of your old toybox that your mother stores in her basement. Leave town. (CWC)

Be gracious. Say, "Oh, you *really* shouldn't have." Or say, "Oh, I really *can't* accept this." Remember one thing, though: If the gift was given with a true heart, accept it with a true heart. (JW)

MODERN MORTALS

To ease the confusion of a friend who is facing the imminent death of someone very close to her, stay by her side emotionally and have her tell you *exactly* what she would like you to do to help. When death does come, call her lawyer and funeral home and notify the cemetery. Call all her friends and family and tell them what's transpired and when the funeral date is and where. Stay by the phone for incoming calls. Make sure the remaining family is fed and comfortable, allowing your friend time for mourning. Organize a lunch or dinner for after the funeral, if that's what your friend wishes. (EL)

In the case of a death in the family of a friend or family member, offer to take care of the children. Take them to your home, or quietly stay in their home if you are very good friends. (TD)

Send flowers to the funeral home with an unobtrusive card stating your sympathy and name. (EL)

After an appropriate period of time has passed since the death in the family of a friend, ask them over to a family dinner. Don't ignore your friend or assume she wants to be left alone. (TL)

IN CARPOOLS

No excuses: If you're going to be a part of a carpool, you'd better be on time — precisely and utterly life-and-death, to-the-very-second prompt and punctual.

Don't smoke in the car without asking. Be sure to open your window a little bit. If you are in the front seat, remember that your burning embers may land in the laps of people in the backseat. Also, remember that the snow and rain and sleet will also land on the people in the backseat. Remember the wind, too. All those carefully combed heads back there are going to get the wind. It might, in fact, be better to refrain from smoking and to leave the window up.

The big picture: Remember that the driver is supposed to be able to see. Do what you can not to block the view. In other words, be conscious of the driver.

Don't brush your hair until you are out of the car. Nobody wants your little hairs all over their coats. (NLW)

AT THE TABLE

Euro-silver: It's perfectly acceptable to keep your knife in your right hand and the fork in the left, Euopean style. And, yes, by all means, cut your salad with a knife. After dinner, place the fork and knife diagonally across the center of the plate. The tines on the fork should point up. (OT)

Never salt or pepper your food before you've tasted it. And never ask for ketchup or any other condiment — the message you'll be giving is that the food was improperly prepared. (SK)

If you need to spit something out of your mouth — bones or pits, maybe — put the objectionable object onto your fork and then place it on your plate. (RP)

If you should find an insect in your food, pick it out with your fork and put it in your napkin. No comments allowed. Same goes for a hair. You needn't continue eating if your sensibilities are in an uproar, but try to fake it. (TO'D)

When you're served chicken or game hens, try to cut as much meat as possible off the bones first, before you really get down to enjoying it. (OT)

Don't serve corn on the cob unless it's a very informal dinner. (TY)

DINING OUT

The person who invites you out for dinner is the one who pays — as you do when you invite someone out. (TR)

Wait for your guests at a designated area — the bar, for instance. Never wait for your guests at the table. Arrive at the restaurant *before* your guests. (MN)

You must wait for at least one-half hour for tardy guests. Call their home or workplace to see if some kind of emergency has come up before you leave. (OT) *If you're going to be unavoidably late* to dinner, make every effort to call the restaurant (or the home, if that's where you've been invited) and explain to the host that you'll be late and say when you will be arriving. If there's a party of people waiting, tell them to go on with the meal and you'll join them for dessert or drinks. (PL)

If you're called on to order first, order modestly. If the host orders first, and orders lavishly, so can you. Don't *expect* the host to order wine. If you want wine with dinner, offer to buy a bottle for the table. (TO'D)

Arf: It's perfectly all right to ask for a doggie bag from the waiter. (RLi)

BAR ETIQUETTE

Although it may seem otherwise, a combination of common sense and basic courtesy are the groundwork of bar etiquette in today's saloons.

Tipping: Bartenders derive a large percentage of their income from tips, and several factors should be considered when doling out the dough:

- *How long* have you been occupying that barstool? Think of it as paying rent.
- *How was the service,* attitude and efficiency?
- Were the *drinks up to snuff?*
- *Will you be back* again and, if so, how do you want to be remembered?

Leaving a percentage of your total bill doesn't always make sense. Again, use common sense. But remember that most bartenders will turn up their noses and won't remember you fondly if you simply empty your pockets of excess change. (SWa)

Working for stiffs: The bartender is working and it is rude to engage him in long conversations, as then he can't attend to his other patrons. If he wants to talk to you, you'll know it. (VS)

Sending a drink is a nice way to start up a conversation. It is perfectly acceptable to buy another customer a drink (but never the bartender, unless you're in Europe). You must allow the bartender to inform the customer before serving, as no one should become indebted without his consent. (AP)

A dissent: Offering to buy a bartender a drink is a friendly tradition, one appreciated by many barkeeps. (RGR)

Final judgment: Always accept the bartender's judgment on when you've had enough to drink. Arguing this point proves you have. (SWa) **You'll need to see** *Hangover Therapy* **in** *CHAPTER ELEVEN: MODERN WOMAN AT EASE.*

ONE-WOMAN SHOW

Modern single women should entertain as much as they are entertained. No matter how modest your circumstances may be, it's the proper thing to do. (TO)

When you are invited to a cocktail party or dinner, never assume you can bring a date. You must ask the hostess if it's all right if you do. If she hestitates, be gracious and don't press the issue. (PL)

A hostess may ask you to bring a date. If you don't know anyone at the moment and don't have any men friends that you could invite, tell her. Or say that you'd prefer to come by yourself. (OT)

When you want to pay for a business lunch or for taking a man out to dinner but you sense that it may cause embarrassment, excuse yourself from the table and quietly settle up with the captain. (RL)

Gag chow mein: Your cooking leaves a lot to be desired? Reciprocate an invitation by taking your friends out for a Chinese dinner. (NC)

It's perfectly all right to ask a man out for a date. If you feel too uncomfortable asking him face-to-face, write a little note. But be sure your phone number is on it. (NC)

GOOD FORM

No bleachers: There aren't many occasions when you must worry about seating people correctly for a formal occasion, but you never know. Here's the program:

• *The male guest of honor* sits on the hostess's right, and the next most important man sits to her left.

• *The female guest of honor* sits on the host's right and the second most important woman on his left.

• *You should stagger the seating* between men and women, although it's not always possible to do so. Husbands and wives should not be seated together. (FR)

• *Place cards* should be used for seven or more guests. They need not be printed — a clean and clearly typed card will do. Place the card against the stem of a wine glass or set it on top of the plate. (TR)

• *Don't worry about seating two men* or two women together if you have an guest list with a gender imbalance. Two people of the same gender can have a marvelous rapport, especially if you live in Los Angeles. (TR)

Don't bring your children or an unexpected house guest to a dinner party unless you clear it with the hostess. (RL) **See** *How to be a Guest,* **below.**

Wait to eat until your hostess and host have begun, unless otherwise urged on by the hostess. (OT)

You needn't serve hors d'oeuvres before dinner, but if predinner cocktails are being served, you may want to have a platter of raw vegetables or a dish of nuts placed about for munching. (OT)

If you're on a diet, be gracious and take small portions. (TY)

WINE TIME

Never pour red wine into the glass your guest has been drinking white wine from. Be sure you supply another glass. (OT) **See** *GLASS MENAGERIE* **in** *CHAPTER NINE: HOME EC* **for guidance.**

With a first course (chicken, fish or fruit), serve a chilled white wine. A nice Chablis, Johannisberg Reisling, Pinot Chardonnay or Chenin Blanc is appropriate.

With a main course of meat — and even with the after dinner cheese — you'll want to serve a room-temperature red wine like Bardolino, Valpolicella, a Burgundy, Bordeaux or Zinfandel. (AB) **For more wine info, see also** *Wine* **in** *CHAPTER ELEVEN: MODERN WOMAN AT EASE.*

Remember that certain people like certain wines. It's really inappropriate to insist that a guest must drink red wine with the meat course. If she prefers white wine with everything, it's okay. It's your job to offer, not dictate. (OT)

If you can afford it, serve a nice bottle of champagne with or after dessert. Make it dry, make it great. (AB)

Hosting a dinner party takes confidence and a great deal of work. A way to get into the moment is to rise, wineglass in hand, and make a toast to all your guests, thanking them for their friendship and for coming. (OT)

As a guest at a dinner party, it's very nice to toast your host and hostess at dessert time. Thank them for the superb dinner and for the good company. (BT)

AFTER DINNER

After the dinner is over, **encourage conversation.** Make sure the most talkative of your guests circulate. Play some nice music at a volume that can be talked over. Never turn on the television unless there's a war on. (TO'D)

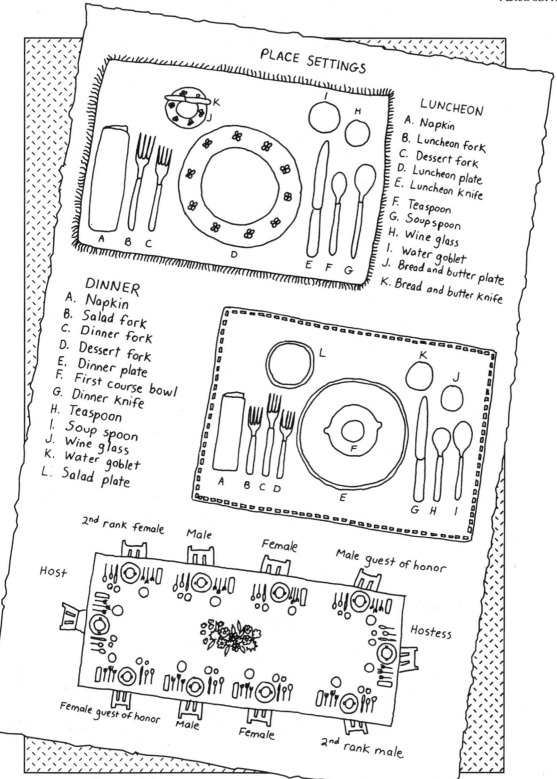

PLACE SETTINGS

LUNCHEON

A. Napkin
B. Luncheon fork
C. Dessert fork
D. Luncheon plate
E. Luncheon knife
F. Teaspoon
G. Soup spoon
H. Wine glass
I. Water goblet
J. Bread and butter plate
K. Bread and butter knife

DINNER

A. Napkin
B. Salad fork
C. Dinner fork
D. Dessert fork
E. Dinner plate
F. First course bowl
G. Dinner knife
H. Teaspoon
I. Soup spoon
J. Wine glass
K. Water goblet
L. Salad plate

2nd rank female
Male
Female
Male guest of honor
Host
Hostess
Female guest of honor
Male
Female
2nd rank male

Leave a dinner or cocktail party on time. Don't overstay your welcome. Don't get drunk and make your hosts have to worry about you. **See** *Drunk Driving Guests* **in** *CHAPTER ELEVEN: MODERN WOMAN AT EASE.* Send a thank-you note and reciprocate. (OT)

THE COCKTAIL PARTY

How to host a cocktail party: As with all things, *planning* ahead puts you on the road to success.

• Take a good look at the actual floor space, the number of couches and chairs, and imagine how many people could fit in that space comfortably.

• Now that you've come up with a number, invite those people over the telephone — that way you'll get an immediate answer.

• At least four weeks in advance of your party, hire a bartender and waiter. This is not very expensive, and it allows you time to relax and circulate and lends a certain air to the occasion. Tell the help what you'd like them to wear, and ask them to arrive at your home to help you set up at least half an hour before your guests arrive.

• Since guests usually start arriving half an hour after the stated time, if you want to start at seven o'clock invite them for six-thirty.

• Figure twelve hors d'oeuvres per person in a two-hour period. Catered hors d'oeuvres are wonderful but expensive, so if you make them yourself, do it early in the day. Also, have bowls of nuts and platters of cut fruit and cheese at several areas around the room, since people tend to congregate around the food.

• Buy ice the day of the party.

• When you're choosing drinks, buy as much wine as you do spirits, and don't forget beer.

• For fifteen people you should have on hand: one fifth each of vodka, scotch, gin and bourbon; two bottles each of red and white wine; and twelve bottles of beer. Don't forget to buy seltzer, mineral water, club soda and orange and grapefruit juice.

• If you don't happen to have forty appropriate and matching glasses on hand, rent them from a party supply rental store. (SJ)

POOL PARTIES

Invitations: If you're lucky enough to have a pool, have invitation-only pool parties, specifying the hours of the party and that food will be served.

The idea here is to have a great time at minimum expense.

• Set up an outdoor bar for the adults and a soda bar for the kids.

• For food, put together a hamburger and hotdog barbecue with a large salad and fresh fruit.

• Have plenty of towels, sun screen and water toys on hand.

• Hire a student to watch over the kids and to keep them busy with games so you can actually visit with your guests.

ENTERTAINING ON THE EARTH

Picnics are a great way to entertain, and you won't have to clean up your house the next day. They can be fancy or plain. Just keep in mind what you think your guests would most enjoy. For example, if many of your guests have children, a baseball and hotdog get-together is more appropriate than a linen napkin and wine affair. (GH)

In planning a picnic party, first consider the site.

• If there will be kids at the picnic, choose a place where there is something for them to do, like a playground area nearby with swings and slides. The beach or a site that has a stream are good places for kids on outings, but you must then also plan on having somebody in charge of the children.

• If only adults are invited, choose a place away from playgrounds.

• Make sure you've covered every possible need from diapers to ice.

• Always take along more supplies than you think you'll need, because chances are everyone will want to stay longer than you've expected. There's something about a picnic that makes people groan at the thought of it, but once they get there, they never want to go home. (SM)

HOSTING WEEKEND GUESTS

Plenty of notice: Invite your guests one or two months ahead of time. Say exactly when you want them to arrive and what time you expect them to leave. Clue them in on what activities will take place so they'll know what kind of clothes to bring. (RL)

It's your responsibility to make your guests comfortable. Never imagine that they will remember to bring toothpaste or shampoo. Have necessities on hand. These should include hair dryers, toothpaste, shampoo, hand lotion, a razor and packet of blades, a radio or small television, a reading lamp, matches and ashtrays, a bottle of aspirin, books and current magazines, a small coffee maker, a comfortable bed with plenty of blankets, a well-ventilated room and a fresh bouquet of flowers on the night stand. (OT)

If you plan on entertaining overnight guests, you must provide transportation from and to their place of arrival — the airport or train station. (RL)

HOW TO BE A GUEST

The most important thing to remember about being a weekend guest is not to overstay your welcome. (OT)

Always ask before you bring your children to weekend invitations. You should assume your pets are not invited. (KK)

Bring a present for the hostess. It doesn't have to be extravagant, but it does need to be nice. A large, beautiful plant, a few bottles of wine, or a pound or two of exotic coffee would be nice. (BT)

Keep your bed made and don't make long-distance telephone calls. If you break something, tell your hostess immediately and try to replace it. (YL)

JERK DEFENSE

Don't get angry with a jerk. That only makes the situation worse and creates two jerks instead of one.

Instead, manipulate him. Don't say things that will inflame him or send his defenses sky-high. Listen to what he says, then rephrase his remarks and ask questions. It will appear as though you are an interested and caring person, when really you are ordering him to self-destruct. When jerks have to actually hear what they are saying and then respond to questions about their beliefs, they disintegrate before their very own eyes. (RD)

Never put yourself on the level of the jerk. You must be beyond reproach. Do nothing to justify the jerk's words or actions, but continue to act as if the person were a decent human being. (GG)

Say, "Excuse me, but I hear the phone," no matter where you are. Then leave. (HN)

The problem with jerks is that it's difficult to know when you've run across one. They will confuse and upset you before you know what has happened. But a good way to deal with jerks once you have identified them is to say as little as possible. Give them next to nothing to twist or mangle. (HPD)

Give it some thought. Maybe *you* are the jerk. Keep an open mind about who is being what. (EA)

Is he a jerk? Or just awkward or shy or unhappy? Give people a chance before you hurry to dismiss them from your life. A bit of jerkness is not really such a bad thing. You want some egotist who spends all his spare time cultivating fake charm? (FDD)

BAD HABITS

Many people have their whole personalities tied up in bad habits. Break a habit if you can, but if you can't, don't don't let it break your heart.

HOW TO BREAK BAD HABITS

Break a bad habit on a special day. Christmas Eve was a good one for me. I stopped smoking at 11 P.M. on that evening and didn't smoke again for eight years, so it worked pretty well. I wouldn't recommend New Year's. Pick a day that will be your own. (UJ)

Some habits are next to impossible to break. Tearing at your cuticles, for example. If you have done this since childhood, you don't even know you are doing it. Quitting smoking is a snap compared to cuticles. You can't throw your cuticles into the trash, can you? (TP)

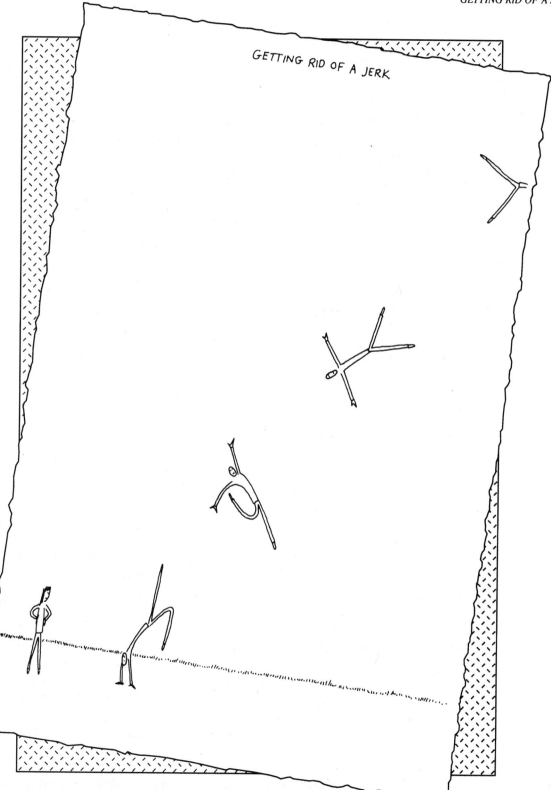

GOOD BAD HABITS

I need my bad habits. They round out an otherwise goody-goody personality. I cultivated them on purpose so that people wouldn't think I was a jerk. (BB)

CHART YOUR PROGRESS

For years, my mother had us make monthly tooth-brushing charts. We'd get red and gold stars for brushing teeth. So make yourself a calendar and buy a box of stars. Reward yourself. A red star for every good day and a big gold one for a perfect week, that's how it works. Ask my mom. (DK)

GOD WILL GET YOU

Make breaking a habit a moral issue. Predicate all your integrity on stopping doing something. Make smoking a cigarette, for example, worth your soul. (PAN)

TALK SHOPPE

Language is the great divider. A well-timed verbal thrust can knock the wind out of a bully, and a well-placed *bon mot* can bring a dead party back to life. So watch what you say.

THE SIMPLE RULE OF CONVERSATION

Here it is: One person's turn leads to another person's turn. When you're asked a question, don't answer with an abrupt yes or no, but don't go into too much depth, either. And ask the other person about her own experiences. Leave enough room in the conversation for genuine dialogue. (ER)

SILENT LANGUAGE

You can do a lot silently to put people at ease. It is especially easy if you work in a government office where the employees are known for their abrupt manners and poker faces. Any sign of kindness by you will be gobbled up by the public with whom you come into contact. If you work in a really dreadful place — say, an employment office — your clients will be very anxious. They may be confused or angry or worried. Look them in the eyes and smile at them. It doesn't happen very often in those places. Touch them. Not so that you go to jail, but if you are explaining something complicated on some horrible government form and your hands are pointing to something and their hands are on the desk, too, you can kind of touch them on their hand. That little touch can change the whole course of the interview. Instead of two natural enemies, you become two human beings. (WL)

Don't explain and don't complain. There's nothing wimpier than the sound of an excuse, and there's nothing more boring than a complainer. Be a big cowboy, strong and silent. (EC)

If you have doubts about what you are about to say, don't say it. People will think you are elegant and mysterious if you don't blow it by opening your mouth. (TP)

You can chatter away to your heart's content with your dear friends, but in the workplace you must think before you speak. Don't gossip about coworkers. On the other hand, you don't want the folks to think you are unfriendly and aloof. When the people at the lunch table start gossiping, you must not rise up in a huff and stalk out. Just be careful with the words you contribute. You have to get along. (RO)

SMALL STEPS TO SMALL TALK

There is no such thing as useless conversation. No one should be expected to leap immediately into The Truth. It's not natural. Small talk is an essential skill. It makes a little bridge. Once you've got the bridge made, you can send in the big trucks. (BV)

Let's talk: Leaping into an intense, meaningful conversation is like sex without foreplay. (TT)

Small talk is a wonderful art. To be able to put others at ease through meaningless conversation is difficult. Being good at small talk in social situations will help you out in your business transactions, too. It's a treat to be able to convince other folks through skillful small talk that they interest you, because people shine when they believe they are liked. (FL)

Sniff: The awful thing about lacking the skill of small talk is that people tend to see quiet types as snobs. (RP)

If you make your small talk slightly outrageous, people will dislike you for being eccentric. If you make your small talk utterly commonplace, people will dislike you for being a big bore. I think it's sensible then to be slightly outrageous, since nobody is going to like you anyway. *(Anon.)*

The secret to making good small talk is to state the obvious with humor and charm. (VS)

TIPS FOR GOOD CONVERSATION

• Remember, it's the ones who talk too much who get into trouble, not the ones who talk too little.

• Don't rattle on and on. Stop and think about what you are doing. Is everyone glassy-eyed?

• How many times do you hear yourself using the pronoun "I"? Cut down on your use of that word. It will do wonders for everyone.

• Don't try to make everyone laugh all of the time. Most people aren't funny enough to pull it off.

• If you can't think of a thing to say, try asking for advice about something — *anything*. People are flattered to be asked and will love telling you everything they know, and meanwhile you can relax.

• Learn to accept a compliment gracefully. If someone tells you that you look nice, don't go on and on about the pimple on your nose. Simply say, "Thank you."

• If you have a chance to give a compliment, give it. The world is a mean place, and any nice word will be well received.

• If someone says something that enrages you, try to change the subject. If you think you can keep a cool and level head about it, go ahead and state your opinion. (LG, BR)

A WOMAN OF LETTERS

The one rule of informal letter etiquette:

Don't apologize.
It's been fifteen years since your last letter? So? *You* know it. *They* know it. Don't start by going on and on with sorry and gosh and, oh, I've been *sooo* busy, or, gee, but not a *thing* has happened in the last fifteen years. Face it, there *is* always time to write a letter, something *has* happened in the last fifteen years, and there *are* no excuses. So, no apologies. Just get to it.

Not to put a damper on your drive, but do remember that once you have written something and sent it away, it is forever. You can't get it back. You can't cancel it. The written word has impact. You may have written one fleeting thought out of millions of fleeting thoughts, a thought that you don't even remember thinking by the next day, but to the receiver of the letter, there it is. Your thought. In stone. But don't get all crazy over this. All you have to do is write your letter, and put it away for one day. If it still looks okay in one day, send it off.

Nothing wrong with a little heart. You don't have to put on a big show about your delightful, successful, riveting life. This letter isn't business. You're not marketing yourself, for Pete's sake. Let your heart write.

It helps to start by finding a stamp and addressing the envelope. Often, that is the hardest part, and if you can get that done, the rest is a snap. (EC)

If you have lots of letters to write, start with the person you love the most. That one's always easy, and it'll get you going for the rest. On the other hand, you could try beginning with the one you love least. That way, by the time you get to the one you love, you'll be going full blast. Or you could do it alphabetically. (VP)

Modern Men

Suddenly, the landscape is filled with New Men, victims of pop-politics and social engineering. Sometimes it seems that what was once a man's world is now a land of living wimps where men take daily meetings with their feelings and spend all night reading you the minutes of the meeting.

Where did these guys come from? Did *we* create them or did they spring full blown from some dark pit inside Phil Donahue's closet?

Thankfully, there are still large numbers of regular guys out there — hard-working, courteous, Modern Men who are not only holding open doors but also holding families together and generally trying their best to survive in a era of good intentions and confused results.

The distinction between a New Man and a Modern Man, then, is obvious: you can cry with a New Man, but you'd *die* for a Modern one.

C O N T E N T S
Chapter Five: *MODERN MEN*

DATES: Blind Date — How to Meet a Lover — Where
to Meet People **— How to Flirt — How to Send Silent
Signals — Be Brave — Death of Courtship — Better
Than Buns — Recognizing a Come-On — How to Tell
If a Guy Likes You — Good Dates —** Impress Your
Date **— Dressing for the First Date — Recognizing the
Married Man — Six-Shooter — Date Rape — To Date
or Not to Date — Don't Date — How to Deal with an
Unruly Drunken Date — Gold Rush — Single Life —
A Date Dispatch — Don't Advertise — Things You
Can Say to Drive Men Crazy — Manipulation by Guilt
— When It's Okay to Go Out with Other Guys —
May-December-May — 180° Relationships — SEX:
Five Sure Signs of Lust — Scalp Message — First Aids
— Staying Alive — Latex Love — Dealing with
Men's Sexual Inadequacies — Dealing with Your
Own Sexual Inadequacies — You Want Me to *What?*
— Public Displays — Exhibitionism — Oral Sex —
How to Talk About Sex — Lesbianism — Celibacy —
Touching — Excuses for Not Having Sex —
BREAKING UP: Leaving a Lover — Ways to End the
Relationship Peacefully — Get Away — Not Good
Enough — How to Tell When It's Time to End It —
The Other Woman — Some Clues That He May Be
Fooling Around — Many Happy Returns —
MATRIMONY: Wedding Invitations — Red-Lining —
Kneel — Fare Weather Friends — Screening a Mate —
Sign Here — A Couple — Power — Oops! — On the
Street — Two Carriers — Divorce Prevention — Go
Samoan — Selfishness — Trouble Sneaks In — The Ex
Factor — Incest and Battering — DIVORCE: The
Rush to Split — Altered State — Divorcing Dad — Not
in Front of the Children**

DATES

Hell at night, that's what most dates are. The kids at school wised up —
nobody under the age of 21 *dates* anymore. They hang out, instead — and
usually in large, roving groups, like wildlife.

As a result, there's a generation of oafish men, inexperienced in basic social graces,
holding their hand out for *your* share of the dinner *they* invited you to.

Modern Women understand that the dating ritual no longer has much to do with mating. It's a training procedure, designed to give young men a little experience out alone with
a woman. Train them well. Some other Modern Woman will thank you for it.

BLIND DATE

What a place to start a relationship — trying to draw a conversation out of the telephone
with some jerk your cousin Becky knew in junior college. *Don't go,* if in your gut you know
you're not going to have a good time. If you can't sustain a ten-minute phone call with the
guy, how are you going to live through an entire evening? (GSt)

So what do you do?

HOW TO MEET A LOVER

Lovers arrive as friends of friends. That's a good way. You can trust someone a little
more when he's the friend of a friend. You're not looking for him or expecting him, and one
day you go over to your pal's house and she introduces you to So and So. And you greet So
and So with nothing on your mind at all, and then by and by it just clicks. Now, if this friend
of your friend is your friend's *special* friend, maybe you shouldn't get too close. But I am
talking about unattached friends of friends. (NC)

If you're in school, it's a snap. Just go to class. (AO)

If you work, just look around. Offices and factories are *lousy* with men, most of whom
are too shy or too awkward to know how to approach you. Send up flares. (LOP)

If you belong to a health club, go often. Don't go shimmying in like you're looking for
a lover, because you'll look like an idiot and end up with a one-night stand. Go in like a good
sport. Laugh. Be honest and sweat. Make *friends* with people. It's a decent way of locating
a lover. I'm talking about a *lover* here — one who loves. (TP) **See** *Recognizing a Married
Man,* **below.**

Allow a man to approach you in a supermarket or other nonthreatening environment.
If someone asks you a stupid question about canned soup, assume he's trying to start up a
conversation and needs a little help. *(Anon.)*

Don't anticipate rejection. It takes a special measure of courage for a man to walk up
to a strange woman and try to initiate a civil conversation. He can be quickly discouraged

if you telegraph your fears — he'll probably read them as get-lost messages. Similarly, don't assume every man who talks to you is a boor. If he is, you'll find out soon enough. *(Anon.)*

When I was a junior in high school, I asked my best friend how she always managed to start talking to people. She said, "Find something you both have in common, and break the ice."

The weather is enough. That you are both alive and walking down the same street can be enough. That he is reading something you enjoyed reading is enough. It doesn't matter, since *it's what comes after the first thing you say* that determines the length of the conversation or relationship.

Just break the ice. If you find nothing in common, compliment him on his shirt, body, eyes, or hair — or ask him a question. (GSt)

HOW TO FLIRT

flirt (verb) 1. to move erratically; FLIT *2. to behave amorously without serious intent 3.* TOY.

All right, what we're after, we Modern Women, is the second definition, the one about "behaving amorously without serious intent." If flirting is not approached with the right technique, we end up with definition number one. And if we approach the subject with no thought — relying on instinct alone — we're in danger of sliding into definition number three.

Eye contact: Eye contact is the most common way to begin a flirtation. This is basic and simple, yet effective. Look deeply into the eyes of your subject, longer than is usually thought polite for the situation. For example, if you are introduced to someone for the first time, let your eyes linger even after the verbal niceties are completed.

The more advanced form of eye contact used to be called *bedroom eyes.* This is for experienced flirts only. For those who wish to learn, seat yourself comfortably in front of a mirror. Close your eyes. Relax. Imagine yourself as the single most sexy woman ever born. (That may be the hardest part.) Picture someone you find attractive, someone you'd like to flirt with if you only had the chance (out-of-reach movie stars usually do the trick). Think of this someone smiling at you. With this vision in mind, *slowly* open your eyes, but don't bother opening them *wide*. Look in the mirror. If you think you look pretty good, you're ready for a test drive. If you look like a hay fever victim, forget it and try the wide-eyed innocent flirt — it'll probably suit you better anyway. **See** *How to Send Silent Signals,* **below.**

Touchy: Only use physical contact when flirting if either you are in a public place or you are in a private place with someone you know is a gentleman. Otherwise, *physical contact can be dangerous*. After all, an attractive woman can make a man lose his head.

Appropriate places to touch during light flirtation include the forearm, the shoulder and the lapel of his jacket. These areas are socially acceptable, yet still intrusive of his personal space. The pressure of your touch should be light and playful and the frequency should be selective. *The more serious the flirt, the longer the touch.*

Hand touching can be tricky. It is most effective when used sparingly. Let your fingers pass over his when he hands you a glass or your dinner napkin. Other types of touching, such as pressing your leg against his or your breast against his arm, fall under the category of making a pass and are not considered flirting.

Last laugh: To round out your flirting repertoire, laugh at his jokes, unless they are racist, sexist or tasteless, in which case you might consider either ignoring the joke or drop the flirting and tell him what you think of him — or gracefully extract yourself from the room. Pay attention to what he says and smile when appropriate.

Basic conversational skills are a bonus but are usually not necessary for flirting. On the other hand, if the extent of your conversation consists of monosyllabic muttering, you're a lousy flirt. **For guidance, see** *Small Steps to Small Talk* **in** CHAPTER FOUR: MODERN P's & Q's.

A good flirt knows her limits. After lots of practice you begin to sense when to start, when to stop and, most importantly, with whom to flirt.

A good guide for selection of flirting partners:
• He flirts with you first.
• He seems shy but interested.
• He makes your mouth dry, your knees weak and your heart flutter.
• Any normal man nearby when the urge strikes to flirt.

In other words, *it's okay to flirt with anybody* you're attracted to — except a police officer giving you a ticket, a judge handing down your sentence, your doctor, dentist or lawyer, a door-to-door salesman, your minister or priest, your boss, your assistant or your psychiatrist or marriage counselor. (AAT) **But also see** *Don't Date,* **below.**

You know you are acting in a flirtatious way when you realize that someone you didn't even know was there has been observing you with the one you did know was there. If you feel sort of silly, then you know that you have been caught flirting. (TP)

HOW TO SEND SILENT SIGNALS

Use eye contact. Don't look away when he looks at you. Let your eyes sort of linger on his. (VDV)

Exchange looks that imply comradeship or a sense of alliance. For example, if you are both at a cocktail party listening to a bore, catch the eye of the man you admire and give him a "this-is-all-just-too-boring" look. (JDP)

Let him catch you looking at him while you're talking to another man. (JDP)

Glance at his crotch once in a while. (You must have very serious intentions before you do this. (BNo) See *Date Rape,* **below.**

CONVERSATIONAL GAMBITS

Ask him where the hot spot in town is. Pretend you're new to the city and don't know a thing about the night life. (LS)

Suggest times you are free in the course of conversation. (JDP)

Express an interest in the things he talks about. Give him lots of compliments. (LS)

Ask him questions about his work and his life. Don't move from subject to subject, either; try to have a follow-up question ready. (JDP)

BE BRAVE

Men love women who are confident Don't give a second thought to your perceived physical shortcomings. Be confident of your abilities, your skills, your sexuality — your *womanliness*. And by the way, despite every woman's favorite myth, men are *not* preoccupied by things like breast size. In fact, they are almost always attracted first to a woman's face. So if body-shame is one of your problems, forget it. On the other hand, nothing creates an asexual atmosphere faster than a woman with low self-confidence. If you find you have far more male friends than you want or need, you're probably hiding your sexuality too well. *(Anon.)*

DEATH OF COURTSHIP

Women are suffering the death of courtship. Once upon a time, the dates, the uncertainty and the anticipation gave form and structure to a blooming relationship and gave each party the necessary distance in order to become closer. Romance depends on the earn and yearn system. These modern days, everyone just wants to earn. (MT)

Insist that a man court you before you settle comfortably into a relationship. Don't be a tease, and above all, don't be silly or coy, but I mean really *court* you — flowers, dinner dates, the works. Most men appreciate the opportunity to woo and win a woman, and it establishes a certain elegance for the relationship that will follow. *(Anon.)* **See the list under** *Manners and Men* **in** *CHAPTER FOUR: MODERN P's & Q's* **for the things you** *should* **expect.**

BETTER THAN BUNS

Something about the eyes and his having a sense of humor are the two things that most women notice first about a man. If these two things are present, look deeper for sincerity, compatibility and if he has an ability to have fun. (PS) Look for *reliability* in a man; it's nice when there is a certain predictability there, too. (MT)

The attractiveness of any given man equals the amount he wants you times the length of time you've been alone. *(Anon.)*

RECOGNIZING A COME-ON

Everyone in the world can recognize a come-on. Something in our genes makes us instantly aware of it, no matter how subtle the come-on is. After all, the survival of the human race depends on it. You know how it goes: One set of eyes meets another set of eyes for one second too long. Isn't it absolutely *wild* how long one extra second can be? (AJ) **See** *How to Flirt,* **above.**

You can recognize a come-on when either you feel intensely irritated or your blood begins to boil in a nice way and you feel light-headed. (JJ)

You can be sure a man is coming on to you at a party if he presupposes a certain exclusivity in talking to you; you'll know he's succeeding if his conversation tends to make you feel that the two of you are alone. (CO'N)

HOW TO TELL IF A GUY LIKES YOU

The guy's a goner if
- He asks for your phone number and actually calls you.
- He asks your friends about you.
- He finds excuses to run into you.
- He invites you over to his place for dinner.
- He introduces you to his friends or family. (AP)

GOOD DATES

We've all been out on lousy dates — and occasionally on good ones. Enjoyable dates all share some of the same things, and the tips that follow will help you make them all good.

- Don't plan anything that could be potentially embarrassing to the other person. (RF)
- Enjoy yourself; have the best time you can manage. Try not to go out with anyone who's not in your league. For instance, if you love bowling and he prefers croquet, the relationship could get bumpy. (AAT)
- If you're only going out for lust, don't go out with him again — it's just too dangerous. (MT) **Certainly see** *First Aids* **and** *Staying Alive,* **below.**
- If it's a first date, help the guy out. Express pleasure in his choice of restaurants or movies. Ask him about himself. Instead of concentrating on having a nice time yourself, try to help him have a nice time. For some men, a first date is traumatic.
- Don't give out crosssed signals. If you have no intention of sleeping with the guy in the near future, don't wear sexy clothes and act like a tease. You could be setting yourself up for date rape. (LK) **See** *Date Rape,* **below.**

DRESSING FOR THE FIRST DATE

- Consider where you will be going.
- Wear clothing you will be comfortable in.
- Wear clean underwear. A traffic accident, maybe.
- Don't dress provocatively. Save the French maid's outfit for later. (LK)

RECOGNIZING THE MARRIED MAN

With the man shortage being what it is, it might be tempting to grab onto the first available man who looks your way. However, some of the things your mother told you are true. There are married men out there wanting and waiting to deceive you. These men are

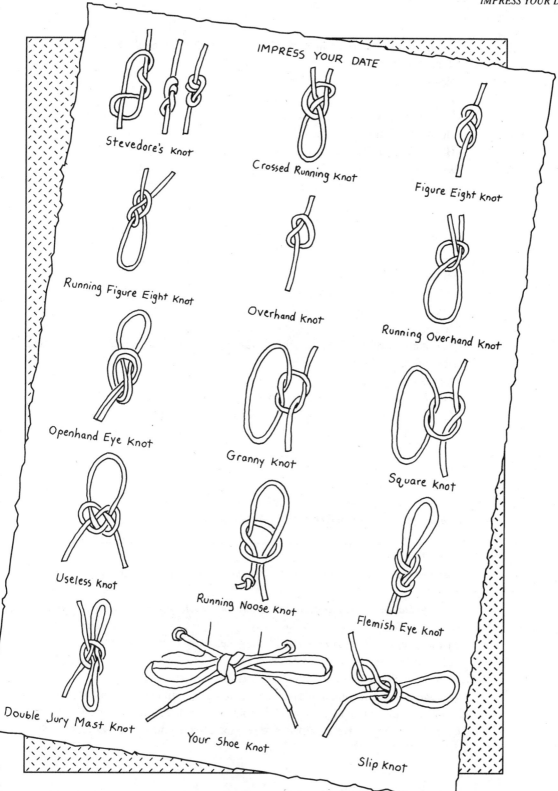

IMPRESS YOUR DATE

Stevedore's knot

Crossed Running Knot

Figure Eight knot

Running Figure Eight Knot

Overhand knot

Running Overhand Knot

Openhand Eye Knot

Granny Knot

Square knot

Useless Knot

Running Noose Knot

Flemish Eye Knot

Double Jury Mast Knot

Your Shoe Knot

Slip Knot

to be avoided at all costs. Here are some clues — but definitely not *all* of them — that may suggest that Mr. Possible is leading a double life.

- He can never be with you on a holiday.
- He never stays overnight at your place.
- He asks you never to call him at home or at work, or he won't tell you where he works.
- He insists upon taking a shower before he leaves your place.
- He doesn't seem to have any friends.

Any of these circumstances — by itself — may be explained in perfectly innocent terms. But combined as a pattern, they suggest something's wrong. For your own piece of mind, it's important to satisfy yourself that his explanations are not just put-offs to keep you on the string. If he can't or won't assuage your suspicions, dump him and dump him *fast*. (MK)

SIX-SHOOTER

It's very difficult to get rid of a guy you really can't stand, especially if he's hound-dogging you. Let's assume the guy's a real jerk, and you have to dump him. Here are six ways to ditch him:

- *Take him to a big party and disappear*. Have a girlfriend inform him of your departure and offer him some dip and chips.
- *Dance with somone else all evening*.
- *Introduce him to your sexiest girlfriend*. Then he's her problem.
- Get your friends together and *overwhelm him* while you duck out. Have them talk about sex and laugh.
- *Talk about your former boyfriends* and how wonderful the dates were. Offer to introduce him to the coolest one of them.
- Find out his *allergy* and expose him to it every chance you get. (KSS)
- *Just tell him*. Tell him you're not in love with him and that you never will be. (ARo)

See also under *CIVILITY* **in** *CHAPTER FOUR: MODERN P's & Q's.*

DATE RAPE

Don't say yes when you mean no. Be passive towards any preliminary sexual moves. (KG)

Be very clear of his intentions from the moment he picks you up. Set a time for yourself to be home. (SN)

Be aware of an increase in tension during the course of the date. (SV)

After a date, *don't invite him up* to your place and don't accept an invitation up to his place, unless you're willing to deal with a possible confrontation (SV)

If it does happen to you, don't pretend that it didn't. Call the cops, call your friends. Take photos of yourself immediately if he has physically abused you. Spread the word loud and clear about this guy. He's a rapist, after all; there's a big difference between a dating

misunderstanding and rape. Don't allow him to duck the punishment he deserves. (SV, CP)
See also under *RAPE* **in** *CHAPTER TWELVE: MODERN WOMEN IN DISTRESS.*

TO DATE OR NOT TO DATE

There are good guys and bad guys in every profession, but what he does can be a clue to what he is.

Ten Bad Professions to Date (in alphabetical order)
• Actors, artists, male models, musicians
• Bartenders
• Cab drivers
• Dentists
• Gynecologists
• Insurance salesmen
• Lawyers
• Middle management men
• Politicians
• Toll booth collectors

Ten Good Professions to Date (in alphabetical order)
• Blue-collar workers
• Comedians
• Educators
• Engineers
• Independently wealthy men or professional dilettantes
• Industry magnates
• Old, sick rich men
• Surgeons
• Symphony conductors
• Writers (GTB)

DON'T DATE:

• Anyone who is looking for a mom. **See** *Wedding Invitations,* **below.**
• A guy who makes you feel like you're a status symbol or his possession.
• Anyone who is obsessed with designer anything.
• Someone who always has a hot deal, and you find yourself waiting for him alone in the car a lot.
• A guy who drinks too much or seems overly dependent on drugs.
• A man who is too loose or too tight with his money.
• Anyone who dresses funny and is *sure* it's part of his personality.
• A guy who avoids certain situations or conversational subjects and can't tell you why.
• A guy who won't let you be your own person.

• Anyone who downgrades your apartment, car, job, family or body.

• A guy your friends hate.

• A man that you can't talk to honestly or with whom you find yourself avoiding talking about the past. (YB)

HOW TO DEAL WITH AN UNRULY DRUNKEN DATE

• Get him some food.

• Never give him coffee.

• Get him out of the bar by lying, deception or any kind of wild promise.

• Trick him into talking to his mother on the phone.

Under no circumstance take a drunk home to your place. If you feel trapped or unsafe, call a cab and go home on your own. (DO)

GOLD RUSH

Don't be dumb. If that guy you've been slobbering over finally asks you out and after a few dates you're thinking marriage, not only are you being foolish but you're probably acting stupid. For instance:

• Don't hang around when it's obviously time for you to go.

• Get out of his apartment on Sunday afternoon when his buddies come over for their weekly poker party.

• Don't offer to do his laundry and dishes or to clean his bathroom.

Don't rush it, you could end up doing these yukky things for the rest of your life and his.

Never disconnect yourself from your friends and rituals; keep your personal life going on as usual. After all, the relationship just may not work out and you'll need those friends.

Don't allude to marriage or ask him how many children he would like to have someday. He'll feel the bricks being laid around him.

Likewise, if he begins pulling these situations on you, watch out! (LK)

SINGLE LIFE

You've met a truly terrific man and you've started seeing each other on a regular basis. It may be that you're so intensely infatuated that you've lost all interest in the rest of your life. One of the worst mistakes you can make is to let this happen, and, even worse, to let him know about it.

Few things will make a man reconsider a new relationship quicker than getting the impression that you're going to turn into a clinging vine who wants to spend all of your time wrapped in his arms. Although it may seem old-fashioned, *force yourself to play the game.* Don't buy him those cute little gifts. Don't drop everything to run off and be with him. Don't sit home and wait for the phone to ring. Having a life of your own will make you much more interesting to him and, if things should go sour, you'll still have a life to go back to. (MK)

A DATE DISPATCH

I didn't have a proper date until I was eighteen years old. Sure, things *happened* to me. That older boy who went to jail for six months. Or the young man who climbed into my window at three in the morning when I was sixteen. (My mother heard the noise. "Simon," she said, "could you possibly arrive at a more suitable hour?")

But it wasn't until I was eighteen that a certain boy roared up on a BSA Victor 441. He slung a camera around my neck, handed my mother a bunch of daisies, and said to me, "Got a sack of cherries here. Let's go up into the park and spit out the pits." The daisies won my mother over on the spot, and I fell in love for five years.

Here are some of the things this guy did:

• He worked as a cook in a steakhouse. One night the doorbell rang at midnight. When I opened the door no one was there, but on the front step was a steaming baked potato in tin foil with a cocktail stirrer stuck in it. On the stir stick was a piece of a napkin. He had written on it, "You're beautiful."

• In the middle of the night he drove eighty miles in a rented delivery man's suit. He arrived at my dorm room with my birthday present in a big box with a ribbon.

• He gave me a gallon jar filled with fortune cookies. He had taken the fortunes out with tweezers and inserted his own messages.

• He had a neon sign especially designed with my name on it that flashed on and off.

• He let me wear his favorite flannel shirts.

• He sincerely believed that I was beautiful even though I know I am not.

• He wouldn't drive anywhere unless I fastened my seatbelt.

• When everyone knew that the concert was sold out, I found a note in my mailbox: "Got two tickets, twelfth row, center. Pick you up at seven."

Maybe it wasn't so good for me. I don't know. Because now I am forever spoiled. One cannot realistically expect twelfth-row tickets and baked potatoes for the rest of her life, yet I do. *(Anon.)*

Everyone should expect at least one romance that's so rotten and heartbreaking that you experience at least nine months of full-blown grieving when it's over — crying jags, no appetite, feeling you're losing your mind. It's normal. It will pass. (ADe)

DON'T ADVERTISE

As tempting as it may be to extol the virtues of the one you love, be careful whom you may be tempting. Sad but true, there are women who would have no compunction about going after your very own glowing example of masculinity at its best. While it's not necessary to paint a picture of an illiterate bum who pees in the sink, keep in mind that she who toots the horn too loudly may soon be playing taps. (BB)

THINGS YOU CAN SAY TO DRIVE MEN CRAZY

• In answer to the question "What's wrong?" always say, "Nothing."

- In answer to *any* suggestion say, "That's fine."
- Use words they don't know the meaning of.
- "If you don't know, I'm not going to tell you."
- Smile sweetly and say, "I love you." *(Anon.)*

MANIPULATION BY GUILT

Guilt is one of the most useful emotions you can ever inspire in a man. With many men, it doesn't take much before they're groveling and begging for forgiveness. The following techniques will almost always produce in him the desire to do whatever you want him to do:

- Break into tears.
- Look pensive.
- Refuse to say what's wrong.
- Confess your inadequacy — tearfully if possible.
- Do sweet little things for him.
- Accuse him of something that he didn't do but *could* have. (MK)

To really get the upper hand, be absolutely honest. They'll feel guilty because you've been honest — and they know they haven't been. (ARo)

WHEN IT'S OKAY TO GO OUT WITH YOUNGER GUYS

Don't worry about age. There are plenty of other things to worry about. If you meet a younger man you like and he seems interested, go ahead, provided

- He doesn't act his age.
- He's independently wealthy.
- He has to be at the office every day.
- He integrates well within your social group and your friends accept him.
- He's not your associate, your ex-husband's best friend or your son's best friend.
- Your daughters don't mind.
- Your daughters recommend him.
- You can arrange the lighting during sexual encounters. (JGu, LOP)

MAY-DECEMBER-MAY

There are no age differences — there are only people differences. A twenty-two-year-old can be more mature than a forty-four-year-old, or he can be hopelessly adolescent. If you have a relationship that's truly satisfying to both of you — and you're not trying to regain lost youth and he's not trying to gain experience at your expense — then who cares if people keep assuming he's your son? *(Anon.)*

Does age matter? It depends on the people involved. We are all so different, how can we set up one rule for everyone? I have seen hundreds of men eighteen years my junior whom I wouldn't think of dating. On the other hand, I have lived happily for over fifteen years with my beloved companion, who is eighteen years younger than I.

We each are interested in the same things, understand each other, appreciate each other; our backgrounds are similar, we agree on major issues, respect each other's space and, above all, we have *fun* together.

So what if I am old enough to be his mother? Somehow that doesn't seem to matter when you love each other. So go for it if you are fortunate enough to attract and be attracted by a man or men younger than you are, and let the rest of the world take care of itself. After all, is it so bad to be recognized as a woman who is obviously so fascinating that young men find her glamorous and desirable? (AW)

No man is worth beans until he is at *least* forty. (EC)

If you are twenty-five you might want babies. If he is fifty-nine he is probably divorced and his babies already grown. You have to think about things like that. (TD)

Trust your friends to make all kinds of cracks. They're just jealous. Don't let them get you down. (AB)

My partner is very much younger, and the world is bright and lovely again. (GC)

Look at all the divorces among people of similar age. That should say something positive about May-December romance, don't you think? (AP)

We go from one dumb stage of life to another until the day we die. How depressing to have two people in the same ridiculous stage at the same time.(FU)

I thought I could never be attracted to someone much younger than I. And then along came this boy eleven years younger than I. He was good and kind and smart and made me laugh. I was delighted by him, but I never said anything. I never did anything about it. (CH)

Where have you gone: When I first saw *The Graduate,* I was so grossed out by Mrs. Robinson. Now I am Mrs. Robinson's age, and I think young women are pretty intolerant. (NLW)

Triple dissent: When we were eighteen, one of my closest friends had a love affair with the father of another girlfriend. I felt sick. It wasn't fair of him. Even in the modern world, there is such a thing as too young. (CWC)

I think true love should be able to conquer all. However, a big age difference can possibly make it a little more difficult for the younger one to truly empathize with the older. After all, the younger person won't be there for another fifteen or twenty years. It's hard for the older person to have to wait that long. (DK)

Being with men very much younger is just so wearisome. They have this embarrassing joy of life that makes me roll my eyes. For heaven's sake, I don't *want* to be enchanted by the sweetness of a flower or the glory of a sunset with a bunch of noisy *oohhs* and *aahhs*. (KT)

180° RELATIONSHIPS

If you're looking for good companionship, always go for a contrasting partner — someone completely different from you in race, age, beliefs and ethnic background. He will always prove to be the best lover and the best teacher. Who wants to learn from someone who is a mirror of herself? (LB)

SEX

The three-lettered monster of love, the verbal approximation of Aphrodite bowling in the nude.

This is the steamy part of the book, where we all sit around on the living room floor drinking more than we've ever drunk before and talking about . . . well, talking about *things*. You know.

FIVE SURE SIGNS OF LUST
He's bothered if
1. He drops his drink when you bend over.
2. He sprinkles his conversation with double entendres.
3. He invades your personal space often and to an unnecessary extent.
4. He tries to get you drunk.
5. He tells you he doesn't have a sexually transmitted disease. (DRW)
Men express themselves sexually more easily than they do emotionally; women express themselves more easily the other way around. (JGu)

SCALP MASSAGE
The most erogenous zone on a man or a woman is the brain. Stimulate that and you've got it made. (JGG)

FIRST AIDS
The Big Question: You've been dating Mr. Wonderful for a while now, and while in years past your considerations over whether to sleep with him would have been mostly moral, nowadays you have the added complication of sexually transmitted diseases to think about. How do you raise the question without creating that awkward moment? And can you believe what he tells you?

Since every situation is different and each requires its own solution, I offer only my own opinion on this touchy subject. If you don't feel comfortable enough with him to ask him this vital question, you shouldn't be sleeping with him. If you don't know him well enough to be able to tell if he's lying to you, you shouldn't be sleeping with him. And if you sleep with him without finding out about his history, figuring that such a wonderful guy would never put you at risk, he shouldn't be sleeping with you. (MK)

STAYING ALIVE
The way you inquire about sexual history is by asking. Anyone who is going to be insulted by a question in this age of death is a fool. So ask. Just ask. (EL)

First of all, ***don't take strangers to bed.*** Just don't do it. Don't take new friends to bed, either. Wait long enough until you know the person well. Get it? When they know you, maybe even love you, they're not going to storm off in a rage when you ask them about their past and their health. And you know what else? If they love you, they are not going to want to give you a disease that will hurt you. Maybe there is something to love. Love combined with sex. What a wild combination. (LH)

LATEX LOVE

Sure, condoms are dumb-looking, ugly little things. But diaphragms full of spermicidal jelly look pretty icky, too. Condoms are no worse than any other part of this sticky, sexual mess we're all involved in. If you can't bring yourself to ask your partner about his sexual history, at least pull a condom from your purse. And even if you *do* ask, consider pulling a condom from your purse anyway. If he doesn't want to use it, remind him that he has a life to save, too. His own. (AK)

Guts up. Go to your local drugstore and buy a package of condoms. Never buy old-looking packs or ones that may have been damaged by heat or direct sunlight; they may not be reliable. Most condom packages have an expiration date on them, so check it out.

There are several styles and colors, but most are made from latex or lambskin. The lambskin types are more expensive and are AIDS ineffective. *The safest and most effective are latex condoms with a spermicide that contains nonoxynol-9*. (KL)

DEALING WITH MEN'S SEXUAL INADEQUACIES

You can lead a horse to water, but you can't make him drink.

• Don't ever put him down or laugh at him. Really, he can't help it. *(Anon.)*

• Suggest nicely that perhaps he should go to a physician. There are physical reasons and cures. (LKe) Suggest a doctor only if it is a recurring problem. Otherwise, it will be. *(Anon.)*

• Turn the focus of the encounter to yourself, you'll feel good and he can let go of the pressure or embarrassment he's feeling. *(Anon.)*

• Change the whole subject. Suggest a late night snack. *(Anon.)*

• Give him a massage, get him to relax. (MK)

• Be nice and let it go. Don't make him feel guilty — he really doesn't need another ego blow. (ST)

• Don't let it be an ego blow to you, either. It doesn't have anything to do with you, unless he really hates you. (LPo)

• It's his problem. Send him home. (CGr)

• Remember, it's not a crime. Get used to it. *(Anon.)*

• Wait till he leaves or goes to sleep, then masturbate. *(Anon)*

• Masturbate for him. Aside from turning him on, it will lessen the pressure he feels to perform in order to meet your needs. *(Anon.)*

DEALING WITH YOUR OWN SEXUAL INADEQUACIES

If you spend too much time worrying about the Big O, you'll never get the big *ah.* *(Anon.)*

Faking orgasms is the same as lying to your partner. *(Anon.)* Or lying to yourself.

Tell him what you like and how you like it. Make it part of a sex-talk ritual, if necessary. It's pointless to pretend that you're enjoying something a lot when in fact you're enjoying it very little. All women are different and all men are different, and without communication you'll both be operating on false assumptions. *(Anon.)* **See** *Sex Talk,* **below.**

It's about as good as you're going to feel in your life, so enjoy it. *(Anon.)*

YOU WANT ME TO *WHAT?*

He comes home one night with a new pair of red heels and a garter belt. They're for *him.* So how are you supposed to handle this one?

Don't let your inexperience or fear of looking foolish deny you what could be an enjoyable new experience. Depending on how comfortable you feel with your partner, and unless he wants to do something physically dangerous or basically impossible, why not give it a try? Live a little. And by the way, don't be afraid to suggest something *you'd* like to try. Turnabout is fair play. *(Anon.)*

Find the limit: Weird, fantasy sex acts are only weird when they go beyond your personal sense of integrity and tolerance. If they get beyond that point, stop immediately or you'll end up feeling guilty about it. (SV)

If your lover suggests that you go beyond the norm in sex, ask for time to think about it. Sometimes, the whole scenario needs to be talked about and prepared for. And other times, sponteneity is best. Play it by ear. *(Anon.)*

Willingness to try and take part in sex fantasies is really dependent on what your own limits are. Figure out if it will make you feel turned on, or degraded, or just left cold. (LD)

Once you have participated in living out your partner's sex fantasies, it's wise to make it a kind of physical territory, with defined boundaries. The first time sets a precedent. *(Anon.)*

If it turns you on, go ahead and do it. It's perfectly all right if no one is hurt. (AAT)

Don't confuse repulsion with repression. If it seems like it *might* be worth a try, then it probably is. *(Anon.)*

PUBLIC DISPLAYS

What's wrong with a little semi-public romance? Maybe not dry-humping in the park, but wonderful kisses under doorways and in the backs of libraries and in the middle of crosswalks? Every day we see people angry and yelling and making mean faces and honking horns. Let's hear it for a few wild kisses. (HL)

Passion is so wonderful. Let's have more of it. Everywhere. All over the place. Any time. (EC)

Why should only the high school kids have all the fun? Let's all of us kiss by the lockers and in the center of the hallways. The world will improve. (MC)

PDA: Public displays of affection are absolutely necessary. The extent to which one is willing to get physical in public says much about how involved he is in the relationship. *If a man doesn't want to be emotionally involved,* he won't want you to be touching him "in front of people." (GSt)

EXHIBITIONISM

If you've got it, flaunt it. Or even if *he* thinks you've got it, flaunt it. Walking into a room — a restaurant or a casino or a nightclub — in a frankly revealing outfit produces an incredible adrenaline-like rush. It's like a wild drug. Every head in the place turns and you suddenly are the center of everyone's attention for as long as you're there. It's incredible that a woman can have that much power over men.

If you're nervous the first time, think of it like jumping in a cold stream. It doesn't take long to get warmed up. *(Anon.)*

A little flash every now and then is fine with me — in fact, I think it's fun — so long as it isn't going on in the middle of a room where there are children. *(Anon.)*

ORAL SEX

Cunnilingus: When on the receiving end of oral sex, the most important things to remember are to relax and to enjoy. Women spend more time worrying about how they smell or taste or look than experiencing what their partner is doing for them.

Many women cut it short or avoid it altogether for fear of turning off their partner. Or they may think, "He only does this because he wants me to reciprocate," or "He just *thinks* I want this — he doesn't really like doing it."

Let's get real, ladies. No man is going to perform oral sex unless he wants to. *Who cares* why he wants to — he *wants* to.

As far as smell or taste goes, it's purely an animal instinct. The whole reason women have a scent or taste is for the basic sexual attraction of the male. In other words, most men like that female sex odor. It's not the same as not being clean.

If the hang-up is more along the lines of "good girls don't like this," then you should think about all the women in the world and how many have had oral sex. Are they all bad? No way.

There's nothing wrong with sharing in this special way. But, for heaven's sake, keep yourself *scrupulously* clean. Pure glycerine soap is best. *(Anon.)*

Women who've been without a lover for a long time enjoy oral sex rather than intercourse. (BNy)

A great part of oral sex is enjoying your partner's responses. (AW)

If you would really love your partner to give you oral sex, tell him so. See how he feels about it. If he hates it, there's not much you can do. (BNy) If your lover refuses your requests for oral sex, refuse it to him as well. *(Anon.)*

During lovemaking gently push his shoulders down. He'll get the hint. *(Anon.)*

Tell him you have a wonderful game involving strawberries and champagne. (SV)

Fellatio: The more the giver enjoys giving, the better it feels to the receiver. Take your cue from your partner, he'll let you know what he likes. (AAT)

Men absolutely love to be orally stimulated. The right technique does take some practice, but they won't mind your experimentation. Sends them to the moon. *(Anon.)*

The most important thing is to *genuinely* like doing what you're doing. If you like what you're doing to your partner, if you like the feeling it's producing in you, if *you* like the whole idea of it, you'll do wonderfully. *(Anon.)*

If you don't like to swallow after fellatio, tell him first. It apparently makes a difference. *(Anon.)*

HOW TO TALK ABOUT SEX

Sometimes you just have to.

Occasionally it's difficult to talk about sex to a man without it seeming like a come-on. So talk about it while you're driving to the grocery store. (LP)

Take turns discussing your sexual fantasies or dreams in a disconnected way — it's a subtle way of telling your partner what you might like to try. (SV)

If you're having a sexual problem don't approach the subject in an accusatory manner. Work it out together, and if that doesn't work, go somewhere for help. *(Anon.)*

LESBIANISM

In a cruel world, loving a woman is safe and familiar.

Never feel ashamed of feeling homosexual tendencies or emotions. Everyone has that attraction, so you're not alone and you're not bad. (ML)

Sometimes it's easy to confuse love or admiration for someone of the same sex as being homosexual. This isn't always true. *(Anon.)*

CELIBACY

In our society, eroticism and sexuality are not dealt with openly on a nonsexual basis. In fact, women are taught that we're whores if we let men touch us. Men are uncertain what to do. It all seems such a mess that being celibate erases a lot of tension from our lives.(WL)

TOUCHING

We are taught as children that touching between men and women is sexual. Women need to drop that, because if we don't, the stigma will continue and we'll float even farther apart. (TM) **See also under** *Sexual Harassment* **in** *CHAPTER ONE: WOMEN AT WORK.*

EXCUSES FOR NOT HAVING SEX

Even in the best relationships, there will come a time when your partner turns to you with love in his eyes but the idea of having sex is about as appealing as a GYN exam. You say:

- "I'm sore down there."
- "My dad's calling tonight. I don't know when."
- "Leave me alone, I don't like you tonight." (This is also good for guilt manipulation.)
- "Let me take a shower first." (Stay in the shower until you look like a California raisin; with any luck he will have fallen asleep.)
- Use any postponing technique you can think of — the last part of a TV program, the last chapter of a book.
- Tell him you have a doctor's appointment the next day.
- But always remember, sometimes it's easier to give in, get it over with and go to sleep. (CBC)

A dissent: If you don't want to make love, just say so. *(Anon.)*

BREAKING UP

We assume you want to dump the guy or you wouldn't be here.

Trying to protect the feelings of someone you once cared for is one of life's Barnum-quality juggling acts. Something is going to slip, something's going to get broken. Be kind.

LEAVING A LOVER

Nonstop: Seems like the process of leaving a lover is endless. It goes on and on for weeks and months and even years. I hear about quick breaks, but that has never happened to me. Breaking up is just a long, horrible slow ache. It is hazy and confusing and I can't understand what is happening and I can't think straight and I don't know who is right and who is wrong. It's like going insane. *(Anon.)*

It didn't really hurt. When my boyfriend and I finally broke up for good I felt strangely calm. I couldn't figure it out, because I had loved him like mad. Several years later I ran into him. It was a nice meeting, but after we parted I felt like my heart was full of rocks. My heart hurt and I was so depressed. More than depressed. Sad to my very *soul*. I couldn't shake the feeling for weeks. I guess that's what you call a delayed reaction. In some ways I was relieved. It hadn't seemed natural not to grieve all those years before, and now I had. (TM)

WAYS TO END THE RELATIONSHIP PEACEFULLY

If he still loves you and you no longer love him but he's still an okay guy and you don't want to sear him for life, here are some ways to let him down gently.

- Make sure your partner's ego is left intact and that he doesn't feel like a loser.
- Do not insist on a friendship.

• Be honest. Sometimes that works.

• Don't make the decision based on affection for someone else. Discuss the decision to split based on the disintegration of the relationship itself.

• State that you are really not good enough for him, that he would do much better without you. **But see below under** *Not Good Enough.*

• If possible, put some physical distance between the two of you. Go visit a friend for two months. Absence doesn't always make the heart grow fonder. (THMcP)

GET AWAY

Sometimes it helps to leave town. If your heart's broken and the whole break-up is just too painful and messy and turning you into puréed vegetables, get away from it all. Just get in your car and leave. You can do that if you are young enough or free enough or rich enough. It is hard to leave a lover if you stay in the same small town or if he works in the same office. (CP)

Claim some vacation time and go away to stay with your best friend. Stay for two weeks minimum and you'll come back home a better, healthier person. *(Anon.)*

NOT GOOD ENOUGH

You can always try the old line "I'm just not good enough for you." Nobody believes that kind of thing, but you can always try it. (WP)

A dissent: Try your very hardest to figure out what went wrong *in concrete terms.* Be excruciatingly honest with yourself and your lover. Talk and talk and talk until you get it figured out. Never say something as intellectually bankrupt as "Well, I guess it just didn't work out" to someone you suspect may have some measure of intelligence; don't leave the responsibility for the collapse in mid-air. *Work hard to achieve a resolution.* It'll be worth it — not only for your self-esteem, but also for the good friend that you will make after the wound heals. (BPr)

HOW TO TELL WHEN IT'S TIME TO END IT

The telltale signs of decay:

• Everything he wants to do bores you to tears.

• You can't stand to have him touch you.

• You avoid phone calls from him.

• Being nice requires a major effort on your part.

• The smell of his cologne makes you ill.

• He makes you feel claustrophobic.

• You hope he meets someone new, and you allow him every advantage to do so.

• Communication has stopped and you don't care.

• You have fantasies about other men.

• All the sounds he makes, from brushing his teeth to eating, drive you crazy.

• You don't care or want to help him when he is ill.

• You don't care or want to hear about it if his car breaks down or if things are rooten at the office.

• You avoid any situation where you'll have to be alone with him for any length of time, i.e., train trips, long car rides, dinners for two, movies.

• You don't want to be seen in public with him. (LFD)

THE OTHER WOMAN

A sure bet: Men who cheat, *cheat.* Men who have cheated, will cheat again. So if you're helping him to do one dirty, someone else will help him dirty you. Take it from a man.(GSt)

SOME CLUES THAT HE MAY BE FOOLING AROUND

• He smells freshly showered when he comes home.

• He comes home missing pieces of clothing. Now where *did* that green sweater go?

• He has a sudden lack of interest in sex.

• He develops an interest in trying a new sexual routine.

• He *starts* remembering your anniversary, Valentine's Day, or your birthday, which he has always forgotten before.

• His life becomes more complicated. He becomes difficult to keep track of.

• He runs a lot of small errands.

• He has frequent late-night emergencies. (MK)

MANY HAPPY RETURNS

My favorite expression is "They all come back."

I have found that it helps to remember that saying when I need to let go of someone or something in either a business or personal relationship. I find that when I have truly let go of the situation, and that person calls — *and he always does,* even if it takes a long time — it gives me a double pleasure — one because I know I let it go way back then, and two because that person called back. (LHo)

MATRIMONY

When you say "love" to somebody in a free-association test, you'll likely get one of two responses: "marriage" or "hate." Ironically, there's a finer line between love and hate than there is between love and marriage.

These days, that has created a great deal of confusion. Today, self-justification has a social and institutional dimension that it has never had before. We are encouraged to indulge ourselves and to believe that constant change and aborted commitments will somehow inevitably lead to personal happiness. Further, we are led to believe that our happiness has an *ultimate* value and that we are allowed to pursue this ephemeral and vague goal at the expense not only of others, but also at the expense of our souls.

ADVENTURES IN MATRIMONY

Modern Women know that happiness isn't a place or a situation that you find if you look long and hard enough. Instead, it's a mammoth do-it-yourself project, something you build yourself down there in the messy, hot and sweaty workroom of your heart.

To Modern Women, marriage has a bottom line: It's a promise. We have the right to assume that if we are women of our word, we are creating a circumstance likely to lead to happiness. After all, if you can't keep your word, you'll never keep your husband.

WEDDING INVITATIONS

Men want mothers to take care of them. Unfortunately, most men had mothers that did indeed take care of them. Your role is not to manage his life, but to take care of each other. (JGr) Don't make the common mistake of imagining your husband is your father. (DBG) *People should not get married to make each other happy.* It's not our job or men's jobs to supply each other's happiness. The best we can do is to make each other comfortable and secure in a very insecure world. (KO)

Marriage gives you a sense of certainty and completion. You can then live out the cultural fantasy of living happily ever after. Fairy tales and movies give you the indoctrination You believe it. Walt Disney and your mom wouldn't lie to you, or would they? Marriage meets that need for an indefinable satisfaction. It's rare and, naturally, you must work for it. Marriage gives you a false sense of security, and most of us are terrified of commitment. (BNo)

Marriage is the great demonstrative act. You'll be suddenly committed to the whole program of economical feats and defeats, children, illness, weird vacations, forgiveness and death. Make sure you're ready to partake in the joy and depression that's certain to erupt. So, what else are you going to do with your life? (KK)

You must devote yourself to your marriage or else you become a woman who is living her life as a hobbyist. Why not take up tennis with the girls instead? Marriage is a *real* commitment. You have to be serious and industrious. Maintaining a husband, a home, children and perhaps an outside job takes loads of stamina and willpower. You must consider every single part of yourself before you make such a commitment, or you will fail. (DLe)

Get married to protect yourself from the unmarried world. (KF) Marriage gives you a place in society, security and safe sex. We all need to belong to someone emotionally. (SMcP) Being married is easier than not being married; it's comforting and above all it keeps you from growing old alone. (JGu)

Marriage is a ceremony of commitment, something we don't see much of anymore. (TRe) The ceremony of marriage makes the relationship seem more substantial in the eyes of others and to each other. (JGu)

The bottom line: Being married is great for tax purposes, affecting each partner in a postitive way. It also protects the woman's right to child support. (TO'D)

RED-LINING

It's very important to know when you're at your partner's tolerance level and when you're at your wit's end. Protect your pride and self-esteem, practice give and take. (JGu)

Pay attention to your inner reflections after an argument. What are you telling yourself? More importantly, what was the argument *really* about? (KHe)

KNEEL

Men want adoration. They want you to be in awe of them. They want you to think that they're always right. By the way, they're not. (CGr)

FARE WEATHER FRIENDS

An anecdote: The old man and the old woman ride the number five bus. I've crossed their path a hundred times in the past three years. They go downtown when it is 105° and when it is 10°. He always wears a suit and a hat. She always wears a dress and a coat. They walk arm in arm. I think perhaps they are eighty years old.

One day I saw her alone on the bus, and I fretted for two weeks. Then I saw them again, arm in arm, walking slowly up the street.

I am comforted by them, by the way they comfort each other. *(Anon.)*

SCREENING A MATE

Warranty not included: There's no way to tell for sure if your one and only is the one for you, but it's not a bad idea to inspect the goods before making a final purchase. Here are some screening techniques:

Make sure he goes to a family event and note carefully how your family reacts to him. You know you love him, but do you want to spend the rest of your life explaining it to your relatives? *(Anon.)*

Take him on an obstacle-course trip. Forget the directions, lose the hotel reservations, book the most uncomfortable room, and watch how he deals with adversity. (EH)

Make it a point to *meet as many members of his family* as you can manage. Tell him you'd love to go to his uncle's funeral. (DRD)

Show up inappropriately dressed for a date. For example, go to a symphony date in jeans and a sweatshirt and see how he reacts. (SBB)

See what you can find out about how he spends his money — not what he spends on you, which will decrease after you get married, but the rest of it. (KH)

Listen to the stories he tells about work. If he tends to blame everybody else for his problems, watch out. *(Anon.)*

If he ever uses drugs or alcohol as an excuse for unpardonable behavior, get rid of him. *(Anon.)*

If you catch him lying to you — a big lie like former marriages, children, job status — give him the gate. (JAO'N)

Marriage won't change him. If he cheats on you when you're dating, you can bet he'll cheat on you when you're married. (GI)

If he ever hits you, even once, for any reason, drop him *now*. (AG)

SIGN HERE

Prenuptial agreements seem to be all the rage these days. But they're also a sure-fire way to remove the romance from relationship. If he won't marry you without one, perhaps you should reconsider. (JAO'N)

Prenuptial agreements can be helpful in a situation where there is a desire to limit the amount either party can take away from a failed marriage. If, for example, you wish to make sure that your children inherit your estate, rather than your spouse, you might consider a prenuptial agreement. Or if you had a lot of money going into the marriage and your partner had very little, you might want to stipulate how much he could take with him if he should go. As long as it is made on an informed basis, with the participation of counsel, it will probably be upheld by the courts. (PSD)

A COUPLE

You have to learn to share your life, and that's not easy at all. If you don't much like to talk, perhaps you should not get married, because talking is necessary in a marriage. You need to talk often, not just when the Big Events happen. If you only talk when the Big Events occur, you will tense up and feel miserable and defensive anytime he opens his mouth, rather like when a telegram arrives. (DJ)

You will find yourself socializing with other couples once you become one. Probably two of you actually like each other, but you bring your mates along and then there are four of you. The possibilities for encountering problems are endless. You will long for your high school and college days, when people arrived in ones or transitory twos. (GJ)

POWER

One of you will have more power. It's never equal, so get used to it. One or the other is going to rule. If it's you, be benevolent. (EP)

OOPS!

Being half of a couple means that you have to learn to be considerate. You have to apologize when you are wrong and even when you are right. (CO'N)

ON THE STREET

You have to include your partner in your life, and that means you can't decide on everything all by yourself anymore. You have to check with the other person to see how he feels about it. It's just not easy to cooperate and share. That's why they spend so much time on it on "Sesame Street." (KK)

TWO CAREERS

In a two-career marriage, compromises are going to have to be made. But in the more important decisions — relocation, child-care — sacrifices should be made for the good of the partner with the more lucrative job or the one with the most potential — the job that could pay for the kid's college or win a Nobel Prize. (ADe)

DIVORCE PREVENTION

Notes from all over: There's no sure-fire way to keep love alive, but here are tips from correspondents:

• *Don't take him for granted.* Don't let him take you for granted.

• *Fighting can be constructive.* Allowing resentment to fester can give your marriage gangrene.

• Remember what Mr. Rogers says: "Sharing is good." *Involve your spouse* in the important parts of your life.

• *Your husband is not the enemy.* Don't make him responsible for all the things that are wrong in your life. Don't put all the problems on his shoulders and shove him out the door. You'll only end up with one more problem — divorce.

• *Always let the man think he's the boss,* and then do what you damn well please. (MHL)

• *Fight like hell. (Anon.)*

GO SAMOAN

I am a forty-four-year-old woman married to a twenty-eight-year -old Samoan. I have three teenage sons and a career as a manager of five dry-cleaning stores. I do not have an "average" life, but one filled with joy and challenge. My only advice to other women would be to relax and enjoy what comes your way. Don't sweat the small stuff. (KDa)

SELFISHNESS

In order to maintain your identity in a relationship, you have to be a little bit selfish. Don't be afraid to suggest the activity for an evening out or to tell the truth if you need a night to yourself. Just don't go overboard. (HYW)

TROUBLE SNEAKS IN

Being married to a "communicator" can have its problems. After a childhood and first marriage where strong emotion was forbidden and feared, it's a real change. I like being able to share what's happening with my husband. I value the vulnerability of telling how I feel and sharing the positives and negatives of our lives.

Our teenage daughters have learned that it's okay to tell what they feel or worry about, because we share ourselves with them. However, my husband believes that we should communicate all the time, and there are times when I would rather *not* talk and keep my feelings secret, as I have learned to do for thirty-four years. I guess life is never everything we want it to be. (MKa)

One of the most painful times of life is when a husband who has had secretaries to do his bidding all during his professional life, retires and carries such expectations into his home. It is hell for the wife, and there is a real need for negotiations at this point.

Unfortunately, many men are inflexible and actually unable to make adjustments in their expectations. Solution? Perhaps all marriages should end when the children are grown. (*Anon.*)

What hope is there? Everyone is right. How can two people be right and have totally different opinions? That's how it always is. How easy it would be if one person were clearly a villain. *"Ha!* You Hitler, you!"

If you listen to the man he is certainly justified. He is hurt. He has been good.

Then you listen to the woman. She is certainly justified and hurt and good, too. Everything everyone says makes sense, yet each person is saying completely different things. Then you just sigh. There is no justice. No right and no wrong. Just a bunch of different sides. If only it were as easy as World War II. (BV)

THE EX FACTOR

If you are a second wife, especially if your husband and his ex have children, you must take care not to escalate the difficulties that will certainly arise. To keep it together emotionally and with your husband, here are a few tricks to remember:

• Stay uninvolved and neutral in any disputes between your husband and his ex.

• Don't compete with his ex. He's all yours now.

• For his children's sake, allow their relationship to be agreeable.

• Make sure all financial and custodial agreements between them are in writing and filed with a lawyer. (BL)

On being number two: In the best of all possible worlds, if you marry a man who's been married before, his ex-wife will be nothing more to him than a memory (hopefully a distant one).

However, in a lot of cases, there will still be some ties that bind, and the two of you are going to have to hammer out a relationship with her that works. Usually, the ties are children, and no matter how amicable their parting was, relations can become strained when he remarries. It is essential that you do everything possible to make sure than the children are not adversely affected by any conflicts that arise. In fact, do everything you can to avert any friction at all.

Perhaps you can suggest that your husband and his ex put all their agreements in writing and have any changes legally noted (especially in cases of custody or child support). If she goes crazy every time she sees you, be an adult and don't insist you go along to pick up the kids.

Don't put her down to the kids or even to your husband, and don't try to compete by spoiling the kids. Basic common sense can tell you most of the do's and don'ts. (MPN)

INCEST AND BATTERING

Save yourself, save your kids. Get out! There are shelters, federal and private funds available, and many support groups in almost every city. Take advantage of all these alternatives *immediately*.

DIVORCE

The double-barreled failure.

A million new households are created every year by divorce. Millions of household furnishings and utensils must be purchased, because couples have just one toaster. After the divorce, someone is going to need to buy one. Divorce is a cottage industry. This country wants you to divorce. It is good for the economy. *(Anon.)*

THE RUSH TO SPLIT

A huge industry has grown up around divorce: legal services, child-care services, counselors, women's groups, state programs. *You may find a high degree of supportiveness for a situation that perhaps would have been only temporary.* Your divorce lawyer is not there to stop your divorce. You are his livelihood. You are an industry. Be cautious. (LL)

ALTERED STATE

Divorce will change your life even more than your marriage did. Here's what you can do to ease the pain:

• Develop a support system. Women's groups, church organizations, friends all have a part to play in your life.

• Don't terrorize the children or his family. The divorce is between the two of you — nobody else.

• Reassure your children. Make sure they don't try to absorb the guilt.

• Don't be a victim and don't make your ex a villain. Divorces occur for a number of complex reasons. You both played a part.

• Don't try to use the children as a weapon. *Never try to convince your children that their father is a bad man.*

Don't expect miracles from friends. The turmoil you're feeling is completely internalized. Nobody else can know the pain, guilt, relief that you're feeling. (GT)

Wise monkey: If you can say nothing good about your ex to your child, then say nothing at all. (DDK)

They say the feelings you have at a divorce are similar to those you feel because of a death. So don't expect to bounce right back. Grieving takes time, and it helps to realize that. (TEs)

DIVORCING DAD

As soon as you know a divorce or separation is certain, *tell the children.* Hopefully, you can do this while the family is still intact. Try to get the father's cooperation. Give the children a chance to prepare. (LOP)

NOT IN FRONT OF THE CHILDREN

Tell your children over and over again that the divorce is not their fault. You love them and it has nothing to do with them or their behavior. Try to explain the divorce without blaming one parent or the other. Don't give the children every bloody detail. Tell them that you have tried, but it just hasn't worked out. Hopefully, both parents can tell the children at the same time. This way the same story gets told. (HPD)

Whew: Chances are your children will even breathe a sigh or two of relief after the divorce. All the tension of the bad relationship will no longer exist in your house. (NAR)

6

Modern Merchandise

Shopping comes in two basic styles: It's either a troublesome necessity, an intolerably inefficient way of obtaining the stuff of sustenance. Or it's a way of life.

C O N T E N T S

Chapter Six: *MODERN MERCHANDISE*

PLOTTING TO SHOP: Emergency Instructions — Control Your Impulses — Family Lists — SHOPPING TIPS: Take Your Husband — Reach for It — Delivery Service — Backtracking — Discounting Discounters — Gifts — Sticky Stickers — Will You Still Love It Tomorrow? — Impulse, Mark V — Hierarchy — On the List — Season Ticket — Toys-R-Them — Knock, Knock — Second-Hand Rose — ...But You Know What You Like — Two Time-Savers — SHOPPING AT HOME: Home Television Shopping — COMPLAINTS: Think Positively — A Federal Case — AUCTIONS — THRIFT SHOPPING: Flea Markets — Factory Outlets

PLOTTING TO SHOP

"The trouble is, I think too much," said Tammy Faye Bakker. "And the only way I can stop thinking is to go shopping."

So now you know. It's just the devil making you do it, so succumb to the temptation. And since it's only a peripheral sin we're talking about here — shopping creates jobs and feeds children, after all — we don't have to take our excesses too seriously. At least not until the bill comes. **See** *INCOME: Secure Credit* **in** *CHAPTER TWO: MODERN MOOLAH*.

EMERGENCY INSTRUCTIONS
Shopping can boggle the mind and even make you feel faint. The following tips are designed to take the edge off, to calm you, to make the transition from prosperity to indebtedness smooth and easy.

So, before you leave the house:

Why are you going shopping? Decide exactly what you want. Always make a list, whether you're embarking on a major spending expedition or just going to the supermarket for a few odds and ends.

Figure out how much you're willing to part with for each item and, if you're going to purchase many items, how much the whole enterprise is going to cost.

Know where you're going. Make a list of places where you've had luck before. Don't base your list on whether or not you have a credit card at any particular store.

Geography: Don't backtrack from one store to another. Give your shopping expedition a circular route.

Wear comfortable clothes that will be easy to change in and out of if you're shopping for clothes. Take your smallest purse, preferably with a shoulder strap so that your hands are free. Wear your most comfortable shoes. In the winter time, it's better to wear a big sweater rather than a big coat because you'll only end up carrying the coat.

If you're shopping for clothes, bring along color swatches, a shoe, a bit of cloth, whatever, to make sure you get the right match.

Eat and go to the bathroom.

Once you get to the store, don't waste time wandering around looking for the item you have in mind. Go to a salesperson and ask. (AAT)

CONTROL YOUR IMPULSES
When you walk into a store and something catches your eye, control yourself, don't grab it. *Stop and think.* Advertisers, display managers and product representatives have all been working in collusion to make sure they have every advantage. For example, they place certain items at eye level just so you will grab them. If you realize suddenly that you must

have something, and it's not on your list, look high and low for the best buy. (SBl) **See** *Impulse, Mark V,* **below.**

FAMILY LISTS

Keep an order list on your refrigerator of all the things you're out of, so when you go shopping your list will be made and you won't forget anything. Insist that all family members participate. (SBl)

SHOPPING TIPS

If you tell a friend you're going shopping, she'll send you away with a cart full of advice.

We received handy hints from all over. Here's a shopping list of the best ones:

TAKE YOUR HUSBAND or boyfriend with you when you're shopping for clothes. He can coax you to try a new look and tell you how it looks. (AM)

Advice for hire: If you really detest shopping or don't have loads of leisure time *consider hiring a personal buyer.* Call a quality department store and ask about what they have to offer. The only disadvantage is that it may take too much time. But, once you've set the service up, it's wonderful. (JL)

REACH FOR IT

Always *choose food from the back* of the shelf — it's fresher. And always check the expiration dates, especially on dairy products. Remember that the "sell-by" dates vary from state to state and usually allow for adequate shelf life at home. (JS)

DELIVERY SERVICE

Try mail-order shopping. First, of course, you'll have to order the catalogues. Also consider the time factor: It takes from four to six weeks to receive your item from the time you've ordered. If you receive something that doesn't meet your expectations, most good mail-order services will pay the freight for returns. (CK)

BACKTRACKING

You can return shoes that make your feet hurt, even though you've worn them for a few weeks. When buying anything, but especially shoes, save the receipt, bag and box. When making your purchase, make your transaction as personal as possible so that the salesperson will remember you; make eye contact, comment on her clothes, tell her a personal anecdote.

Then when you return the shoes, approach that same salesperson reminding her when you came in, and state factually that the shoes simply aren't comfortable, don't fit correctly — whatever — and ask for your money back, or say that you want to trade for another pair. Smile and be friendly, but firm. State the problem and the solution. You want her to know what you want and what you expect to be done for you. (HN)

Taking advantage of this technique would be sleazy. **See also under** *SHOES* **in** *CHAPTER EIGHT: THE MODERN MODE.*

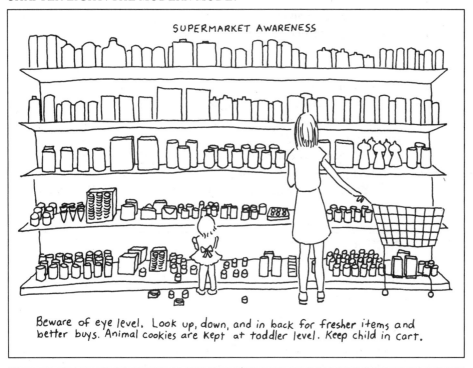

SUPERMARKET AWARENESS

Beware of eye level. Look up, down, and in back for fresher items and better buys. Animal cookies are kept at toddler level. Keep child in cart.

DISCOUNTING DISCOUNTERS

You can get an additional price break on small appliances and electronic consumer goods in discount houses by buying floor samples. There are some important points to bear in mind, however:

• *Two types:* Discount houses sell floor samples only when the item is the last one in inventory. If the item is to be reordered by the store, the price reduction will range between ten and twenty percent. If the item represents a discontinued line, the discount will be much higher — some place between thirty-five and fifty percent.

• *No guarantees:* Floor samples are usually sold as-is and without any warranties. Often, the item will come without the packing crate it was shipped in, and sometimes the instruction manuals will have been misplaced.

• *Watch for* items that have been used for display only. Check the power cord; if it's still tightly coiled and shows no sign of use, then the chances are good that the item was never actually used, but only displayed. Check appliances that use remote control to be sure the remote unit is still around some place.

• *The department manager* is usually the person who authorizes the sale of floor samples and sets the additional discounts. *(Anon.)*

GIFTS

Ask yourself questions about the person for whom you're buying a gift:

• What does the person do for fun? If she dreams of traveling, buy her a book about where she wants to go.

• What does she wear? Buy something that will match the colors she likes most. Pay attention to her personal style.

• What does she already have? For instance, if she has a great poster taped to her bedroom wall, buy a nice frame that will fit the poster.

• Give yourself a price limit, and once you've hit on the perfect item, figure the best store to buy it from. (TMK) **See** *Gifts* **in** *CHAPTER FOUR: MODERN P's & Q's.*

Blind hunt: Don't just go to a store and wander around until you find something that catches your eye. You'll probably choose something *you* want and spend too much on it. (AAT)

STICKY STICKERS

Ever run up against ***the problem of a stubborn sticker?*** Even if you manage to get all of the paper off, you usually manage to end up with that sticky glue that just *won't* come off. Here are some things that usually work:

• *Spray hair spray* on the glue and then rub it off.

• *Use lighter fluid.*

• *Rub in some peanut butter* and then wash the item.

• *Laundry stain pre-treaters* can also remove leftover glue. (YL)

• *Use the sticky side of tape* to pick up any remnants of a messy price tag. (CMF)

• *Rubber cement thinner,* nail polish remover or rubbing alcohol will remove glue from glass surface. (AR)

WILL YOU STILL LOVE IT TOMORROW?

Shopping satisfaction is like sex. If you wake up the next morning and you can live with it, you're doing great. (KPH) *Note:* Check the returns policy for sex. **See** *COMPLAINTS: The Right Way,* **below.**

A *dress you wear once* is about as gratifying as a one-night stand. (AR)

IMPULSE, MARK V

There are two kinds of shopping. *Impulse* buying and the *wait-for-the-sale* buy. Impulse shopping is like trout fishing — you've got to have the right lure. Sale buying is a waiting game: Figure out what you really want, and eventually it will be marked down, allowing you to be impulsive again. (JGu)

HIERARCHY

When you go to a store, go to the basement first and work your way up. (DDy)

ON THE LIST

Write a check or charge it on a card and you'll automatically get free catalogs. (VS) Some retailers have different marketing strategies for different parts of the country. In Pocatello, Idaho, expect to get a cheaper, less fashionable catalog; in Beverly Hills, expect to get the very best. (TC)

SEASON TICKET

Buy furs and winter coats in June. Most items are least expensive just after their season has passed. (AAT)

Buy bathing suits in March. Stores will be putting out last season's leftover stock. (LG)

In January, purchase sheets, towels and Christmas decorations, cards and wrap. Buy calendars in February. (VS)

TOYS-R-THEM

Go to *garage sales,* especially if you're looking for toys and bicycles. Kids — especially very young ones — don't mind second-hand items. In fact, kids can make a new toy very, very old in a matter of minutes. (DK) **See** *TOYS 4 TOTS* **in** *CHAPTER SIXTEEN: THE MODERN MOM* **for loads of toy advice.**

KNOCK, KNOCK

Convertible: Always buy a sofa that folds out to a bed. You never know. (ML)

But you do know one thing: Sofa beds have a bar that hits a sleeping guest in the middle of the back. Keep a mattress board handy for those staying more than one night. (AR)

SECOND-HAND ROSE

Never buy children's clothes new. Ask your friends for their outgrown children's clothes or go to children clothing exchanges. (TR) Don't spend a lot of money on kid's clothes; they seem to grow out of them weekly. (JS)

... BUT YOU KNOW WHAT YOU LIKE

When you want to buy art but can't spend a fortune, try art schools, auctions and estate sales. (JG) **See** *Auctions,* **below.**

To find good prints, try a second-hand or rare bookshop. (AR)

TWO TIME-SAVERS

Always try it on, even when you're absolutely *sure* that it's the right size. (HG) ***Buy your new accessories*** when you buy your new outfit. Don't try to do it by memory. (AL)

SHOPPING AT HOME

As if television weren't insidious enough.

HOME TELEVISION SHOPPING

is big business these days. Almost every time you turn on the set you can find someone trying to sell you a cubic Zirconium this or a Capodimonte that.

You can get some good values if you keep a few facts in mind before you reach for the phone:

• The company offering the products is trying to make money — your money. *Never buy something unless you know what the retail price really is.*

• Remember that most sale prices don't show the *shipping and handling charges.* When you call, ask what the extra charges are and decide if the product is still a good buy.

• *When you call to order* a product, ask the operator if the product is in stock. If it's an item that has to be shipped by the manufacturer, you may not see your authentic Louis XIV telephone for months.

• Most importantly, *don't buy on impulse.* Listen to the entire description of the product and, if possible, do some comparison shopping before you dial the phone. Don't be suckered in by the implied threat that you must buy an item while it's on the screen. If the home shopping service wants to behave that way, don't buy anything from them. They're simply pressuring you — and probably have something to hide, pricewise at least.

• *Round the clock:* Most shopping shows or direct response companies have operators on duty twenty-four hours a day. (MK)

COMPLAINTS

Taken one way, this could be the longest chapter in the book. So let's take it another way.

THINK POSITIVELY

Dale Carnegie once said,"If you get a lemon, make lemonade." That's fine if you want to go into the juice business. But these days things cost too much and time is too precious to waste haggling with anyone. Every once in a while you *must* complain, haggle and bitch. The constructive moan and groan is an art.

The wrong way is to go into the shop ranting and raving, being discourteous to counter people and patrons alike. Never throw the product, sweep things off the counter, use abusive profanity or threaten to kill anyone. You really won't get your way if you do this; it only works with your parents. **See** *CIVILITY* **in** *CHAPTER FOUR: MODERN P's & Q's.*

The right way: Any complaint has five simple elements, easy to learn and practice.

1. State the problem. Get to the point right away.

2. Get your facts straight. Be clear on when and from whom you bought the product. Bring your receipts with you.

3. Have a solution in mind.

4. Set a reasonable deadline on how long you are willing to wait for a solution. If the person is unwilling to negotiate, go to her superior.

5. If you're getting nowhere fast, make a threat, but only one that you can back up. Say that you will stop payment on the check, or you will tell others how rotten the store or product or service is, or you will take the matter to small claims court. Make your threat in a calm and cool manner.

If the dealer is unwilling or unable to right the wrong, you may have to go to the manufacturer. If that doesn't work, go to the Better Business Bureau, contact your state or local consumer protection agency, or contact your local newspaper or television consumer action line.

Keep accurate records of all transactions, photocopy every letter sent and received and note everyone you speak to and when.

Complaining by telephone: It's better to bitch live and in concert, but sometimes the phone has to do.

• *Think it out:* Before you make a complaint by telephone, clear your thoughts. Collect your sales receipts, and jot down the problem of that malfunctioning lemon sitting before you.

• *Decide beforehand what you want* from the company that sold it to you. Do you want a free repair? Do you want a brand-new lemon? Do you just want to get rid of it and receive a full refund? A partial refund? Credit for some other item? Make sure your pencil is sharp and you have space on your pad.

• *Hello?* Now, who do you ask for when you call? "Customer Service" is the new title for "Complaint Department," so try that first. If there is no "Customer Service," ask for the department manager or the store manager.

• *Once you get someone on the line,* make sure you write down her name, and the date of your call, and the time of day, and what she promised to do.

• *If she promises to do something,* repeat the promise back to her to be sure you've got it straight.

• *Be polite,* but don't be weak.

• *If you decide that a letter* of complaint is the action to take, then keep it neat and type it if you can. Don't freeze up. You are not out to win a writing award. Try to keep it brief, one page or less, and never send it without making a photocopy of it for yourself. Mind your manners in the letter. Who can tell how big this problem is going to become or how many people may end up reading your letter? You don't want to come off sounding like a hysterical, abusive person. Immediately explain what it is that you want done. Next, describe what it is that you bought. If there are any serial numbers on the item, write them down. Tell what day you bought it and what it cost. Give the name of the salesperson, or describe that person as best you can if you do not know the name. Include a copy of your receipt. Now give the problem. Keep it brief. Don't go on about all the grief and inconvenience it has caused you to see the television image sideways for the last two days. Just tell them the image is sideways. Close your letter by repeating what it is you want done to correct the situation.

• *Don't assume:* If this is your first letter to them, don't assume that they will try to get away with highway robbery. Don't threaten; assume that they will *want* to correct the problem. Photocopy the letter, and send it off to the retailer. If the retailer gives you no help, send a letter to the manufacturer. There are reference books in the library with addresses, and reference librarians to help you locate the reference books. (FL, *Anon.*)

A FEDERAL CASE

The Federal Trade Commission investigates false or misleading advertising. The FTC usually will not go after something or someone unless it receives many complaints, but don't let that stop you. Be one of many complaints. Something might get done because of it.

The National Advertising Council is a division of the Better Business Bureaus. This agency is sponsored by the ad industry and concerns itself with national advertising. They've been pretty tough on misleading ads. If you are thinking of complaining to them, know that it will take longer than next week to solve your problem.

The Better Business Bureau in your area is concerned with local advertising. They're a good bet for complaints against small businesses. They may be able to help you get your money back or the item repaired or replaced. They may be able to get the business to change its ads. Your complaint will go on file at BBB. If they receive too many complaints, BBB will give unfavorable reports to those who call wondering about a firm's reputation.

The state consumer protection agency handles complaints about advertisements that are misleading or out and out lies. It may be within or separate from the state attorney general's office. (PM)

AUCTIONS

When that special something is going, going, *gone,* make sure your budget didn't go with it.

Viewing: Always examine potential purchases carefully before the auction. Most auctions sell items as-is.

Bidding: Keep your limbs in control. If you fidget a lot in your daily life, you might think twice about attending an auction.

Floor price: The highest bid in an unrestricted auction does not have to be accepted if it is obviously terribly low. The seller may place a minimum price on an item, and the auctioneer will begin at that price.

Caveat emptor: If an article is presented as-is, then you cannot complain about whatever damage you may discover after you've bought it. But you do not need to accept something that has been offered as perfect if you find that, in reality, it is not.

Delivery: You must pay the delivery charges. You should have the item picked up the day you purchase it, or make certain everyone is aware that you have made arrangements for later removal. Remember to insure valuable items before the moving van comes for them.

Order of sale: Least expensive items are usually offered first, but you'll just have to wait for the one you are waiting for. A certain item will not be offered at a particular time just for your convenience.

Payment: Full payment or a deposit is expected right away. As a rule, an auctioneer will accept only cash or some other form of guaranteed funds. (ITG)

Estate auctions: An auction just may be the result of a disaster in someone's family. That family may be in attendance, so mind your manners when you are there. (KK) **See also under** *Auctions* **in** *CHAPTER NINE: HOME EC*.

THRIFT SHOPPING

Thrift shops can be veritable bonanzas of bargains in clothes, housewares, books and, generally, stuff you didn't know you needed.

But the good ones aren't places that you can just give a quick once-over and expect to find that perfect little skirt to go with your green blouse. You've got to be prepared to invest some time in exchange for the money you save. Poke around, look behind and under things (the staff often hide things that they want for themselves). Think of it as a treasure hunt.

Thrift shops that are connected with churches or charities are generally pretty good bets to have some quality merchandise at great rates. And consider that by buying in a church or charity thrift store, your money is going for a good cause. (MK)

There are thrift shops and there are thrift shops. Most cities have several *boutique-type thrift shops*, each carrying a second-hand inventory that reflects the taste of the owner. Find the one that most closely approximates the kind of clothing you collect and befriend the owner and sales help. They can keep an eye open for you at auctions, estate sales and other places where they pick up their stock. (AR)

When you buy second-hand furniture, spray it with an insecticide. Cockroaches often hide in nooks and cracks and breed. (PAN) **See also** *Buy, Buy Love* **in** *CHAPTER NINE: HOME EC*.

FLEA MARKETS

You'll need a second sense to locate some of the best flea markets, because they often seem to hop around. Look in your weekend or Friday afternoon paper to see if there is a notice for one.

• When you locate a flea market, be sure to take a tape measure with you because there will be no place to try on clothes.

• Take cash.

• Be either late or early. If you're early, you'll be able to snap up the best items. If you're late, you'll be in a good position to bargain with the vendors who don't want to have to cart all the stuff back home again. (RM)

FLEA MARKETING TIP

Bring your tape measure.

FACTORY OUTLETS

No bronze medals: Firsts are considered perfect. Seconds have some slight flaw somewhere that, chances are, is not even noticeable. Seconds end up in factory outlet stores or other discount stores. Thirds get torn apart and made into new fabric. (PL)

Samples are size 8s that were modeled in the showrooms. These arrive at the discount houses and other bargain outlets in the first half of August and in February. You won't have too much luck in locating these unless you live in New York. (YT)

Note: Most large cities have a fashion district where samples can be purchased cheaply.

The Vanities

The perception of our beauty changes as we grow older.

When we were babies, we were "perfect" because we had dual arms and legs and a solo head. "She's just perfect," Mom said. "A beautiful baby," agreed the nurse.

Well, things change. Sort of. Now we look in the mirror and realize we're almost as wrinkled as we were when we were born. And in order to get someone to say, "You're beautiful, baby," we have to commit to twenty minutes a day minimum just for camouflage.

C O N T E N T S
Chapter Seven: *THE VANITIES*

MAKEUP PRIMER: Makeup Definitions for Those Who Know Nothing — Mirrors and Lights — The Kit — The Hard Part — Buying Makeup — Get It On — Eyes Have It — Eyeliner — Eyebrow Pencil — Aw, Shucks — Lip Pencils — CAMOUFLAGE: Five Ways to Camouflage "Bad" Points — FACIALS: Seven Homemade Facial Mixtures — Steam Facials — Skin Care Basics — Pelt Types — Skin Warriors — Skin Ailments — HOMEMADE BEAUTY: Skin Cleansing — Moisturizers — Conditioners — Stimulators — Bleach — Exfoliating — FOLLICLE FOLLIES: Shapes and Styles — Hair-Care Products — Homemade Hair Care — Read All About It — EYES: Contact Lenses — Shades — Glasses — SCENTS AND PERFUMES: Perfume — How to Pick a Perfume — Putting It On — Home Brews — pH DELUXE — IMPROVED NATURE

MAKEUP PRIMER

Wearing makeup is a sort of rite of passage. The application of a variety of different goops and dusts and paints changes us from girls to women, and all the Janes, Myrtles, and Ruths become Jacquelines, Michelles, and Racquels.

Why? What's the importance of the paint pot?

I know a woman who won't leave the house without lipstick. She doesn't wear anything else on her face, but if her lips aren't bright red they won't see the light of day. The reason behind it is simple: It's her mask, her glamor, her personal best. Red lips make her feel finished, complete. (EC)

Women who wear makeup do so in order to feel better about their looks. So, if we're going to do it, where should we start?

How about with a batch of

MAKEUP DEFINITIONS FOR THOSE WHO KNOW NOTHING

and who are reading about the whole sordid business here because they're too embarrassed to ask their moms or friends — or because they're too cool to *really* care about makeup but are, well, sort of *curious?*

• *Foundations* are supposed to make the skin look better. They cover small imperfections and can alter skin color. Use foundation the same way an artist might prepare a canvas for a painting.

• *Powders* give makeup either a sheen or matte look.

• *Blushers* add color, shading, warmth, luminosity.

• *Eye-shadow* adds color, contour and dimension to the eye.

Best specific advice: Don't wear blue eye shadow.

Best general advice: Makeup has a function. Decide what you want the makeup to do for you, then apply only enough makeup to achieve your goal. *Don't apply makeup so you can look like a woman wearing makeup.* Cosmetics are a means, not an end. (ESP, KK)

MIRRORS AND LIGHTS

First, let's get set up. *The lighting of the place* you apply your makeup is very important. *Incandescent light* will show your natural skin tone. Stay away from *fluorescent lighting* for the initial application. You should have a nearby window for checkups in *natural light.*

The mirror should be a good one, well-silvered and without distortions. If you get one with lights along the sides, you'll eliminate shadows created by single-source lighting. (ESP, KK) **See** *Buying a Mirror* **in** *CHAPTER NINE: HOME EC.*

THE KIT

The trouble with arts and crafts is they always require specialized tools. Makeup is no exception.

Obviously, you'll need

• *A mirror* (see above)

• *Facial tissues*

• *Cotton balls* or cosmetic balls (cotton balls are preferable, since the synthetic fibers in the other can be harsh to your skin)

• *A makeup sponge* (make sure you rinse the sponge thoroughly after each use)

• A small, flat *brush for concealer*

• A **powder puff,** brush or, better, cotton balls, which are more hygienic since they're used only once

• **An eyebrow brush** and eyelash comb combination

• A small *lip brush*

• A large *blush brush* (say it three times, fast) with soft, natural bristles, preferably sable

Go ahead and make an investment in these tools. A twenty-dollar blush brush will last for years, and the results you'll get are worth the money. (ESP, KK, AAT)

To keep your brushes for years and to protect your skin from harmful bacteria that can accumulate in brushes, wash them every now and then in cool water and mild liquid laundry detergent. Let them soak, then swish them around gently; rinse under cool, running water. To keep the bristles soft, use a mild hair conditioner, then rinse again. Shake out any excess water and place them on a towel to dry. (ESP)

THE HARD PART

Now, *take a good look* in the mirror at your naked face. Not just a glance, either. Look at your face until you gain some objective distance on it. Look at your skin tone. Are you pale, sallow or rosy? Is your skin dry, oily or a combination of the two? Do you have dark circles under your eyes or shadows cast from bags? Your face is your canvas, so examine it, get to *know* it.

BUYING MAKEUP

The next step is buying the right makeup. Remember, when you approach the cosmetic counter, that the counter personnel are often paid on a commission basis, so are trained to sell you as many products as possible. Learn to say no, but learn what you can from the demonstration. You might pick up some techniques you can try at home in front of your own mirror.

• It is best to *shop for cosmetics under incandescent light.* At the very least, natural light should be available. You'll need an atmosphere conducive to accurately judging colors. Unfortunately, department store lighting is not the most flattering. On the other hand, it's probably no worse than the fluorescent lighting in most offices, so if you're choosing make-up for daytime use, bad light may be the right light.

• *Foundations* should match your neck, not your face. It is too difficult to judge the base color of your face with its uneven tones. Pick a type of foundation that will aid your skin. If your skin tends to be oily, select a water-base foundation for oily skin. If you are in the sun too much, get one with sunscreen.

• *Powder:* Loose, translucent powder is generally chosen over pressed powder by most makeup artists. Loose powder gives better coverage, and provides an even matte finish. Pressed powder is handy, however, for traveling.

• Powder *blush* in either a single color or a blush duo or trio are good choices. Pick one that is only as intense as your own skin tone. If your skin tone is pinkish, use a pink shade. Don't fight your face. If you'd rather try something other than powder, cream blushes and color washes are also available, but more difficult to apply..

• There are a variety of *eye color products* available — powders, pencils, crayons. Some of the best guides for choosing eyeshadow are current magazines. Whatever is "in" for the season is the best bet for the most up-to-date look. If you do not care to follow the trends, the best bet is a neutral color in the same family as the blush. Remember that iridescent eye shadows have a drying effect.

• *Never use a product made for any other part of your face on your eyes.* There could be dyes or formaldehyde derivatives in them that are not safe when used in the eye area.

• *Eyeliner* is optional. Women with big, round, wide-open eyes can wear eyeliner pretty much anytime. When purchasing eyeliner, get whatever color you like, but remember to stay within the realm of your own possibility. Don't go with a jet black kohl pencil or liquid liner if your hair is platinum, your eyelashes blonde, and your skin snow white. Liner can be found in powder, liquid, or pencil form.

• Black-brown or dark brown *mascara* is most preferable. If you are teary-eyed at movies and weddings, get a waterproof brand. This is also good if you live in a rainy place or in a freezing place where your eyes tear up in the cold — or if you are a sweaty person. *Caution:* Although it is desirable to lengthen and thicken your lashes, mascaras with claims to do so have small fibers that can irritate your eyes, especially if you wear contact lenses.

• If you want to darken your eyebrows, get an *eyebrow pencil* close to the color of your hair. Some makeup artists will use two pencils, each a different color found in the client's hair.

• Complete your cosmetics collection with a *lip color and lip liner.* Both should be within the same color family. If your skin tone has more of a yellow cast, go for peaches or corals. Pink-toned skin looks best with pink, rose, or mauve shades. Small lips are prettier in sheer colors because dark tones emphasize their smallness. The liner pencil or lipstick should be just slightly darker than the lip color. The lip color can be in the form of lipstick, lip gloss, or slim-sticks, whichever you prefer. Slim-sticks are the same diameter as your lips, and make the color easier to apply. (AAT, KK, ESP)

GET IT ON

To apply makeup:

• First *clean your face* with a facial soap or cleansing cream and tepid water. Don't use hot water — it can dry your skin out. Splash your face several times to remove all traces of cleanser residue. Pat your face dry.

• *Use toner or astringent* and cotton balls to clean away soap film and close pores, thus retaining the water absorbed from rinsing. Make this thorough cleaning part of your routine both morning and evening.

• Immediately, while your face is still damp from the toner, *use a light moisturizer or sunscreen.* Be sure to cover your face completely. For oily skin, use a light oil-free moisturizer. Moisturizer not only helps retain the moisture in your skin, it also protects it from impurities in the air, such as smog, fumes and pollen.

• Apply *foundation* with a damp sponge. Dot foundation in the center of your face and then gently blend out. This will provide an even coverage and will make it easier to blend from made-up skin to bare skin at the neck, jaws, and hairline. Go ahead and put foundation on your lips.

• *Powder your face* all over with a brush, cotton ball or powder puff. Brush off the excess, including around the lips. The foundation and powder will set while you get dressed.

• After dressing, apply one coat of *mascara.* To avoid clumps and flakes, remove the wand from the mascara bottle and wave it gently in the air for thirty seconds before applying. If your eyes are more almond-shaped than round, you may want to apply mascara on the upper lashes only.

• *Eye shadow:* There are many ways to apply shadow, and a million colors to apply. Going with the latest style will only work if you do it absolutely right and change the style every month with the beauty magazines. (AAT, KK, ESP)

EYES HAVE IT

Here are *two very flattering tried and true methods* of applying eye shadow:

Method one, for close-set or well-contoured eyes:

• *Apply lighter shadow* at inside corner of eyes and blend out just past center.

• *Gradually darken the lid* toward the outer corner.

Method two, for wide-set eyes or for eyes that do not have well-defined contours:

• *Apply the lightest shade on the brow bone* and the eyelid from the inner corner to the outer corner.

• *Use the darker shade* in the crease blending up and down along the lash line and joining them up at outside corner of your eye. (ESP, *Anon.*)

EYELINER

A guideline: If you want to use eyeliner, go lightly.

For the most subtle approach, use a powdered eye shadow that's one shade darker than the *darkest* color on your lid.

• Wet a very thin liner brush with water and roll it across the shadow.

• Next, draw the brush across the top lid lash line. Liquid liner should be drawn across top lash line as well. Do not pull the skin taut, though, since that will stretch the skin and age it prematurely.

For a softer line, apply the shadow dry with a #0 brush. If any flakes of eyeshadow get on your cheek, simply brush them away with a fluffy brush.

If your eyes slope down on the outside corner, draw the line on the outside and only to just below the inside corner of your eye.

For a different look, try a liner pencil in black, gray, brown, or another color that's one shade darker than your darkest eye shadow.

• Line along the upper lash line. If your eyes are wide-set, line the lashes from end to end. If your eyes are closer set, line only from inside edge of pupil to outside corner eye. Make sure to hold your head straight and look straight ahead when applying.

• Women with wide eyes can line under the eyes as well, from the inside edge of the lash line to the outside corner of the eye, not from corner to corner. Although it has been popular to line the lower lids on top of the lash line, *that can easily cause serious eye infection.* Line the lower lids below the lash line only.

• Apply second and third coat of mascara, if desired. (ESP, KK, YML)

EYBROW PENCIL

Apply *eyebrow pencil* with a light hand. Make easy, feathery strokes on the brow hairs. *Do not try to draw them on,* or reshape brows with a pencil. Use an eyebrow pencil for color only. The light, short strokes should just fill in where hair is sparse. (KK)

For those with a steady hand, it's possible *to augment thin eyebrows* with a slender, brushed mascara, usually in a brown shade. Start at the part closest to the nose. Brush up and out in short, light strokes that extend to the outer point of the brow. (ESP)

To shape darker, thicker brows, spray hairspray onto a brow brush, then brush the eyebrow into the desired shape. Be careful not to get hairspray on your skin. (ESP)

AW, SHUCKS

Applying blush is where the most mistakes are made. Before you begin, you must understand that *the function of blush is to add color to your face, not to contour or emphasize your cheekbones.* As you examine your face without makeup, you'll see your natural color somewhere on top of the cheekbone.

To apply blush:

• Start by putting powder on your blush brush. Blow off excess.

• Beginning at the highest point of your cheekbone, lightly apply the color in a pork chop shape from below your mid-eye to halfway up your temple.

• Blend in an upward manner up to the hairline.

• Add a touch of blush to your temples to accent and frame your eyes. (AAT, ESP, KK)

LIP PENCILS

If you're wearing a light shade, lip pencils should be used to keep the edges of your lips neat. Match the color of the pencil to your natural lip shade.

If you're wearing a bright, rich shade of lipstick, have the pencil match the lipstick. You can use a lip pencil to both line and fill in the lips for a longer-lasting color.

Before applying lip pencil or lipstick, apply a lip balm, let it sit for a minute or so, then blot it off.

- Apply the lip pencil, starting with the top lip, working from the middle to the end.
- Soften the pencil line with a brush.
- Finally, put on lipstick and blot with a tissue. (AAT)

Reapply lipstick as needed, especially after a meal — but not at the table, okay? (KK)

CAMOUFLAGE

Let's be honest. Let's not mince words. Let's camouflage.

FIVE WAYS TO CAMOUFLAGE "BAD" POINTS:

1. Lose ten pounds by standing up straight.

2. Wear something you really like and throw away everything you don't feel comfortable wearing.

3. Color can give you an instant face-lift. Light colors make you look heavier; dark colors, thinner.

4. Don't try to squeeze into clothes that are one size too small.

5. If you want to lessen the size of your breasts or hips, wear a dark color on that area combined with a light color on the other. Just the opposite goes for breasts or hips that are too small. (CLC)

See also *Three Rainbow Rules* **and** *But Which Colors?* **in** *CHAPTER EIGHT: THE MODERN MODE.*

FACIALS

Wipe off that smile, soldier. Or wipe it on, depending on your point of view.

How to apply a facial:

1. Tie your hair away from your face.
2. Apply the cleanser gently, then tissue or rinse it off.
3. Apply a freshener to remove traces of cleanser.

4. Blend a moisturizer onto your forehead, cheeks and chin.

5. Rinse with lukewarm water.

6. Apply a masque on your face and throat, but not near your eyes.

7. Cover your eyes with cotton pads soaked in milk. Leave the masque on for twenty minutes.

8. Remove masque, blot your face and throat, and apply a thin film of moisturizer. (FD)

SEVEN HOMEMADE FACIAL MIXTURES

Get up close and personal with the natural world:

1. Crushed strawberries, either alone or with oatmeal
2. Mashed cucumbers
3. One teaspoon of powdered yeast and two teaspoons of warm water
4. The beaten white of one egg added to one quarter teaspoon of lemon juice
5. One beaten egg white with a tablespoon of skimmed milk
6. An egg yolk, a few drops of cider vinegar and a dash of vegetable oil
7. Two tablespoons honey and a half teaspoon of lemon juice (FDD, *Anon.*)

For an extensive list of mixtures for specific uses, see *Homemade Beauty*, **below.**

STEAM FACIALS

Steam facials are not for sensitive skin or skin with broken veins, since steam encourages pores to push out impurities. It does, however, promote perspiration and improve circulation.

To make a steam facial, pour boiling water over herbs and make a towel into a tent. Steam your face for about ten minutes.

Natural cleansing agents: Chamomile, lady's mantle, nettle, rosemary, or thyme are good for cleansing and soothing.

Natural tightening agents: Peppermint, elderflower, tincture of benzoin and gum arabic are good for tightening.

Yarrow is good for *drying*, and leek, comfrey and fennel are fine for *healing*. (EC, CF)

THIS WON'T MAKE YOU HAPPY

A grim statistic: It takes a quarter-million frowns to make one wrinkle. Therefore, if you frowned approximately 700 times a day, or about 30 times an hour, or once every two minutes, you'd get a wrinkle a year. *(Anon.)*

SKIN CARE BASICS

• *Keep in mind exactly what you need,* and stick to that. It is not necessary to buy an entire line of skin-care products, for example, to reap the benefits.

• You might simply *buy a cleaner* and moisturizer and ask for sample sizes of other products to test at home. That way you'll have the heart of the regimen and can buy whatever extras you find you need later on.

• *Other useful skin-care products* should include an *astringent or toner* for the oilier areas of your face, a *moisturizer* for night or under makeup, and a mild *cleansing cream* or soap. Even gentler creams should be used for the delicate area around the eyes.

All of the above should be chosen with your own skin in mind. If you have oily skin, avoid products with mineral oil in them. If your skin is very dry, choose an alcohol-free toner for dry skin, rather than the more drying astringent. (ESP, KK, *Anon.*)

PELT TYPES

There are only *two basic skin types* — *dry* and *oily* — but a million variations. So it's possible to have an oily nose and a dry scalp, for example. Compounding all that is the fact that skin can be dry or oily and extremely *sensitive*. Not only that, but after the age of twenty-four or so, your skin begins to age as your body ceases to make the chemicals that keep kid skin alive. (FC)

SKIN WARRIORS

The world is full of dermatologic villains—conditions and substances that, in the words of TV, rob your skin of its valuable natural nutrients.

Airplanes and *forced air heating* provide the driest air on earth. *Alcohol* also dehydrates the skin.

Dust, smog and *pollution* clog pores. So do deodorants with aluminum chlorhydroxide.

Sunshine is profoundly carcinogenic. Tans look good on twenty-two-year-old kids. They look like leather on thirty-six-year-old women. *(Anon.)*

SKIN AILMENTS

Acne is related to stress and diet.

Stress: Adult acne can sometimes be reduced by using some sort of antistress routine. Here are some other tips to try before you run to the dermatologist:

• Drink eight glasses of water a day.

• Try to get at least seven hours of sleep each night.

• Try a stress-reducing activity, such as yoga, meditation, sex or reading.

• Get some form of aerobic exercise that induces perspiration.

• Reduce the amount of makeup (foundation or cover-up) that you use. (AR)

Diet: If you eat fatty, oily foods, you'll make the problem worse. Clean your face three or four times daily and use masques as often as you like. (**See also** *Homeopathy* **in** *CHAPTER SIXTEEN: MODERN MEDICS.*)

Age spots: Nothing you can do about these except buy a cream that gets rid of those brown, freckle-like spots that usually appear first on the hands. From the mid-twenties on, your skin loses its ability to dissolve melanin, the pigmenting substance that lives under the skin.

Pimples: There are two exciting flavors here. *Blackheads* are caused by clogged pores blocking the excretion of waste material. Steam helps, and so does cleansing. But try not to pop them — you'll do more harm than good. *Whiteheads* are more difficult to treat because they are subcutaneous. If proper cleansing doesn't do it, consult a dermatologist about the possibility of electrolysis. They are caused by bad diet and a build-up of skin oils, by the way, so watch what you eat (sometimes they can be symptomatic of calcium deposits, and dairy products will be the likely culprits). If you eat greasy, oily stuff, you could end up looking like your food.

Enlarged pores are hell to deal with because there's really nothing you can do about the resulting oily condition — except to try to tone and tighten up the skin. Regular cleansing is exceptionally important in preventing the more serious consequences of enlarged pores. (ESP, FM, AR, *Anon.*)

HOMEMADE BEAUTY

Retin-A aside, Modern Women know that the ridiculous prices charged for some beauty products are cynical efforts to dupe women who don't know better.

Is it worth it to spend thousands on skin-care products? Of course not — unless they *really* will make us all look twenty years old. If they can do that, then we say they're damn cheap and could we have seconds?

Meanwhile, here are folk recipes from all over. If we charged $50 for each of them, they'd probably work better than they already do.

SKIN CLEANSING

Remove makeup with cream or oil. Wet skin with lukewarm water. Work up a lather with a mild facial soap. Rinse and pat dry. That's how to wash a face.

Fresheners rinse away all traces of cleanser and dirt. They help to restore circulation and they help retain the moisture that plumps out your skin cells. Astringents are the strongest and are best for oily skin. Fresheners and toners are for dry to normal skin. Apply fresheners after cleansings.

• Try a teaspoon of cider vinegar with a cup and a half of water.

• Or rub the skin with slice of raw potato.

• Or rub the skin with a lemon slice, or splash on lemon juice and water.

• Or squeeze the juice out of two cucumbers, heat it to boiling, skim off the froth. Bottle it and refrigerate it and use it when you want.

• Or try a few drops camphor in rinse water.

• Or soak a cotton ball in Witch Hazel and pat it gently on your face. (ESP, RE, *Anon.*)

MOISTURIZERS

Moisturizers smooth and plump the skin surface, improve the feel of your skin and protect your skin from the pollutants in the air. Apply a moisturizer when your skin is damp.

• *Milk of almonds:* Skin one ounce of almonds by dipping alternately in boiling water and cold water. Grind the nuts into a powder. Add one half pint of distilled water very slowly — literally drop by drop. Blend the mixture until the liquid is milky. Strain, then apply. (RE)

CONDITIONERS

Conditioning keeps skin soft and smooth and is usually best done at night. If you have oily skin, don't use a conditioner.

Apply conditioners on clean, moist skin.

• For *extremely* dry skin: Melt one teaspoon butter and beat in two tablespoons milk. Leave the mixture on for several hours.

• Try a thin film of petroleum jelly. *A dissent:* Smearing your skin with petroleum jelly will add nothing to your skin; in fact, it will keep your skin from breathing.

• Moisten your face and massage in some raw honey. Leave it on twenty minutes. (ESP, JNT, RE, ATT)

STIMULATORS

Stimulators activate circulation and bring nutrients and oxygen to the surface of the skin. This is usually done with a masque, which can be either rinsed off or peeled off. Rinse-off masques are better cleansers. (JNT)

BLEACH

The old wives' tale that lemon juice is a good natural bleaching agent for hair and skin is unfortunately just another myth. Lemon juice has never been proven to have any bleaching properties at all. (MK)

EXFOLIATING

The mortuary end of cosmetic care, exfoliating is the removal of dead surface cells from the skin and is done after cleansing.

Occasionally, the older, upper layer of skin needs to be helped away so that a new, softer layer of skin can come to the surface. Exfoliation shouldn't be done more than once a month.

• *Mix plain yoghurt with cornmeal* until you have a very moist paste. After cleansing, but before applying toner, apply the paste to your wet face. Use your fingers and scrub gently in a circular motion. Avoid getting the stuff in your eyes.

• For rougher skin, *mix honey and crushed, blanched almonds* and apply as above. Rinse and finish off with toner and moisturizer. (ESP)

• Try non-iodized *salt on a wet washcloth.* Rub face gently, and then rinse. Use a toner and a moisturizer immediately afterward. This obviously is not for sensitive skin.

• *Papaya mint tea:* Pour two cups boiling water on two papaya mint tea bags. Steep. Soak a washcloth in the tea, wring it out and apply it to the face. The tea *must* be hot. Keep heating and renewing the cloth for fifteen minutes. (RE)

FOLLICLE FOLLIES

Hair, shoulder length and longer — and shorter. Hair is the symbol used by children to distinguish them from their parents. Once upon a time, hair was a political statement. Now Modern Women see hair for what it always was — a visible headache.

SHAPES AND STYLES

Hairdressers won't tell you, but never allow anyone to give you a style the shape of which is the same as the shape of your head. Too many hairstylists simply see *hair* when they go to work. It's up to you to keep the whole picture in focus. If you have a round face, don't get a round hairstyle. If your face is long, don't let anybody convince you to go for some lanky look. And if your head is small — and especially if small and very round — never, ever let anyone cut your hair short. *(Anon.)*

Round-faced women should never wear bangs with a hairstyle that doesn't reach their shoulders. (SLo)

You can be first with the latest hair fashion. But don't let yourself be last. Don't fall so in love with the way you look in this year's cut that you let it slide on into next year. (SPo)

Whether you have *straight or curly hair,* leave it alone. Deal with what you have or what you'll have is a mess. Color changes and cuts are less problematic and cheaper. (KL)

Just ask: If you see a woman whose hair looks great and who has both a facial type and hair similar to yours, ask her who cuts her hair. She'll probably take it as a compliment, and you'll get a great lead on a good stylist. (MHi)

HAIR-CARE PRODUCTS

Send it to charity: The difference between a bottle of shampoo that costs $20.00 and one that costs $2.00 is psychological. Chemically, there is no difference at all between a gentle dish soap and the standard salon-formula goo. The added "conditioners" and such are often only chemical or natural equivalents of vegetable oil (some manufacturers at least actually list it as such on their ingredients list). And protein cannot enter the body through the follicles; you have to eat the stuff. Next time, buy the cheap stuff and send a check to your favorite charity. (SF)

Baby shampoo is essentially watered-down liquid dish soap. If you wash your hair every day, it's the best stuff to use. (AJ)

HOMEMADE HAIR CARE

Homemade shampoos:

• *Bar brand:* Shave a portion of a bar of pure castile soap into warm water and let it dissolve. Do not boil. The resulting liquid should be strong enough to lather instantly. Don't rub bar soap into your hair, as it is resistant to rinsing. (ESP)

• *Herbal shampoo:* Add rosemary or thyme to any castile shampoo. (SF)

• *Egg yolk shampoo:* Beat two egg yolks into a cup of warm water, then massage it into your scalp and hair for five minutes. Leave it on for ten minutes, then rinse thoroughly. (SF)

• *Oily hair formula:* Pour four whole eggs, beaten, over your hair. Massage thoroughly and leave it on for fifteen minutes. Rinse first with water, then with a cup of rum combined with a cup of rose water. (SZ)

Rinses:

• *To add sheen:* Boil parsley in water for twenty minutes. Strain and use as a final rinse.

• *To add luster to dark hair,* pour a pint of water over two tablespoons of rosemary and steep for thirty minutes. Strain the mixture and add it to final rinse.

• *To improve natural hair coloring,* simmer a handful of nettles in a pint of water until they're soft; strain and add to final rinse. Gives hair body.

• To restore light tones to blonde hair, simmer a cup of dried chamomile flowers in a pint of water. After thirty minutes, strain and use as a final rinse. Catch the liquid in the sink and repeat the process a few times. (SZ, *Anon.*)

Conditioning:

Instant conditioners are gooshed through and rinsed away. They soften and untangle hair and can be used after every shampoo.

Deep conditioners are rich in creams and oils and are left on for ten to thirty minutes. They should be used once a month or so.

• For *brittle, dry hair,* warm two tablespoons of olive oil and massage it into every part of the scalp. Wring out a towel in hot water and wind it around your head. Repeat the process two or three times as the towel cools. Shampoo and rinse.

• *The Modern Woman's Universal Hair Restorer:* Beat two eggs, then slowly add one tablespoon of olive oil, one tablespoon of glycerine and one teaspoon of cider vinegar. Apply the mixture after shampooing and leave it on for fifteen to thirty minutes. Rinse.

• *Hair Salad:* Mix one egg, one tablespoon of vinegar and two tablespoons of vegetable oil. Massage and comb through hair. Leave on for fifteen minutes, then shampoo and rinse. Helps moisturize and lubricate dry hair. Or leave the mixture on your hair and add tomatoes and a head of lettuce. (SZ, SF, AJ, GY)

READ ALL ABOUT IT

If you have color-treated hair and you're in a big hurry with no time for touching up or toning down, rub the morning paper through your freshly washed and dried hair for several minutes. Follow with a light hair spray. This gives your hair a natural ash-blond look that won't rub off in the course of an evening.

Note: USA Today is not recommended for this purpose unless you want a fright wig. (SJH)

EYES

Once you had to make a choice. You could either look beautiful or you could look where you were going.

Now you can have it both ways, of course. Modern Women consider that a mixed blessing: It's great to look good — but it's an ugly, ugly world.

CONTACT LENSES
Corneal lenses fit only over the cornea, while larger *haptic lenses* fit over the whole eye and are excellent for spots where eye protection may be necessary.

Hydrophilic lenses — the so-called "soft" lenses" — cover only the iris. While they are extremely comfortable, *long-term, uninterrupted use can cause damage to the surface of the eye*. The lenses keep necessary oxygen from reaching cells on the eye's surface, resulting in a deterioration of the surface. If you use soft lenses, never wear them for longer than twelve hours or so — and then make sure your eye gets plenty of recovery time. Hence, the *permanent-type soft lenses* are especially treacherous.

All soft lenses must be *discarded and replaced* every year or eighteen months. (VL)

CONTACTS AND COSMETICS
If you wear your lenses too long and your eyes get tired and bloodshot, *line the tops of your eyes* with *bright* blue or *bright* green eye shadow or eye pencil. While this makes the whites of your eyes look whiter and thus less tired, it also makes you look like you haven't opened a fashion magazine since 1963. (ESP, VB)

If you wear contacts, *avoid greasy eye makeup* and use waterproof mascara. (CFu) If you wear contact lenses, you should make sure to *use a good moisturizing cream* around your eye area. Contact lenses usually make your eyes more light-sensitive, causing you to squint more, thus increasing the production of crow's feet. (MK)

SHADES
Another must for contact lens wearers is a good pair of *sunglasses* — or two — with lenses specially designed to cut down glare on hazy days. (MK)

Try to appreciate fully how ridiculously *affected* you look wearing sunglasses indoors.

Don't talk to people when your eyes are covered by dark glasses — it's not fair. *(Anon.)*

Theraputic angle: Good sunglasses help absorb infared and ultraviolet rays. (MK)

GLASSES

Try on glasses in front of a full-length mirror for a correct sense of proportion. Make sure the glasses sit securely on your nose and don't squeeze your brains. The tops of the frames should line up with your eyebrows. (EL)

Always *wear your earrings* when you are trying on new specs. (AR)

There are always lots of rules about what looks best on each facial type, but *get what you feel good wearing.* (WN)

Remember, *eye makeup* often needs to be altered with glasses. (EL)

If you have to wear glasses, *don't go designer crazy.* Find simply designed frames that fit your face, and choose a subtle color, not white or electric blue. Take a friend with you to help with the frame choice — she knows what you look like a lot better than you do. (AA)

SCENTS AND PERFUMES

We all have a unique musk, a chemistry that is ours alone. That's why choosing a perfume is a difficult task. Modern Women don't go with the crowd when it comes time to select a perfume. They, uh, know that common scents reek of a certain mundane vulgarity.

PERFUME

Perfumes are as complex and subtle as wines. Here are the principal varieties:

Floral: Single florals produce the effect of one flower, even when a number of different essences are blended. *Floral bouquets* are a combination of several flowers.

Citrus: Fresh, woody, crisp, clean.

Woody scents, such as pine and cedar, are blended with ferns, grasses, flower stems, and mosses.

Modern: Developed over the last few decades, these synthetic oils are pleasant, uncomplicated and bright.

Spicy perfumes are pungent, heavier than florals. They are made with the essences of cinnamon, cloves, vanilla, and ginger combined with exotic flowers.

Sweet: Jasmine, tuberose, gardenia. Many skins react by turning a perfume's scent even sweeter, so use sweet scents carefully.

Oriental scents are robust and full-bodied. Eastern woods and grasses like sandalwood are used to produce Oriental's characteristic sultriness. Musk, ambergris and civet.

Toilet water and cologne are diluted perfumes containing a greater percentage of alcohol. *(Anon.)*

HOW TO PICK A PERFUME

There's no secret here. It's all trial and error. Use tester bottles in the stores and find the scents that break your heart. Sniff cologne right away for a first impression, then sniff again in an hour. *Your sense of smell is better later in the day,* so think about doing your testing in the afternoons. (NNR)

Nicotine alters skin chemistry and will reduce a perfume's staying power. Medications can also alter your skin's reaction. (ARL)

PUTTING IT ON

Apply perfumes on pulse spots — ankles, behind the knees, between thighs, on the bosom, the throat, the back of the neck, wrists, the crook of elbows. Behind the ear is not the best place, because oil secretions there are different from other areas of the body. (RT)

Store perfume in the cool and dark. Maybe in your wine cellar. (RT)

HOME BREWS

Save those little vials of perfume samples and add them to the unscented bottles of lotion recommended by your dermatologist. The mix will keep aging skin supple and yet smell wonderful. (FW)

pH DELUXE

These days, it seems just about every woman is concerned with her pH balance.

While there are many products on the market designed to correct pH imbalances, most if not all are topical applications to apply to your skin and hair. Does this make sense when the balance of acid and alkaline is an internal function of the human body?

I find that when my pH balance is on the more acid side, I drink one glass of cold fresh water with one tablespoon apple cider vinegar in the evenings. I will do this for several evenings or until my pH balance has been restored. Also, tonics of this sort are mild relaxants and, because of the high potassium content, useful food for soft skin tissues — what calcium is for teeth and bones, potassium is for skin and flesh tissues. And potassium is, I believe, useful in recovering from surgery. (MH)

pH is measured on a 14-point scale. Values between 0 and 7 indicate an acidic content; 7 and up indicate alkalinity. Incidentally, pH stands for *pouvoir hydrogène,* which, literally translated, means "hydrogen power." You could look it up. (KK)

IMPROVED NATURE

Plastic surgery is *surgery*.

Ask the surgeon *everything* — what will be done, how long it will take, how long you will have to stay in the hospital, what sort of anesthetic will be used, when the stitches will be removed, when the marks will disappear, how long the results will last. The only surgery that lasts forever has to do with bone structure or areas not influenced by muscles or fatty deposits, like chins and noses and ears.

Don't forget your psychological self. Physically, you might look better, but you could possibly miss your old self, imperfections and all. Think hard. (NO)

If you are considering plastic surgery, by far the best way to select a surgeon is to get recommendations from friends who have had a procedure done that's similar to the one you're considering — and are happy with the results. But don't stop there. Once you've got a name, make an appointment for a consultation (which should be free) to be sure you feel comfortable with the doctor and his or her suggestions as to what needs to be done to get the desired results. (JWe)

Liposurgery — the removal by suction of fatty deposits — seems to have no more and no fewer bad aspects than any other type of plastic surgery. There is an oddly irresponsible aspect to it somehow reflective of modern life: If you make a mistake — say, you eat too much — and Modern Science can absolve you by *sucking away* your guilt. And that's a modern curse. *(Anon.)*

The Modern Mode

The distinction between a Modern Woman with clothes and a Modern Woman without clothes is not a fine line.

A Modern Woman without clothes on lives on the far side of fear, close to truth and next door to nature. It's a dangerous neighborhood.

Modern Women prefer to stay closer to home, with all their belongings gathered close to their bosoms.

C O N T E N T S

Chapter Eight: *THE MODERN MODE*

THE BASIC WARDROBE: Color Analysis — Three Rainbow Rules — But Which Colors? — What Is "Celadon"? — What to Do When You Discover Your Color — Self-Analysis — Taille of Two Cities — Don't Dress for Cartoons — The Skirt Issue **— Details — Kids 'N Klothes — Jean Dreams — SHOES: Alternate — Size Change — Trying Experience — Throw Down Your Cloak — Work Shoes — High Heels — LINGERIE: Spend Money — Size Right — Panty Hose: The Two Terrible Shades — In Brief — Eek! A Repairman! — ACCESSORIES: A Rule That's Too Good to Be True — Liberace Look — Earrings — BARGAIN BASEMENT: Boys' Department — Antique Clothing Care — Wearing Somebody Else's Skin — Wearing Your Own Skin — Killer Clothes — A DIFFERENT DRUMMER: How to Do a Striptease**

THE BASIC WARDROBE

Catholic schools have the right idea: It's not what you wear but who you are.

Unfortunately, what we are is clothes junkies. And worse, we're *insecure* clothes junkies. Where once we had good taste, now we have things like

COLOR ANALYSIS

There are several different approaches to finding your best colors — those that make you look most vibrant and hence are most flattering. One of the more popular methods is *color analysis,* an approach that divides skin types into one of four categories, each corresponding to one of the four seasons of the year.

Skin undertones: According to adherents, *summer* and *winter* people have *cool undertones* to their skin; *spring* and *autumn* types have *warm undertones.* It works this way:

Winter types can get away with murder. They can wear bright reds and deep pinks, rich blues, warm grays and even blacks and whites, but not orange. There are no red-headed winter types, but plenty of well-tanned blondes fit into this category.

Summer types are essentially the pastel versions of winter types. They can wear any color with blue or pink undertones, but only in the more muted shades. Taupe, brown and lavender are summer colors, but yellow isn't and neither are colors with warm tones. People with medium complexions would do well in summer colors, but brunettes do less well than others.

Spring people can wear muted shades of warm colors — shell pink, for example, rather than the soft pink worn by summer types. There are very few blonde spring types, and anyone with very a light complexion would tend to disappear in spring colors.

Autumn types can wear vibrant colors with warm undertones — orange, brick red, beige — but no blues. Brunettes with darker complexions tend to be autumn types. (*Anon.*)

THREE RAINBOW RULES

1. Lighter colors receive more attention than darker ones. Therefore, if you do not wish to accentuate an area, cover it with darker clothing.

2. Dark colors absorb heat. That is why folks go white or light in the summertime.

3. Generally, use strong colors in small amounts and calm colors in big amounts. (KF)

BUT WHICH COLORS?

If you have pale skin, you can wear dark blues and browns, but not lighter colors like tans or yellows or pale grays. (NNR)

But be careful: Browns, grays and yellows have base colors that may not be flattering to you. Some browns and grays are cool, with a blue-green base, while others have been mixed with reds, purples and pinks to create a warmer color.

If you have dark skin, you can wear the colors people with pale skin can't wear, but not the colors that they can wear — and especially not dark browns.

If you're a blonde: You can wear blue, gray, turquoise, red and green. You can't wear orange or any shade of brown, light to dark.

If you have black hair, you can't wear darker blues. But dark gray is okay, and so is tan, red, green and pale blue.

If you're a redhead, never wear reds, pinks, yellows or pale grays. Instead, try greens — all shades — darker browns in warm tints, blues and dark grays.

If you have brown hair, you can wear gray, beige, blue, red and mid-range browns (unless you have exceptionally pale skin). You can't wear darker browns or greens.

If you have silver or gray hair, you can wear anything you damn well please — except yellows.

Black and white are free for all.

Outlaw: Your ability to alter your coloring with the artful use of makeup will allow you to break some of the rules of color choice. (AR, GY, NNR) **Check out** *MAKEUP PRIMER* **in** *CHAPTER SEVEN: THE VANITIES* **for step-by-step directions.**

WHAT IS "CELADON"?

The ad describes the dress as being a "lovely celadon." What is that? Who makes up these words? Are we supposed to understand them because we are born female? Have you ever read the simple words, *pale gray-green* in any advertisement directed at a woman? And have you ever read the word *celadon* in an ad for men's clothing?

Here's a glossary for the color-simple:

- *Aubergine:* dark burgundy
- *Azure:* deep blue-green
- *Bisque:* light grayish brown
- *Celadon:* pale gray-green
- *Cerise:* cherry red
- *Chinese red:* dazzling red
- *Heather gray:* muted purple
- *Heliotrope:* pinkish purple
- *Loden green:* dull, muted green
- *Palomino:* slightly yellowish bone
- *Parchment:* grayish yellow
- *Sepia:* reddish brown
- *Slate blue:* gray-blue
- *Taupe:* dark brownish-reddish gray
- *Teal:* dark greenish blue
- *Vermillion:* brilliant orange-red (EC)

WHAT TO DO WHEN YOU DISCOVER YOUR COLOR

Choose one color and make it the star of your closet. Never buy anything that doesn't work with that color. (GY)

Ideally, you should build your wardrobe around one central color and no more than two secondary colors. (VS)

That goes for accessories, too. Find out the color that works for you and only buy accessories that work with that color. (DL)

Matching: Don't try to be cute by matching a belt to your shoes, especially if they are red or any color close to it. Gray works and so does black. Remember, white never works. (JL)

SELF-ANALYSIS

Color analysis is fine for those who lead simple lives in need of complication. For some of us, however, the wardrobe is simply an expensive investment, one we can't afford to repeat every season. We just want clothing that is attractive and practical, sophisticated and comfortable, that's all.

Look in the mirror. Start shaping your wardrobe by looking at your own shape. Come on, *look.* Are you fat? Short? Tall? Don't confuse self-characterization with self-criticism here. What we're trying to do is discover what you *really do look like*, not what you're *afraid* you might look like or what your cousin says you look like or what you *want* to look like. Aside from downright terrible taste, most wardrobe gaffes come from wearing clothes that are appropriate for somebody else's body. (KK)

There are new *shoulder pads* on the market that don't require snaps or Velcro to stay in place. They're available in flesh tones as well as other colors to suit your wardrobe. (AR)

If you feel that you are too tall, or if you actually *are* tall, break up your body by using different colors. Instead of a dress with no break at the waist, try wearing separates that actually are separate: a light blouse, a belt, a skirt. If you wear vertical stripes, you'll look like a missile.

Too short? Match the color of your shoes, hose and skirt — but keep it subdued, with black, taupe or natural colors. Wear shoulder pads and a large beaded necklace in the same color field as your top. In other words, let the colors flow up your body; don't chop it up. And remember that shoes that are cut narrow and low in the toe will make your legs look longer. If you have short legs, never wear running shoes with a skirt or dress; it'll look like you're walking on your knees.

Overweight? Dark colors, no frills. *Whatever* happens, don't wear something a size too small because you're trying to convince yourself it's your size. Err on the side of bigness.

To be thin was once in. Now it's out. If you're thin, wear light colors, especially skirts and pants. Avoid body-hugging dresses, but don't wear the living room drapes, either. Silky, frilly tops will work well for skinny girls. Don't dress timidly. (AAT, AR, GY)

TAILLE OF TWO CITIES

Eurosize conversions for dresses:

American	8	10	12	14	16	18	20
British	10	12	14	16	18		
Continental	38	40	42	44	46	48	50

. . .and for shoes:

American	4 1/2	5 1/2	6 1/2	7 1/2	8 1/2	9 1/2	10 1/2
British	3	4	5	6	7	8	9
Continental	35 1/2	36 1/2	38	39 1/2	40 1/2	42	43

In Europe, clothing sizes vary from country to country. An American 6, for example, is a size 40 in Italy and a size 38 in France.

British and American stocking sizes are the same. (AKP)

Italian clothing usually is designed for women who are broader in the shoulders, have a somewhat straight waist and smallish hips. Italian fashion is *not* designed for tall people.

French fashions generally favor small, shapely women with very small waists.

If you buy *European clothing* that is cut to be worn close to the body, you may want to choose one size larger than your American size. (AR)

DON'T DRESS FOR CARTOONS

Select a style that will work for you at all times. A selection of blue-striped tops and red bottoms will give you a wardrobe perfect only for children's birthday parties.

Build your wardrobe around a conservative core. Don't try to develop a wardrobe based on ephemeral fashions purchased at stores that specialize in leisure wear. You'll look like an unemployed cosmetologist. Instead, think like a boring grown-up and let accessories or the vagaries of your mood lighten your closet.

Give some thought to clothing you already own. Which clothes are most comfortable? Which items reap the most compliments? Which things make you feel sexy, professional or innocent? Don't confuse dissatisfaction with yourself with what you wear. You may have the makings of a good core wardrobe in your closet, but you might be too depressed to see it. So throw out that bad boyfriend or whatever before you gut your wardrobe.

Purchase quality and you'll find that you've also bought a good measure of self-confidence. **See also under** *Budgets* **in** *CHAPTER TWO: MODERN MOOLAH*. Find a few elegant blouses; you'll get more mileage from them than from a closet full of garish, once trendy rags. If you want to achieve some sort of informal look, then simply add a pair of jeans or a cotton skirt to a silk blouse.

Your core wardrobe should be able to provide the basis for any look you want. Anything else — including, say, the jeans we discussed above — should be seen as a sort of accessory.

Every women's magazine — except *Ms,* of course — has a list of what should be considered the foundation blocks of a wardrobe. If you're too lazy to look, you'll have to take

THE SKIRT ISSUE

Trumpet : good for fairly narrow hips.

Pegged : not for larger hips.

A-line : for broader hips.

Gored: for larger hips.

Pleated: pleats should not open across stomach or hips.

Straight: ideal for most women.

Gathered: for larger hips.

Circle or double circle: for heavier hips.

Egg-shape: for narrow hips.

our word for it. So, ***here's a basic list of components*** for a core wardrobe:

• Light-colored blouses, including at least two in near-white. Silk is best, synthetic isn't. Cotton is the most practical.

• A simple, black dress. But if black isn't your best color, pick a dark and elegant neutral that suits you better. Pick up some scarves in more flattering colors to frame your face. If you feel that you must have a classic black evening dress, even though the color isn't the best for you, get one with a very open or cutaway neckline so that the color of your skin and your jewelry flatter your face.

• Two suits, blue and gray if you have normal coloring, beige and brown otherwise. This bit is optional if you don't need suits for work. And be careful of those beiges, grays and browns — they may have a base color — green or purple, for instance — that isn't flattering to you. Be consistent; buy either all cool or all warm neutrals.

• Two or three skirts, one black and simple, one in an earth tone and one rather flamboyant.

• Two or three pairs of pants. Choose black, navy or olive, or something like taupe or rust or some other warm earth tone.

• Sweaters, including at least one turtleneck.

• If you have to choose just one coat, make it a classic raincoat with a zip-out lining. Get something flattering, but neutral: Try olive, black or beige. If you can't stand raincoats, pick up something that looks like Pat Nixon's plain cloth coat.

• One very good quality pair of pumps and a good pair of flats for daytime wear. Choose a neutral color.

You can add other items to this wardrobe, but never consider them to be part of this core. Scarves, jeans, T-shirts, off-the-shoulder sweatshirts, whatever, should all be chosen for their ability to work well with the core wardrobe. (AR, GY, NNR)

DETAILS

Simplicity is the key to a basic wardrobe. For evening wear, there's nothing more appropriate or alluring than a basic black dress, with simple, elegant accessories. (TR)

Triple match: Never buy anything that doesn't coordinate with at least three things you already own. (BH)

Solids are more practical than prints. (ARo)

Start off with a few well-made, classically styled ensembles, preferably ones that can be combined to give different looks. Unless you suddenly strike it rich, you can buy just a couple of new outfits a season and keep your look current and stylish. (ID)

Buying more expensive clothing can actually save you money. The clothing is usually better made and more classically styled so you can wear it for several years. Also, the sales clerks in a more upscale store are usually knowledgeable about colors and styles and can help you to pick out clothes that will really suit you. (MHi)

If you positively know you look great in a color or style, buy only that. ***Uniforms are*** *great.* You don't have to worry if this will go with that—everything's right there. You won't have to worry about what's at the dry-cleaners, and you'll always have something to wear. (KK)

KIDS 'N KLOTHES

Don't be afraid to let your teenage daughters help you select clothes. They generally have a good knowledge of what's in style and they won't let you go out looking ridiculous. (LEv)

But caution: Teens, having a false sense of the importance of age, may also dress you too old. (AR)

Dressing too young doesn't make you look younger — it just makes you look silly. (MK)

JEAN DREAMS

Go to a large store and invest an hour or so trying on every brand of jeans you can lay your hands on. If you still haven't found a pair that makes you look the way you want to, try another store and more brands. With all the cuts of jeans available, if you look hard enough, you'll find the jeans of your dreams. Then buy twenty pairs and you're set for life. (MK)

A dissent: Styles and cuts change with jeans, as they do with everything else in clothing, so buying more than two pair is silly. (AR)

SHOES

We treat them like men — we hate them, we love them, we walk all over them and we can't get along without them.

ALTERNATE

Once you've chosen the key colors for your wardrobe, find shoes that match or accent your clothing. You'll need at least two pairs. *Alternate your shoes every day.* Never wear the same pair twice in a row. Give them a day or so to recover. Following this simple rule will prevent your shoes from stretching out and falling apart and will increase their lifespan twice over. (NNR)

A shoe tree will extend the life of your shoes by four to five years. (PL)

Well-heeled: Money spent on shoes is a decent investment. Cheap shoes fall apart quickly and they may damage your feet. The materials and craftsmanship that go into making a good shoe are reflected in its price. So spend what it takes to get something that will last — and look good. (KK)

SIZE CHANGE

Remember that your shoe size will probably change during your lifetime. ***Have your size checked every few years.*** There should be a finger's width of space between the end of your longest toe and the end of the shoe. The width should be such that you can pinch the leather on the sides. Your heel should not slip in back. (MHo)

TRYING EXPERIENCE

Try new shoes on tired feet. Happy feet will accept most anything. Tired feet will be discriminating. (BC)

If one size is a little too small for you and the next size is a little too big, choose the bigger pair. Don't expect the smaller pair to stretch into a comfortable fit.(LL)

For that special medical look: Ask a podiatrist to recommend a shoe. (SS)

THROW DOWN YOUR CLOAK

Protect your shoes with a water and stain protector. Then, after you come indoors from the rain or snow, wipe the salt marks off with a damp rag. Reapply the protector every few weeks. If your shoes are soaked, wet the shoe all over when you get home or you'll end up with a water line. Keep wet shoes away from radiators and fireplaces. Shoes need to dry naturally or they will stiffen and crack.

To remove white water stains try a tablespoon of vinegar in a quarter cup of water. (ES)

WORK SHOES

Here it is, the one you don't want to read. But we're going to say it, and we're going to say it loud: ***Don't wear white socks and athletic shoes as part of a semiformal ensemble.*** All over the world, men and women are going to work dressed like people with good taste and common sense — except in certain large cities in North America, where women have adopted the pseudo-therapeutic affectation of wearing jogging shoes and white cotton socks with suits. It looks really stupid, no way around it, and long after very busy women with lots of places to go have stopped yelping about how God never meant for them to walk on pavement without Nikes, the grandkids are going to chuckle over how silly they looked. Wear flats if you have to, and if the commute to work is too much for normal footwear, take a bus. (KK)

HIGH HEELS

The safest and by far most flattering heel is stacked or curved. It should feel centered under your heel and should not give as you take a full stride. Check the sole for reinforcement at the instep. The heel backs should be cut in a way that doesn't slice into your Achilles tendon.

A shoe made wholly from leather allows the foot to breathe and is more comfortable. Look at the outside sole of the shoe — there should be a stamp telling you if the shoe is all leather or manufactured of man-made materials.

Remember that feet change as you grow older — they often get larger and wider.

Contrary to popular belief, *shoes will not stretch* enough to make a difference if you buy them too tight. Try on shoes that are one-half size larger if your feet feel cramped. Wiggle your toes, bend the ball of your foot. Your toes should not be pinched, and the sole should bend easily at the ball and remain on your heel. If your foot slides forward slightly, you can have a sueded piece put on the inside of the heel to take up the slack.

Sandal straps should not pinch, cut into, or rub on any part of the foot or ankle.

After a few hours wearing heels, you may want to stretch out your calves and hamstrings gently to avoid sore muscles.

It's a good idea to *vary your heel heights* from day to day in order to protect your back and legs and to avoid foot problems in the future. (AAT)

High heels are a must in almost every situation, but never take them off in public. (MT)

LINGERIE

Good lingerie looks good — and feels better.

SPEND MONEY

Everything about your lingerie should be skimpy — except the price. The cheap stuff will only make you look and feel cheap. (SBA)

SIZE RIGHT

Nothing spoils the scenery like a woman wearing lingerie that is too tight under a knit dress, with bulges and lines everywhere. Start at the bottom and buy the right size bra and panties. Then buy the right size dress. *(Anon.)*

PANTYHOSE: THE TWO TERRIBLE SHADES

What's more appalling than having your legs wrapped up in coffee- or taupe-colored hose that you bought at the supermarket, or anywhere else? Those two shades in particular highlight the stubble, the little red dots (from only God knows where), the bruises and the capillaries of a Modern Woman's leg — even if you don't think they do. It's disgusting. And they sound funny, too. (RGR)

It's better to wear colored sheers that match your shoes or skirt. *(Anon.)*

Invest in a garter belt: Garter belts are comfortable and slightly sexy — and they're especially nice to wear at very long, boring business meetings. *(Anon.)*

IN BRIEF

Don't be afraid to wear cotton underwear. You won't turn into a Methodist or anything. On hot, muggy days, they're a wonder. (RK)

EKK! A REPAIRMAN!

Roll your own: Ever notice how your dirty underwear jumps out of the laundry basket and onto the floor about the time the plumber arrives? Here's a tip: *Always* roll up your dirty underwear — fold crotch in, then roll up to the waistband — then knot it. This costs precious little time, but it saves endless embarrassment. (AR)

ACCESSORIES

Don't overdo it here. Accessories are the special effects department of the Modern Woman's wardrobe. Too few accessories is boring; too many is science fiction.

A RULE THAT'S TOO GOOD TO BE TRUE

Almost everything looks great with gold; only a few things look good with diamonds. (DLe)

It's better to buy lower-priced but *real* jewels, than high-priced junk. (TO'D)

A vigorous dissent: Most clothing needs larger gems than anyone could ever afford. Accessories are like everything else in your wardrobe — you must buy the right size. (AR)

THE LIBERACE LOOK

Don't be a jewelry junkie. There's nothing more disconcerting than trying to talk to someone who has eight different kinds of simulated stones on her hands or a junky gold lasso around her neck. (TO'D)

On the other hand, don't wear the same jewelry every day, unless you're still a college student. Wedding bands, engagement rings and sentimental rings are obvious exceptions. (AR)

EARRINGS

Clip-ons: Stop heavy clip-on earrings from hurting by padding them on both sides with the soft, sponge-like nose pads made for eyeglasses. If this doesn't do the trick, take them to a jeweler and ask for help. Bending them yourself is not advisable since base metals can snap easily.

Pierced: If your ear lobes are sensitive to the cheaper types of pierced earrings, try dipping the wire or post and back into a cortisone cream or analgesic first aid cream. When removing the earrings, clean them with alcohol or hydrogen peroxide and use cortisone or analgesic cream on your lobes, front and back. (AAT)

Sense of scale: Like eyeglasses, earrings should be tried on in front of a full-length mirror to see if they really suit you. (KAL)

BARGAIN BASEMENT

This is where we offer advice on clothing that didn't fit anyplace else. Free with purchase.

BOYS' DEPARTMENT

Save money by buying some of your clothes in the boys' department. This works best if you are slim and small-busted. Clothes very similar to the clothes in the women's section may be as much as fifty percent less in cost. A boys' size 18 compares to a women's size 6 or 8, 16 compares to 6 or 4, and so on. (RF)

ANTIQUE CLOTHING CARE

So you've found something wonderful to wear in a junk store, right? And now you're fretting about how to care for it. Don't fret too much, because how did it get to be an antique in the first place if it was going to evaporate after one cleaning? Bear in mind, though, that women didn't have fabric-chomping washers and dryers throughout most of history.

White cotton: If your newly purchased ancient white garment has bad stains, boil it in a pot on the stove with some powdered bleach mixed in. Hang it to dry, and iron it before it is completely dry. Hand wash from then on. Remember that very old snaps might rust during washing, so it may pay to remove them before all that boiling.

Colored cotton: Wash gently in moderately warm water. A little vinegar in the rinse can brighten colors.

Silk and rayon: Stains can usually be removed at the dry cleaners. Have the garment steam pressed while you're at it.

Lace: Never use bleach. Wash in moderately warm water with a gentle cleaner. Sugar in the rinse will stiffen it.

Linen: Treat like white cotton.

Beads: Silks, rayons, and chiffons that are beaded should be dry-cleaned. Wash sweaters in cold water and dry flat. Don't wring them out. (GG)

A note on dry cleaners: As a rule, dry-cleaners take every care not to damage your garment, but sometimes it seems they just can't help themselves. Not only that, but dry cleaning is very harmful to most natural fabrics — you're almost always better letting something air out rather than rushing it off to the chemical bath. This is especially true of woolens. (VP)

For more specific info about stain busting, see under *THE PAIN OF STAINS* **in** *CHAPTER NINE: HOME EC.*

WEARING SOMEBODY ELSE'S SKIN

Probably, you should do as the Indians do and draw the line at wearing only the skins of animals that you eat. So if you haven't had a mink burrito lately, maybe you should leave the little critters with their clothes on.

Without getting into sartorial vegetarianism, you should be aware that fake furs will keep you just as warm as real ones, and you won't be able to hear the little squeals of death-pain coming from some place up your sleeve. (DB)

But if you just can't stop yourself:

What to look for: There are three basic methods of making skins into a coat, and the process used determines the quality and final price of the garment:

• *Let-out:* In this painstaking method, skins are cut into thin diagonal strips and reassembled into one long, thin strip. This produces the most durable (and therefore as a rule the most expensive) fur.

• *Skin-on-skin:* In this process, whole skins are attached vertically with leather and joined together to form the garment. The coat will usually have variations of shading that can add to its attractiveness.

• *Pieced:* Leftover pieces of fur are sewn together to form large pieces that are cut into coats. The leftover pieces often include castoffs such as paws, tails, and so on. This method produces the least expensive but the most durable coat. (ELe)

Check the nap of any fur coat sold at a discount. Sometimes they are selling let-out mistakes, in which the fur brushes upward, instead of down and toward the hem, as it's supposed to. (AR)

Where to buy: Department stores usually sell fairly high quality furs at fairly high prices.

• *Manufacturer's showrooms* have better prices, but be sure you check carefully for quality.

• *Fur salons* are good because the staff are specialists, but because most shops are small, they may not have the variety of styles you need to decide on the right coat for you.

When to buy: Although you may find the best prices at spring sales, keep in mind that you'll be buying last year's styles - so shop for classics. (ELe)

WEARING YOUR OWN SKIN

How to select a bathing suit: This is where exhibitionists get to go conventional. Use the same sense of style you use with the other garments in your wardrobe.

• *Blue* compliments most complexions, especially after modest exposure to the sun.

• *Black* is the most slimming.

• *Heavy thighs* can be minimized with very high leg cuts.

• *Age-to-flash ratio:* The younger you are, the more revealing you can be. (*Anon.*)
See *Season Ticket* **in** *CHAPTER SIX: MODERN MERCHANDISE* **for best times to buy.**

KILLER CLOTHES

Sexy clothing catalogs have been around for decades. Frederick's of Hollywood, Victoria's Secret and dozens of other retailers circulate some really steamy catalogs to prospective customers. Ironically, the merchandise in their catalogs is *much* bolder than the inventory they carry in their showrooms. **See** *Delivery Service* **in** *CHAPTER SIX: MODERN MERCHANDISE.*

Using catalogs, you can construct complete fantasy outfits easily and fairly inexpensively. Victorian frills and lace, French maid outfits and the like are all available. But shop carefully and be sure of your size. Nothing's less appetizing than a size 10 belly-dancer squeezed into a size 6 outfit.

There are no real fashion trends or styles in a sex wardrobe, so indulge your favorite fantasy. Look for fun accessories, including wigs (do blondes really have more fun?) and costume jewelry. And don't forget shoes. Whether you prefer spiked heels or "hurt-me-hurt" pumps, shoes are an important addition to anyone's fantasy closet. (ESR)

A DIFFERENT DRUMMER

There. Now, as long you've got all that wardrobe *on,* you might as well take it all *off* — with a little backbeat, please, maestro.   .   .

HOW TO DO A STRIPTEASE

No Trini Lopez: Choose your music carefully. It must speak to you, make you feel sexy and be easy to move to — in your own manner of moving. Sexy, heavy-breathing music only works for some; I prefer a honky-tonk piano or jazz, but others move best to a pop love song. Whatever you choose, the music should tempt *you.*

First, put it all on: Your most available crutch is your costume. Simply to go from fully clothed to naked is easy, but not interesting. *The costume must tempt your audience* — but remember, the club owner is the one you must ultimately impress because he makes or breaks you.

You must start with a look. Choose an image or a theme that suits you. A blue-eyed blonde might consider a cowgirl or Viking theme (your music may inspire you). One of my more successful costumes was a 1950s circle skirt topped by a varsity cardigan with a soft white blouse underneath. From there I stripped to a pastel peek-a-boo teddy dolled up with sequins. Somehow it seemed exciting to the audience, even though I continued to wear the club trademarks, fishnets and stilettos.

All together now: The important part of music and costume selection is making sure the costume and music come off together. That means that the costume must *lead* you to the end of the music and vice versa. Nothing can turn off your tips faster than taking off too much too fast. The audience *wants* to be teased.

Please pass the fiery hoop: Now, if your intention is to strip down and perform sexual "tricks," the rules are a little different. The music must still drive you and suit you, but the costume must come off a little quicker. Your performance must be carefully choreographed to allow enough time to get your act in and still not leave you hanging, as it were. Usually a set lasts five or ten minutes, and you'll do one set per hour. Depending on the club, the state and the degree of stripping you do, a good stripper can make about $50 per hour, counting tips.

Give yourself some room and let 'er rip. Work out your routine in front of a mirror and in front of friends that strip. Allow enough time between items of clothing to provide for any accidents. I remember, one girl stepped out on stage and got a run in her stocking, down by her ankle. She made it work for her by slowly ripping the hose up her leg to her thigh. She made *major* money in tips that set.

During the performance itself, remember the routine you practiced, and remember that you are in control. You have the power to turn them on, turn them off and tune them out. Make eye contact only when you can be assured of nearby protection — a bouncer or an escort. Play to the tables with several patrons sitting at them — the loners are more dangerous. And remember to include your face in your act — if you *look* turned on, you'll make more tips.

Always perform sober. There'll be less chance for mistakes and less chance of ending up in the can. Never work in a club with unprotected dressing rooms; make sure there's a bouncer and a strong and reliable man to escort you to your car. And *never* work where the pay is based on how many drinks you sell. Pay-per-set, plus tips, is the only way to fly.

Learn the laws and stick to them. They vary from state to state. In one state you may be required to cover almost the entire breast and the cleft of your cheeks. In another, you may not even need a G-string. Wherever the line is, make sure never to cross it. Prostitution and entertainment laws can be very tricky. You may, for example, be allowed to take tips — but only if you do not touch the money while it's in the patron's hands. (We could only take tips in our garter belts.) Vice squads can be a real pain, so run a clean show and disassociate yourself from anybody who doesn't.

Always leave — out a back door and with an escort — as soon as you're through. If you want to have a drink after the show, go to a non-strip bar. That way you won't run into a patron.

Know your associates. Make friends with the other strippers and never give them cause for revenge. Don't hang out with anyone who prostitutes on the side. Don't date the bouncers. Never sleep with, encourage, or flirt with the club owner, and never date a patron. Never do anything obscene with the flag of your country. And never tell anyone at your day job that you strip. Lots of people will hold it against you for some reason. (ADu)

Home Ec

There's a fine line between Home Ec and home ick. You can probably find it just under the bottom front edge of the stove.

It's there for a reason, too. After all, most of us have better things to do with our time than wage a ceaseless battle on filth, a task better left to the morally indignant. Modern Women know that only a dirty mind sees dirt where there's really only charm.

C O N T E N T S

Chapter Nine: *HOME EC*

FLOORS: Refinishing Wood Floors — Sanding Wood
Floors — **Carpets** — **Rugs** — **Painting a Floor** —
Carpet Burns — **THE WALLS: Wallpaper** — **Painting**
— Wallpaper Tips — Painting Supplies —**Paint Tools** —
Taking It Off — **Hole in the Wall** — Bad House Bugs
— **Wall Washing** — **DECORATING: Bare Bones** —
Squeaks, Sticks, Drags, Rattles — **The Big Thing in the
Corner** — **Dollar Deco** — **Buy, Buy Love** — How Ants
Get In — **Good Image** — **Buying a Mirror** —
**DRUDGERY: The Modern Woman's Jump-Start
Cleaning Kit** — **New Leaves** — **Clean Corps** — **Light
Cleaning** — **Pools of Polish** — **Trundle Troubles** —
Heavens Above — **Division of Labor** — **More Chores**
— **Spin Cycles** — **Out of the Closet** — **A Clean Story**
— **And a Last Word** — **THE PAIN OF STAINS:
Generic Stains** — **Now for the Guide** — Windowpane
Replacement — **WINDOW PAINS: The Best Way to
Clean a Window** — Sticky Windows — Screen Repair —
Broken Windowpanes — **MS. FIX-IT: The Basic Tool
Kit** —Some Basic Tools — Some More Basic Tools —
Appliance Repairs — **Water Heaters** — **Toaster
Trouble** — Gas Water Heater — Electric Water Heater —
Irons — **Vacuum Cleaners** — **Clothes Washer and
Dryer Troubleshooting** — **Dishwasher** — **Refrigerator
Maintenance** — Washer/Gas Dryer — **Electricity** —
Electric Plug Repair —Knots, Loops, Splices — **Cutting
the Rates** — **How to Fix a Wobbly Chair** — **Starting
from Scratch** — **HOT AND WET: Troubleshooting
the Furnace** — **Hot Talk** — **Heater Maintenance** —
Hot Under the Cooler — **Pipe Dreams** — **Tampons** —
Toilet Terror — **White Noise** — **Plumbing Tools** —
Leak? What Leak? — **Fixing Leaky Toilets** —

All About Faucets — Drip — **Compression Faucets** —
Washerless Faucets — Noncompression Faucets —
Tub and Shower Faucets — GLASS MENAGERIE —
KNIVES AND SCISSORS: Knife Types — **On Edge**
— Blades — Scissor Anatomy — **Sharpening Scissors —**
MODERN WOMEN ON THE RANGE: Bibliography
— Feasts, Fear and Famine — Two Essential Recipes
— THE PROBLEM: How to Season a Cast-Iron
Frying Pan — How to Preserve a Cast-Iron Frying Pan
— Taking Inventory — Dishwashers — Kitchen
Equipment Must-Haves — Silverware Must-Haves — **The**
Rule of Spices — Men Rule — The Modern Woman's
Kitchen Ditchenary — Easy All-Purpose Dips —
Breakfast — Desserts — Vegetables — Health Food —
Recipes You Should Be Able to Make Before You
Qualify for U. S. Citizenship — Turkey — Lamb —
How to Cook Pasta — Calorie Count — Duck Fat —
Herbs and Spices — Bird Hunting — Thawing Frozen
Poultry — Chicken Cutups — **Chicken — Fresh Fish**
— Shrimp — Mussels — Lobsters — Fish Facts —
Fishy Business — **Oysters — About Meat — Man Meal**
— Perishable Foods — Meat Slicing Techniques —
More Meat Slicing Techniques — **Canning — Pickling**
— Freezing — Drying — Measurements — How to
Determine the Freshness of Vegetables — **How to**
Determine the Freshness of Fruits — Cooking: Good
and Bad News

FLOORS

You have to start somewhere, so you might as well start at the bottom.

REFINISHING WOOD FLOORS

When a floor is badly stained and discolored, the only way out is to refinish it completely by sanding it down to the raw wood and applying a new finish. If you are worried about a few small areas, you can try scrubbing with steel wool or a substance called Mex and a wire brush and then touching up with the original finish.

Don't try to sand a whole floor on your hands and knees. The key to refinishing a floor is to provide a uniform surface, something you're not likely to achieve with a sanding block and a piece of sandpaper.

Rent a floor-sanding machine. Rent a large drum-type sander for most of the floor, and a little disk sander for edges. Remove every single thing in the room — that means the curtains and blinds, too. Drive down any protruding nail heads. Close the doors to the room to keep the dust from the rest of the house. Open windows to keep you from Dust Death.

Start with coarse paper first, then medium, and then fine. If you're using one of those great big floor sanders, keep a uniform pressure on the machine and never stop moving or you can sand yourself straight through the floor and to hell or, worse, end up with a floor featuring a corrugated finish.

Vacuum up all the dust when you are finished. Don't forget the dust that has settled all over the walls, too. Use a tack cloth to get the very last bit. **See illustration.**

Finish: There are two types of finish suitable for bare wood floors.

1.Penetrating sealers soak into the wood and leave a low-luster finish with little surface film. Penetrating sealers can only be used on raw wood or on wood that has been coated previously with the same sealer. Apply the sealer with a large brush or a cloth, and wipe off the excess with a dry cloth. Wait for the first coat to dry and then apply another. After a few days, apply a coat of paste wax and buff.

2. Surface coatings will leave a hard and glossy coating on the floor. There are three types of surface coatings:

• *Shellac* dries quickly to a glossy finish. You can apply more than one coat in a day, and walk on it after only a few hours. It's tough and very resistant to scratches. Mop up spilled water or it may turn the shellac white.

• *Floor varnishes* are hard and glossy and more resistant to water. They take longer to dry than shellac and may darken with age.

• *Plastic finishes and synthetic lacquers* are very resistant to spills. They usually do not result in as high a gloss, and they may require more coats because they are thinner than either shellacs or varnishes. (NW)

If you have a floor that has only been scrubbed clean or partially sanded, use *varnish or shellac.* You can buff on your knees or you can rent a buffing machine.

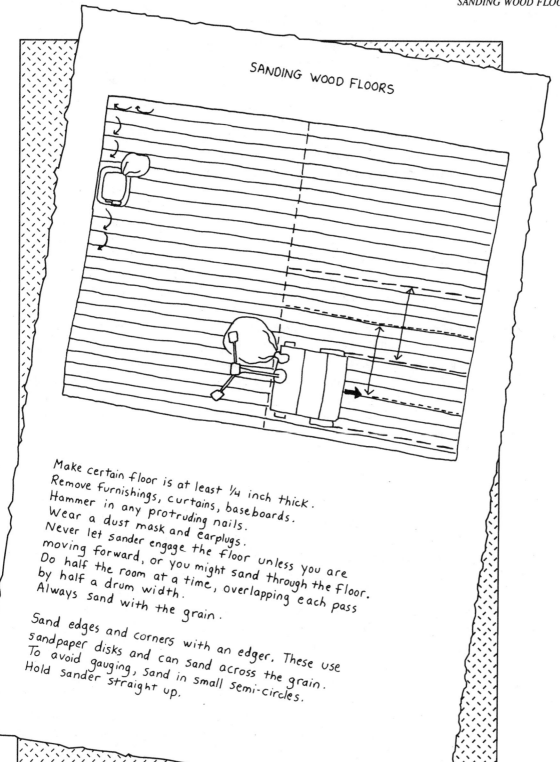

SANDING WOOD FLOORS

Make certain floor is at least ¼ inch thick.
Remove furnishings, curtains, baseboards.
Hammer in any protruding nails.
Wear a dust mask and earplugs.
Never let sander engage the floor unless you are
moving forward, or you might sand through the floor.
Do half the room at a time, overlapping each pass
by half a drum width.
Always sand with the grain.

Sand edges and corners with an edger. These use
sandpaper disks and can sand across the grain.
To avoid gauging, sand in small semi-circles.
Hold sander straight up.

Protect your floors with a good wax that is a type recommended for your particular wood. Wipe up spills as fast as you notice them. Wash only as much as is very necessary, and don't wash wood floors with water. There are cleaning solutions just for wood. (EC)

CARPETS

Carpets are floor coverings that stretch from wall to wall, as opposed to *rugs,* which cover only small areas (see below). In judging the quality of a carpet, it's a good idea to know which *type of carpet fiber* is best for the area you're going to cover. Each has its strengths and weaknesses. The following, while not by any means an all-inclusive list, may help you make a more informed choice:

• *Nylon* is the most prevalent carpet fiber, both because of its endurance and its sensible price. Most nylon carpets these days also have superior stain-stopping treatments incorporated right into the fibers.

• *Acrylic* simulates the warm look and soft feel of wool but sacrifices much of nylon's durability to do so. Acrylics generally work best where looks are more important than performance.

• *Polyester* has neither nylon's strength nor acrylic's warmth. However, polyester does dye extremely well and therefore is available in a wide range of lush colors. If you're trying to match those little green dots in the wallpaper, polyester may be for you.

• *Olefin* has a low moisture-absorbency rate, making it a great fiber for kitchen, bath or beachhouse carpeting, but it lacks durability.

One final note on judging carpet quality: When examining a carpet, check its density, a key measure of quality. Bend back a corner to see how much of the backing shows. Finer-quality carpets have more closely spaced fibers. (MK)

RUGS

Show of hands: The difference between a machine-made oriental-style rug and a handmade one can be determined by examining the bottom. If there is a series of small knots, then it's been done by hand; machine-made rugs have no knots on the underside. (NW)

Go for broke: A threadbare, worn and frayed genuine oriental rug is better than a brand-new, machine-made phony oriental rug. A cheesy, fake rug gives an otherwise well-appointed room a subtle sense of sleaze, while the genuine article, if purchased in good condition, will actually increase in value, making your floor-covering into a smart investment. (ARo) **See under** *Dollar Deco,* **below.**

PAINTING A FLOOR

First, make sure you use a *floor paint.* Normal household paints won't stand up to the wear and tear a floor takes.

Prime the floor before applying the paint, then brush the paint on in a thin, even coat. You will need to give the floor several coats, and each one should be progressively heavier. They should all be extremely even, however. (SG)

CARPET BURNS

1. Clip away burned fibers if burn is fairly slight.

2. If burn reaches backing, scrape away charred fibers. Apply glue. When it turns tacky, replace fibers one by one from carpet scrap.

3. If burn is hopeless, cut out entire section of rug. Replace with scrap. Use carpet tape.

4. Dye rug brown.

5. Remove rug. Install parkay.

6. Rearrange furniture.

If you have a decent wooden floor — on a porch, for example — you might consider preserving the warmth of the wood by using a **polyurethane** finish. This plastic-based substance gives wood the protection it needs while allowing the grain to show. (LP)

THE WALLS

It takes four of 'em to make a room, so you're going to be surrounded by them most of the time.

Don't let that bother you. In a way, walls are what make a home out of thin air. So the next time they start closing in, don't climb them — cover them.

WALLPAPER

Prepasted: It seems sensible to buy wallpaper that already has the paste on the back, although it is possible to apply the paste yourself. If you're going to apply the paste, you're going to need a big surface on which to lay the paper. Spread the adhesive onto the paper with thin, long strokes, taking care not to allow any big globs to appear. To keep from getting paste all over the table, put a few sheets of wallpaper under the one you are working on (face down, of course) so that the paste drips onto them.

Cutups: Cut strips of wallpaper at least a few inches longer than the wall is tall. After it is up there, you can slice off the unnecessary portion. To be sure that the first strip of paper is perfectly straight, hang a string with a weight on the end and follow the line it makes. You can't trust your walls. (ES)

Cornered: When you arrive at a corner, don't crease the paper down the middle. Cut it so that only about half an inch folds around. Always start at the top when hanging wallpaper. (BS) **See illustration.**

Layered look: I hear that one should remove the old layer of wallpaper before hanging the new one. I know for a fact that there are four layers on our walls that nobody ever removed.

Now, this is the deal. We want to put up new paper. That would be the fifth layer. Is that so bad? Why is that so bad? I suppose one day if people kept on in this manner the room would end up teeny weeny, but it won't happen in *my* time, right? (EC)

PAINTING

Interior paints: The whole world can be colored to suit your taste. But start by taking on a corner of the planet you can control — say, the bedroom.

• *Flat paints* have little or no sheen and are usually used on walls and ceilings. They're not as stain-resistant as glossy paints, so you'll never find a kitchen or bathroom painted with flat paint.

WALLPAPER TIPS

Yes

No No No

Mismatches are inevitable. Hang wallpaper so that you will finish in an unobvious area.

Beginners should start in rooms with floor to ceiling fixtures and no windows or doors.

• *Semigloss paints* are also called satin finishes. They're halfway between flat and high gloss. They're often used on windows, doors, and other trim where you want a finish that is easy to clean.

• *High-gloss paints* are also referred to as enamels. They can take very hard wear. Kitchen cabinets are often painted with high gloss, especially the inside, which gets banged a lot. Brush marks can be more noticeable with this paint, so application takes a lot of care.

• *Undercoats* or primer sealers are used as a first coat. They are essential when working on badly worn or unpainted surfaces.

• *Latex paints* thin with water, while

• *Oil-base paints* thin with turpentine. Latex paints are a gift from heaven. They dry faster than the oil-base variety — you can apply the second coat almost as soon as you finish the first — they are more stain-resistant, they cover better, and you can clean the brushes and rollers with soap and water. (LV)

If you are painting over a glossy surface, be sure you sand it thoroughly first. Do you know what will happen if you don't? You'll think you've done a fine job. Months may go by. You won't even be thinking about it anymore. Then it will begin. Your walls will peel off. (EC)

Exterior paints: When you're ready to take on the great outdoors, use *latex* paint. When the clouds suddenly burst open, your first coat will probably already have dried. When you spill it all over your pants, it will come out. You can shut the windows on the very same day. (Be sure to open and close them periodically over the couple of weeks following painting to make sure they don't stick shut.) Latex paints have finishes from nearly flat to satin.

• *House paints* are for wood siding, eaves, and other large areas.

• *Trim paints* are for doors, windows, shutters and any other trim. They dry harder and glossier.

• *Masonry paints* are for brick, concrete, and stucco.

• *Shake or shingle paints* are similar to masonry paints in that they are resistant to moisture. They dry to a dull finish.

• *Deck paints* are for decks, porches, patios, and steps. They are made to withstand abrasion and scuffing.

• *Primers* are to be used as a first coat on new or unfinished surfaces or surfaces that have been scraped bare.

• *Varnish and enamels* are similar, but varnish is clear while enamel has pigment added that makes it opaque. They are both used on furniture, cabinets, and surfaces where you need a very smooth surface and are willing to spend some time. Every flaw will show up under varnish, so the surface must be carefully prepared. The wood needs to be utterly clean. Tack cloths are good for the final wipe. On cabinets, remove all handles and knobs and take out all the drawers before beginning to paint.

• *Wood stain* soaks into the wood and changes the tone without covering the original grain or completely changing the original color. Stains are used to color or darken before a finish is applied.

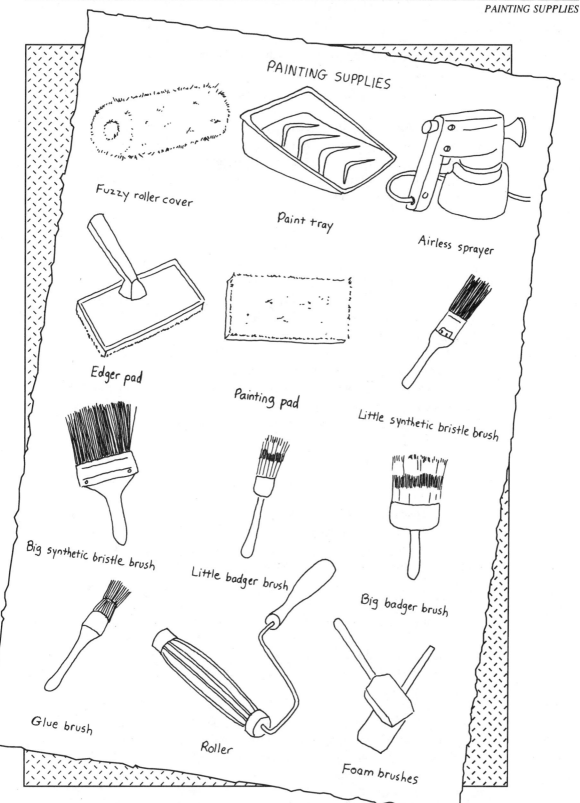

PAINTING SUPPLIES

Fuzzy roller cover

Paint tray

Airless sprayer

Edger pad

Painting pad

Little synthetic bristle brush

Big synthetic bristle brush

Little badger brush

Big badger brush

Glue brush

Roller

Foam brushes

• *Wood sealer* is a transparent finish that also comes mixed with color. It works as both a stain and a finish combined. (LV)

PAINT TOOLS

Use a *roller* on the walls and ceilings. Rollers are fun. Roller covers range from those with a very short nap to those that look like little sheep. Short hair is for extra smooth surfaces, while textured walls such as stucco call for the sheep.

It's not worth it to buy the very cheapest. Why mess with streaks and skips if you can avoid them? Use a brush for the areas around woodwork and in corners and near the floors. *Do the brushwork first,* and then do the roller as a reward. Try to cover as much brushwork as you can with the roller so that the difference between the two is barely noticeable. (LV)

A *wonderful invention* is the little plastic cover you can buy that clicks into place and catches all the drips and spray from the roller. It is essential if you are painting ceilings. (EC)

Brush-offs: Don't mess with those cheap little brushes that look like they are made up of rhinoceros whiskers. They don't work worth beans. They streak, and the little bristles fall out and get dried into the paint, or they just stick all over you. If you want a few cheapies, buy those little sponge brushes that come in several sizes. For windows and baseboards, buy a good sash brush. (LV)

Dry to wet: Start on a dry area and brush into the wet area. *(Anon.)*

Don't let windows worry you. Excess paint is simple to scrape off with one of those little window-scraper razor blades. Trying to protect the glass with masking tape is a whole lot of work for nothing. The paint will seep under the tape anyway — or you will pull the paint off along with the tape. Or you will forget to pull the tape off until the sun has baked it onto the glass for eternity. (LV, EC)

TAKING IT OFF

Paint can be removed by scraping with a hand scraper, sanding with an electric sander, burning with a torch, or by using a chemical paint remover. I can't see myself putting a torch to the walls of my house. And I can't see myself splashing chemicals all over, either. I spent last summer scraping by hand. I *can* see myself using an electric sander. (EC)

HOLE IN THE WALL

Use spackling compound on little holes and fine cracks. You can buy it in a powder and mix it yourself, but that seems like a waste of time when you can buy it ready-to-go at the right consistency. A good, three-inch putty knife is perfect for most jobs. Try to put it on smoothly so that it will blend into the rest of the wall without ridges and lumps. Sand it lightly after it is dry.

Bigger holes and cracks larger than a quarter-inch in width will require patching plaster for most of the job. You can finish it off with spackle. You'll need to patch in two or three layers. Fill halfway, allow to harden, then fill the rest of the way. Before you begin, chip away any crumbling material and wet down with water.

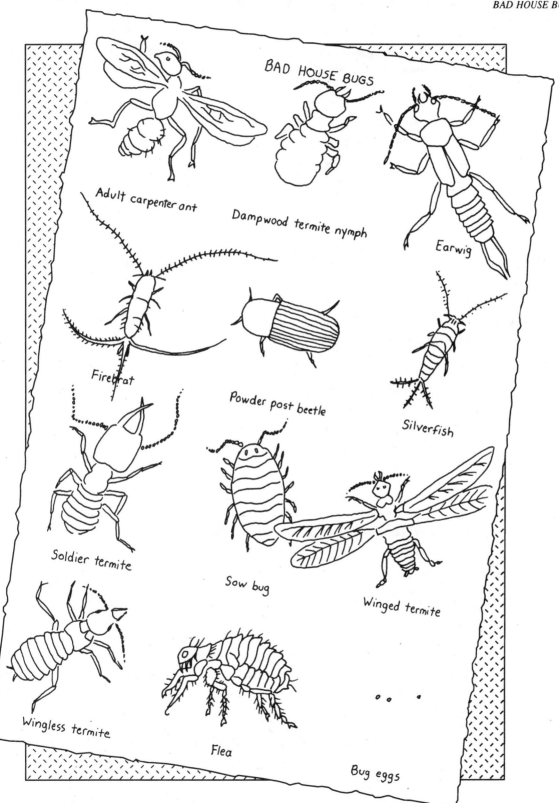

BAD HOUSE BUGS

Adult carpenter ant

Dampwood termite nymph

Earwig

Firebrat

Powder post beetle

Silverfish

Soldier termite

Sow bug

Winged termite

Wingless termite

Flea

Bug eggs

For large, gaping wall-chasms, pack the plaster around the edges first and then work towards the center. Plaster dries pretty fast, so if you mix a lot, it may harden before you have a chance to get to it. If it does, give up on it, and mix more. If the hole seems to lead off into the bowels of hell more or less, crumple up a bunch of newspapers and shove them in there until they form a tightly packed base so that the plaster will have some support. Finish off by working from the edges in toward the center, then sand. (JN)

WALL-WASHING

To clean interior painted walls, first vacuum to remove dust and cobwebs, then wash with a sponge and a mild detergent.

Always wash walls from the bottom up to keep the detergent from running down onto the dirty surface and making those streaks you think will never go away.

If you need *to clean wallpapered walls* and the wallpaper is not washable, wad up a big ball of fresh bread and roll it over the surface of the wall. Keep folding it to expose a clean surface. (ABo)

DECORATING

Nest administration is one thing. Nest decor is another.

The great thing about home decorating is that it's a great leveler. A woman with lots of money can spend herself right to bad-taste hell, while a Modern Woman of any means can arrange her possessions in such a way that her good judgment becomes the centerpiece of the whole show.

We received some demographically balanced contributions that allowed us to divide the question of interior decorating into three parts, each reflecting a budgetary consideration. We'll start in a familiar neighborhood to us — the apartment where the only money hidden under the bed is the dime we dropped last week.

BARE BONES

Throw it all away. The idea here is to reduce the number of objects in any room to a bare minimum.

Concentrate first on *the floor*. If you have a hardwood floor, show it off by polishing it to a high gloss. If you have carpeting, get down and get it clean. **See under** *Refinishing Wood Floors,* **above.**

Now *the walls*. The least expensive thing you can buy when you're decorating a place is latex paint. **See above, under** *Walls.*

• If you have a tiny place, use lots of off-white and ivory.

• If you have a lot of interesting angles, use white. The shadows will provide good lines and contrast.

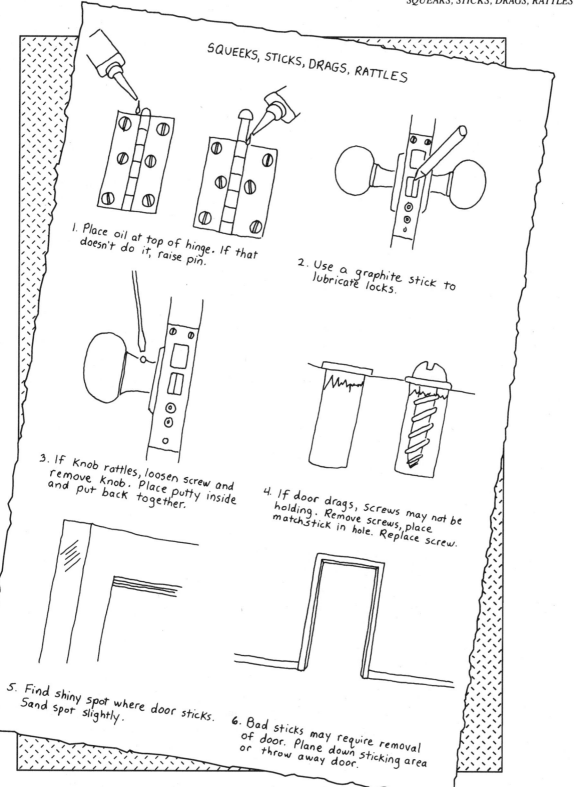

SQUEEKS, STICKS, DRAGS, RATTLES

1. Place oil at top of hinge. If that doesn't do it, raise pin.

2. Use a graphite stick to lubricate locks.

3. If Knob rattles, loosen screw and remove Knob. Place putty inside and put back together.

4. If door drags, screws may not be holding. Remove screws, place matchstick in hole. Replace screw.

5. Find shiny spot where door sticks. Sand spot slightly.

6. Bad sticks may require removal of door. Plane down sticking area or throw away door.

• Warm colors can be used in large rooms, but if you have a limited budget, try to keep to neutral tones.

Keep it clean: You're aiming for a spare and spacious look here, so clutter and disorder are no-nos. **See under** *New Leaves,* **below, for tips.**

Bookshelves and open storage areas will be the place where you'll put most of the material ephemera in your life. Stack books on edge with the bindings showing and keep loose papers to an absolute minumum. Invest in file folders if you have too many odd bits and pieces of paper.

Make an inventory of your possessions. Throw away anything you haven't used in the past three months. **See** *New Leaves,* **below.**

If you have a piece of junk furniture and there's no way to make it presentable, no matter how useful it is, get rid of it. You can get something better for very little money at a thrift shop or auction. (ST, KK, DKu) **See under** *Buy, Buy Love,* **below.**

THE BIG THING IN THE CORNER

If you have a little ready cash that you want to spend on one or two items, you can successfully build a decorating scheme around those major purchases. Incidentally, we're not talking about spending inheritances here. Any of the major pieces listed below can be had for less than $1000 each. If you pay more than that, read on — or open a museum.

In the dining room: Spend money on a hutch or buffet, not on the table. You can pick up a fabulous old tablecloth at auction for pennies (**see below**) and dress up even the scruffiest table.

In the living room: Get a sofa and chair combo, something quite nice, and preferably pieces that go with your other things. All the other incidental furniture will fit around those two large items. Chuck out any smaller pieces that spoil the effect you're trying to achieve. Work on the lighting so that the ends of the sofa and the chair are bathed in a warm light (if you've chosen to go the antique route) or a brighter light (for more modern pieces).

In the bedroom: Obviously, a great headboard is a great asset. But a plain bed can be offset nicely with a good wardrobe or a chest of drawers. Bedrooms are nice places for small things, too — tiny vases or old picture frames.

The kitchen: You can do a kitchen for next to nothing. The most important thing to remember about decorating a kitchen is that clean, open surfaces and color are paramount. Use small touches of color that don't appear elsewhere in your house — like red, for example. (JMcE, KRT, KK)

DOLLAR DECO

If you have a lot of money but you have no taste, hire somebody who does.

To choose a good interior decorator, ask to see interiors the firm has done. Don't settle for looking at pictures. Don't be afraid to talk generally with a decorator about the general mood you want to create, but don't leave it at that. If you don't like a specific color or style, say so. The idea is to get the decorator to help *you* arrive at a good idea of what you want your house or apartment to look like.

If you have a friend whose taste you admire, skip the decorator all together and go with the friend. *(Anon.)*

If you want to do it yourself, do what decorators do and look around at as many interiors as you can. Displays in furniture showrooms as well as interior decorating shows and layouts in magazines will help provide fresh ideas, as will sets in movies and plays.

Don't treat each room as if it were isolated from the rest of the house. Think carefully about how guests will move through your home. But pay even more attention to creating the kind of interior *you* feel comfortable in. Your visitors only have to eat dinner there, after all.

Decide on a style that you can articulate clearly. Try describing your dream living room to a friend and see how clearly you've thought it out. Once you've got the style figured out, decide on a color or two that will predominate.

Choose colors that are flexible. Red is red, for example, and won't tolerate much competition, unless you're going for that special carny look. Browns and other so-called earth tones and greens and blues in muted shades work well with other colors in adjacent rooms.

Buy the best furniture and rugs you can afford. Even new furniture will appreciate in value if you purchase quality stuff. Oriental rugs are generally very good investments. (KRT, KK)

An alternative: Start out with an original piece of art. Take hints from the colors within the image to select rugs, lamps, fabrics and so forth. *Don't use reproductions* or posters. If you can't afford a painting by a well-known artist, choose work by a local artist whose work you admire. (RLe)

BUY, BUY LOVE

Knowing where and how to buy furniture cheaply is as important as knowing what to buy.

Thrift shops and auctions are filled with decent $20 chairs and terrific $30 cabinets.

The Thrift Shop Rule of Three: Never buy anything that has three things wrong with it. (ARo)

Here's an actual list of expenditures on living room furniture bought over the course of a week in early 1988 from various yard sales, auctions and thrift shops:

• *Sofa:* Victorian, dark blue-green, for $60

• *Occasional table:* Octagonal, in cherry, for $20

• *Armchairs:* All late Victorian. Two — one in dark gray-blue with wood trim across the back, and the other in beige, for $20 each — and a third in a slightly lighter shade of blue for $25

• *Carpet:* Dark blue oriental 6' x 9', purchased as unclaimed goods from a carpet-cleaning company for $40

• *Coffee table:* Cherry wood in great shape for $40

• *Lamps:* Two — one, with a brass base, for $35, and a smaller one for $20 from a discount house

Total: $260

See also under *Thrift Shopping* **in** *CHAPTER SIX: MODERN MERCHANDISE.*

Yard and garage sales are the best, and if the items above had been purchased there over a longer period of time, the total cost would have been significantly less. Yard and moving sales are advertised in the paper the day before — usually on Fridays for the weekend. So read up on the sales, then go as early as you can in order to beat the antiques dealers. (ST)

Auctions offer unusual bargains for wary shoppers. But they can also result in a disastrous purchase if you're careless.

• *Auction notices* appear in the classified section of most newspapers.

• *View the merchandise* before you bid for it. All auction notices give a prospective customer two times, one for the auction itself and another announcing the times the merchandise can be seen prior to sale.

• *Remember* that most auctions sell items on an "as is" basis, and if you bid for it and your bid is the best bid, it's yours, no matter what.

• *Know the value* of the items on which you wish to bid. Don't get into an emotional state about something you just *have* to have.

• *An auction is not a competition,* and if some fool wants to bid up an object to some astronomical level, let it go. *At an auction, you can buy anything you want, provided you're willing to pay more than anyone else there.*

• Most auctions are *cash only,* and the stuff you buy has to be paid for and removed at the time of sale. (DB, MS, LT) **See also under** *Auctions* **in** *CHAPTER SIX: MODERN MERCHANDISE.*

GOOD IMAGE

Mirrors are a good and attractive way to cover a wall. Decoratively, they serve part of the same function as a painting, but they're lots cheaper. (EAJ)

BUYING A MIRROR

One way to tell a good mirror from a thin, cheap one is to take a closed penknife (or any relatively heavy, blunt object) and tap the surface of the mirror *lightly.* The sound the mirror makes will tell you the thickness of the glass used. (MK)

DRUDGERY

There's no other word for it.

After all, the compulsion to walk on squeaky-clean, shiny surfaces isn't something we're born with. Ten thousand years ago, when real estate consisted of a hole in the ground,

Ms. Neanderthal didn't waste time dusting in case those nosy Cro-Magnons came by. No. She was busy keeping the sabre-toothed tigers off Junior's back.

So we get better digs, but they come with a steep price. And now it's time to pay.

THE MODERN WOMAN'S JUMP-START CLEANING KIT

Let's say you arrive from Mars and have to move into a one-bedroom apartment and you've got no cleaning equipment. Can we say that? Okay. So what *exactly* do you need before you can spread the bathmat and stack the glassware?

• *Paper towels:* Don't skimp here and get those generic, one-ply tissue-type towels. Get the thick-as-a-brick variety. The one-plys are fine for small stuff, but we're talking *cleanliness* here, for Pete's sake.

• *Spray cleaner:* Fantastik is fantastic and will do fine for most household chores.

• *An abrasive cleanser* like Comet or Ajax. But be careful with some of the newer bathtub and sink installations, many of which are marked with stickers warning against the dangers of using harsh cleansers. Still, there's not a toilet bowl made that doesn't need an occasional dose of the stuff. Bon Ami makes a good nonabrasive cleanser (Pyrex recommends it for their glass products).

• *Toilet brush*: What else?

• *Scrubbing pads:* Get the steel-wool type for use on tough stuff like stove burner rings. And get the nonmetallic type for dishes and everything else. Dobie brand pads work well and seem to stand up to a lot of kitchen torture testing.

MILDEW EQUIPMENT

1. Cover mildew with bleach.
2. Scrub with toothbrush.
3. Rinse bleach thoroughly with water.
4. Wash walls with ammonia. Do NOT mix bleach and ammonia. The fumes could be fatal.

• *Sponges:* A four-pack will do.

• *A pail.*

• *Murphy's Oil Soap,* one of the things you'll want to put in the pail. Murphy's is an excellent all-purpose cleaner, especially if you have a lot of woodwork around.

• *Mop, broom* and *dustpan.*

• *Dish soap* and *bar soap.*

• *A disinfectant* for the bathroom.

• *A window spray* **See under** *Windows,* **below.**

Those are your weapons, the enemy is everywhere, and you know what to do next. *(Anon.)*

NEW LEAVES

Nobody makes a bigger mess than Mom Nature. The outside world is messy and chaotic, a crazy place over which we have no control. Our homes, however, are subject to our own rules and regulation, and the only tidal waves that engulf our living rooms are the ones we make ourselves out of our own lack of organization.

Here's how to keep your home from looking like the Devil's Postpile:

Put it away: After you use something, put it away. As common-sensical as this must sound, it's the best way to minimize your cleaning chores, and if housekeeping is a major assault for you, ignoring this rule might well be the reason. Because if you let this rule slide even three or four times, you've got a mess on your hands — and under your feet.

• ***Chuck it:*** If you don't use something on a regular basis, *get rid of it.* Sell it, give it to a pack-rat friend, or lend it to the neighbor who already has borrowed half your possessions anyway. The rule of thumb here is that *if you don't use it for six months, you don't need it,* so get it out of your house. When you move, you'll thank yourself. (MG) **See under** *Bare Bones,* **above.**

CLEAN CORPS

Clean your house or apartment on a regular basis and you'll avoid large-scale unpleasant jobs. A reasonable schedule calls for a general cleaning once a day and a thorough cleaning once every two or three weeks.

Every day:

• Make your bed.

• Wash the dishes.

• Dispose of routine daily clutter — newspapers and the like.

Every two or three weeks: This regime will take a couple of hours. Try to do it on a routine basis — say, every third Saturday or something — so it becomes part of your regular schedule.

• Wash all counters and floors.

• Scrub sinks, toilets and the tub.

• Clean all mirrors.

• Clean all chrome fixtures — faucets and shower heads, for example.

• Vacuum.

• Dust.

• Clean the kitchen cabinets and the medicine chest.

• Evict the leftovers from the refrigerator and wipe the fridge walls.

• Defrost the fridge. **See** *Refrigerator Maintenance,* **below.**

Windows can be done less frequently — say, once at the beginning of spring and once again at the end of summer. (MG) **See** *The Best Way to Clean a Window,* **below.**

LIGHT CLEANING

Edge of night: It's a good idea to keep a supply of 25-watt bulbs around the house for occasions when company drops in on short notice. Simply replace the bulbs in the living room lamps with the low wattage bulbs and that dust on the bookshelf won't be nearly as noticeable. This trick, of course, works only in the evening. (MK)

POOLS OF POLISH

Dust and polish only those areas immediately surrounding a lamp. When company comes, don't turn on any overhead lights. (GMH)

TRUNDLE TROUBLES

Cover-up: No matter how late you're running in the morning, always take an extra minute or so to make up the bed — even if you just pull up the blankets and sheets and tuck them under the pillows. The whole bedroom will look 100 percent cleaner, and the bed will be much more inviting in the evening. (CB)

Now lie in it. To make your bed while you're still in it, lie in the middle of the mattress, stretch out your arms and legs and straighten out the sheets and blankets around you. Then flip the sheets up and slide out as they fall down. Then all you have to do is straighten the top and you're done. (RFF)

Until the drifts pile up: Every morning while making the bed, powder the sheets with a bit of scented body powder. Smells great, feels great. (MHL)

HEAVENS ABOVE

Water stains on a bathroom ceiling can be removed by sponge-mopping the ceiling first when you clean the bathroom. (EC)

DIVISION OF LABOR

Ask ***him*** *to make a list* of household chores that have to be done; see that it's in his handwriting, if possible. Reach an agreement on who will do what. Then post the list. Avoid being the taskmaster, the dictator, the nag. Simply refer to the list. *Make the list the enemy,* not you and not your spouse. (CL)

MORE CHORES

Spread your housework over a five-day week so that the weekends become free. Nothing like two days away from scrubbing to make Saturdays wonderful — and Mondays hell.

When it's time to go back to work on Mondays, plan your week first thing. Group together jobs that can be done simultaneously. For example, wash the kitchen floor while the laundry's in the machine.*(Anon.)*

SPIN CYCLES

Turn dark-colored socks, slacks, jeans and similar garments inside-out when you put them in the washing machine or the dryer. Then, if they pick up any lint, it'll all be on the inside, where it won't show. (WN)

Never put a towel in a dryer with a sweatshirt — especially a dark one. The sweatshirt will never forget the towel and will carry a small part of it around forever. (LStJ)

Presoak everything and wash everything in cold water. Your clothes will come out just as clean — and they'll last forever. (AM)

Hang the dryer: We all use dryers now, so all our clothes and linens smell like fabric softener and soap. For a real olfactory treat, though, try hanging your sheets and towels outside on a line to dry, the way they used to. You'll see why Grandma did it that way even after she got that new Maytag. (FSR)

OUT OF THE CLOSET

Closet sachets and most perfumes make a terrible combination. Use an open box of baking soda, instead. (EC)

A CLEAN STORY

There's a little part of me that truly enjoys the domestic chores we fight — cooking, shopping for food, doing the laundry. Unfortunately, my job doesn't allow time for much.

My escape is this: Once every two weeks, right after payday, I spend an hour or so with my Sunday paper, cutting out coupons and reading grocery store ads for good buys. I make my choices, go shopping, and pat myself on the back for what I've saved. I freeze meat and vegetables. And I spend the entire afternoon, once a month, baking muffins or bread and freezing it for later.

These are the afternoons when I tell my friends I'm busy and I unplug the phone. With the right attitude, this ritual gets a lot accomplished and provides a tiny holiday as well. (AT)

AND A LAST WORD

I work in an office not for personal satisfaction or to build a career. I work in an office nine to five to get money to avoid having to work eight to six at home. Almost two-thirds of my pay goes to hiring cleaning help. I'd rather push paper than push a mop, that's all. And I think I'm getting a bargain. *(Anon.)*

THE PAIN OF STAINS

Think of your home as your character. Now think about stains.

Stains are what characterize one hemisphere of the world of cleaning. The other hemisphere is filled with messes. And if there's one thing Modern Women know, from hard experience in every aspect of life, stains are what you get if you leave messes around for too long.

TIGHT SPOT REMOVAL

Place back against one side of passage, and feet (or knees) against opposite side. With hands pressed tightly against passage behind you, lift body slightly while taking tiny footsteps.

Incidentally, *the stain, in Spain,* is *la mancilla.* ¿Hokay?

The three rules of stains: Stains can be a pain, as anyone who's ever dumped a drink can tell you. While no treatment will work on every stain, most stains can at least be lessened by remembering three easy rules:

1. Waste no time — get something on it at the first opportunity. A stain, left to itself, could become a companion for life.

2. Spare no effort. Think of stain removal as a challenge. It's you against some foreign agent that's invaded your personal space. If at first you don't succeed, try something else.

3. Don't get frustrated. This is sort of a corollary to rule 2. Patience is a virtue in stain removal and can mean the difference between an item saved and a trip to Goodwill. (MK)

Our stain-removal guide, with a note: Basically, we think stains belong in a man's book. As women, we have already received boundless advice on stain removal by the time we are ten. The first bit of advice generally concerns *grape juice* — the dangers of grape juice. The second bit of advice concerns *blood,* because every little girl in the world will one day bleed. We learned "stain removal" while boys learned "automobiles." So let us not go endlessly into this subject. First, we'll present a few basic tips, enough to get you started. Then we'll list a few of the world's more important stains, in alphabetical order. If you need additional information, *The Modern Man's Guide to Life* is full of stains, if you get our meaning.

GENERIC STAINS

When you talk stains, you're talking grease or nongrease, okay?

• *Greasy stains:* On washable materials, pretreat by first rubbing with detergent. If you have already washed the item, rub liquid detergent into stains and rinse with hot water. You may need cleaning fluid. Let material dry and sponge repeatedly. Use chlorine bleach or hydrogen peroxide to remove any yellow stains that may remain (but check the care tag on the item first). Use cleaning fluid on nonwashable items. Let them dry between applications.

• *Nongreasy stains:* On washable items, some of these stains come out by laundering. Others are set for eternity. Immediately following the spill, sponge with cool water or soak in cool water for at least half an hour. After soaking, work in liquid detergent and rinse. If the stain is old and ironed, the stain is probably there forever.

On *nonwashable items,* sponge with cool water. Try working in a bit of liquid detergent. Rinse. The fabric will dry faster if you give a final sponge with alcohol, but test this first in an inconspicuous area.

• *Combination greasy and nongreasy:* Treat the nongreasy portion of the stain on a washable fabric with cool water and detergent. Rinse and let dry. Then attack the greasy part with cleaning fluid.

If the fabric is nonwashable, sponge with cool water. Try a grease solvent. Chlorine bleach will remove the last bit.

NOW FOR THE GUIDE

Starring, in alphabetical order:

• *Alcoholic beverages:* Sponge fabric right away with cool water. Follow directions for nongreasy stains, or sponge the stain with rubbing alcohol, but test first. Dilute the alcohol with two parts water when working with acetate.

• *Antiperspirants and deodorants:* Wash with warm water and liquid detergent. Rinse. Use chlorine bleach or hydrogen peroxide and rinse.

• *Blood:* Soak or rub in cold water. On nonwashable items, sponge with cold water and then hydrogen peroxide. Spit works well to take blood out of fabric.

• *Candle wax:* Scrape with dull knife. Place stain between two paper towels. Press with warm iron. Sponge with cleaning fluid.

• *Chewing gum:* Rub with ice and scrape.

WINDOWPANE REPLACEMENT

1. Remove glass with pliers. Work from outside of window.

2. Remove putty and glazier points with putty knife and pliers.

3. Place putty around frame.

4. Place pane against putty.

5. Tap glazier points gently into place about six inches apart. Do corners first.

6. Press putty into place in groove and smooth with putty knife.

• *Chocolate:* Follow directions for combination stains.

• *Coffee or tea:* Follow the nongreasy stain directions, unless cream is in the drink. Then follow combination stain directions.

• *Cosmetics:* With washable materials, use liquid detergent and rub. Use cleaning fluid on nonwashable items.

• *Crayon:* See cosmetics.

• *Fish slime:* This is a good one and needs to be understood somehow more metaphorically. Add a half cup salt to two quarts water and soak or sponge stain. Rinse with water and wash with warm water and soap. In the future, avoid slimy fish.

• *Fruit and berry:* Don't use soap and water first. No, no, *no.* Soak first with cool water only. Follow directions for nongreasy stains.

• *Grass:* Sponge with alcohol. Dilute alcohol for acetate materials.

• *Ink:* Ballpoint ink can be removed with glycerine or hairspray. Blot a lot. India ink is a real mess. Put a sponge under the stain and force water through with a medicine dropper. Wash with liquid detergent and soak in warm water with ammonia (one to four tablespoons per quart). Soak for hours. (EC, DB, KK, JGr, JH, NW, *et al.*)

• *Juice:* See *wine*, below.

• *Rust:* To remove nasty rust stains, as well as provide a general cleaning for porcelain bathroom sinks, tubs, and toilets as well as white porcelain kitchen sinks, simply fill them with cold water and add a quarter cup of household bleach to sinks and toilet and a full cup to bathtubs. Don't leave the bleach in too long or your white sink, tub, or toilet will begin to brown. Just wait long enough for the stain to dissolve.

Also, *baking soda* works for light scouring if you run out of regular cleanser. (BM)

• *Water marks on furniture:* Rub with toothpaste. (NW)

• *Wine:* A nasty wine or juice stain on the carpet can be lifted quickly if caught immediately by pouring a mound of table salt directly on the spill. The salt absorbs the spill nicely and you simply vacuum afterwards. (BM)

• *Vomit:* See fish slime. (EE)

WINDOW PAINS

Chances are, at your house you're the only one who does windows. These are modern times, after all, and nobody but *nobody* else will do your windows for you.

THE BEST WAY TO CLEAN A WINDOW

Skip the soaps and sprays. **To get a window squeaky clean,** wad up a bunch of wet newspaper and scrub away. Use dry newsprint to wipe up after. Unlike rags or towels, newspaper will not streak the glass. If the window has greasy marks, a dash of ammonia will cut through them. (SY)

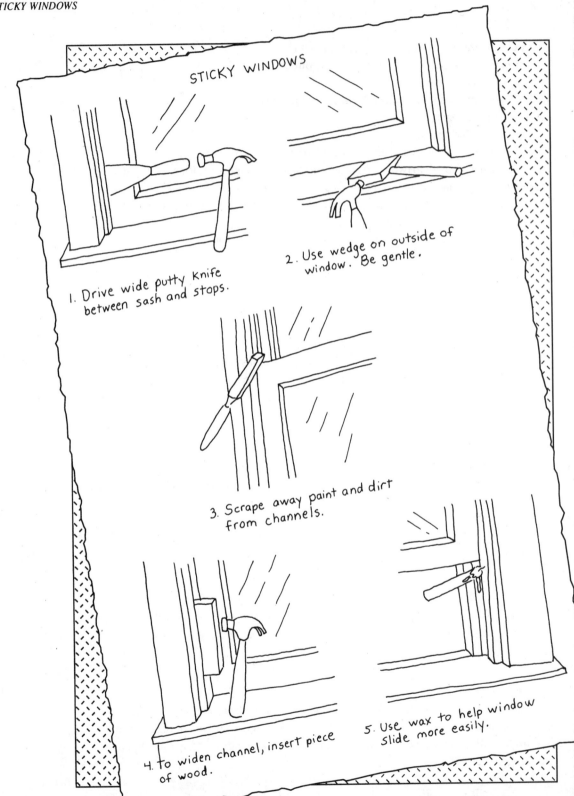

STICKY WINDOWS

1. Drive wide putty knife between sash and stops.

2. Use wedge on outside of window. Be gentle.

3. Scrape away paint and dirt from channels.

4. To widen channel, insert piece of wood.

5. Use wax to help window slide more easily.

SCREEN REPAIR

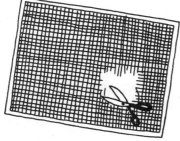

1. Trim hole with scissors to make edges smooth.

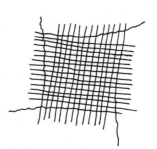

2. Remove three outer wires on each side of screen patch. Patch should be cut one inch larger than hole.

3. Bend wire ends over small wooden block.

4. Press patch over hole from outside of screen.

5. Bend wires toward center of hole.

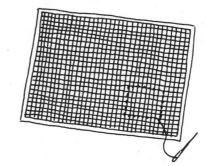

6. Stitch with fine wire the color of screen.

BROKEN WINDOWPANES

Wear gloves and follow these steps:

• First, *remove all the broken glass.* Some pieces may be a little stubborn. Rock them back and forth, but be gentle and careful.

• Then use a screwdriver to *scrape out all the old putty.*

• *Seal* the now-exposed area of wood with thinned-down house paint.

• *Measure* the opening and go to the hardware store for a new pane. The pane should be about one-eighth inch *less* in height and width than the actual opening.

• Apply a thin layer of *glazing compound* to the inside of the groove. This will make a watertight seal.

• *Press in the glass.* Fasten it with little glazier's points — triangular bits of metal that you can buy at the hardware store when you purchase the glass. Just push them in with the end of a screwdriver.

• Now *roll the putty* into strips a bit thinner than a pencil and press it into place around the window. Smooth with a putty knife into a bevel and wipe away the excess. (HT) **See illustration.**

Ms. FIX-IT

A Modern Woman's work is never done — especially now that planned obsolescence makes repairs part of the program.

Things break. Chairs, lamps, hearts all need a minor repair now and then. To fix a broken heart, see elsewhere in this book. But if the water on the floor is coming from a leaky pipe and not your eyes, then the solution is here.

THE BASIC TOOL KIT

Something's going to go on the blink before you know it. So be prepared. Here's the essential contents of a beginner's toolbox:

Saws: All-purpose utility sets are good for beginners. This usually consists of a single handle and two or three interchangeable blades. There will usually be a small pointed blade known as a *compass saw* that has fine teeth. It is good for cutting curves or cutting out holes. There will be a larger blade with coarser teeth for general wood cutting, and a blade for cutting metal. (JJe)

Measuring tools: A twelve-foot steel *tape measure* and a yardstick are important to own. You might enjoy keeping a *level* around. (JC)

A *level* is an amazing tool. It has two sets of bubbles, one parallel to the length of the tool and one at right angles to it. You use it to check to see whether surfaces are level or not. (EC)

Drills: Among other things, a drill is something you'll need to make starting holes

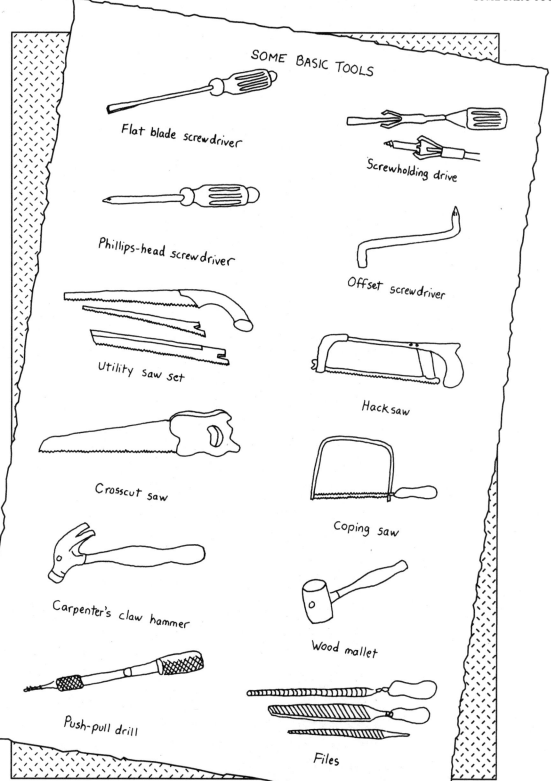

SOME BASIC TOOLS

Flat blade screwdriver

Screwholding drive

Phillips-head screwdriver

Offset screwdriver

Utility saw set

Hacksaw

Crosscut saw

Coping saw

Carpenter's claw hammer

Wood mallet

Push-pull drill

Files

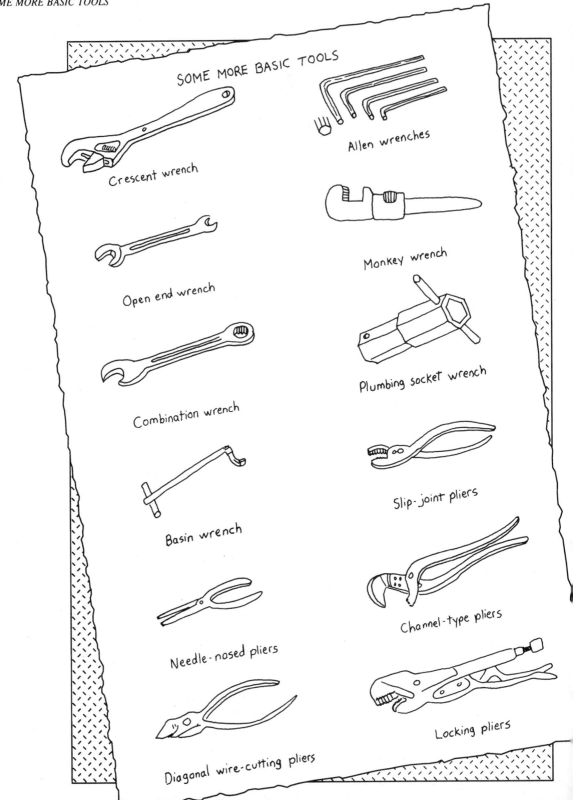

SOME MORE BASIC TOOLS

Crescent wrench

Allen wrenches

Open end wrench

Monkey wrench

Combination wrench

Plumbing socket wrench

Basin wrench

Slip-joint pliers

Needle-nosed pliers

Channel-type pliers

Diagonal wire-cutting pliers

Locking pliers

before driving a screw. A simple *push-pull drill* might do the trick. You just pump up and down on the handle to drive the bit into the wood.

Electric drills can be equipped to bore holes into metal, brick, and masonry. You may be able to add attachments that will let you use the drill for sanding and buffing. Consider a variable-speed control that lets you go faster or slower depending on the amount of pressure you exert on the trigger. (JC)

• **Hammers:** Get two, one with a nail-removing claw and a slightly smaller one with a ball peen. (HJS)

A dissent: You'll almost never need more than one hammer. Get one of medium weight (about ten ounces) with a head of polished steel. (JC)

There's nothing like a good old solid hammer. I keep one under my pillow. (EA)

• An assortment of **nails, screws, tacks and brads.**

• **A set of screwdrivers:** Flat ones and Phillips-type (the X-shaped kind). You'll need long, thin ones and stubby, wide ones.

There's a sort of *variation* on these themes — the "screw-holding" driver. It has little spring claws that can be pushed out past the tip of the blade so as to grip the head of the screw with the blade pressed inside the slot. This way you can insert screws into tight spots that would be otherwise impossible because your hand wouldn't fit. (EA)

• **An adjustable wrench:** Begin with two *adjustable crescent wrenches* for tightening and loosening nuts and bolts. One should be six inches and the other should be eight to ten inches.

A set of *open-end wrenches* is also nice to have. These have fixed jaws with different sizes on each end and can be used to reach places an adjustable wrench cannot.

A *combination wrench* has an open-end wrench on one end and a *box wrench* to fit the same size nut or bolt head at the other end.

The *box wrench* is nice because it wraps around completely for a firmer grip.

Pipe wrenches have two serrated jaws. One is fixed and one is movable. They grip round objects by tightening automatically as more pressure is applied to the handle. For plumbing work, you may need two of them, one to hold the pipe and the other to turn the fitting. (JC, EA)

• **Pliers:** *Slip-joint pliers* are the ones everyone owns — the way everyone owns a hammer, for instance. But there are other types of pliers that are mighty handy, too.

Mechanic's pliers have jaws that can be set for larger size widths and openings, and the offset handles permit greater leverage. They're great for plumbing repairs.

Needle-nosed pliers are perfect for reaching into tight corners and are useful in electrical work.

Don't buy cheap tools. If you get decent tools to start with, they'll perform better and much more reliably (nothing's worse than a cheap screwdriver that bends rather than turns), and you won't have to replace them for many years. (JC, KPF)

• **Others:** You've got to have a *utility knife* around the house. Also, you can't live without one or two *putty knives*. You'll have to have a *plunger* for clogged drains. A couple of *clamps* are nice to have — they're handy when it comes to repairing furniture or toys and can hold things together for you while you are assembling and gluing. And every house needs a roll of *masking tape* and a ball of *string*. (JC)

There are tools for every job. Use the correct ones correctly, and you save hours and hours of labor. I know it is true. After ripping out a forty-year old carpet, I spent the next two days trying to pry hundreds of carpet tacks from the floor. I had blisters and cuts, and the wood had scrapes. Then my neighbor lent me a tool, and I pulled a hundred tacks out of the floor in ten minutes. The point is not to go out and buy every possible tool you will ever need, but just to know that the right tools are out there somewhere. Start off with a basic set. Then, when the need arises, purchase more. (EC)

Screw it. Don't use a screwdriver to do anything other than screw screws. *Never use a screwdriver as a lever,* for example. If you don't bend the screwdriver, rendering it useless, you'll break it in two, a dangerous proposition. If you need a lever, get a lever. (CC)

APPLIANCE REPAIRS

Troubleshoot first. So. The damn whatever has broken down *again?* Here are a few suggestions to follow before you kick it hard. Actually, there is nothing wrong with a little *mild* kick now and then, but you might be better off just giving the problem a quick diagnosis. Here is a step-by-step troubleshooting guide:

1. Take a deep breath. Do not panic. There is more to life than just the whatever it is. The water heater isn't heating? You'll live.

2. Is it plugged in? Maybe it *is* plugged in, but maybe it needs a jiggle because the connection isn't connecting.

3. Maybe the outlet is kaput. Take something that you know is working and plug it into the outlet. If it doesn't work either, your first appliance is fine — or the outlet is fine but everything else in your house is breaking down.

4. Fuses: If you think that electricity is not coming out of the outlet, change the fuse or switch the circuit breaker off and then on again.

5. Ask the neighbors. Are all the lights out in your house, or are they also out all over the neighborhood? Somebody may have banged into a telephone pole. Or it may be squirrels.

6. If there is nothing wrong with your outlets, *read through the manuals* that came with the whatever. You saved them in an easy to locate place, of course. Be sure the proper buttons are pushed.

7. Maybe it's just dirty. *Clean* that baby up. Might do the trick.

Check the warranty. Now that you've checked it all out and it still won't work, you probably want to know if it is under warranty? If it is under warranty, you might consider leaving it alone. *Tampering with the whatever could invalidate your warranty — even turning one screw.*

Surgery: If you decide you are going to take it apart, remember how you did it. Line up the nuts and bolts and screws on a clean surface in the order you took them off, and don't let your arm accidentally sweep them onto the floor.

Zap: Remember to unplug the appliance before you fiddle.

Caution: Watch out for pulleys and gears. Touching one of them in one place can cause a reaction in another place. The fingers you thought were nowhere near the area you were working on could be mangled.

Tie back your hair and roll up your sleeves. My friend was scalped while working on a motorboat (she's okay, but she had to go to the hospital, and it took a long, long time for her hair to grow out, and it scared us all nearly to death). (EC)

Repair tools: The following tools should be enough for all your simple repairs:

- Knife
- Needle-nosed pliers
- Phillips screwdriver
- Pipe wrench
- Adjustable wrench
- Hammer
- Diagonal cutting pliers
- Regular screwdriver
- Channel lock pliers
- Soldering iron (HE, JC, EC)

WATER HEATERS

If you are receiving all kinds of warm water, but no *hot* water, the dip tube may be loose, causing cold water to mix with hot. Here's what to do:

Allow the tank to cool completely.

Shut off the electricity or gas and the water inlet.

Remove the cold-water inlet, reattach the dip tube, and refasten the inlet. While doing this, check the metal rod called the "sacrificial anode." This device is there to protect the metal of the tank by giving up its own life. If it is over half an inch in diameter, it's fine. If it's badly eaten, replace it. It won't cost much. (JC)

If the water isn't heating *in an electric heater,* check for a blown fuse or an open circuit breaker. (EC) **See under** *Electricity*, **below.**

In a *gas heater,* check the pilot light. If the pilot goes out, there is a safety feature that shuts off valves and stops the flow of gas. Follow instructions on the heater to relight the pilot.

If the water is too hot on your gas heater, turn down the temperature control. If the burner continues to burn, the control may be stuck. Call someone to repair it. You can do it yourself, but some states don't allow that for fear you might blow up your neighborhood.

In *an electric heater,* the thermostat may be improperly adjusted. Turn it down. There are two *heating elements* in an electric water heater, and one may be sticking closed. If this is the case, the top of the tank will be terribly hot, and the bottom three-quarters will be cool. You'll need a new thermostat.

If you find that you do not have enough hot water, usually you just need to increase the *thermostat* setting. Remember, though, that overheated water is a primary cause of dangerous burns. (HYW, JC) **See also under** *Heating and Plumbing,* **below.**

TOASTER TROUBLE

If your toast won't stay down or if it won't pop up, you might be able to fix the problem

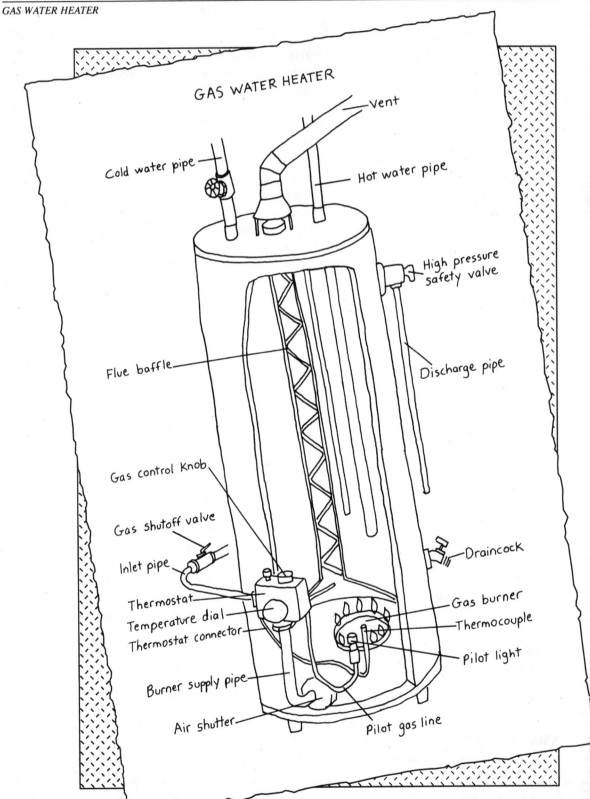

GAS WATER HEATER

Vent

Cold water pipe

Hot water pipe

High pressure safety valve

Flue baffle

Discharge pipe

Gas control Knob

Gas shutoff valve

Inlet pipe

Draincock

Thermostat

Temperature dial

Thermostat connector

Gas burner

Thermocouple

Pilot light

Burner supply pipe

Air shutter

Pilot gas line

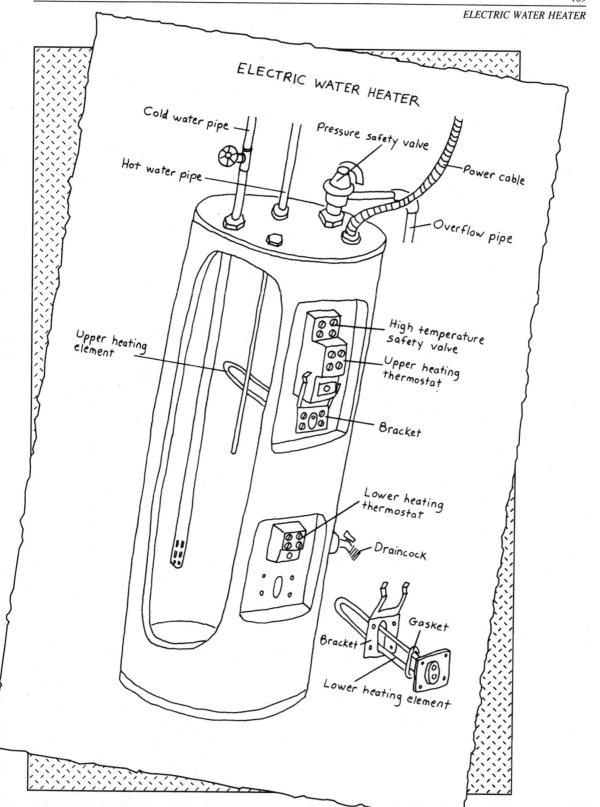

ELECTRIC WATER HEATER

Cold water pipe

Hot water pipe

Pressure safety valve

Power cable

Overflow pipe

High temperature safety valve

Upper heating thermostat

Bracket

Upper heating element

Lower heating thermostat

Draincock

Bracket

Gasket

Lower heating element

easily. In most toasters, bread is lowered in a rack and locked down by a latch that engages the carriage. The latch may be bent. Unplug the toaster and remove the access panel. Operate the lever and watch what happens. Realign any bent parts. If your toast doesn't pop up, the slide lever that lowered the bread may be binding. Free up any binding. Perhaps the latch-down lever is broken.

Remember, value your time. You can always buy a new toaster for peanuts. (EC, HYW)

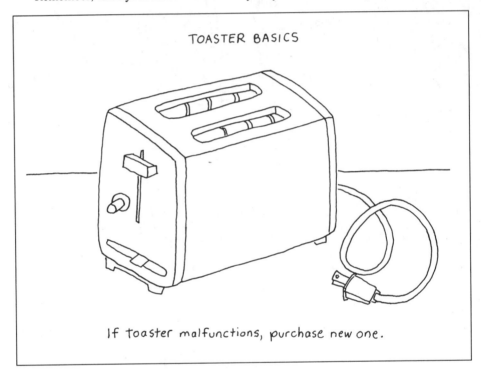

TOASTER BASICS

If toaster malfunctions, purchase new one.

IRONS

Try to *use only distilled water* in your steam iron. It will help keep minerals from clogging the iron. You can unclog those little holes with a paper clip.

To clean the steam chamber inside, mix some vinegar and water and fill up the iron. Turn the setting to "steam" and let it all steam out.

If the temperature of your iron changes but does not seem to match the dial setting, you might be able to fix it if the thermostat adjustment screws can be reached through a hole in the cover assembly. Turn the screws clockwise to decrease the temperature and counterclockwise to increase it. (HYW)

VACUUM CLEANERS

Uprights have a brush and rotating beaters; the brushes raise the dust out of the carpet or off of the floor. **Tank and canister** types do not have brushes and rely on the strength of the vacuum.

Vacuum cleaner bags should be replaced when only half full, not almost full. If the cleaner is not sucking anything up, check the air inlet and pickup tubes — your cat or something may be lodged inside. If the efficency of an upright drops, check the belt that drives the beater and brushes. It can be easily replaced. (KF, WW, *Anon.*)

CLOTHES WASHER AND DRYER TROUBLESHOOTING
Check these things first:
- Is it *plugged in?*
- Are the hot- and cold-water *faucets turned on?*
- Is the *water hose bent* in two?
- Is the hose strainer *clogged with sediment?*
- Is it *out of balance?*
- If it is a gas dryer, *is the pilot on?*

If you turn off the faucets in between washings, it can weaken the valves.

Have you checked *the lint trap* in your dryer? (KGG, JJ)

DISHWASHER
If a dish breaks, turn off machine and clean out the broken glass. If it still makes dreadful sounds, unplug the machine. Remove the trays and take a flashlight to the bowels of the thing. Needle-nosed pliers are helpful in removing debris. (BR)

REFRIGERATOR MAINTENANCE
Defrost regularly. See below.

Wash the inside walls frequently.

Noise could be coming from a loose grill in the back or a loose drain pan underneath.

Brush or vacuum the condenser coils at the back or bottom of fridge frequently.

A fridge should not sit in an enclosed, unventilated corner of a room.

Are the condenser pipes in the back clean?

Does your door shut securely? Close the door on a piece of paper towel. Does it pull out easily? If so, tighten the door hinges. (TY, HPD, JC)

Perma-defrost: If you're unlucky, your refrigerator is not frost-free. You have to do it yourself.

First of all, put your knives and chisels away. Don't come near it with anything sharp. Ice always melts on its own by and by. Just turn the knob to "Defrost" and go away for a while. (EC)

Take all your perishables and put them into an ice chest while you defrost, or wait until winter and put everything on the porch for a couple of hours. (HG)

Cleaning: It's no big deal, okay? All you need is a sponge and a bucket and some baking soda and your refrigerator will look like it belongs in *Good Housekeeping*. (DS)

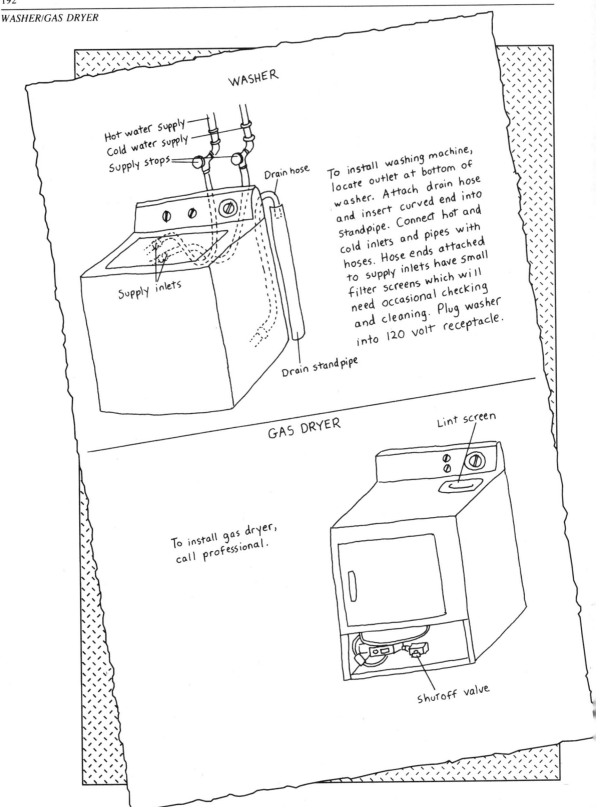

WASHER

Hot water supply
Cold water supply
Supply stops

Drain hose

Supply inlets

To install washing machine, locate outlet at bottom of washer. Attach drain hose and insert curved end into standpipe. Connect hot and cold inlets and pipes with hoses. Hose ends attached to supply inlets have small filter screens which will need occasional checking and cleaning. Plug washer into 120 volt receptacle.

Drain standpipe

GAS DRYER

Lint screen

To install gas dryer, call professional.

Shutoff valve

Zap! You're liquid! My favorite method of defrosting the refrigerator is to use my trusty hair dryer. Just train the nozzle on those pesky chunks of ice and fire away. Just remember you are using an electrical appliance around what will soon become liquid, so take the proper precautions (watch that cord!). (MK)

ELECTRICITY

The most important thing to remember about electricity is that it is there, even if you can't see it. In this, it resembles the abstract concepts that constitute theological and philosophical inquiry. Unlike transubstantiation or beauty, however, electricity can knock you on your ass in a literal kind of way if you don't pay attention.

Never attempt any electrical repair if there is live electricity present. Unplug things, turn stuff off — you get the idea. And one more thing, *never fool with your household electricity unless you first turn off the main switch.*

Plugs: If the plug is jiggly, you can bend the prongs a little bit to make the fit tighter. If the prongs are the doubled-over type, you can pull them apart slightly with a knife to make the fit more secure.

If you need a whole new plug, use wire-cutters to cut the wire a couple of inches from the plug. First, strip the insulation off each wire with a knife, then feed the wire through the back of the plug and tie an Underwriter's knot in the two wires (**see illustrations**). Draw the knot back into the recess between the prongs by pulling back the wire. Twist the wires and wrap them clockwise around the terminal screws. When the screws are tightened, the wires will be drawn tighter. Let no bare ends protrude or you may end up with a short. (HE, JF)

Lamp wiring: A lamp cord runs from the plug through the base of the lamp to the socket. Take apart the socket so that you can disconnect the wires. Unscrew the bulb. The word *press* will be embossed into the metal at the side of the socket near the switch. With your fingers wrapped around the socket, press your thumb hard against this point. You will be able to snap the two parts of the socket apart this way. Slide off the upper half. Slide off the cardboard insulating liner, and you will see two terminal screws with wires attached. Pull up on the socket to pull the wire through the lamp base and loosen the screws and disconnect the wires. Tie a heavy piece of string to the old lamp cord and then pull the old wire out from where it enters through the base of the lamp. When the string comes out, you can untie the old cord and tie on the new wire. Pull the string from the top and the new wire will follow. Once it comes through, strip off about a half inch of insulation and reconnect it to the socket terminals. Twist the strands and wrap them clockwise around the screws. Finally, reassemble the socket. (JC, EC, HG)

Breaker, breaker: Fuses and circuit breakers do the same things, but one looks modern and with-it, and the other is what your mom used to fiddle with in the basement with a flashlight. Both stop the flow of current when it goes beyond a certain point before damage can be done to the wires and units served by the wires. When your mother went into the basement like that, she was probably replacing fuses that had burned out because of an overload. Circuit breakers do the same thing as fuses, but you don't have to replace anything. An overload trips a spring, and all you have to do to reset it is flip a switch. (HC, JC)

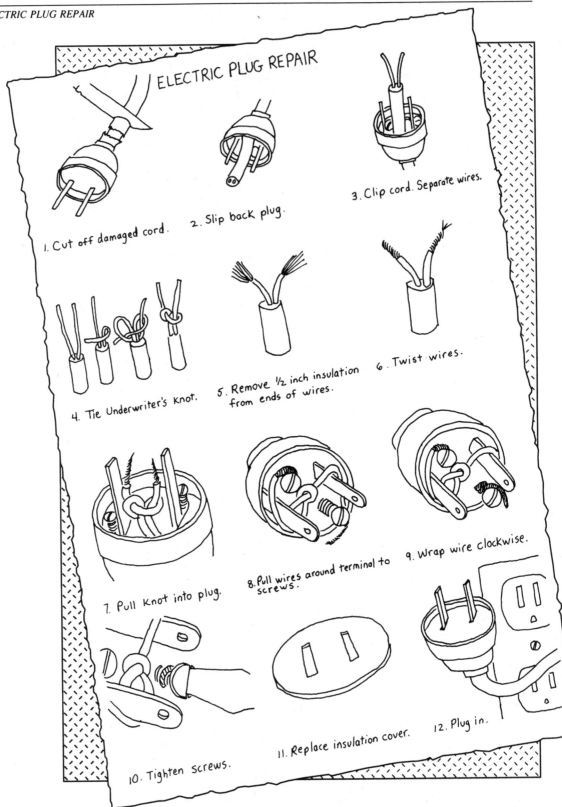

ELECTRIC PLUG REPAIR

1. Cut off damaged cord.

2. Slip back plug.

3. Clip cord. Separate wires.

4. Tie Underwriter's Knot.

5. Remove ½ inch insulation from ends of wires.

6. Twist wires.

7. Pull Knot into plug.

8. Pull wires around terminal to screws.

9. Wrap wire clockwise.

10. Tighten screws.

11. Replace insulation cover.

12. Plug in.

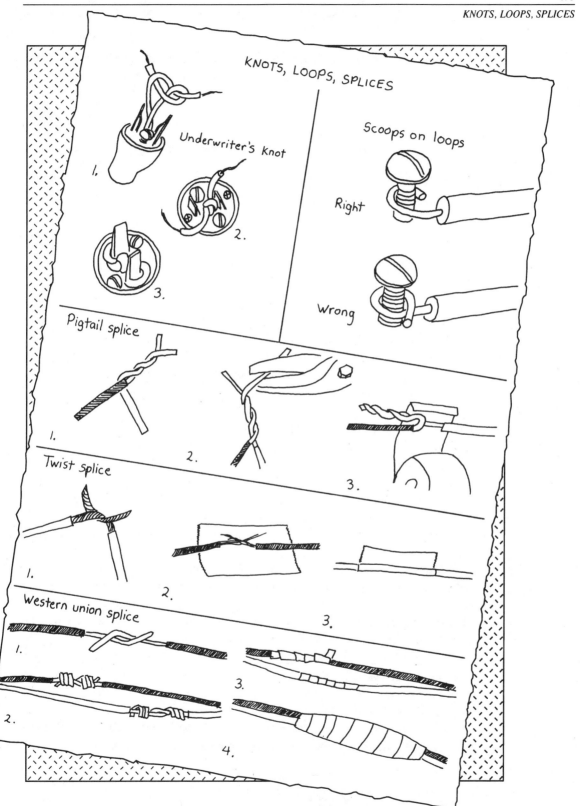

KNOTS, LOOPS, SPLICES

Underwriter's knot

1.

2.

3.

Scoops on loops

Right

Wrong

Pigtail splice

1.

2.

3.

Twist splice

1.

2.

3.

Western union splice

1.

2.

3.

3.

4.

You must remember this: Something went wrong in order for the fuse to melt or the spring to trip. Find out what went wrong before you change those fuses and flip the switches. Did you have every appliance in your house working at the same time? (JC)

CUTTING THE RATES

• *Don't run your dishwasher,* dryer or washer unless it is full.

• *Don't overdry your clothes.* Overdried clothes are greeted by early death and you will have to pay a lot of money for new ones.

• *Lower your hot water thermostat.* Put your hands under the hot water tap. If you have to pull them away quickly, your water is too hot. If your dishwasher needs extra hot water, have a dual-supply valve installed.

• *Insulate* your water heater and the hot-water supply piping.

• *Roast meat* at no more than 350° F. This will reduce meat shrinkage and use less heat.

• *Don't open the oven door* all the time to peek.

• Don't put the *refrigerator* next to a heat-producing appliance.

• Don't allow too much *frost buildup* in your fridge.

• Don't allow the *dryer* to dump moisture exhaust into the house.

• *Remove lint* from lint trap in clothes dryer after every cycle.

• Promptly *repair water leaks.* **See** *All About Faucets,* **below.**

• *Use a water-saver* shower nozzle. (EA, DB, KGG)

HOW TO FIX A WOBBLY CHAIR

Wood shrinks and that may be why your chair wobbles. The joint no longer fits into the hole snugly and the glue breaks loose. What you have to do is build up the end of the shrunken piece.

Start at the end: You can wrap the end with thread that has been coated in glue or you can saw a little slot into the end of the rung and wedge in a little piece of tapered wood. This will spread the sawed end a bit. Scrape off all old glue, apply a new coat, and drive the piece back in.

A frame job: Sometimes the frame against which the upper part of the legs is fastened works loose. If that happens, turn the furniture upside down and wiggle to see where the loose place is. Tighten any nuts and bolts and screws that you see. Some wood corner blocks are held together with glue. If the blocks have come loose, apply fresh glue. Trying adding metal corner braces — available at your hardware store — to strengthen the frame. (JC)

STARTING FROM SCRATCH

Handy hints from our far-flung correspondents: *Tiny scratches* can be eliminated by applying any good oil-base furniture polish. (EC)

• Little *scratches on walnut* can be hidden by rubbing with the meat of a walnut or a brazil nut, so that it matches the wood. Then apply wax or polish. *(Anon.)*

• Apply a little iodine with a swab to cover scratches on dark *mahogany* finishes. If the repair is too dark, use alcohol to lighten it.

Paint stores sell touch-up stain. (JC)

• *Deeper scratches* need to be filled in and then stained. Rub a touch-up stick back and forth over the scratch until it is filled in, then use a piece of cardboard to scrape away any excess material. Use the stain carefully; if the first application seems too light, wait a bit before applying more, since the color will change slightly in the setting process. Go slowly, applying just a bit of stain until you are able to match the patched surface. (KF)

• Try removing *white rings* with alcohol, turpentine, or lacquer thinner (**but see also above, under** *Stain Removal*). Using spirit on any wood is hazardous to the finish, so test very carefully in a hidden area by wiping on and immediately rubbing off. Try lacquer thinner last, because it will remove the finish fastest. (DT)

• *Burn marks* can often be removed by rubbing with #0000 steel wool wrapped around your finger. If the burn mark is very deep, scrape the finish down to the wood with a utility knife or an X-acto blade held at a right angle to the wood. After you have scraped the burn away, rub with fine steel wool, then fill the depression with plastic wood — unless the color of the wood is similar to the color of the finish, in which case, you can simply fill the dent with several coats of varnish, allowing each coat to dry before applying the next. (T6)

HOT AND WET

Heating and plumbing live in the invisible world of household comfort, where everything is dark and mysterious.

It's also where big-buck repairs dwell, since nothing gets our attention faster than a sub-zero bedroom or a coral-reef basement. When water starts gushing out of the kitchen range, most of us rush to the phone and call a guy to come over and unclog the drain on our bank account.

Look here first. Then, if you can't fix it, call the repair company. At least you tried.

TROUBLESHOOTING THE FURNACE

Dead of winter, dead of night, and the furnace goes on vacation. First, curse it, then kick it. Then try one of these likely remedies:

• *Check the fuses* or the circuit breaker to the furnace. If they're okay, check the heating system's master shutoff switch. It may have been tripped by accident. See *Electricity,* **above.**

• *Fill 'er up:* If you use oil, do you have fuel?

• *If you use gas,* is the pilot out? Relight the pilot by following the instructions on the burner. Call the repairman if it keeps going out.

• *Is the thermostat set* properly? You can tell if the thermostat is operating by turning the dial and listening for a click when the dial passes the prevailing room temperature.

• Are the *filters* clogged?

• Is the *fan belt* on the blower broken?

• Is the *register* in the room closed?

• *Check the safety button.* There is a red safety button that pops out to shut off the burner when the chamber pressure has gone too high. Press the button. If it starts but then quits again, open the door of the furnace for a little while, and then try once more. If it goes out again, remove the stack from the smoke pipe and clean the soot off the part that goes into the pipe.

• *Check the water level* gauge on your boiler if you have a steam-heat system. Fill the boiler past halfway. (EC)

HOT TALK

Know what's what with your heating system. By understanding the basic function of the heating system you use, you might be able to get help over the telephone from a friend or a repair company for a lot less money than a repairman will charge for a house call.

Automatic furnaces have a control that keeps the motor from coming on before the water or air has been heated enough.

Furnaces have *a high-limit switch* to keep them from overheating. The switch should be set so that the circulator motor or blower motor keeps running long enough after the thermostat cuts out to the allow the heat to dissipate.

Hot-water systems use a *circulator motor,* and *hot-air systems* use a *blower motor.*

With *hot-air systems,* heated air is forced through ducts by a motor that runs a large blower. The motor and the blower need *regular lubrication.* Add a little oil to the oil cups. The motor is connected to the fan by a *drive belt.* Check to see if it feels slack or is badly frayed and replace it if it is. Check the *blades* on the fan or blower and vacuum them clean. Air *filters* need to be replaced or cleaned periodically. They will be located in a main duct in or near the furnace. Some are meant to be cleaned, while others are meant to be replaced. Hold them up to the light once a month or so. You should be able to see the light clearly through them.

With *hot-water systems,* radiators need to be "bled" at the beginning of each heating season. When the system is running, the radiator should be full of water. If air gets caught inside, the efficiency of the system is lowered significantly. *To bleed the system,* open the vent valve near the top until the air escapes and water starts to come out. Shut the valve. Do this to every radiator, starting at the top of the house. Automatic vent valves will do this for you automatically.

The expansion tank next to the boiler should be kept about half full. It may need to be drained now and then by opening the valve at the bottom. Don't forget to close the valve that lets water from the boiler into the tank. It's best to have a pail handy.

An *aquastat* controls the temperature of the water in the boiler.

Sometimes water gets trapped in *steam systems* and keeps the steam from getting all the way across the radiator. Check the valve, which should be letting cold air escape. If you remove or open the valve and cold air and steam come out, the valve is probably clogged. Replace it. If this doesn't do the trick or if your radiator hammers and knocks when the steam comes up, the radiator may not be sloping correctly. It should be leaning toward the inlet valve. Put a little wedge under the opposite side.

The *radiator valve* should be either shut or open, not in-between. (EC, KF, YB)

HEATER MAINTENANCE

To prevent **sediment buildup** in your water heater, drain a few quarts every six months by opening the faucet-like drain valve at the bottom of the tank. Catch the water in a bucket. (JF)

A malfunctioning **thermostat** can cause a buildup of pressure or temperature. Test the valve when you flush the tank by lifting the test lever on the top of the valve. It is functioning properly if a little water leaks out. (HE)

Check the **turnoff valve** from time to time. It is located on the cold water inlet line to the heater. Find out where the shutoff valves for the gas or electric heating supply are located. These are usually near the thermostat. (EC, JC)

If there is a puddle of water at the bottom of the tank, it probably has **a leak due to corrosion.** It is a sign of old age, I fear. It may be time for a new tank. (BS) **See** *Leaks,* **below.**

Inspect the burner or gas-fired heater regularly. Keep it free of dust and sediment. Don't decide to turn up the temperature unless you want to speed up the corrosion of the pipes, waste energy and scald your children. (HE)

HOT UNDER THE COOLER

Keep heat-producing appliances away from the thermostat to avoid a false reading. (MNF)

PIPE DREAMS

An illustrative tale: The water is rushing to the brim at 1000 miles per hour and you remember that once you received some handy information on this situation, but you can't quite remember what it was. So what you do is lurch backwards about ten feet and watch helplessly and remember the time you stood and gazed at Niagara Falls back in '72.

Now you have time to notice that all the floor drains in the basement are brimming and overflowing with water. Do you call A-1 E-Z Duz-It Plumbing? If you do, this is what will happen. In about eight hours a tiny, thin, craggy, very old man wearing enormous black rubber gloves will come to your door. He will work for an hour or more and mutter things to himself like, "I don't know. I'm not sure, but I think we've got some mighty huge tree roots in this system." He works and slaves with this long chain that has a claw on one end. He tells you he thinks he's cleared about forty feet but for some reason he can't get any farther. He says he thinks it's okay now. He says we can hope there isn't a break in the line.

"What do you mean," you say, "'a break in the line'?"

"Well, ma'am," he says, "that would mean that we would have to tear up your lawn. That's if you're lucky. If you're not lucky, it could mean you'll need your sidewalk torn up. But I think we've got it fixed."

"Oh," you say, sweating, "we do?"

"Hope so, ma'am."

You pay him $41.00 and he leaves. Six months go by. After a while you learn to relax. But then in the eighth month you go downstairs and see water coming up from the bowels of hell, and you know, oh my God, your sidewalk will have to be torn up. What do you do?

As far as trying to save a few bucks goes, take my advice. Remember the Roto Rooter commercial when you were little? Where they sing that little song about how away go troubles down the drain? I am not a Roto Rooter representative, but believe me, these people know their business. Spend a dollar more. Call them.

The Roto Rooter man arrived in twenty minutes. He extended his claw a full 120 feet. "Just roots, ma'am, no problem at all."

"What about tearing up the sidewalk?" I asked, trembling and sweating.

"It's just roots, ma'am." I paid him $46.00 and he left. That's how you handle drains. (LC)

TAMPONS

It says on the box you can flush tampons down the toilet. If you live on a tree-lined street, don't do it. (LW)

To continue: He told me it was "just roots, ma'am," because he was a gentleman. What he wrote on the receipt was "roots and tampons." (LC)

TOILET TERROR

It's early in the morning. One of you is taking a long shower. The other of you goes down to the other bathroom. That other one flushes the toilet. When the toilet begins to overflow, quickly turn the little round knob that is under the toilet and the water will stop. It's as easy as that. (TC)

WHITE NOISE

There's nothing quite so soothing as the sound of water — except in the middle of the night and when it's coming from someplace inside the house. There is water pumping somewhere, and it is exiting at an incredible rate, and you are running frantically upstairs and downstairs in your pajamas looking for it, and you *can't find it*. One thing is certain: It's time to turn off the ***main supply line*** to the house.

Do you know where your main supply line is? You'd better. The main supply line to the house has a shutoff valve near where the line enters the building. It may be under the house in older homes.

To shut off water to sinks and toilets, look for valves under the fixture. ***On a water***

heater, look for the valve on the cold water supply line where it enters the top of the heater.

Most valves close clockwise. (EAn)

Clockwise versus counterclockwise: Imagine the lid to a peanut butter jar. Valves follow the same principle. (EA)

First things first: Always turn water off before attempting repairs. Make sure first, however, that cutting off the water will not do more damage than that which you seek to repair. (JJ)

PLUMBING TOOLS

There are a few tools to have on hand for simple repairs:

- A *pipe wrench,* a heavy-duty tool for repairs on large fittings and pipes.
- Keep a supply of *washers* on hand that fit your faucets.
- A *basin wrench* for hard-to-reach places, like under the sink.
- An *adjustable wrench* for loosening and tightening nuts on faucets.
- A set of *screwdrivers.*
- A *rubber plunger* unstops clogged drains if you cover the drain with the rubber end and use an up and down motion to create suction. This is the indispensable plumbing tool in most households.
- Use a *plumbing socket wrench* to remove the "bonnet nut" on shower or tub faucets. An adjustable or pipe wrench may be fitted to the tool and used as a handle.

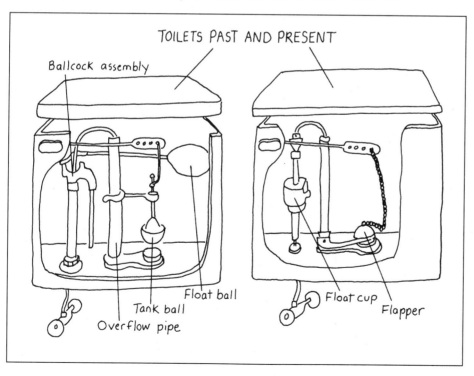

TOILETS PAST AND PRESENT

Ballcock assembly

Float ball
Tank ball
Overflow pipe

Float cup
Flapper

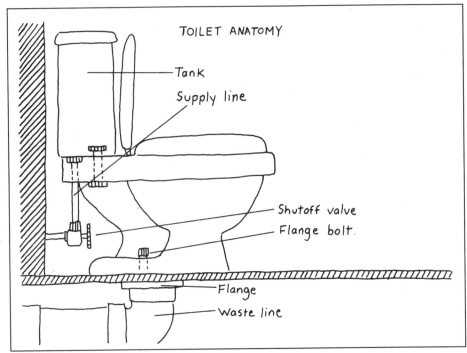

TOILET ANATOMY

Tank
Supply line
Shutoff valve
Flange bolt
Flange
Waste line

• For small water pipe leaks, you can use *plastic electrician's tape* or a piece of sheet rubber held on with hose clamps. (PJ)

LEAK? WHAT LEAK?

First, make sure *all faucets are firmly off.* Next, find your meter box, which is often near the curb in front of your house. Remove the cover and flip open the lid.

On *round-reading meters,* the dial used for testing will either be labeled "one foot" or have no label at all.

Straight-reading meters have only one needle, and that's the one you look at.

The faucets are all shut off, right? Look and remember where the needle is pointing. Check again in thirty minutes. If it has moved, you have a leak. (BB)

FIXING LEAKY TOILETS

• Remove the top of the tank and *check the flushing mechanism.*

• *Make sure the guide rods aren't bent* and that there aren't rusted and corroded parts that may need replacement.

• Check the *water level.* It should remain at least one-half inch below the top of the overflow tube. The water level is controlled by the float ball. You can bend the connecting rod down so that the supply valve shuts off at the proper level. (JC)

To go: A leaky or waterlogged float ball can easily be unscrewed and replaced. Take it with you to the hardware store to make sure you get a match. (KSS)

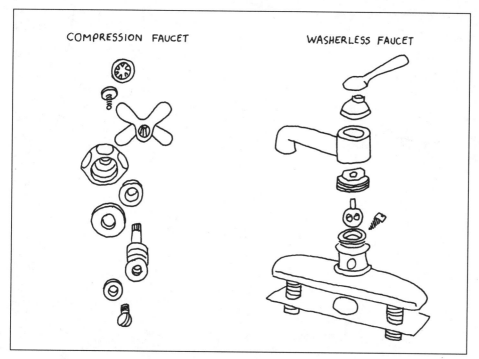

COMPRESSION FAUCET   WASHERLESS FAUCET

The color of leaks: Drop food coloring into the tank to detect *plunger ball* leaks. If color leaks into the bowl, you know you have plunger ball problems. If the plunger ball is worn or rough at the edges, unscrew it and get another. Consider replacing it with a flapper device, which requires fewer repairs. If the plunger ball isn't worn, it may not be seating properly due to a corroded valve seat. Turn off the water supply valve and flush the toilet to empty it of water. Sponge out the remainder. Dry the valve seat and smooth it with an emery cloth. Check to see that the plunger ball falls into place securely, then turn the water back on. (EC)

Hey, good lookin': If your toilet whistles and whines, you may need a new *ballcock assembly.* You can find these in hardware and plumbing stores, but before you go, practice saying "ballcock assembly" without grinning.

To replace the assembly, drain the water from the tank and detach the float ball and connecting arm. With an adjustable wrench, disconnect the supply line beneath the tank. Remove the locknut and washer and lift out the ballcock assembly. Screw the new ballcock assembly into place, making sure you adjust the refill tube on the new unit so it fits into the overflow pipe. Reattach and adjust the float ball, then refill the tank. (EC)

ALL ABOUT FAUCETS

One pinhole leak can waste seventy gallons of water a day — and remember, our planet is running out of water.

Most homes have one of two basic types of faucet: *compression faucets,* which have

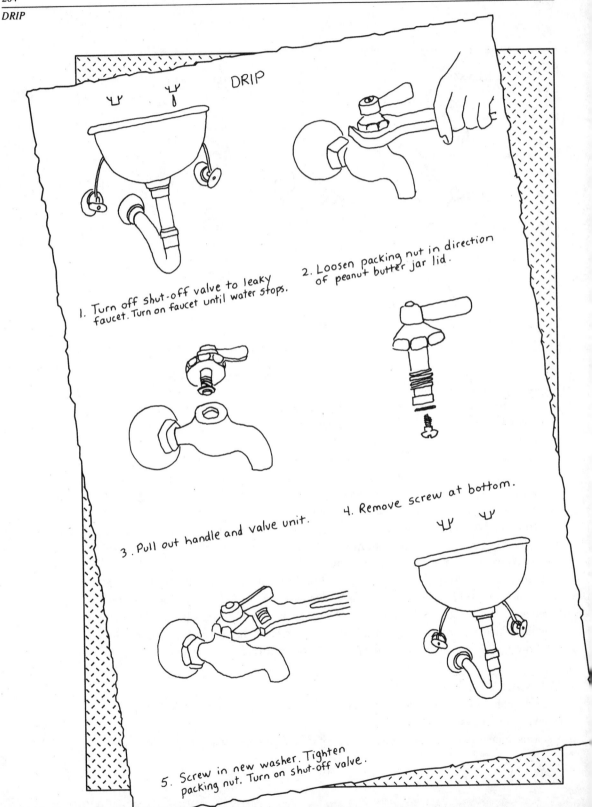

DRIP

1. Turn off shut-off valve to leaky faucet. Turn on faucet until water stops.

2. Loosen packing nut in direction of peanut butter jar lid.

3. Pull out handle and valve unit.

4. Remove screw at bottom.

5. Screw in new washer. Tighten packing nut. Turn on shut-off valve.

separate hot and cold handles, and ***non-compression faucets,*** which have only one knob controling both hot and cold.

Before attempting repairs or replacement, turn off the water supply under the sink or at the main house valve if there is no individual shut-off. (JDP)

COMPRESSION FAUCETS

To replace a washer in a compression faucet, unscrew the faucet stem by turning it counterclockwise. At the end of the stem there will be a washer held in place by a screw. Replace the washer with a new one that is the exact same kind.

The washer should fit easily and spread out to the edges when screwed down. Put the faucet back together, then turn on the water. If you still have a leak, you may have a worn valve seal. (HE)

Replacements: If you need replacements, always take the old part with you. Never rely on memory. (EC)

WASHERLESS FAUCETS

Some compression faucets use a metal disc or rubber diaphragm to control water flow. Follow the steps above for dismantling regular compression faucets, being sure to remove the entire diaphragm assembly after unscrewing the stem nut. Take the assembly to the plumbing supply store to get a matching kit. (HE)

NONCOMPRESSION FAUCETS

Noncompression faucets use one lever or knob to control the flow of water. In most of them, leaks may be repaired by taking the faucet apart and replacing the mechanism with a replacement cartridge rather than individual parts. Take the old cartridge with you to the store. (HE)

TUB AND SHOWER FAUCETS

Often on tub installations, the body of the faucet will be behind the wall. You'll need a plumbing socket wrench to unscrew the large bonnet nut in order to remove the stem. Usually tubs and showers will not have shut-off valves, so you'll need to turn off the main house valve (**see above**). (HE)

GLASS MENAGERIE

Next time your cup runneth over, ditch the mug and go for the right glass.

There is a proper glass for every occasion. In fact, part of what makes an occasion special is the hostess's dedication to tradition. Drinking wine from a tin cup may have a certain *prole* charm, but the wine won't taste very good.

Wine: Wine is a pretty beverage, full of light and color, so the glass that holds wine should be clear to show the drink at its best. The top of the glass should curve slightly inward to help hold the bouquet. The stem of the glass should be long enough to allow the glass to be held without warming the drink with the hand.

Brandy and liqueur glasses should be shaped inward towards the rim to hold in flavor and aroma. Brandy glasses should have short stems to allow the warmth of your hand to reach the brandy. Liqueur glasses should be small and narrow.

Lager should be served in a tall, open glass, preferably one that has been chilled beforehand.

Porter and ale should be served in a thick glass or mug.

Cocktails and highballs should be served in tumblers large enough to leave room for plenty of ice.

Champagne: Champagne glasses should be wide and shallow to allow as much of the carbonation — the "sparkle" — as possible to escape as the drink is being consumed.

Water: In formal settings, place the water glass directly above the point of the knife.

At formal occasions, where more than one glass is to be used, set them in this order, from left to right: champagne glass, red wineglass, white wineglass and the sherry glass last, on the extreme right. (SL, JC)

Store glasses brim down to prevent dust from settling in them. Be careful to dry glasses thoroughly before putting them away so they don't harbor moisture for long periods. *(Anon.)*

A dissent: If you have any kind of shelf liner or paper on your shelves and you stack your glasses upside down, unless they are *absolutely* dry, you'll do nothing but help provide a home to roaches and mildew. (DW)

Don't stack glasses if there's even a *hint* of moisture in them. They'll stick, then crack when you try to pry them apart. (SG)

To clean a tumbler or Collins glass, put a small sponge in the bottom of the glass, then stab it with a fork and swish it around until all the gunk on the bottom is gone. (AL)

Cut-glass, crystal and thick-bottomed glasses should be hand washed. They'll almost certainly crack in a dishwasher. (LG)

To clean a decanter, fill with about a cup of lukewarm water, add a tablespoon of sand and a dose of denture cleanser, then swish, rinse and drain. (LG)

KNIVES AND SCISSORS

Nobody commands respect like a Modern Woman who knows how to handle a blade.

Not that you have to be a Benihana Bitch or anything, but if you're going to survive in the kitchen, you have to identify with your knives — look sharp, be sharp. Get the point?

KNIFE TYPES

Every knife has one or a combination of the following four types of edges:

Cannel: This edge is used for heavy-duty cutting. Meat cleavers have this type of heat-treated edge.

Hollow ground: This edge is used in general purpose cutting. Many pocket knives will be made this way.

Concave edge: Many of the better carving tools are made with a concave edge, which makes very thin slices possible.

V-grind: This is a sturdy cutting edge common on butcher and kitchen knives.

In addition, many knives will have a *serrated* edge in combination with one of the above edge types. (WK)

ON EDGE

A *bench stone* is the most common tool for sharpening a knife. Buy a good combination stone that has a coarse and a fine side; be sure the stone is flat before you begin by sanding it. Place the stone with the coarse side up on the edge of a table and add a few drops of oil to the stone. Honing oil is best, but you can substitute any lightweight oil. Hold the knife at the hilt and pass the blade over the stone. Keep an all-purpose knife at an angle of about 15 degrees. You shouldn't need more than twenty strokes per side. If you want a razor-sharp blade, after you have finished on the coarse side, repeat the process on the fine side.

A *butcher's steel* is great to have around the kitchen. Butchers are always flailing them about before they attack their meat. If you are right-handed, hold the knife in your right hand and the steel in your left. Start at the tip of the steel with the back edge of the knife and swipe down to the handle. Do the same to the other side of the blade. Keep it at 15 degrees. A half dozen passes on each side should do it.

V-type sharpeners: You can buy a system that consists of two stone rods held in a V-shape to a base. As you push the knife blade down along the rods, a 15-degree angle will be maintained for you. This is a good investment if you're not positive about your judgment concerning angles.

If your knife has nicks or is broken at the tip, it will need to be repaired with a *bench grinder.* Don't spend the money to get one if you don't already have one. Most people don't — that's why knife sharpeners are in business. (WK, EC)

Kitchen knives: Every kitchen should have the following knives:

• *A vegetable knife* with a serrated, six-inch edge for easy cutting
• *A carving knife* with a smooth, sharp ten-inch blade
• *A chopping knife* with a ten- to twelve-inch smooth edge

To chop food with a knife, put the point of the knife down, then bring the handle down across the vegetables. Slide the food up, then repeat. Use the knife like a sort of paper cutter. (JDD, WK)

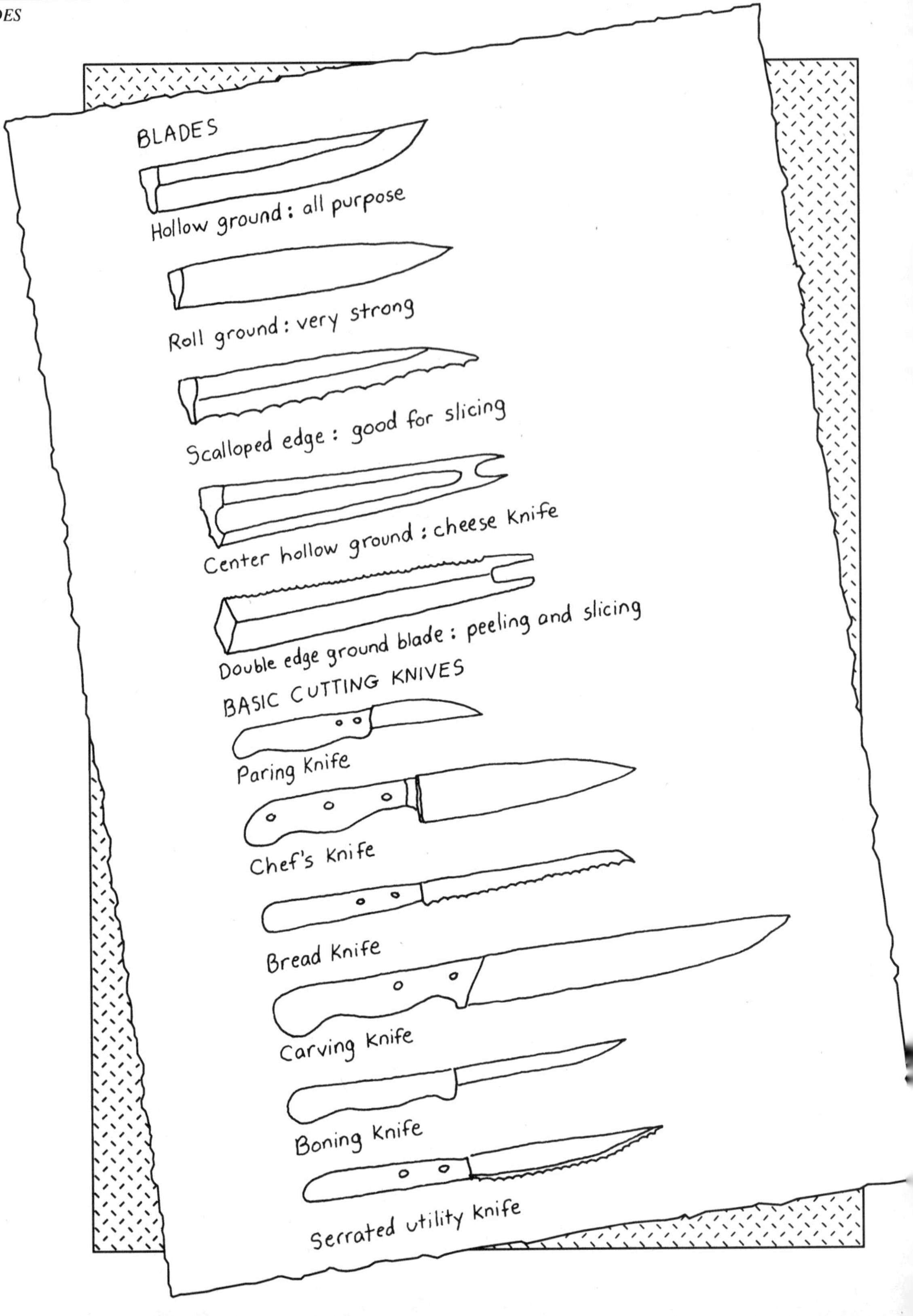

BLADES

Hollow ground: all purpose

Roll ground: very strong

Scalloped edge: good for slicing

Center hollow ground: cheese knife

Double edge ground blade: peeling and slicing

BASIC CUTTING KNIVES

Paring Knife

Chef's Knife

Bread Knife

Carving Knife

Boning Knife

Serrated utility knife

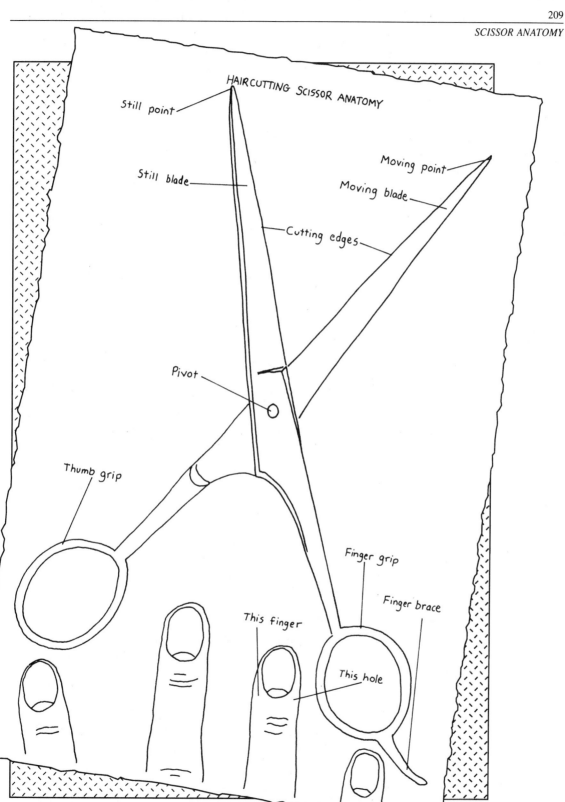

HAIRCUTTING SCISSOR ANATOMY

Still point

Moving point

Still blade

Moving blade

Cutting edges

Pivot

Thumb grip

Finger grip

Finger brace

This finger

This hole

SHARPENING SCISSORS

Tighten up: Before you go to the trouble of sharpening a pair of scissors, check and see if the screw is tight. Check that first, because a loose scissors won't cut very well.

Sharpen up: Be careful when sharpening scissors to keep the bevel edge at about 80 degrees. Stroke the blade several times on a fine-grained stone. Remember to use a little bit of oil on the stone and clean it with a cloth afterwards. Then apply 10-weight oil to all surfaces of the scissors and work it in by opening and closing them. Clean with a cloth. Now, cut it out. (IM, WK)

In case of mishaps while sharpening knives or scissors, see *Bleeding,* **under** *REAL FIRST AID* **in** *CHAPTER THIRTEEN: THE MEDICINE CABINET.*

MODERN WOMEN ON THE RANGE

Food is one of those things that haunts Modern Women, disturbs their restful nights and plagues their busy days.

Here's the horrible truth about food: It's a necessity. And here's the ancillary terror: Sometimes you have to cook the stuff before you can eat it.

That brings us to the kitchen. And that brings us to the room of gender guilt, where we feel like we *ought* to know what's what. No? Then this is the cheap and easy stuff that may not be enough to help you talk your way *through* a kitchen but may at least provide you with enough info to talk your way *out*.

BIBLIOGRAPHY

The best all-round cookbook is probably the ironically-titled *Joy of Cooking.* Especially for novices, it presents basic recipes in a straightforward fashion. (ATT)

FEASTS, FEAR AND FAMINE

The easiest recipe for entertaining yourself, your friends or a roomful of strangers, according to Spence Waugh, a Modern Woman First Class, is also the best one: Serve lots of booze and forget dinner. **But see also** *Recipes You Should Be Able to Make Before You Qualify For U.S. Citizenship,* **below.**

After all, do Modern Women *really* need a section on cooking? All our friends were *born* with a flair for cooking. Back in high school they used to read cookbooks for fun. And we are talking *intelligent* young women who scored in the 780s on their SAT's and majored in biochemistry.

We asked some of them to supply us with rock-bottom kitchen lore. But what we got floated on the surface. Things like

TWO ESSENTIAL RECIPES

Nutty Lentil Salad

Two and a half cups dried lentils

Three carrots, quartered

One medium yellow onion, peeled and stuck with three cloves

A quart and one-half of chicken stock

A bay leaf

Two teaspoons dried thyme

A third-cup of white wine vinegar

Three garlic cloves peeled

One-half cup walnut or corn oil

Salt and pepper

One cup thinly sliced green onions

One cup walnuts

Some chopped parsley

Rinse the lentils. Place in pot with carrots, onion, stock, bay leaf, and thyme. Bring to boil; reduce to simmer and skim off the foam; cover and cook about 25 minutes. *Do not overcook.*

In a blender, whiz the oil, vinegar, and garlic together as a dressing. When the lentils are done, drain and discard the carrots, onion, clove and bay leaf. Pour the lentils in a bowl and pour the dressing over the still-hot lentils. Toss gently and season with salt and pepper. Let the salad cool to room temperature. Toss again, then cover and refrigerate overnight.

Just before serving, add green onions and walnuts. Sprinkle heavily with chopped parsley, but don't get carried away. If you turn it green, you'll be in trouble. Makes *lots*.

Western Chili

A pound of ground beef

Cooking oil

One large onion, chopped

One clove garlic, mashed

One green pepper, chopped

Two one-pound cans red beans

One number 2 1/2 can of tomatoes

One cup tomato juice

Two bouillon cubes

One-half teaspoon each of basil, oregano, cumin, and thyme

One tablespoon of chili powder — or more

One cup chopped ripe olives

Brown the beef in a little oil, adding the onion, garlic, and pepper when the meat is about half done. Then dump everything together into a large kettle and simmer, covered, for at least an hour. That's it. You can add celery seed and Tabasco sauce and cayenne pepper if you want. You can change the amounts of things. You can throw caution to the winds and put in three tablespoons of chili powder. No matter what, it *always* comes out good. (PAG)

THE PROBLEM

See the problem here? Lentil salad and chili, the two *essential* recipes?
　　Who knows what's essential in a kitchen and what isn't?
　　Are frying pans essential?
　　If so, we've got

HOW TO SEASON A CAST-IRON FRYING PAN
　　To season a cast-iron frying pan, coat it inside and out with Crisco brand shortening or a similar product. Put the pan in a 200° oven for two hours or so. The time and temperature are extremely variable. (ARo)
　　And we've got

HOW TO PRESERVE A CAST-IRON FRYING PAN
　　After washing iron skillets, rinse them and place them on a warm burner to dry quickly. Drop several drops of vegetable oil in them till heated, then smear oil on entire inside surface of skillet with paper towel, then store. This protects them and treats the cooking surface for future use. (LJ)

So, who knows? What we decided to do was just sort of stroll through and clean up the joint, in a nonliteral kind of way, putting things away as we find them and stacking them up in bunches. Starting here:

TAKING INVENTORY
　　This is what you should have in your basic kitchen:
　　1. Basic basic:
- A wooden cutting board
- A set of knives for chopping, carving, slicing, utility, paring or. . .
- At least one steak knife to do all of these
- A timer
- A metal spatula
- A long-handled fork, spoon, perforated spoon
- Four measuring spoons from 1/4 teaspoon to one tablespoon

- A bottle opener
- A can opener
- A rotary beater
- A rubber scraper
- A vegetable peeler
- A mixing bowl or two
- A one-quart and a three-quart saucepan, with lids that fit
- Big and little skillets with lids
- A tea kettle
- Liquid measuring cups
- A rolling pin or empty wine bottle
- Oven-to-table casserole dishes with lids, in one- and two-quart sizes
- A rectangular roasting pan
- Dry measuring cups
- A corkscrew

2. More than basic:
- Another cutting board (one for meat, one for everything else)

If you cut raw meat on your wooden board, scrub it with hot soapy water. Once a week run a weak bleach solution over it. Use a scrub brush. If you're very worried about sanitation, buy a cutting board made of polyethylene, hard rubber, or acrylic. (EC)

- Cookie sheets
- A coffee maker
- A griddle
- A muffin pan
- A pair of kitchen shears
- A Mouli grater for nuts
- A wire whisk
- A spatter shield
- A deep-fat thermometer
- A six- to eight-quart kettle
- A colander
- A vegetable brush
- Bread loaf pans, five to nine inches
- A sifter
- A pepper mill
- A funnel
- Cooling racks (EC, FDD, PAG)

DISHWASHERS

Keep these items out of the dishwasher: First, everything wooden. (Dishwashers will

KITCHEN EQUIPMENT MUST-HAVES

Butter curler

Cake dial divider

Cherry pitter

Ebleskiver maker

Egg scissors

Egg sectioner

Escargot dish

Fish scaler

Lady finger tin

Meat baller

Wedding cake pillar

Radish cutter

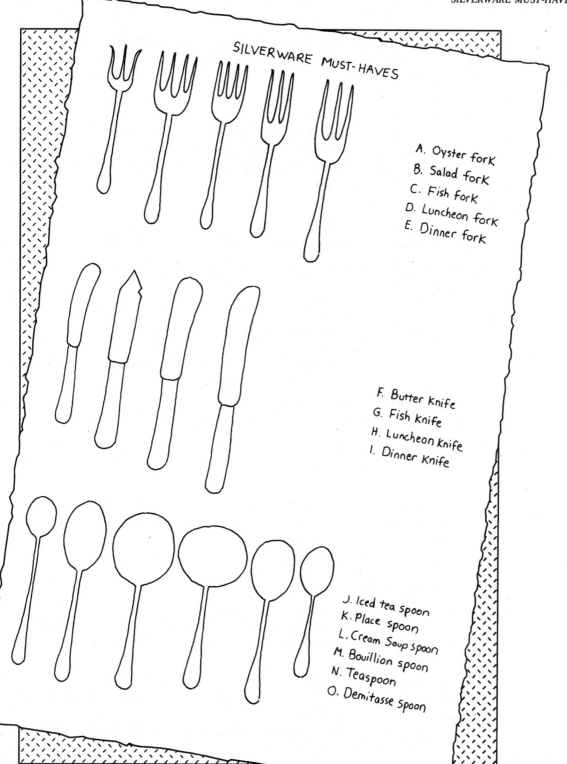

SILVERWARE MUST-HAVES

A. Oyster fork
B. Salad fork
C. Fish fork
D. Luncheon fork
E. Dinner fork

F. Butter knife
G. Fish knife
H. Luncheon knife
I. Dinner knife

J. Iced tea spoon
K. Place spoon
L. Cream soup spoon
M. Bouillion spoon
N. Teaspoon
O. Demitasse spoon

dry them out and crack them by and by.) Plastic and rubber. Rustable items. Wash kitchen knives by hand and dry them immediately. Dishwashers will ruin the seasoning of ironware. Do plated silver knives by hand.

THE RULE OF SPICES

A cooking rule of thumb: Never be afraid to use spices. Just because we were raised on bland frozen food doesn't mean we have to eat that way for the rest of our lives. Remember, you can make almost anything taste better if you use garlic, mustard and thyme. (TO) **See** *Herbs and Spices,* **below, for what to do with them.**

MEN RULE

Leave the fancy cooking to the men. They're the ones who think it's seductive. (DW)

THE MODERN WOMAN'S KITCHEN DITCHENARY

You want to talk food? We'll talk food.

• *À la carte:* Ordering individual items from a menu rather than a complete meal.

• *Al dente:* (Usually in reference to not quite cooked pasta.)

• *Antipasto:* An assortment of appetizers.

• *Aperitif:* A drink that is supposed to set you up for the main meal.

• *Au jus:* Unthickened natural juices from a roast or chicken.

• *Au lait:* French, literally "with milk."

• *Baste:* To moisten food while it cooks, preferably with its own juices, but sometimes with butter.

• *Bone:* To remove all bones from poultry, fish or meat.

• *Bouquet garni:* A bundle of several herbs, tied up in cheesecloth and dropped into a stew or soup.

• *Braise:* To cook food over a low heat with a small amount of liquid.

• *Bread:* To coat the food with breadcrumbs or cracker crumbs.

• *Broil:* To cook food under direct heat.

• *Broth:* The liquid in which meat, poultry or fish has simmered.

• *Coat:* To sprinkle with or dip into flour or sauce.

• *Compote:* A dessert of fresh or dried fruit.

• *Condiments:* Sauces, relishes or seasonings.

• *Cream:* Check the recipe. It can mean heavy cream, light cream or half and half. Or it can mean to blend several ingredients together into a smooth, creamy texture.

• *Crepe:* A thin pancake.

• *Crustacean:* Shellfish with segmented bodies, like lobster or shrimp.

• *Cut in:* To distribute butter, shortening or lard into flour by using a pastry mixer or two knives.

• *Deep-fry:* To cook food in hot fat (shortening or oil), so that the food floats on top of the fat.

• *Demitasse:* A tiny little cup of coffee, with a saucer.

• *Dice:* To cut food in small pieces.

• *Dot:* To place little pieces of butter all over the dish, cut of meat or whatever.

• *Draw:* To remove the guts from poultry and fish.

• *Dredge:* To cover the food with oatmeal, corn flakes or flour.

• *Drippings:* The juices from meat and poultry with which you make gravy.

• *Escargot:* Snails from France.

• *Filets:* Meat or fish that has been boned (q.v.).

• *Foie gras:* Goose liver.

• *Fold in:* Use a circular motion, cutting down into the mixture, bringing some of it up. Repeat, repeat.

• *Fondue:* Melted cheese or hot oil in to which meat, bits of bread, cheese and so forth are dipped.

• *Fricassee:* A stew made from chicken or veal.

• *Fry:* To cook over high heat, in a little fat.

• *Garnish:* To add a decorative touch.

• *Glaze:* To coat food with a glossy mixture.

• *Gratin:* To bake or broil food with bread crumbs or cheese on top.

• *Grill:* To cook food on a rack above a high flame.

• *Kosher:* Foods that by Jewish Law are accepted to be fit for consumption.

• *Lard:* The white fat from pork. Find an alternative.

• *Marble:* Visible fat in red meat.

• *Marinade:* A seasoned liquid that you soak meat in, especially if it's cheap meat.

• *Meunière:* Something made with a sauce of butter, lemon, and parsley.

• *Mince:* To cut into very fine pieces.

• *Mollusk:* Shellfish that have unsegmented bodies, such as oysters and mussels.

• *Monosodium glutamate:* A white salt that makes a lot of people go nutso. MSG, as it is known, often is an ingredient in Chinese food.

• *Panbroiled:* Cooked over a high heat with little or no grease or fat.

• *Panfry:* To cook food over a high heat in a very small amount of fat.

• *Parboil:* To boil food until it's almost done. You're usually going to serve parboiled food in a casserole.

• *Parfait:* Layers of fruit, ice cream and whipped cream — good for Jello.

• *Pilaf:* Seasoned rice.

• *Poach:* To cook food over low heat in simmering liquid.

• *Prawn:* A large shrimp.

• *Purée:* A thick mixture made from a vegetable base. Or to press any food through a sieve.

• *Reduce:* To reduce volume of a liquid by boiling rapidly in an uncovered pan.

• *Score:* To cut shallow slits on the surface of meats.

• *Shred:* To cut food into slender pieces.

• *Steam:* To cook food in a rack, covered, over boiling water.

• *Stir-fry:* To stir thinly sliced food very quickly, while cooking it in a wok or over very hot heat in a skillet.

• *Tempura:* Seafood or vegetables cooked with a batter covering.

• *Whip:* To beat rapidly with a whisk or electric mixer. (JLo, MA)

EASY ALL-PURPOSE DIPS

• *Guacamole:* Peel and dice one tomato. Peel two ripe avocados and remove the pits. Mash the avocados in a bowl with two tablespoons fresh lemon juice. Stir in one teaspoon of salt; the tomato; half an onion, minced; a clove of garlic, minced; and a fourteen-ounce can of green chilies, drained. Serve with tortilla chips. (AY)

• *Green Onion:* In a bowl, mix one cup sour cream, one envelope of beef flavored bouillon, one-fourth cup thinly sliced green onion, and one teaspoon Worcestershire sauce and refrigerate for an hour. Serve with potato chips or with fresh vegetables. (AY)

• *Chili Dip:* In a blender at low speed, mix together a twenty-eight-ounce can of tomatoes, drained; a small onion; a quarter cup parsley; one-fourth cup of green chilies; a clove of garlic; one tablespoon of white vinegar; a teaspoon of oregano; and a half teaspoon of salt. Refrigerate. Serve with fresh, cleaned and cut-up celery, zucchini, mushrooms, green onions and tortilla chips. (KK)

BREAKFAST

A fancy breakfast is a nice thing to do. It's an even nicer thing to have done. **See** *Men Rule,* **above.**

• *Eggs Benedict:* Prepare a hollandaise sauce (recipe below).
Poach four eggs as you like them. Keep them warm. Split two English muffins, spread them with butter, then put them on a broiling pan, buttered side up, with cooked ham along the side. When the muffins are toasted and the ham is warm, put the ham on the muffin halves and place an egg on top of the ham. Place the muffins on a heated platter, then pour some hollandaise over the eggs.

• *Hollandaise sauce:* Put three egg yolks and two tablespoons of lemon juice in the top of a double boiler. Mix it up well with a whisk. Put the pot on top of the bottom part of the boiler that has very hot, but not boiling water in it. Add two tablespoons of butter to the egg yolk mixture and mix it constantly until the butter is melted, then add two more tablespoons of butter and allow it to melt. Then add two *more* tablespoons of butter and do it again. Butter, butter, butter. Beat until the mixture becomes thick and is heated all the way through. Remove from heat. Add salt. Hollandaise is good for the soul, but rough on the heart. (PC)

• *Crepes:* Make the crepe batter at least two hours ahead of time and refrigerate for best results. You should have a crepe pan, but if you don't, use a small skillet. With a wire whisk beat two tablespoons of melted butter, one and a half cups of milk, two-thirds cup flour, some salt and three eggs together until the mixture is smooth. Pour just enough of the batter to cover the bottom of the pan which has already been greased with butter. Cook the crepe over medium heat for two minutes, then loosen the crepe from the bottom of the pan with a spatula and turn the crepe over into another heated, greased skillet and cook on the other side for about thirty seconds. You can stuff crepes with cooked frozen spinach, sliced mushrooms, sour cream, diced tomatoes, shrimp — just about anything you want. (CO'N) Crepes made with farina flour are called *galettes* and are great with savory fillings.

DESSERTS

Forget about making fancy desserts — they're fattening and not good for you anyway. Every meal is nicely ended with fresh fruit and cheese. Serve several different types of cheese on a platter, and green and red apples and ripe pears in a separate bowl. Give each guest a knife to cut her own fruit and pieces of cheese. (SV)

VEGETABLES

Spuds: Almost any meal can be served with boiled, red new potatoes. Buy them small, wash them very well, and steam them until they're just done. Serve whole with a garnish of parsley or sprinkled with chives. (PS)

Asparagus: Get down and get fancy with some asparagus served with that Hollandaise sauce (**see above**). (PS)

HEALTH FOOD

- Onions and garlic are good for your heart.
- Cabbage juice may heal ulcers.
- Broccoli, Brussels sprouts, cabbage, and carrots help fight cancer. *(Anon.)*

RECIPES YOU SHOULD BE ABLE TO MAKE BEFORE YOU QUALIFY FOR U.S. CITIZENSHIP

Meat Loaf

One cup bread crumbs or oatmeal

One teaspoon salt

Pepper

Three-quarters cup ketchup, divided in two equal portions

An egg

Two pounds lean ground beef

One and a half cups of shredded cheddar cheese, divided in two equal portions

One half cup each minced onion and minced celery

Combine the bread crumbs, salt, pepper, half the catsup, and the egg. Add the beef, one cup cheese, celery and onion and mix well. Shape the loaf into a ball and put it in a greased baking pan. Flatten it a bit and brush remaining ketchup over the top. Bake for one hour at 350°. Sprinkle with the remaining cheese before serving. (PS)

Chicken Breasts

Four chicken breast filets
One small can of crab, drained
One cup chopped mushrooms
One cup shredded mozarella cheese
One beaten egg white
One and a half cups of dry bread crumbs, combined with
Two tablespoons of grated parmesan cheese

Pound the breast filets. Put the crab, the mushrooms and the mozarella cheese on each breast. Roll it up jelly-roll style and fasten with a toothpick. Brush with beaten egg white, then roll in the parmesan cheese and bread crumb mixture. Bake for thirty minutes at 375°. (HP)

Tuna Casserole

One can tuna
One small onion, chopped
Two stalks broccoli, steamed and chopped
Small can of corn or peas, drained
One can each of condensed cream of mushroom and cream of celery soup
Parsley, thyme, salt and pepper to taste
One twelve-ounce bag of egg noodles, cooked, or six cups of cooked rice.

Mix everything together and put the mix in a greased casserole dish. If you're using noodles, top with fine bread crumbs; with rice, use smashed potato chips. Or you can top with shredded cheddar cheese. Bake for about half an hour at 350°. (BD)

Stew

Wash and cut up:
One medium yellow onion
Three small carrots
Two red potatoes
One small tomato
Two stalks celery
One pound stew meat
One can tomato paste
One cup hot tap water

Heat three tablespoons oil in a three-quart saucepan over medium heat. Brown meat in oil. Dissolve one-fourth cup cornstarch in one-half cup of the water. Dissolve tomato paste in cornstarch mixture. Stir into meat. Season with one tablespoon each: thyme, basil, and dillweed. Turn heat to medium low. Add vegetables, then stir in remaining water. Cover and simmer on low for one and a half hours, stirring the the stew every twenty minutes or so. (ATT)

Coleslaw

One small head cabbage

Four green onions, finely chopped

Paprika, salt, pepper and garlic to taste

One cup mayonnaise

One teaspoon red vinegar

One tablespoon sugar

Wash, drain and dry the cabbage, then shred it. Add onions, seasonings, mayonnaise, vinegar and sugar. Chill and serve. (ATT)

TURKEY

Turkey is the ultimate American food. It has a variety of cuts, can be served hot or cold, keeps for a long time, is the basic ingredient for many recipes, helps you sleep and there's usually enough of it to supply sandwiches for what seems like perpetuity.

Try to find a fresh bird; the difference between fresh and frozen is remarkable. As with other poultry, wash the turkey thoroughly, and don't forget to take the gizzards out. (Never leave stuffing in poultry either before cooking or after!) Put it on a rack in a large baking dish and cook at 350°, twenty minutes for each pound. You don't need to salt it or butter it. Once in a while, baste it with its own juices. (KK)

LAMB

Easy, expensive and delicious Marinated Lamb Racks (or chops)

One quart dry red wine

Two tablespoons salt

Two tablespoons oregano

One and a half tablespoons course black pepper

One cup onions, chopped

One-half cup finely chopped fresh parsley

One-half cup soy sauce

A rack of lamb or lamb chops

Prepare a marinade by combining wine, salt, pepper, oregano and thyme. Stir in onions, parsley and soy sauce. Place the lamb in a container and pour the marinade on top. Refrigerate overnight for racks and several hours for chops. Remove lamb from marinade and grill over medium coals for approximately twenty minutes, turn occasionally. If you don't have coals, broil for thirty minutes. This recipe gives you enough marinade for several lamb dishes and will keep in the refrigerator for two weeks. (SA)

HOW TO COOK PASTA

Cook pasta in a large, deep pot containing at least two quarts water and some salt. Let the water come to a high boil, then add the pasta gradually, so the water doesn't stop boiling completely. Hold the spaghetti vertically to the water and ease it in slowly. Coil the spaghetti around until it's submerged in the water. You can also break the spaghetti in two. Cook it uncovered, stirring occasionally. Cook until it is just tender but still firm. Drain it thoroughly in a colander. *Don't rinse it.* Instead, add a bit of olive oil to keep it from sticking together. (BD)

CALORIE COUNT

These foods just act fat — they're really not:
- One cupcake: 90 calories
- One-half canteloupe: 60 calories
- An omelet made with two eggs, milk and butter: 215 calories
- Four ounces of cod: 90 calories
- Four green olives: 15 calories
- One dill pickle: 10 calories
- One Fudgesicle: 70 calories
- One cup beef noodle soup: 60 calories
- One ounce Camembert cheese: 85 calories
- Three ounces clams: 45 calories
- Four ounces crab: 105 calories
- Lamb chop: 140 calories
- Four large mushrooms: 10 calories
- Eight oysters: 75 calories
- One baked or boiled potato: 90 calories
- One-half cup mashed potatoes with milk and butter: 95 calories
- One-half cup canned salmon: 120 calories
- Eight scallops: 90 calories
- Fourteen shelled shrimp: 90 calories (KK)

DUCK FAT

For your heart and your figure, try to avoid fats. Staying away from fatty foods also reduces calorie intake substantially. Here are a few things to keep in mind to help:
- Don't eat the skin of poultry.
- Trim all the fat from roasts and chops.
- Cut down on your meat intake and eat more seafood.
- Don't fry meat, broil it.
- Munch on popcorn rather than chips.
- Flavor vegetables with seasonings instead of butter.
- Eat rye bread.
- Eat eggs poached or boiled, instead of frying them. (LDS)

HERBS AND SPICES

Store herbs and spices in cool areas, away from the stove or sunlight. Keep the containers tightly closed. You can store red spices, like chili powder in the refrigerator.

When it's time to cook, add ground herbs or spices near the end of cooking time — their flavor disappears during prolonged cooking. (WH)

What herbs and spices to use with which foods:
- Basil: Tomato dishes, gravies, soups and dressings
- Bay leaves: Soups, roasts, stews and spaghetti sauce
- Chili powder: Mexican food and cocktail sauces
- Chives: Eggs, fish and potatoes
- Dill: Fish and shellfish.
- Mint: Fruit salads and in drinks
- Oregano: Mediterranean dishes and in some seafood recipes
- Paprika: Chicken and cheese dishes and cocktail sauces
- Rosemary: Fish and lamb
- Sage: Stuffings for meat and poultry
- Thyme: Meat, poultry, seafood, soups and stuffings (PL)

BIRD HUNTING

Choose a bird that has well-rounded breasts and skin that is clear of bruises. Sometimes poultry skin looks a bit yellow, which is okay. It doesn't mean that it's old. The coloring comes from what the bird was fed. (MP)

A "dressed" turkey is not a "ready-to-eat" turkey. Dressed turkeys don't have blood and they don't have feathers, but they sure have little heads and sorry little feet and a little oil sack — and you have to deal with all those things all by yourself.

Make sure your turkey is young if you want it for more than stew. (PAG)

Turkey roasts are birds that have been manipulated into loaf shapes after all their bones have been removed. Sort of unappealing, actually, the stuff that was once TV dinner material. (EC)

THAWING FROZEN POULTRY

Be careful: This is tricky because poultry can go off very easily. The best and safest way is to allow it to thaw gradually in the refrigerator. But that takes two or three days, so you may need an alternative method. Try this:

Put the bird in its wrapper in a large pan and cover with cold water — or fill a sink and put the bird in there. A chicken or game hen takes from one to two hours to thaw; a medium-size turkey will take from seven to nine hours.

Don't let it sit around. The minute the bird is thawed, put it back into the refrigerator. (LK)

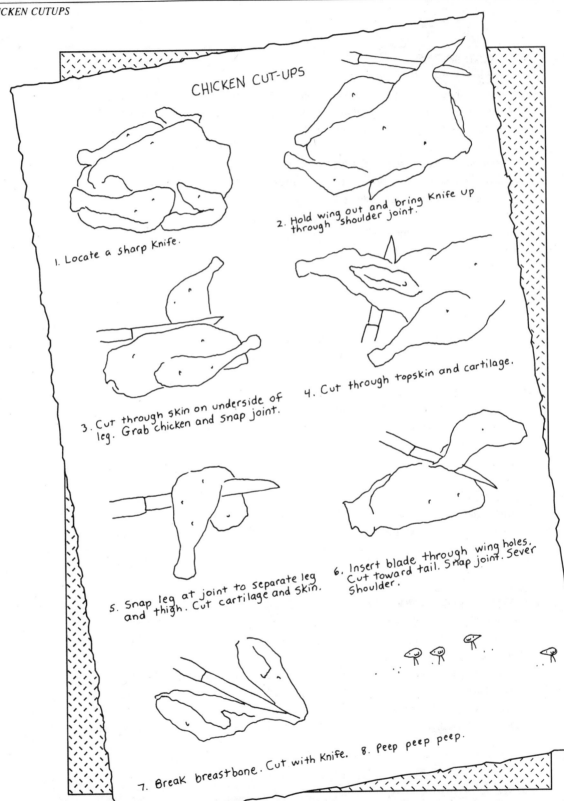

CHICKEN CUT-UPS

1. Locate a sharp knife.

2. Hold wing out and bring knife up through shoulder joint.

3. Cut through skin on underside of leg. Grab chicken and snap joint.

4. Cut through topskin and cartilage.

5. Snap leg at joint to separate leg and thigh. Cut cartilage and skin.

6. Insert blade through wing holes. Cut toward tail. Snap joint. Sever shoulder.

7. Break breastbone. Cut with knife.

8. Peep peep peep.

CHICKEN

Buy chicken whole and disjoint it yourself to save lots of money. If you are squeamish, put a plastic bag over each hand and squint.

Types:
- Broilers are chickens that weigh two and a half pounds or less.
- Fryers weigh two and a half to three and a half pounds.
- Roasting chickens weigh three and a half to five pounds.
- A capon is a castrated male bird and they can be enormous.

Old chickens make the best soup stock. (ML, EC)

FRESH FISH

Avoid buying any fish whose eyes are cloudy. The eyes should be clear and bulging, as though the fish has only just come to the grim realization that there was a catch to that free lunch. It should have a very mild odor, or no odor at all.

Filets of fish should be moist and firm with no weird discolorations and should have very little or no odor. Cook fresh fish within a day after you buy it. Never freeze, thaw, and then refreeze fish. (MP)

SHRIMP

Fresh shrimp should have a mild odor and firm meat. Never buy or eat a shrimp that has lost its curl. *The easiest way to cook shrimp,* in the shell or unshelled, is to put it in boiling, salted water and cover. Reduce heat and and simmer one to three minutes, until the shrimp are reddish on the outside and opaque on the inside. (ML)

If the shrimp smell like ammonia or are slippery, they are not fresh. Cook fresh shrimp within one or two days. Frozen, cooked shrimp should not be kept in the freezer for more than six weeks. If you buy frozen, raw shrimp, you can keep them in the freezer for up to half a year. (EC)

MUSSELS

Mussel bitch: Mussels have seasons and are toxic if eaten at the wrong time of year. Only buy mussels at a reliable fish market.

Rinse them thoroughly under running water to remove all the sand and throw away any mussels whose shells are open or broken. Scrub shells with a metal brush and remove any barnacles and clip off the "beards" with cooking shears.

To steam mussels, put them in a small amount of boiling water, cover, and simmer for ten minutes. The shells will open. Throw away any mussels that have remained closed. (ML)

LOBSTERS

Blackish or blue-green when they're alive, they all turn red after cooking. The peak

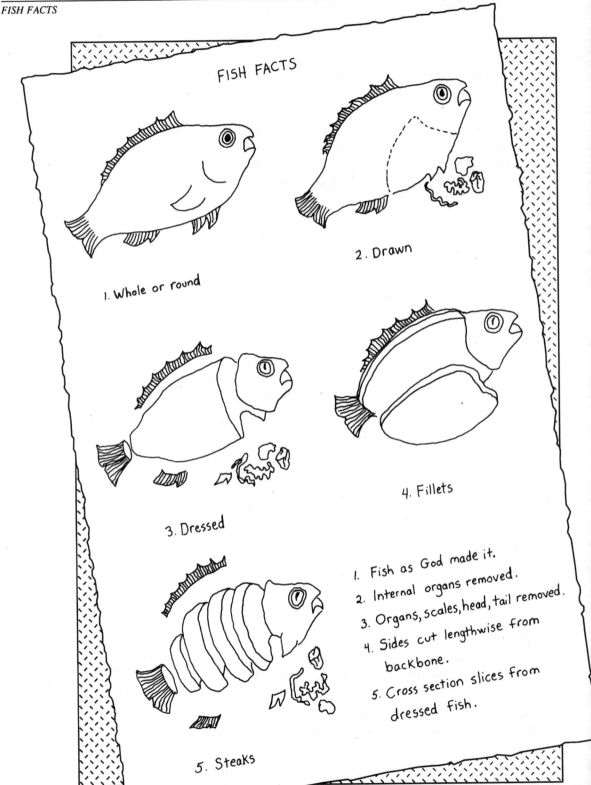

FISH FACTS

1. Whole or round

2. Drawn

3. Dressed

4. Fillets

5. Steaks

1. Fish as God made it.
2. Internal organs removed.
3. Organs, scales, head, tail removed.
4. Sides cut lengthwise from backbone.
5. Cross section slices from dressed fish.

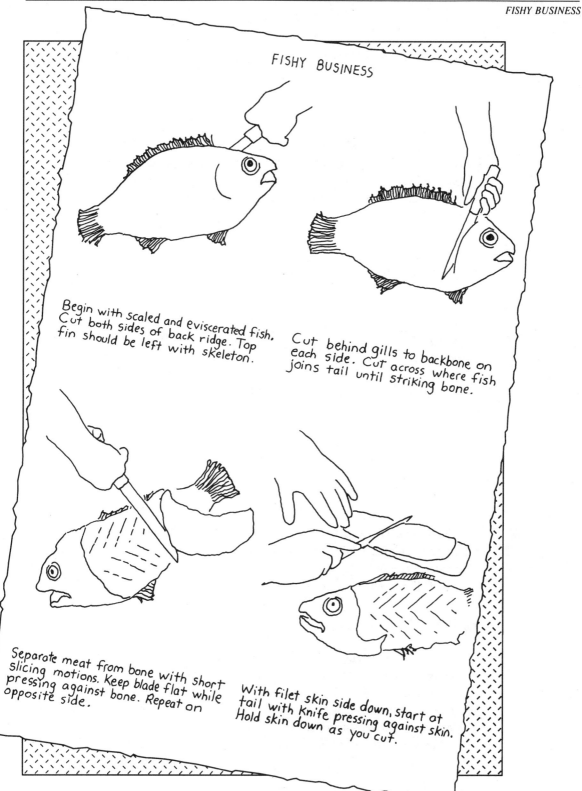

FISHY BUSINESS

Begin with scaled and eviscerated fish. Cut both sides of back ridge. Top fin should be left with skeleton.

Cut behind gills to backbone on each side. Cut across where fish joins tail until striking bone.

Separate meat from bone with short slicing motions. Keep blade flat while pressing against bone. Repeat on opposite side.

With filet skin side down, start at tail with knife pressing against skin. Hold skin down as you cut.

season for lobster in the Northeast is from May through December; on the West Coast it is from October to March. Cook a lobster the very day you buy it. Always try to buy live lobster. (KD)

OYSTERS

You can buy oysters alive and keep them alive for a month if you store them shell down, unopened and dry in the coldest part of your refrigerator. If you see any gaping shells, your oyster is dead. A refrigerated, shucked oyster will stay fresh for three days.

If you don't like the raw bar approach to oysters, toss them on a barbecue for a few minutes. (KAD)

ABOUT MEAT

There are eight grades used by the USDA to indicate the quality of beef.

• *U.S. Prime* is the highest grade. Prime beef is very well marbled with fat, which makes it excellent tasting and very tender. The best stores and restaurants snatch this stuff, and it's not found in most supermarkets.

• *U.S. Choice* is a little leaner than prime. It's found in many supermarkets and restaurants.

• *U.S. Good* is followed by

• *U.S. Standard.* Less juicy and tender than Choice, but terrific in stew and great as burgers.

• *U.S. Utility, Cutter* and *Canner* grades are not found in supermarkets except when disguised as sausage or cold cuts.

Pork should be fine-grained and firm and have white fat. Cook pork to 170° to kill trichinae, but don't burn it to a crisp like your mother did. (EC, PA)

MAN MEAL

There's not a man alive who doesn't love sandwiches. Give him one when you don't want to cook, or just anytime. It will make him very happy. There's something about making a sandwich for a guy — they think it's a sign of true love. They won't care what's in it either. Get rid of all your leftovers at once. (FL)

PERISHABLE FOODS

Fruit:

• *Apples:* Use ripe apples within one week. Store apples in the refrigerator uncovered. Unripe apples should be kept at coolest room temperature.

• *Apricots, avocados, grapes, nectarines, pears, peaches, plums, rhubarb:* Use or preserve within five days. Store ripe fruit uncovered in refrigerator. Unripe fruit should be stored at room temperature out of the sun.

• *Bananas:* Keep out of the sun and unwrapped at room temperature.

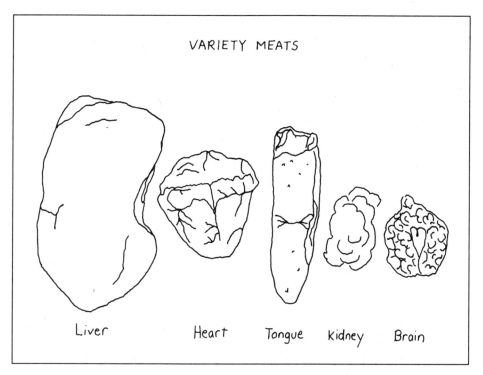

VARIETY MEATS

Liver   Heart   Tongue   Kidney   Brain

• *Berries, cherries:* Store unwashed, whole and uncovered in refrigerator until ready to use, which should be within two days.

• *Citrus fruits, melons:* Use within one week. Store at cool temperature.

Vegetables:

A vegetable crisper works best when at least two-thirds full. If it is less full than this, place the food in plastic bags and then place in crisper.

• *Asparagus:* Use within two days.

• *Cabbage, cauliflower, snap peas:* Use cabbage within two weeks and the rest within five days.

• *Carrots, beets, radishes, turnips:* Remove tops. Use within two weeks.

• *Green peas, lima beans:* Use within two days. Store in pods.

• *Lettuce:* Wash first, dry, use within two days.

• *Onions:* May be kept for several months at room temperature. Keep green onions in refrigerator and use within one week.

• *Potatoes:* Store in a dark, ventilated, cool room.

• *Spinach, kale, collards, chard, turnips, mustard greens:* Wash in lukewarm water first, then in cold water. Drain and store in crisper. Use within a couple of days.

• *Sweet potatoes:* Store at room temperature for a week or for months at 60° F.

• *Tomatoes:* Store uncovered in refrigerator for a week.

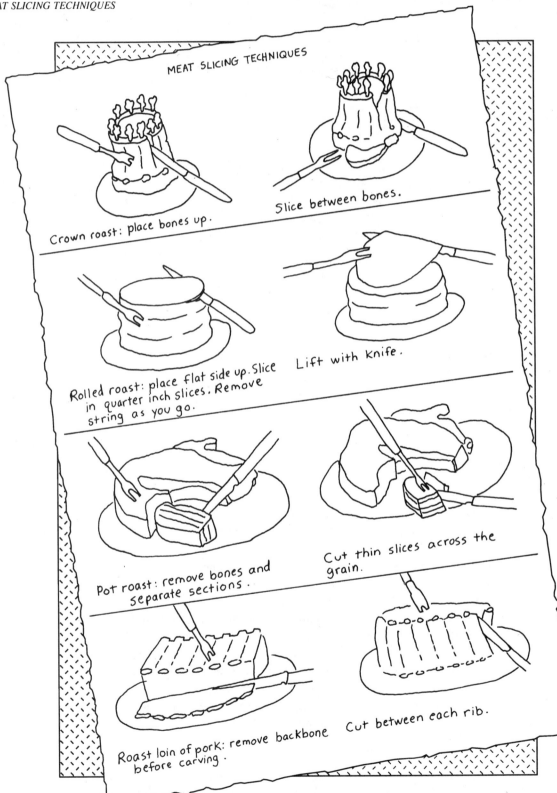

MEAT SLICING TECHNIQUES

Crown roast: place bones up.

Slice between bones.

Rolled roast: place flat side up. Slice in quarter inch slices. Remove string as you go.

Lift with knife.

Pot roast: remove bones and separate sections.

Cut thin slices across the grain.

Roast loin of pork: remove backbone before carving.

Cut between each rib.

MORE MEAT SLICING TECHNIQUES

1. Ham: flatten bottom by removing a few slices.

2. Place ham on bottom. Cut wedge from shank end.

3. Starting at wedge, slice down to bone.

4. Sever slices by drawing blade underneath against bone.

1. Rib roast: Place fork between ribs. Cut slices to bone.

2. Remove bone to free slices.

3. Support slice with fork while lifting with knife.

4. Serve with the juice of the meat.

Meat:

• *Cold cuts:* Keep in refrigerator and use within five days.

• *Cured and smoked meat:* Ham, franks, bacon, bologna, smoked sausage should be kept in refrigerator and used within a week.

• *Seafood, poultry, roasts, chops, steaks:* Poultry should be removed from the original wrap and loosely covered in the coldest part of the refrigerator. Meat stored in original wrap can be kept for one to two days. If unwrapped and loosely stored, it can be kept slightly longer. Use poultry and seafood within two days. Use roasts, chops, and steaks within five days.

• *Ground meat:* Store in the coldest part of the refrigerator and use within two days.

• *Liver, kidneys, brains, giblets:* Store in the coldest part of the refrigerator and use within two days. Giblets should be rewrapped.

Fats and oils:

• *Mayonnaise* and *salad dressings* should be refrigerated after opening.

• *Margarine* and *butter* should be covered and kept in the refrigerator for no longer than two weeks.

• *Hydrogenated shortenings* and *lard* may be stored at room temperature.

Everything else:

• *Honey* and *syrup* should be kept at room temperature until opened and then refrigerated. If crystals form in honey, put the container in hot water.

• *Jellies, jams, preserves, catsup* and *chili sauce* should be refrigerated after opening.

• *Leftover cooked meats, stuffing* and *gravy* should all be quickly cooled by placing the container in cold water. Cover and refrigerate right away. Remove stuffing from poultry, cool immediately and store in refrigerator. Cover gravy and refrigerate immediately. Use all these foods within two days.

• *Eggs* should be stored in refrigerator and used within a week. Egg whites and yolks should be covered and refrigerated and used within two days.

• *Cheese spreads* should be covered and refrigerated after opening.

• *Hard cheese* should be kept tightly wrapped in refrigerator. It can be kept this way for months.

• *Soft cheese* should be used within two weeks, and cottage cheese within five days. (EC, MC, PA)

CANNING

Fruits, vegetables, and meats can all be canned.

How it works: Canning jars have self-sealing lids. When the jars are heated, dangerous organisms are killed. The heat causes gases in the food to expand which drives out most of the air within the jar. A vacuum is created inside the jar when it cools, which pulls the lid down against the mouth of the jar. This creates a very tight seal. No organisms can enter to cause spoilage.

What you'll need: Canning jars are made of tempered glass. They can withstand heat and heavy treatment. They come in half-pint, pint, and quart sizes.

You will need a *canning kettle* if you wish to process acid foods such as fruit, tomatoes, and certain types of pickles. This can be any kettle in which you can completely immerse your jars in hot water. Specially made canning kettles have a metal basket which separates and holds the jars off the bottom so that heat can circulate.

You will need a *steam-pressure canner*, which is a heavy kettle with a cover that locks to become steamtight. This is necessary to apply heat high enough to ensure safe canning of vegetables, meat, poultry, and fish.

You will also need *rubber-tipped tongs* to handle the jars, a good *thermometer, measuring cups* and *measuring spoons* and *a funnel* to help you fill the jars, a *colander,* some long-handled *ladles* and *spoons,* and a food *chopper.*

Safety first: The important word is *safety* because you don't want your canned foods to kill your family and friends. Do you? Don't take any shortcuts. Follow all instructions exactly.

Water bath canning: This method is used for fruit, tomatoes, pickles. These acid foods are put into jars and heated in a hot water bath using a canning kettle. The water should be 180° to 190° F., or simmering. This will destroy organisms that could cause spoilage in these foods. For low-acid foods such as vegetables, meats, poultry, and fish, the steam-pressure method must be used with a steam pressure canner.

Botulism usually occurs in low-acid foods. The organisms that are responsible can live well without air, will not be killed by being processed at 212° F. (the boiling point of water) and can't be detected when a jar is opened. This is why foods other than acid foods *must* be processed at 240° F. in a steam-pressure canner. *If you have the slightest doubt about any food, throw it out. If a jar has a bulging lid, if it is oozing, or has bubbles, throw it out. If the lid is corroded, throw it out. If the food looks mushy or moldy, throw it out.*

How to dispose of contaminated food: Absolutely **never pour polluted food down the drain.** It will contaminate the water supply. Instead, you *must* boil the food for at least ten minutes. *Then* you can flush it down the toilet. Boil the lid, ring, and jar in detergent and water before throwing them away. Wash your hands in a bleach solution..

Remember that sealing lids may only be used once. Don't overpack food. If you are worried about the food even though you can see no particular reason to be, you can bring the food to a boil and then simmer for fifteen minutes. Then serve. (EC, PA)

PICKLING

Pickling is a method of preserving food in brine or vinegar. Pickles are usually made out of cucumbers. A relish is a blend of vegetables, fruits, spices, and vinegar.

Never use a salt substitute. Noniodized salt is best for pickling.

Distilled white vinegar preserves food color. Cider vinegar has good flavor and aroma but may cause darkening. Vinegar should have 4 to 5 percent acetic acid.

It is best to use fresh herbs and spices when pickling.

Use granulated cane or beet sugar.

Use only aluminum, stainless steel, enamelware or glass utensils. Copper will turn your pickles a sick green and iron will turn them black. *Galvanized containers will poison your pickles.*

You'll need a big pot and a canning kettle in which to process your jars and also for sterilizing them. Use a small pan for the lids. Process pickles between 170° and 180° F. Use a cooking thermometer. You can use your ring bands over and over, but use sealing lids only once. (EC, PA)

FREEZING

At 0°F., food won't spoil because freezing causes the bacteria to become inactive.

Freezing food fast will produce the least change in the food. Water in food turns to ice crystals, which can puncture cells. These crystals are much smaller the faster the freezing process. The freezer compartment of a refrigerator usually does not keep food at 10° or below. If this is the case, use these foods within two months. Use a mercury freezer thermometer to test the temperature.

Defrost your freezer regularly because built-up frost raises the temperature.

Freezer burn is caused when air inside a freezer container dries out frozen food and changes its color and flavor. Use glass, metal, rigid plastic containers, heavy aluminum foil, or clear plastic adhesive wrap to package your food. Thaw food in the refrigerator, at room temperature or under running cold water, and use it right away. It's all right to refreeze food that has been partially thawed if it feels cold and has ice crystals — but use it fairly soon.

DRYING

Drying means removing moisture from food by exposing it to increased temperature and moving air.

The temperature and circulation must be controlled so that the food does not spoil. *Sun drying* is a method that is inexpensive. Large quantities can be done at one time, but it takes a number of days at a certain temperature and low humidity. A minimum temperature of 85° F. or more is ideal.

Oven drying is done at a temperature of 130° to 150° F. Some older ovens have a minimum temperature of 200°F. and so cannot be used for this. Dehydrators maintain a low and even temperature and have a fan to circulate air. You don't have to pay them much attention. They generally have from six to twenty shelves. (EC, PA)

MEASUREMENTS

A pinch or a dash or a few grains of something means less than one-eighth of a teaspoon. A dash of liquid means a few drops.

Three teaspoons equal one tablespoon.

Four tablespoons equal one-fourth cup.

Two cups equal one pint.

Two pints equal one quart.

Four quarts equal one gallon.

One cup of pastry flour is the same as one cup of all-purpose flour, *less* two tablespoons.

When used for thickening, *one tablespoon cornstarch* is the same as two tablespoons flour.

One teaspoon of baking powder is equal to one-fourth teaspoon baking soda plus one-half teaspoon cream of tartar. (GB)

HOW TO DETERMINE THE FRESHNESS OF VEGETABLES

Green beans should not have spots or bruises, nor should they be coarse or limp.

Broccoli should have closed flower buds and the stalks should be firm and tender, but if they smell too strong, get away.

Brussels sprouts: Bugs have been around if you see black spots or holes. If they are puffy or smell too strong, don't buy them.

Cabbage should be firm.

Carrots: Smaller is better because the outside is the sweetest, and small carrots have a small fibrous core. Carrots should not bend.

Cauliflower should not have speckles. The head should be tight. As with all of us, a loose head is a sign of age.

Corn should have nice, green husks and kernels without dents.

Cucumbers should not be dull or yellow or have dark, recessed areas.

Eggplants are best in July and August.

Garlic: White skin is the strongest. Pink and purple are milder.

Lettuce should be crisp.

Mushrooms should not reveal their fluted gills. They are old if they do.

Onions should be firm and rustly.

Peas: If they are bulgy, they are probably old.

Potatoes should not be bought in big sacks because many will probably be cracked or decayed.

Scallions should have bulbs no larger than one-half inch in diameter.

Shallots are best from July to October. Bulbs should be about three-quarters inch in diameter and should be smooth and dry.

Sweet potatoes and yams should be small to medium in size and tapered on each end.

Tomatoes should be red and firm. (GB)

HOW TO DETERMINE THE FRESHNESS OF FRUITS

Apples: The best eating apples are Red or Golden Delicious. The best for baking are Golden Delicious and Rome Beauty. McIntosh and Cortland are good for eating and cooking. All apples should be firm, with tight skin.

Apricots: Best from mid-May to August. Should be golden yellow with a bit of red.

Avocados should not be black or have dark, soft spots. They should feel slightly soft, but not mushy.

Bananas are ready to eat when the green is gone and the brown spots just begin.

Grapefruit should have thin skin and not be puffy or pointed at the end.

Lemons: Rough, thick skin means a dry inside.

Limes should have no yellow. Brown spots are okay. Hard limes mean bad news and thin skins are best.

Grapes should have firm, green stems.

Kiwi fruit should give a little when squeezed a little.

Nectarines: If they are hard, green or dull-colored, they are not ripe and never ever will be, either.

Papayas can ripen once you get them home. They are ready to eat when they smell lovely.

Peaches are ready to eat when they smell fresh. Buy them already ripe, because they won't get done at home.

Pears will ripen at home. They are ready to eat when they give a little.

Pineapples should have golden orange or yellow scales. (GB)

COOKING: GOOD AND BAD NEWS

Charcoal broiling: Charcoal is not good for you. It is potentially cancer-causing. Try to cook only lean meat placed on the grill away from the coals. Place foil under the meat if you can.

Frying destroys vitamin A. It also provides fifty times more fat than baking or broiling.

Boiling kills vitamins B and C. Try to use as little water as possible and only *add the vegetables after the water has boiled.* Use a lid that fits. Never use baking soda to keep the greens green; it, too, kills vitamins.

Microwave cooking: There is more nutrient loss from dripping meats than when the meat is cooked in a conventional oven.

Crock pots can destroy the nutrients that calm the nerves. If you can use the cooking liquid, you will save those vitamin Bs.

Roasting loses you less of the nutrients than many other methods — unless you overcook. Go light on the salt while roasting.

Broiling allows the fat to drain and it saves most nutrients.

Stewing is good news as long as you cook slowly.

Baking is the best way to prepare fish.

Stir-frying cuts down calories because so little oil is used, and it saves nutrients because the food is cooked so quickly.

Steaming uses no fat; it's much better than boiling because it loses far less protein, minerals, vitamins.

Pressure cooking uses little water and saves most of the nutrients. (EC, MC, PA, SEM)

Modern Vegetation

Listen, there's more than hell and kids a Modern Woman can raise around the house.

There's something essentially rewarding about growing a rosy, red radish or nurturing a healthy strawberry. You break your back for them, sacrifice your time for them, worry about them all winter, and hope they're okay in the spring.

They become like members of the family. You shower them with love and fertilizer, and they grow strong and healthy and never sass you back.

Then, one day, you go outside, yank them out of the ground, toss them into a salad and eat them.

That's life in the food chain for you.

C O N T E N T S

Chapter Ten: *MODERN VEGETATION*

GROWING YOUR OWN OUTSIDE: Available Area — Sunlight — Soil — How to Make a Compost Heap — Seeds — Arranging Your Vegetable Garden — Garden Tools — Easy-to-Grow Veggies — Garden Tools — Some More Garden Tools — **Garden Pests** — Worm Begone — **FLOWER GARDENS: Perennial Favorites — Cheap Horticulture** — Gazebo City — Fences — **E-Z Grow — Undergrowth — APARTMENT FARMING:** Planters — **Plant Lights — Vegetables — Pet Food — HOUSEPLANTS: Bulbs** — Bulb Basics — **The Great Indoors — Deserting Your Vegetable — The Easiest Plants to Maintain** — Easy Plants — **Flower Paddies — Pests**

GROWING YOUR OWN OUTSIDE

Why waste all that real estate growing lawn when you could be growing dinner?

When it comes time to move your food supply outdoors, there are *three basic considerations* to keep in mind:
1. Available area
2. Sunlight
3. Soil

AVAILABLE AREA

Apartment dwellers have little choice about where to plant a garden. You can, however, grow a useful garden on a terrace or fire escape, provided you take care and make special provisions for the peculiarities of the environment.

• *Ensure proper irrigation.* Apartment terraces — especially those facing south or west — are baked by the sun all day. A feeder-type bottle plunged into the soil will help keep moisture to an acceptable minimum — but only temporarily. Proper and regular watering is essential.

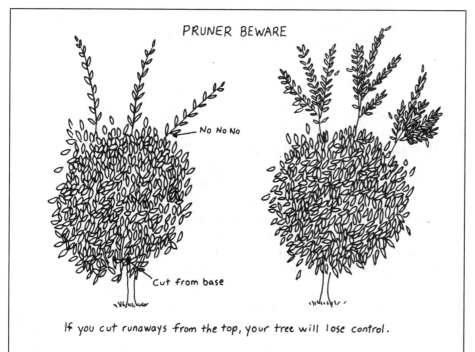

PRUNER BEWARE

No No No

Cut from base

If you cut runaways from the top, your tree will lose control.

• *Diffuse harsh sunlight* by means of a slat blind or screen.

• *Use planters designed for your purpose.* Many apartment garden tubs have reservoirs to make sure the plants don't dry out. (RHW) **See also under** *APARTMENT FARMING,* **below.**

Kitchen gardens should be situated near enough to the house to allow for easy access, but far enough away to avoid the harsh, reflective sunlight that can come off a nearby building.

• *Pay attention to drainage.* You don't want your garden to become a springtime swamp or a summer desert. Carefully survey the lay of the land surrounding your house before you plot a garden.

• *There's no such thing as a garden that's too small.* A bean plant and a tomato plant and a handful of herbs is enough to justify planting a garden. (RHW)

• *A dissent:* Your time is worth money. Calculate how much time and money you will spend on a garden and you will most likely decide to pick your vegetables from the produce section of the local supermarket. (HS)

SUNLIGHT

Some flowers like full shade, others like partial shade and many prosper in full sunlight, but *vegetables need at least six to ten hours of direct sunlight.*

When you've chosen an area, watch the sunlight pass over to make sure there is exposure to continuous sunlight.

Remember that *areas next to a wall* — especially a light-colored one — will get a sort of double dose of light because of the reflected sunlight they'll receive. (HWY)

SOIL

Soil quality is crucial to creating a successful garden. Make sure you're not planting in clay or sand, and don't start working the soil or planting anything if the soil is too wet or cold.

To test, dig down about six inches into the soil and check for moisture and temperature.

The best soil contains balanced amounts of sand, clay and decomposed organic matter. When the soil is workable, break it up down to twelve inches below the surface.

• *If it is a heavy clay or extremely sandy soil,* improve it by working in organic matter, such as manure or compost. **See** *How to Make a Compost Heap,* **below.**

• *Test the pH* to determine the alkalinity or acidity of the soil. You can buy a pH test kit at your nursery or, in the United States, you can send some soil to a county-run laboratory (usually operated by the county agriculture department). The home testing kit will have directions and what to do with your soil to fix it up. (RL)

HOW TO MAKE A COMPOST HEAP

Ideally, you should *start your compost pile in autumn* for the following spring's planting.

WATER WASTE

Avoid sprinkling in the wind.

• Place a dozen eight-foot posts, two feet deep, in a four- to six-foot square, four posts to a side. String chicken wire or nail loose boards (leave space between the boards) between the posts until you have an enclosure about four feet high.

• Spread a layer of plant remains like old vegetables, grass cuttings or leaves on the ground in the enclosure. On top of that sprinkle a cup and a half of fertilizer — a 10/10/10 mixture has equal parts nitrogen, phosphorus and potash and seems to do the trick best under most conditions. Your nursery can help you with this if you're unsure.

• Then add about an inch of garden soil and lightly moisten the heap. At this point, check the salinity level with a testing kit from the nursery — you may have to add some limestone to bring the pH balance into line.

• Add new plant garbage every day until the layer is about a foot thick. Then repeat the layering process, the 10/10/10 fertilizer and more soil and water.

• Keep this up until the heap is about four feet deep. Keep the top slightly concave so the pile can collect rainfall.

• Let it sit over the winter and then turn it with a pitchfork in the early spring, making sure that all parts of the heap are moist.

Start a new pile every year, using the previous year's supply. Turn it into the soil for use as a fertilizer, applying it to the soil a few days before planting your seeds or seedlings. (AP)

SEEDS

Timeliness: You must buy your seeds for the current season; the date is printed on every seed packet. If it isn't, don't buy them. Never plant seeds packed for the previous year, no matter how cheap they are. (ALy)

Get your seeds from a reputable company. There are many mail-order seed catalogs available, and you can find them at most libraries or send away to obtain your own catalog. The seeds available at your nursery will probably do just fine. (TF)

ARRANGING YOUR VEGETABLE GARDEN

You can plant seeds two ways, in rows or in beds.

Everybody knows what *rows* look like. You simply build up the soil in long mounds about twelve inches wide and twelve inches apart. Some people prefer planting in rows, as it is easier to reach, weed and mulch your plants.

With *bed planting*, it actually looks like a small bed — the mound is raised to be about three feet wide and six feet long. The bed sowing method is more space-efficient and easier to water, but it's harder to reach individual plants.

Always plant *the tallest vegetables* along the north side of the garden. According to mature height of each plant (look on the seed packet for this information), gradually plant towards the south, with the smallest plants along the southernmost border. (RL)

Plant *corn* at least three rows deep, not in one long row. (FG)

Creeping vegetables, like *squash and melons,* should be planted at the edge of a garden. They can send runners as long as ten feet. (HPD) **See** *Easy-to-Grow Veggies,* **below.**

Growing *nasturtiums among tomatoes* helps keep down insect infestation. Creeping thyme also helps. (TP) **Also see** *Garden Pests,* **below.**

GARDEN TOOLS

Here's a list of *essential tools.* You really will need them if you're going to garden with any seriousness, so buy, borrow or rent

- A spade
- A spading fork
- A steelbow rake
- A common hoe
- A trowel
- A wheelbarrow
- A wheel hoe, if you have a garden larger than 2,000 square feet (AS, RL)

EASY-TO-GROW VEGGIES

There are lots of vegetables that practically grow on their own. If you don't want an extensive garden, or if you don't have room for one, you can still harvest your dinner with minimum effort. Give them full sunlight and water as necessary.

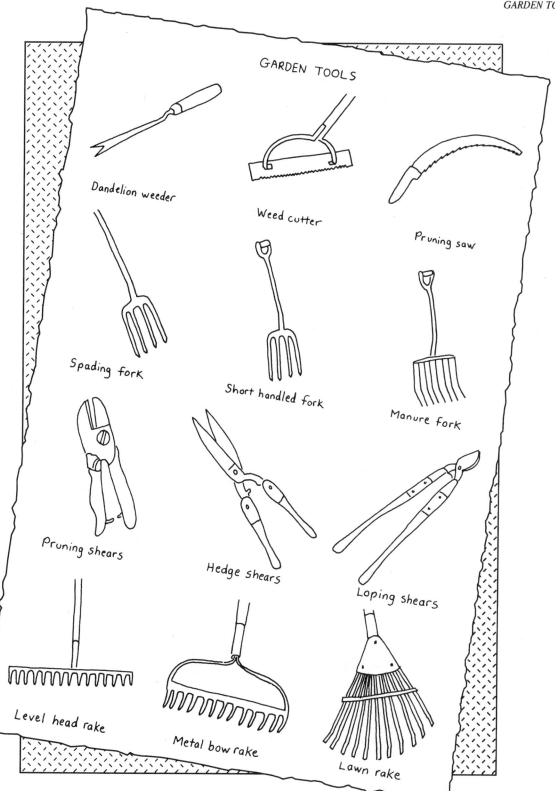

GARDEN TOOLS

Dandelion weeder

Weed cutter

Pruning saw

Spading fork

Short handled fork

Manure fork

Pruning shears

Hedge shears

Loping shears

Level head rake

Metal bow rake

Lawn rake

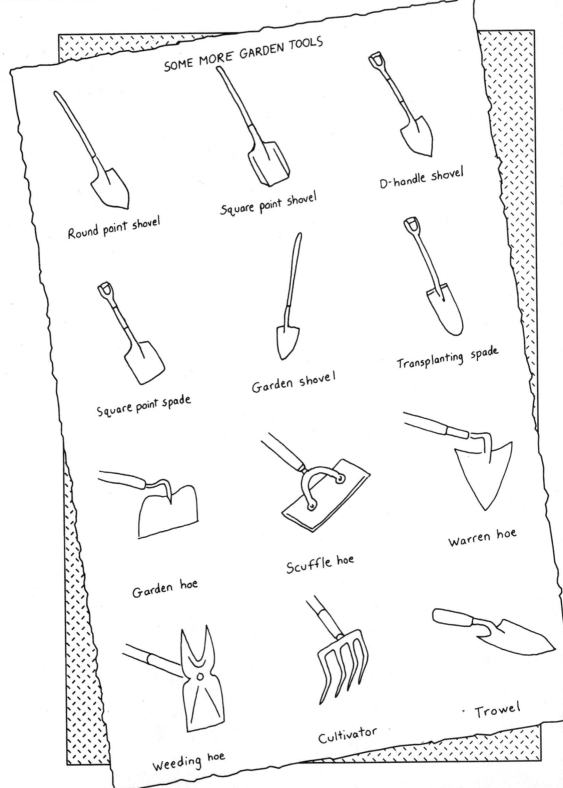

SOME MORE GARDEN TOOLS

Round point shovel

Square point shovel

D-handle shovel

Square point spade

Garden shovel

Transplanting spade

Garden hoe

Scuffle hoe

Warren hoe

Weeding hoe

Cultivator

Trowel

Minimum-care vegetables:

- Cucumbers
- Potatoes
- Corn
- Tomatoes
- Radishes
- Carrots
- Green onions
- Swiss chard
- Spinach
  . . .and every squash in the world (HPD, RL)

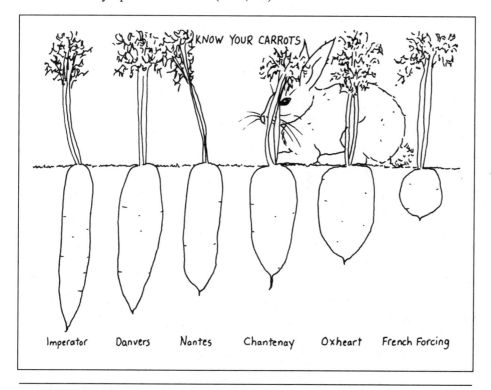

KNOW YOUR CARROTS

| Imperator | Danvers | Nantes | Chantenay | Oxheart | French Forcing |

GARDEN PESTS

are the Vandals, Huns and Visigoths of your peaceful, green empire. To keep the barbarians at bay:

Gophers: Place a six-inch strip of window screen around the bottom of the plant — three inches below the ground, three inches above. (MD) *When you find a gopher hole,* put the garden hose into the hole and turn the water on full blast for about fifteen minutes. Or use poison. (TC)

Birds can be tricked into eating something other than your plants. Plant a bunch of sunflowers or a berry bush nearby. (RL)

Don't hang a bird feeder around your house if you're worried about birds eating your plants. You'll have birds from all over the county to your place for dinner. (TP)

Rabbits should avoid your garden if you surround it with nicotiana or rosemary. (RL)

Insects and worms can sometimes be diverted by sprinkling cigarette ashes or coffee grounds all over your plants or by spraying them all with garlic juice. (TC) **See also under** *Pests,* **below.**

Take *a sample of the worm* you hate to your nursery person. She'll give you a specific cure. (SK) Or curse.

FLOWER GARDENS

A flower garden is a manifestation of the ultimate outdoor alchemy — all that beauty from all that mud.

PERENNIAL FAVORITES

Basically, there are two types of flowers, *annuals* and *perennials.* Annuals bloom for only one season, while perennials will bloom for two or more years. As you plan your garden, take this into account; if you choose a variety that has to be dug up and replaced annually, you might want to make sure you don't have to put the rest of your flora under your jackboot in the process. Seed packets will tell you if the varieties you've chosen are annuals or perennials as well as how deep to plant the seeds, when to plant them and how much sunlight and moisture they'll need to survive.

CHEAP HORTICULTURE

There are a few considerations you must make before planting a flower garden.

Tend the soil, working in lots of leaf mold, compost or peat moss to ensure good drainage. **See above under** *GROWING YOUR OWN OUTSIDE.*

Prepare the planting beds by digging the soil to a depth of twelve inches, thoroughly turning the compost into it, and breaking up large clumps of dirt and chucking out rocks.

Colors: Plan in advance what colors you want in the garden to achieve harmonious color blends. White flowers can always be used as fillers. Try not to put several different types of flowers of the same color together.

Space seedlings properly, as crowded plants grow less vigorously. If you sow seeds directly into beds, thin the emerging seedlings to leave space for the remaining plants.

When planting seedlings make sure all the roots are covered with soil and press the soil firmly all around the plant, then water thoroughly.

Fertilize annuals and perennials at planting time. This gives them a good start. (KF)

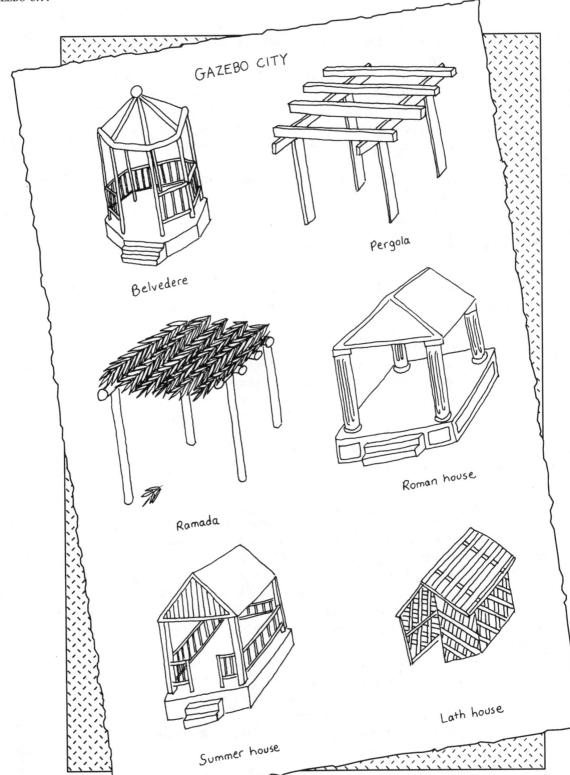

GAZEBO CITY

Belvedere

Pergola

Ramada

Roman house

Summer house

Lath house

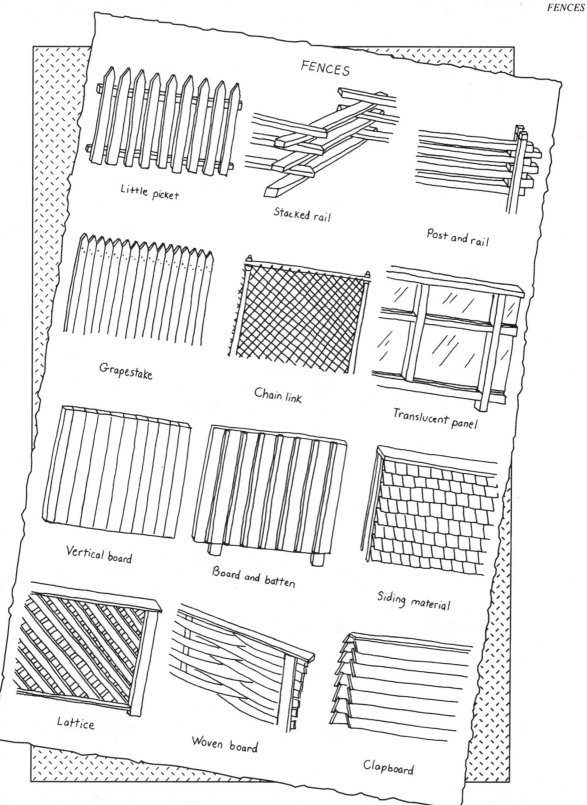

FENCES

Little picket

Stacked rail

Post and rail

Grapestake

Chain link

Translucent panel

Vertical board

Board and batten

Siding material

Lattice

Woven board

Clapboard

E-Z GRO

There are some *flowers that are easy to grow* for beginners and are also perfect for cut flower arrangements:

- Daisies
- Zinnias
- Bachelor buttons
- Carnations
- Cosmos
- Nasturtiums
- Forget-me-nots
- Phlox
- Marigolds
- Geraniums
- Calendulas
- Peonies (TR)

UNDERGROWTH

If you have only a small patio or balcony, or have very little time to devote to maintaining a garden, you can buy dwarf roses or fruit trees, grow some *vegetables* in pots (tomatoes, green onions, cucumbers or green peppers), or enjoy an array of *flowers* and vines grown in pots or planter boxes or on trellises. **See** *Available Area,* **above.**

Herbs can also be grown on a sunny kitchen window or out on the balcony. **See below under** *APARTMENT FARMING.* It takes very little effort and time for such a lovely reward. (RL)

APARTMENT FARMING

Many recipes call for a weird ingredient — some small, leafy rarity — that you have never heard of but *must* have just this one time.

When you finally find it in the store it costs $6 for an ounce of the stuff. So you buy it and you never use it again for twenty years.

Why not grow it instead? Then it won't matter how often you actually use it in your recipes, because in its spare time, it's busy decorating your apartment with its little spikes and leaves and buds.

It's easy to do. You say you live on the twelfth floor? No problem, you can grow crops on your windowsill. No windows? No problem, you can grow salad in an air shaft.

Don't put roadblocks in your way. Think of this as agriculture and reap the benefits.

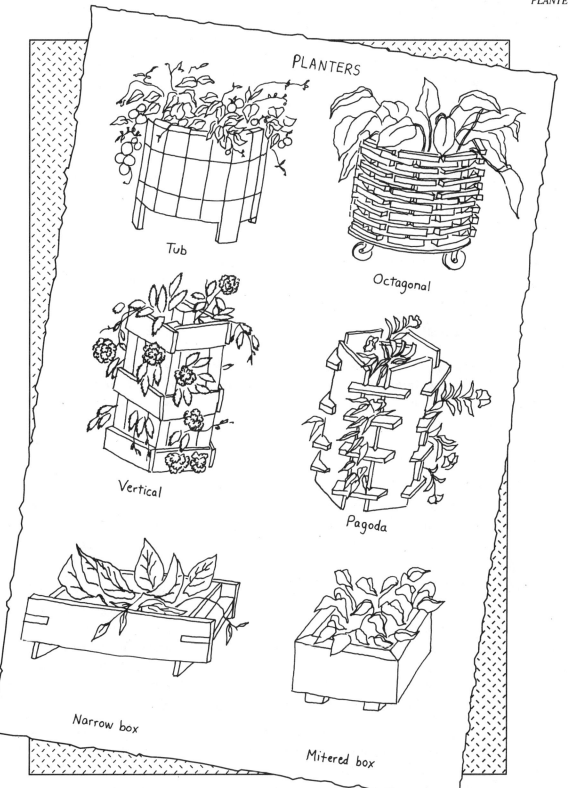

PLANTERS

Tub

Octagonal

Vertical

Pagoda

Narrow box

Mitered box

PLANT LIGHTS

Plants look fine, but they aren't long on thought. For example, you can trick any plant into growing in an otherwise dark room simply by turning on a plant light. Because you can monitor them and achieve an ideal amount of growth light, plant lamps are as good as — if not better than — a sunny exposure.(BG)

VEGETABLES

Burdock: This plant is used in many Oriental dishes. Sauté very thin slices of the root in oil and mix with other vegetables. To grow, plant seeds two inches apart and a quarter-inch deep in four-inch pots.

Chinese cabbage: Plant anytime indoors, but keep out of the hottest sun in the summer. Plant seeds eight inches apart and a half-inch deep. Thin to twelve inches.

Collards: Plant in four- to eight-inch pots. These plants are tough little bunnies and can stand the heat of summer sun and the freeze of winter, if you like your windows open in January.

Cress: You can grow cress in a shallow tray by sprinkling seeds on wet cheesecloth that has been placed on top of potting mix. Keep the cheesecloth moist. Use cress as a garnish.

Endive: Plant in four- to eight-inch pots. Blanch — first draw the outer leaves together and tie with string — to lessen bitterness. Use in sandwiches and salads.

Horseradish: Place roots a foot apart in a large container. The small end of the root should face up, and the large end should be two inches below the surface. Horseradish needs plenty of sun and grows the most in the late summer to be ready in the early fall. Give the plant sun from a south- or east-facing window. Pull the whole root up when ready.

Purslane: Some people think this is a weed, but you can steam it and serve it with butter and be very happy with the result. Plant in four- to eight-inch pots about three inches apart and then thin to six inches. Pick the leaves when young.

Rocket: For a surprise blast, put a little rocket in your salads. It's strong and tastes like horseradish. Plant in four- to eight-inch pots. Does best at about 60° F.

HERBS

Basil: Plant basil in an eight-inch container, leaving about two inches between each plant. The more you cut, the more they grow, so snip snip snip those stems. After the plants flower you should cut them about six inches from the ground. Dry them and strip them and store the flowers and leaves in a jar.

Chives: Chives are among the easiest herbs to grow. Simply plant them in a sunny window and clip off what you need.

Marjoram: Plant in a pot at least four inches big. The leaves may be pulled at any time, and they will quickly be replaced by new ones. To dry marjoram, pick the leaves just before the blossoms appear.

Oregano: Oregano is a perennial but should be replaced every two to three years. Grow in four-inch pots. Pick the leaves as you need them, or dry and store them.

Rosemary: Rosemary is a perennial that grows to six feet tall, but you can buy a dwarf variety for your apartment window farm. Buy a little plant from the nursery and grow in a four-inch pot. Cut off the leaves whenever you need them. Water well only when the soil begins to feel dry.

Summer savory: Grow in four-inch pots in full sun.

Tarragon: Tarragon can be grown in a four-inch pot from cuttings, from seed, or from seedlings purchased at a nursery.

Thyme: As easy as tarragon and all the rest. Cut the plants when they are in full bloom, then cut them back to the ground after they flower.

Sprouts: This is the food that's too cute to eat. Grow sprouts by soaking the seeds in water until they are saturated (large seeds take overnight). Sprinkle sprouts on a damp cheesecloth in a Pyrex baking dish. Spray several times a day with lukewarm water and drain while keeping them moist and at room temperature. After they sprout they will need lots of light. (EC, KJ, FDD)

PET FOOD

Got a cat? She like to eat grass? You live on the twentieth floor? *Grow grass* on a sponge!

• *Put your sponge into a bowl* and fill the bowl halfway with water.

• *Sprinkle some grass seeds* onto your sponge and push them gently down so that they are soaked but not drowned.

• *Keep adding water* every day so that the sponge stays wet.

Pretty soon you'll have a little lawn for kitty.

If you don't have a cat, you can use your sponge to grow *chives* or *parsley*. (EA)

HOUSEPLANTS

Cuter than pets, quieter than kids, houseplants are a gorgeous way to brighten up your home.

BULBS

One way to make it easier to get through a dismal winter is to have pots and bowls of forced bulbs everywhere. The bulbs are very inexpensive and the process effortless. Here's how it works.

Buy your bulbs at a grocery or hardware store or at a nursery in October. *Hyacinths, daffodils, narcissuses, crocuses* and *tulips* are best for forcing blooms indoors. Amaryllises are easy, too, and deliver a good show, but you can't force the bloom in water.

Grounded: You can either place bulbs in soil — one part loamy soil, one part peat and one part sand — or place bulbs in cleaned pebbles and cover with water three-quarters of the way to the top of the pebbles.

BULB BASICS

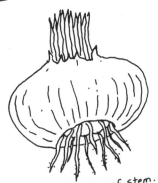

True bulb: short stem surrounded by fleshy leaves and dry outer scales. Bulblets can be divided and replanted.

Corm: swollen portion of stem. New corms form on top of old ones. Save them for future planting.

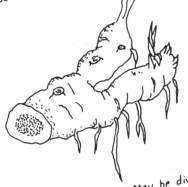

Rhizome: creepy stem. May be divided as long as each division has a growth bud.

Tuber: Short and fat stem. Not creepy like rhizome. Lots of eyes. Divides like rhizome.

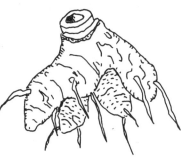

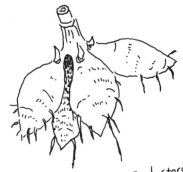

Tuberous rhizome: Slender. Tubers may form at end of each branch.

Tuberous root: roots with food storage structures. Divides like rhizomes or tubers. Each section must include an eye.

• If they are planted in soil, they need *sharp drainage*, otherwise they will rot.

• In the water/pebble method, the plants will only last a few weeks due to rot.

If you choose to plant in soil, fill the pot loosely with soil; don't compress the soil and don't fertilize it. The tops of the bulbs should be even with the rim of the pot. Keep them in the soil for about five weeks in a cool and dark — but not damp — place, then bring them indoors. The warmth and light will trigger growth and blossoms.

Bulbs grown in pebbles do not need to be put in the dark; they will bloom within two weeks if they get enough light. You will have continuous blooms well into the spring. (RL)

THE GREAT INDOORS

No plant was made to grow indoors. Through hybridization and lots of fooling around with nature, however, some plants can actually thrive indoors if they are properly cared for.

Light and water are the two critical factors in successful indoor gardening, so avoid overwatering and don't keep your plants in too dark a place.

Most plants, when domesticated, need bright indirect sunlight. While many houseplants will tolerate a few hours of direct winter sun, they won't put up with direct summer sun. (RL)

In winter, cut down on watering, as most plants go through a sort of off-season hibernation. (DU)

Check for moisture: The best way to see if your plant needs water is to put your finger into the soil. You'll be able to feel the moistness or dryness easily.

• If your plants' leaves turn yellow and become droopy, you're probably *overwatering*.

• Brown foliage and falling leaves usually indicate the plants are *not getting enough light* or *enough water*.

• *Too little light* causes a plant to lose or elongate leaves.

• *Too much light* causes a plant to wilt and lose its color.

• *Forget misting* your plants unless you plan to mist ten times a day. Instead of misting, buy a small air humidifier and place it in the room. Keep air circulation constant and dust or sponge leaves once in a while, as dirt and dust can clog up the plant's pores. An easier way to wash your plants is to give them a shower once a month.

Water plants thoroughly — no half cups — so that you do more than darken the soil on the top. The water must seep through the bottom to ensure all the roots have been replenished.

Don't allow the plant to sit in the water in the dish. Throw out the water after draining the pot. Use only tepid water, not hot, not cold.

When applying *fertilizers*, read the label and follow directions — with this modification: Generally, use only half the amount recommended, but twice as often.

Dormant or sick plants never benefit from fertilizer. (RL)

DESERTING YOUR VEGETABLE

Leaving town for a while? Can't find anyone to feed your plant? Here's a survival guide for lonely houseplants:

• Give it *lots of water*. Soak the soil.

• *Wrap* your plant up in a large plastic bag. Loosely.

• *Poke* a few holes through the plastic at the bottom.

That's it. Your plant will survive your vacation quite happily. In fact, it may never even know you've gone. (JL)

THE EASIEST PLANTS TO MAINTAIN

Don't sit around like the Fisher King wondering why your thumb is so apocalyptic. Here's a list of plants that can outwit even your deadly touch:

African violets: These will bloom almost year-round if given indirect sunlight and soil that hasn't been over-fertilized and kept well drained and rich in humus. Water with moderate frequency; never let plants dry out completely. A constant temperature should be maintained — 60° to 70° F. is ideal.

Aloe: Aloe does the best in dry air and with plenty of sunlight. Water just enough to keep it from shriveling. If you snap a leaf you'll see a sort of gummy substance that is excellent for healing cuts, burns and other skin irritations.

Asparagus fern is a great plant for a hanging pot. It likes just ordinary soil and filtered sunlight. Allow the soil to dry out between watering.

• *Aralia* likes good indirect sunlight and shade — an east window is ideal. An aralia prefers some humidity and won't grow in dry air.

• *Avocado:* The Universal Kid Science Project Houseplant. Halfway down the pit, insert three toothpicks. Then fill a glass of water and rest the toothpicks on rim of glass so that the half of the pit with the rounded end hangs down into the water. Leave this attractive arrangement of avacado pit, toothpicks and jelly glass in a bright window and soon the miracle of rebirth will block your view of the neighbors' pool. Pinch back the seedling regularly or it will become very tall and leggy. In a no-frost climate, you can transplant the plant outside; avocado trees are quite attractive and make good medium-size shade trees.

• *Baby's tears* is especially nice as ground cover around other plants. The plant must be constantly moist and shielded from direct sunlight.

Begonias: When in the growth period, keep begonias fairly well watered. When the growth cycle ceases, reduce your watering and let the plant rest until the next cycle. Begonias require good light, but not direct sun. Pinch back regularly.

Bird's-nest ferns need regular potting soil with good drainage. Place the plant near a window woth a northern exposure so it will receive indirect light only. Water thoroughly. Bird's-nest ferns love high humidity.

Bromeliad: Keep warm and moist. Water right in the center where there is a little cuplike formation. Light is necessary, but this plant also prefers some shade.

Cacti are surprisingly delicate. Most species must have sandy soil and good light and drainage. Be careful of overwatering.

Caladiums are draft sensitive, so don't place one in an air-conditioned room. They grow

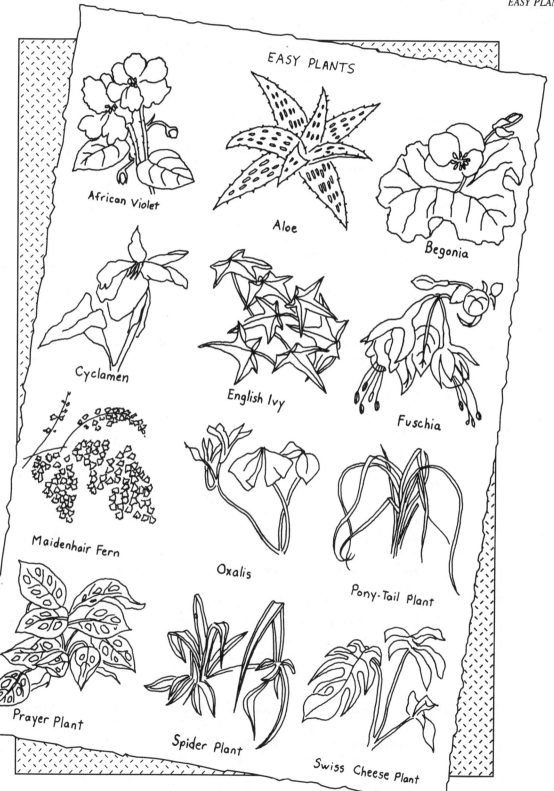

EASY PLANTS

African Violet

Aloe

Begonia

Cyclamen

English Ivy

Fuschia

Maidenhair Fern

Oxalis

Pony-Tail Plant

Prayer Plant

Spider Plant

Swiss Cheese Plant

best in rich soil and should be placed in a warm, well-lighted place — but *not* in direct sunlight. Water just enough to keep the soil damp to the touch.

Chinese evergreens are great indoor plants because they can stand both poor light and a reasonable amount of brown-thumb neglect. Allow the soil to dry between soakings.

Coleus: Everybody's easy-to-grow indoor favorite. Good light encourages strong colors; pinch back the purplish flower stems for continued leaf growth.

Cyclamen: The soil used to pot a cyclamen should be well drained, but never allowed to dry out completely. Give a cyclamen moderately good light but keep the plant cool when it's in bloom. High temperatures or too little light can cause leaves to yellow and the buds to drop.

Corn plants will grow in poor light but like warmth and constant moisture at roots. Protect them from sudden chills or drafts.

Dumbcane: Don't chomp on the leaves! They aren't called dumbcane for nothing: one good bite can leave you with temporary mouth or tongue paralysis. The plant can withstand moderate heat, dry air, poor light and needs only moderate watering. But if you allow chill air to reach it, it goes quick.

English ivy can grow twenty feet high along a wall or trellis or it can be used as a ground cover. English ivy requires little sun and you can allow soil to dry completely between waterings. It's most attractive when used as a hanging plant but grows better when allowed to climb a trellis.

Ficus: Likes moderate to good light and an even supply of moisture at the roots. The common variety can stand air conditioning. Ficus will grow very tall, so pinch it back from time to time. It will propagate in water.

Fuchsia is an ideal hanging plant that likes good light but not too much hot or dry air. Water frequently when blooming. Give it a water rest in winter. Pinch back to prevent legginess.

Grape ivy is very adaptable vine with no special needs. Give it ordinary soil, light and water. Nothing extraterrestrial.

Geranium: Loves sunshine and moderate watering. A geranium must be pot-bound or it will not produce flowers.

Jade plants like sun but will survive in shade nicely. Allow the soil to dry for several days before rewatering.

Maidenhair Fern: Keep out of sunlight and away from heat sources. A maidenhair can't tolerate drafts and likes warmth. Never allow the soil to dry out completely.

Palm: Good in shady places. Keep evenly moist. Doesn't mind air conditioning.

Pineapple: Take off the top with all the leaves and a piece of the core from the fruit — twist it out, don't cut it. Peel off some of the short leaves at the bottom so the stem is one and a half inches long. Let the top dry for a day. Plant the core so the stem bottom is covered. Keep the soil slightly moist. After a couple of weeks in a sunny place, your plant will begin to sprout. (EA)

Orchids grow well in pots of fern root, fir bark or shredded tree fern. They need warm, moist air and good light. Avoid placing them in direct sun. Make sure they get a thorough weekly watering.

Oxalis: Needs a sunny, airy window. Keep soil evenly moist.

Philodendrons prefer warmth and reasonably good light but will tolerate just about any condition. Does better if trellised rather than hanging. Along with the *rhododendron* (no relation), philodendrons take the survive-at-all-costs prize.

Evidence: I once grew a philodendron in a closet. (CK)

Piggyback plant: Requires ordinary conditions and moderate light. Don't allow the soil to dry between waterings.

Ponytail plant: Give this one sun and warmth and a rare watering. In winter, don't water at all.

Pothos can withstand heat or poor light but should be kept fairly dry at roots.

Prayer plant: Moderate light and warmth and constant moisture, please.

Rubber plants are easy and have no special requirements. Water them occasionally, keep them away from direct sunlight and wash their leaves every few weeks. Pinch the plant back if it gets too tall and starts leaning over. Try to avoid those ten-foot redwood stakes unless you're going for some sort of primeval ooze look.

Silver-laced fern can grow with an absolute minimum of care and is good for terrariums or as a ground cover for larger plants.

Snake plants can grow through total neglect. Water only occasionally.

Spathiphyllum: Tolerates moderate room temperatures and light. Keep soil evenly moist.

Spider plants grow under nearly any condition but "spider" better in sunny, airy spaces. Propagate by cutting and planting offshoots in ordinary soil.

String-of-hearts: Keep moist in summer, drier in winter, but always in well-drained soil. Needs moderate light and warmth.

Sweet potato: Fill a glass jar with water to one inch from the top. Find a sweet potato that has little buds near the top, and set it into the jar so that a third of it is in the water. You can hold it in position with toothpicks. Place it in light, but avoid the direct sun. Keep the water at the same level. After about a month you can pot or plant your sweet potato. Keep it in a light place and train your vine to grow round and round your room, hither and thither.

Swiss cheese plants need minimum care, with only a piece of wood to cling to. Water sparingly.

Velvet plant: Give plenty of sun to encourage deep purple colors, and moderate amounts of water. If it gets too leggy, pinch it back. You can root cuttings in water, then transplant them to soil. (EA, DB, PL, RL, CK, KK, DY, JJ)

FLOWER PADDIES

A number of plants can be grown in water, then transplanted. *African violets, begonias, coleus, geraniums, grape ivies* and *philodendrons* are all amphibians at heart.

To take a shoot for propagation: Cut the plant just below the point at which a leaf is growing. Cut off the top of the cutting, leaving a stem (**see illustration**). Put it in a clean glass, jar or bottle, removing any leaves that are under the water. When roots appear, place in a nice soil mixture and jump back. (RL)

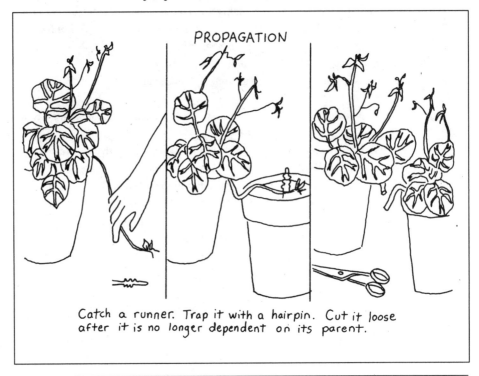

PROPAGATION

Catch a runner. Trap it with a hairpin. Cut it loose after it is no longer dependent on its parent.

PESTS

Nicotine is not good for humans and just as bad for bugs — but unlike humans, insects have the good sense to avoid the stuff. Try sprinkling the contents of a couple cigarette butts on the soil of your houseplants to repel harmful pests. (LE)

Modern Woman
at Ease

You run ragged all day in a world so complicated you don't understand half of what's going on.

So you come home, prop up your feet and turn on a little gadget that's so complicated you don't understand half of what it does.

Free-time enthusiasms come in different styles. Subjecting yourself to voluntary incomprehension is sometimes called "leisure." If you actually understand what you're doing, it's called "a hobby." If it's something that requires no thought and lots of expensive clothes, it's called "fitness." None of this stuff, though, is ever called "fun."

Modern Women know that *fun* isn't something you make, that it's not the result of a long, exhausting pursuit. Modern Women know fun is something that finds *you*.

C O N T E N T S
Chapter Eleven: *MODERN WOMAN AT EASE*

TECHS/MECHS: The Rule of the Moving Part — The Ancillary Rule — Life on Videotape — First Things First — VCR: The Next Step — Choosing the Right VCR — Happy Hooking — VCR Tip — Home Movies — TELEPHONES: Information — When You Hear the Beep... — PHOTOGRAPHY: Some Cameras — **How to Make a Pinhole Camera — COMPUTERS: Compute Your Uses — Software First — Apple or IBM? — Glossary — A Bolt from the Blue — Changing Tunes — THE GREAT OUTDOORS: Camping — When You Have the Urge to Sleep Under the Stars —** Ant, Centipede, Tiger Awareness — Bad Sea Items — **Emergencies — Camp Life —** Bad Outdoor Bugs — **Basic Camp First-Aid Kit — FOOTBALL:** Football Field — **The Object — How They Do It — Touchdown — Equal Time — Femme Fan Hints — SAUCE STUPIDE: Ice Breaker, Breaker — Basic Liquor Lore — Wine — How to Read a Wine Label — Boy Booze, Girl Booze — Don't Water the Animals — Drunk Driving Guests — Daily Dumb — Firmly Dumb — Strange Cities — How to Crash a Party — How to Make a Great Martini — Hangover Therapy — BOREDOM: Alien Experience — Booked Up — Docu-Roids — Bored Working Stiff — Twenty-Minute Burnout — Boredom Deluxe — Modern Ed — HOW TO SET UP AN ART STUDIO: Space: The Final Frontier — Adjustable — Distraction — BIBLIOPHILIA: How to Preserve Papers**

TECHS/MECHS

Modern technology is marked by the rise of electrical gadgets that are exceedingly small and move in mysterious ways. In this, they resemble seraphim and cherubim. Except in price and comprehensibility. A bell and a whistle and a little red light on something unfathomably technical will boost its cost to heaven.

THE RULE OF THE MOVING PART

Here's the bottom line on technology: The fewer moving parts a gadget has, the less likely it is to break down. (JNT)

THE ANCILLARY RULE

The fewer moving parts a gadget has, the less likely it will be to break down, but the more expensive it will be to repair when it does. (DB)

LIFE ON VIDEOTAPE

If life isn't good enough the first time around, put it on tape and replay it with special effects. Live through the best moments in slo-mo, then fast-forward through that blind date back in '73 and the time you walked out of the ladies' room with your skirt tucked neatly into your pantyhose. That's what progress is all about. **See** *Home Movies,* **below.**

FIRST THINGS FIRST

Before you start worrying about video-cassette recorders, worry about the TV on which you'll watch all your videotapes.

Choosing a TV: The best place to find the television of your dreams is a large appliance or department store, the kind with a whole wall of TVs tuned to the same channel. Look at the pictures, not the brand names. Use *your* eyes and *your* head, not the salesman's. (MK) **See also under** *Backtracking* **in** *CHAPTER SIX: MODERN MERCHANDISE.*

Features: If you think you will be using your TV set as a component in a larger audio-video set-up, then remember what you're shopping for is a monitor, not just a TV. In a monitor, compatibility with component systems is as important as a good picture. (LDC)

A bedroom TV, if you must have such a thing, should be equipped with a remote unit. It's the most important feature next to the picture, especially on cold nights when the only person who will talk to you is Ted Koppel. (LDC)

VCR: THE NEXT STEP

Very Careful Reaction: While the letters VCR have been known to strike fear into the hearts and minds of the hardiest, all a VCR really is is a machine to either record images or play previously recorded images on magnetic tape. In this it's strikingly similar to an audio cassette deck.

Tape: The only reason videotape is wider than the tape in an audio cassette is that it has to hold more information. The VCR reads this information and processes it, then sends out signals to the TV set, which then makes a picture. That's all — no black magic. (MK) **See under** *Happy Hooking,* **below.**

CHOOSING THE RIGHT VCR

There are two important factors to consider when deciding on the type of video cassette machine you need — format and use.

Format: There are basically two formats to video cassettes: VHS (which stands for Video Home System) and Beta. VHS is much more prevalent, and if you're looking to use your machine for playback of movies from the video store or with tapes you make with a VHS video camera (VHS-format cameras are also the most common type), you should be looking for a VHS machine.

Use: Are you going to use your machine just for playback of prerecorded tapes? If so, you can save some money by buying a video cassette player with no recording capacity. However, if you want to record programs from your television or an outside source, you'll need a video cassette recorder (VCR). There are gradations of quality and function (and, correspondingly, price) in VCRs, but there are two basic things to look for: ease of programming and quality of playback. (See below.)

Shopping tips: When you've decided on your basic video needs, it's time to visit the store. Your best bet for a research visit is the biggest, most expensive electronics store you can find. Look for one that carries as many brand names as possible. The salespeople in these stores should be fairly knowledgeable and able to answer most of your questions. However, they may also throw a lot of techno-jargon at you, so insist that they explain things in layman's terms. Look for a VCR that has a programming system that makes sense to you. Remember that the quality of picture reproduction of any VCR can be affected by the quality of the picture your TV produces and the quality of the tape you're playing, as well as the quality of the VCR itself. (MK)

Take notes: When you've picked a model you feel you can live with, note the brand and model number. Then make your way to a discount electronics store and start shopping for your best price. Work really hard to buy cheap, because the video industry is constantly upgrading and you could find that your machine has been completely outmoded in a relatively short time. You won't feel so bad about this if you've gotten a good buy. (CS) **See under** *Backtracking* **in** *CHAPTER SIX: MODERN MERCHANDISING.*

HAPPY HOOKING

Why is it that most VCR manuals have hook-up diagrams that look like wiring plans for the space shuttle? Some of the smartest people on the planet have found themselves

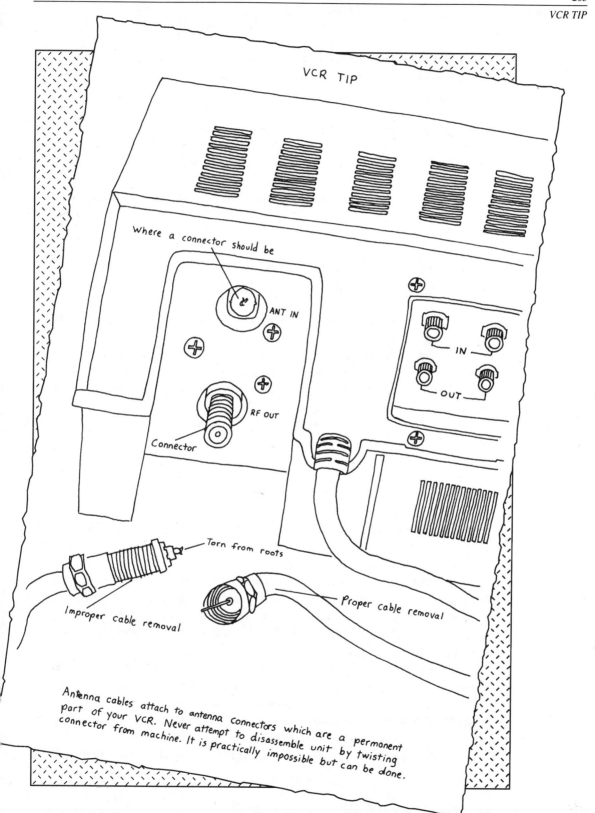

VCR TIP

where a connector should be

ANT IN

Connector

RF OUT

IN

OUT

Torn from roots

Improper cable removal

Proper cable removal

Antenna cables attach to antenna connectors which are a permanent part of your VCR. Never attempt to disassemble unit by twisting connector from machine. It is practically impossible but can be done.

totally baffled as to how to get the digital clock to stop blinking high noon. But it really isn't that hard. Here's what to do:

1. Plug in the VCR. The little clock will begin flashing 12:00. Don't worry about it.

2. If you're hooking your VCR directly up to your TV set (and you aren't using a cable system box or a satellite dish): Just take the cable that comes with the VCR (it may be called the "RF" cable) and attach it to the place on the back of the VCR that says "Video Out" or "To TV" or something like that. Then plug the other end of the cable into the back of your TV set.

On newer TV sets there will be a silver threaded connector just waiting for you. If you have an older model set, you may find that there is no such thing and you have to attach the cable to two little screws that say UHF. You'll probably need an adaptor (called an "RF adaptor") for this. The VCR may come with such an adaptor; it will have the silver threaded plug on one end and two wires ending in small, flat, double-pronged connectors (called "spade" connectors) on the other. Or you may have to go to the electronics store and ask them for an adaptor (they're not expensive).

3. Turn on your TV set. Most VCRs will give you a choice of setting your TV to channel 3 or channel 4 (there's a little switch on the back of the VCR that you need to set to 3 or 4). You may find that you get a better picture if your TV is set to one rather than the other, depending on your area. (You may also need to use the fine tuning knobs on your TV set to zero in on the channel of your choice.) Next, look for a switch or button on the VCR (or the remote control if you have one) that says "TV-VCR." Make sure it's set to VCR. Now you should be able to insert a prerecorded tape into the VCR, press the play button and see a picture.

4. If you're hooking your VCR up in conjunction with an outside source (i.e. cable service or satellite dish): Here, things get a little more complicated. If a cable service is involved, in many cases they'll send someone over at no charge to do it for you. This is the easy way out for both you and the cable company. It's great for you, since you don't have to do anything but stand there and watch the silverware. It's good for the cable company, since you aren't going to be calling them for service twice a day because your VCR is acting up and you can't figure it out.

If you have to do it yourself, first study the manual carefully. Different brands of VCRs have totally different ways of utilizing outside sources. But in a lot of cases what you have to do is hook up the wire from your cable or dish to the connector on the back of the VCR labeled something like "Video In" or "RF In." You then follow the instructions above for hooking the VCR up to your TV set.

Your TV (or cable converter box) must still be set to either Channel 3 or 4, and the TV-VCR switch should be set to VCR to enable you to see a picture from your VCR. If the TV-VCR switch is set to TV, your set should show whatever is on channel 3 or 4 in your area. If the TV-VCR switch is set to VCR but the VCR is in the stop mode, you should be able to switch broadcast channels using the VCR's remote control. (MK)

Recording on a VCR: This is the part where most everybody runs into problems. One of the reasons this is so is because almost every brand of VCR has a different method of programming (see below). The easiest way to record something is with a straight TV-VCR hook-up. Here's how:

1. Insert a blank tape into the machine (remember to turn the VCR on).

2. Use the channel selector on the VCR (or the remote control) to choose the channel you want to record.

3. Press the Play and Record buttons simultaneously. (Most VCRs take a brief moment to get into record mode, so give it a little slack.) You should see a small light go on to indicate that the machine is in fact recording. (MK)

If you want to watch the program at the same time you're recording it, turn your TV set to channel 3 or 4 (whichever you've selected) and you should see the program you're recording, assuming the TV-VCR switch is set to VCR. (MK)

If there's a commercial broadcaster in your area using channel 4, your VCR should be tuned to channel 3 to avoid interference. (KJS)

If you want to watch a different program, just set your TV to whatever channel you want and make sure the TV-VCR switch is set to TV. This should not affect the VCR's recording (assuming the hook-up is correct).

Programming: As for programming your VCR to record something on its own, as mentioned above, almost every model has a different method for doing this. Basically, the VCR has a timer mechanism— like a clock radio's — that requires you to tell it what time it has to get up and go to work. Set the day first, then the hour, then the minute. Be sure to tell it what channel you want to record.

But that's just a general view. If you get confused, the only advice we can give is to study the manual. If that doesn't work, call the store where you bought your VCR and make them tell you step by step which buttons to push. Make them go slowly enough for you to take notes. If you're still stumped, screw up your courage and try to find a friend who understands this stuff to explain it to you.

The good news is that VCR manufacturers are responding to the public outcry over the complexity of programming the suckers and are coming out with new models that have simplified programming systems. (MK)

HOME MOVIES

Whether you're looking to make a tape that will be an artistic masterpiece or just a family record of Cousin Cecilia's wedding, here are a few things you can do to give your tape a more professional look:

1. Make your movements as smooth as possible. Nothing looks more amateurish than a picture that jerks all over the place. (A tripod is never a bad idea.) Also, movements will be magnified if you're zoomed in for a close-up.

2. If you're shooting indoors, try to keep any lights out of the frame.

3. Make sure there's some movement in whatever you're shooting. Still-lifes are great for painting and photography, but they make lousy video. If you're shooting the scenery, add movement by panning (moving the camera from side to side) or zooming (using the telephoto qualities of the lens) to add interest. But use restraint.

4. A thousand words: Remember that each shot should make some sense, so try to tell a little story every time you use the camera. If you want to get a shot of a pretty valley, for example, choose one thing of interest in the valley, then pan the camera back and forth, and finally zoom in to the object of interest.

5. Cut! Don't be afraid to turn off the camera. Don't let it linger endlessly on something. Watch TV and time how long the average camera shot lasts before there's an edit or a cut to a different camera. In most cases it's just a few seconds.

6. Charge it: Pay attention to the battery indicator. Change batteries when the warning light comes on.

7. When using an autofocus, remember that it will focus on the closest object in the camera's field of view. If you're trying to shoot the mountains in the distance, you may end up focused only on the trees in the foreground. (MK)

TELEPHONES

Hello? Is anybody home? I can't hear you, but if you can hear me, listen to this: In an age where the telephone company doesn't own any telephones, a simple call can become a complicated piece of business.

INFORMATION

Dialing for dollars: A cheap telephone can knock your home's phone wiring for a loop. A perfectly good telephone can be obtained for only $10 more than an unacceptable one. Spend the money on the phone and save in the long run. (JK)

You can save big bucks on long-distance calls by putting a timer next to your telephone. When you're talking to long-distance friends, it's easy to forget the time. The timer will remind you. *(Anon.)*

The features offered by the telephone company are ones you can usually live without. *Call-waiting* is especially offensive. If you're busy, you're busy. (WW)

A dissent: Homes with teenagers should be equipped with call-waiting. Otherwise, you can never get through, even to leave a message. (NF)

Telephones that offer *memory-dialing* are usually not worth the extra money. You usually remember the numbers you frequently call, and you won't save more than two seconds dialing the extra digits. You can look up other numbers faster than you can remember the codes you gave them. *(Anon.)*

WHEN YOU HEAR THE BEEP. . .

Here's the message: An answering machine is a dangerous thing. It means that every telephone call is a passive confrontation, where you either offend the calling party by not returning the call or face the burden of calling a bunch of people you'd rather avoid. But if you're going to have an answering machine, here are some good features to have:

• Beeperless remote, so you can retrieve messages from a touch-tone phone without using a beeper.

• Toll-saver, so you can tell if you have messages before the answering machine picks up. (Great when calling for messages is a long-distance call.)

• Variable incoming message length.

• Remote programming, so you can change messages or even turn the machine on from a touch-tone phone.

• Call screening, so you can hear who's calling before you answer the phone. (RE)

Well-chosen words: Don't make your answering machine message cute, ever! Clever is okay, but don't overdo it. (RE) If you can't be terribly witty, simply say, "This is 555-5555. Please leave a message when you hear the beep." Don't make your message too long; a short message is less likely to encourage a hang-up. (FD)

Don't give your name on your answering machine message — it's an invitation to weird guys. (JL)

Always leave your phone number when you leave a message. If a person retrieves messages from a remote location, she may not have your number at hand. (NF)

PHOTOGRAPHY

Picture this: Let's say there's a bright golden haze on the meadow, the prettiest thing you ever saw, ever. And there you are with no Brownie. How can you describe it? Either you have to take a picture, or you have to be there.

The great thing about cameras is they make all fish stories come true. As a rule, photographs tell the truth about their subjects, as every Modern Woman knows, usually much to her chagrin. And when pictures do tell a lie, we call it art.

Good old technology: Once upon a time, you could slug a roll of 110 film into a $10 camera and take pictures of proms and moms and always get it sort of right.

But at a certain age, every woman feels the near-biological need to upgrade, and presto! there's a $500 Nikon sitting in the closet that nobody can make work as well as the good old trusty proto-camera that you consigned to the rubbish.

Relax and say cheese, because photo technology has come full circle. Now you can upgrade and be right back where you started.

Modern autofocus cameras are the most significant advance of equipment design in fifty years. Liberation from tedious focusing allows greater spontaneity and fewer missed shots. In still photography there's no such thing as "creative focus." It's only a distracting chore. (NK)

It's a snap: If you're going to buy a camera, get the autofocus kind. If you take more than thirty-six pictures a year, replace your conventional equipment with the automatic focusing type. You'll be glad you did. All types are available, from the tourist pocket camera to the professional rig. (FU)

Instant photography (Polaroid) and other new developments have taken the dark out of the darkroom. Nowadays, building a light-tight room is nearly senseless. In only a few years, chemical photography will be over, too. Electronic images will replace Daguerre's silver process that we now use. Those dark cubicles full of noxious fumes mercifully will be the province of artists, rather than of normal photographers like you or me. (WB) **See** *HOW TO SET UP AN ART STUDIO,* **below.**

Less is less: Cameras with a film format smaller than 35mm (110 or disc) yield image quality so poor that they're hardly worth the effort, even for snapshots. The primary advantage of these tiny film sizes is that the cameras can be made very small. Modern 35mm cameras are now so compact that the portability of 110 or disc is not worth the sacrifice in picture quality. Make 35mm your minimum format camera. (TR)

Expiration dates on film boxes are not engraved in stone, they're printed on paper. Those dates are generally conservative, and using color film six months or even a year out of date usually will work out fine.

Black and white film that is years past the expiration date can provide perfectly acceptable results. (ARo)

Negative space: Years of memories in those photo albums could be lost or ruined in a fire or flood, so keep your negatives in a safe place — maybe at your mom's house. (PG)

Don't touch: Unless you're going to do your own darkroom work, don't touch the negatives that come back with your film. Label the negative strips and file them away in case you ever need dupes. *(Anon.)*

HOW TO MAKE A PINHOLE CAMERA

In the world of photography, there's a long jump from the Nirvana of a Nikon to the funky charm of a pinhole camera.

To make a pinhole camera successfully is fairly easy. To use one successfully isn't. It takes a lot of trial-and-error experimentation and a good deal of patience. Just remember: It can be done.

First, make the pinhole. And by pinhole, we mean pinhole. The opening should be very, very small; if the pin itself can fit into the hole, it's too big. Just the tip of the pin is sufficient.

The hole should not only be small, it should be very clean, with well defined, crisp edges. One ideal material to use is a one-inch square of aluminum cut from a beer or soda can. Aluminum foil is too flimsy; paper material has too many small fibers that can blur the edges of the picture.

Then make the camera. A shoe box will work fine. Cut a small opening in one end of

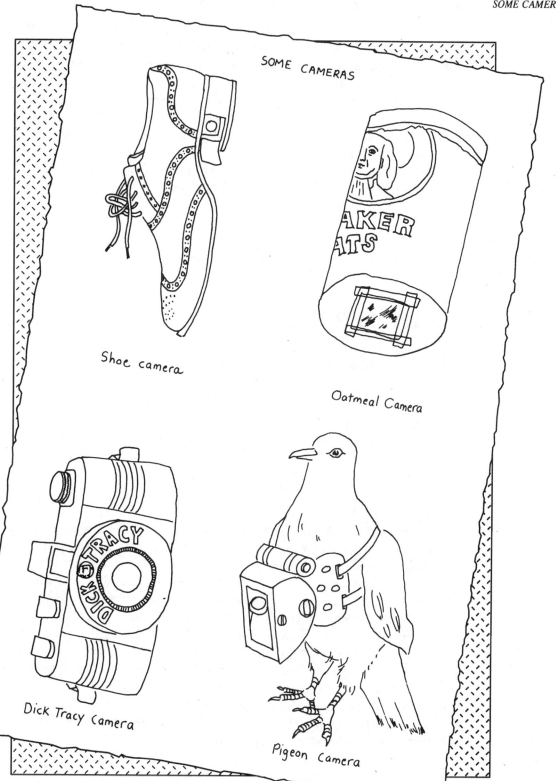

SOME CAMERAS

Shoe camera

Oatmeal Camera

Dick Tracy Camera

Pigeon Camera

the box and tape the aluminum square with the pinhole in it to the opening. Use the bit of cardboard you cut away as a sort of hinged lens cap to cover the pinhole aperture.

Now load the camera. You can get cut film from a photo shop or you can cut apart some 120 film and make your own. Either way, go into a pitch black room and tape a piece of film, emulsion side (the dull, nonglossy side) up, to the inside of the shoe box opposite the aperture. The film should be as flat against the side of the box as possible. Put the lid back on the box before you leave the dark room.

Finally: Take the picture. Place the camera on a steady surface and direct the aperture at the object you wish to photograph. Open the hinged lens cap and allow the light to pass through the pinhole for several minutes. Then cover the aperture again.

After you see the results, you will probably want to reload and try again. The possibilities for getting the right exposure and the correct distance between the aperture and the film are endless. You may have to cut up the shoe box or use a Quaker Oats box instead. (GL)

COMPUTERS

Computers are like babies. Everybody thinks they should get one before it's too late.

But think it over. If all you need is something to take care of household accounts, recipes and the like, then use a box full of index cards and a ledger book. On the other hand, if you want to track your earnings and investments, write a book, and other assorted upwardly mobile activities, then megabyte the bullet and get with the program.

COMPUTE YOUR USES

Know yourself: Decide what you really need a computer for. Don't let some smarmy salesman seduce you into buying more computer than you need or less than you want. If you need a word processor, don't let them talk you into the super-duper mega-unit. (JK)

If you're going to buy a computer *for strictly personal use*, you can save some money by buying a brand that's not one of the biggest sellers. However, make sure it's compatible with a major brand so you won't find your software options limited. (PR)

Add-ons: When you look at computer store ads and they're running a big special on the Mighty Max personal computer, keep in mind that probably only the computer itself is on sale. Essential add-ons like monitors, disk drives and printers are probably not on sale and may set you back some big bucks. (AM) **See under** *Glossary,* **below.**

Hardware is the machinery of the computer: keyboard, disk drive, hard disk, etc. It's the equipment that processes and stores information. The *software* is the instructions that tell the hardware how to process the information. (JK)

SOFTWARE FIRST

There are very few ways to recommend one brand of computer over another. One way to choose is to decide what you'd like your computer to be able to do, find the software to do it and buy the brand that runs the software. Most salespeople in computer stores are pretty knowledgeable (if you can get them to speak nontechnical English) and can fill you in on which computer companies have the best reputations for innovation in software and technology. (AP)

Mini-business: There are four basic programs you need for any small business application.

A *database program* is the computer equivalent to index cards. Let's say you are running a book store and you keep a list of all your clients' addresses and the kinds of books they buy. With a database program, you can ask the computer to sort through all the clients with an interest in history, or all the clients with the same ZIP code or all the clients with a first name beginning with the letter *C*.

A *spreadsheet* takes all the hard facts you can give it and shows what happens if you introduce variables. For instance, let's say you are buying widgets for 3 cents and selling them for a nickel and you see that you need to sell 1000 widgets a day to make your rent and overhead. What happens to the price of widgets if your rent is increased by 5 percent? A spreadsheet will tell you.

An *accounting package* will help you do basic bookkeeping. It will *not* take the place of a good accountant, however.

A really flexible *word processing program* is also a useful addition. It will file your correspondence and help you write error-free letters, among other chores. Working in tandem with your database, for example, a word processor will enable you to send out personalized form letters. (KM, DB)

APPLE OR IBM?

Fanatics: There are people to whom computer brand loyalty is more important than religious heresy or treason. If they have one type of computer and you buy another, they'll actually *hate* you for not going with their brand.

Like most things with computers, the choice between IBM and Apple should be based on application.

• *An IBM PC* or compatible computer requires learning something about how a computer works before you can use it. IBM's operating system (MS-DOS) tends to be more sophisticated, thus more complex than Apple's and there is widespread acceptance of IBM data in the business, scientific and engineering communities; there are a wide range of IBM-compatible computers, including some very handy, small portables. If you have sophisticated engineering or technical applications or if you need to be able to have your PC communicate with other PCs and IBM mainframe computers, then IBM or compatible is for you.

• The latest *Apple Macintosh* computers are as powerful as IBM PCs, plus they're phenomenally easy to use. However, because of the closed architecture on some of the older

Macs, you can't easily program on them, and for technical applications they aren't as useful. If you need a computer for general applications, though — word processing, database management, spreadsheets and accounting, for example— you can't do better than an Apple Mac. But, be aware that the Macintosh is much more expensive than an IBM compatible. Macintosh computers are also the best for graphics and for desktop publishing — programs that allow you to produce professional-quality newsletters, pamphlets and books. (CFo) In this area the gap between Macintosh and IBM is ever narrowing and in a few years may not even be noticeable. (DE) This book was produced using Apple technology.

Second-hand Apple II-series computers occasionally show up in the classifieds. They are perfect learning computers for children and can do most of your household computing chores, as well. There are more games and entertainment programs for Apple II computers than for any other type. You should be able to pick up a good second-hand system with monitor, dual disk drives and a printer for less than a grand. (CFo)

GLOSSARY

Here's a list of common computer terms:

• *Bit:* The smallest unit of information used by a computer – usually expressed as either a "1" or a "0". The term is a contraction of the term *binary digit.*

• *Byte:* A group of pieces of digital information. As a rule there are eight bits to each byte.

• *CPU:* Central processing unit. The guts of a computer.

• *Disk drive:* An external or internal device that reads information from floppy disks and sends it to the CPU for processing. Disk drives also work in reverse, taking information you have entered into the computer and recording that information on disks for storage. A double-sided disk holds a little less 900,000 bits of information.

• *Floppy disk:* A small magnetic disk that holds recorded information. Most disks can fit a little more than 400,000 bits of information on each side.

• *Hard disk:* A large storage device. Hard disks can hold much more information than floppy disks. For most personal computers, hard disks come in sizes ranging from 20 megabytes to 80 megabytes.

• *Interface:* A coupler that allows the CPU to communicate with peripheral devices, such as monitors and printers.

• *Kilobyte:* One thousand bytes.

• *Megabyte:* One million bytes.

• *Modem:* A device that allows for the transmission of computer-generated information over telephone lines from one computer to another.

• *Monitor:* The TV-type screen on which information is displayed.

• *Operating system:* The program a computer uses to accomplish internal functions.

• *Printer:* The typewriter-like device that allows for the production of "hard copy" — printed sheets of information, letters, documents and so forth. As a rule, "dot matrix" printers produce letters that are less crisp than those produced by "daisy wheel" printers. Dot matrix printers are much, much faster, though, and the letter quality of the latest models rivals those produced by daisy wheel printers. Laser printers print in near typeset quality.

• *RAM:* Random access memory. RAM is available for use by the computer to process information before storing it.

• *ROM:* Read-only memory. ROM is unalterable information, usually reserved for the internal requirements of the computer.

• *Software:* The preprogrammed set of instructions — usually contained on floppy disks — that tells the computer what to do with information you enter. A word processor, for example, is a piece of software — not a machine. (CFo)

A BOLT FROM THE BLUE

Protection: Always make sure that your computer is protected from electrical surges, which can blow programs and destroy data. Get something called a line-filter or surge suppressor to protect your system. Sometimes a spark caused by static electricity you picked up walking across the rug can be enough to give your computer the hiccups. This is also a good reason to back up programs and data. (MK)

CHANGING TUNES

Obsolete: Be wary of computer brands that have limited software and hardware. There's nothing more frustrating than being stuck with an outmoded computer that works just fine but for which you can no longer get programs, parts or service. (MK) Think of a computer as a tool to do a job — a bigger hammer. No need to have a pile driver to kill an ant. (DE)

THE GREAT OUTDOORS

Not every woman thinks it's so great. Those who *do* don't need us to provide a handbook. Those who *don't* can look here for a little get-by advice — just enough to keep you out of the poison ivy, maybe.

There's wilderness and there's wilderness. The national park variety is tame compared to the singles-bar variety, where there are no deer and no antelope because the wolves ate them all up.

CAMPING

This is what happens when you camp. You drive somewhere that is beautiful and you pitch a tent and you make a fire and you roast some weenies. Then you wonder what to do with yourself until bed. If you are in a national park, you can go down the path to the restrooms. There might be a shower there; you will have to put dimes in the timer for the hot water. There will be a lot of strangers in the restroom brushing their teeth. Then you return to your tent. If it is in a national park, you will hear the sounds of all your neighbor campers. They will be playing poker and board games and what-not and having a whale of a good time at top volume. The stars in the sky will be gorgeous. At about 7:45 P.M. you will crawl into your tent and there will be a dip in the ground right under the middle of your back, and there will be some little gravel-type things here and there in other places under you. Your feet will be *freezing* in spite of the hot rock wrapped in paper that you placed at the bottom of the bag. After about an hour you will drift into an uneasy sleep only to be awakened because you have to go to the bathroom. This is just after you realize that your feet are warm. So you don't go and you don't go until you *really* have to, and you don't want to go all the way down the path so you just creep behind a nearby tree. The next day you come down with a rash all over your private parts. (EC)

Tips for hardy campers:

• *Don't trespass* on private property. Ask permission.

• *Don't go off* and leave the fire burning unattended.

• *Don't trust your neighbors* in the next camp. They are not necessarily trustworthy simply because they appear to love nature. And who says a thief can't wear a flannel shirt?

• *Sound really carries* out there in the grand outside. Keep your voice down and your radio at home. Listen to the crackle of the fire and the buzzing of the bugs, instead.

• *Leave your area as clean* or cleaner than you found it. Don't leave a speck of garbage. And don't throw your dishwater out near the campsite, because insects love dishwater.

• *Consider the direction of the wind* when you build your campfire.

• *Don't pee in the dark* if you are a woman unless you know for certain what kind of foliage is under you. *(Anon.)*

WHEN YOU HAVE THE URGE TO SLEEP UNDER THE STARS

Avoid nasty accidents by not camping or sleeping under rocks or boulders that could fall or under or near trees that have dead branches that could crash on you in the night. (BR)

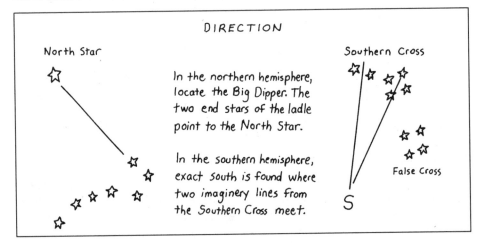

DIRECTION

North Star

In the northern hemisphere, locate the Big Dipper. The two end stars of the ladle point to the North Star.

In the southern hemisphere, exact south is found where two imaginary lines from the Southern Cross meet.

Southern Cross

False Cross

S

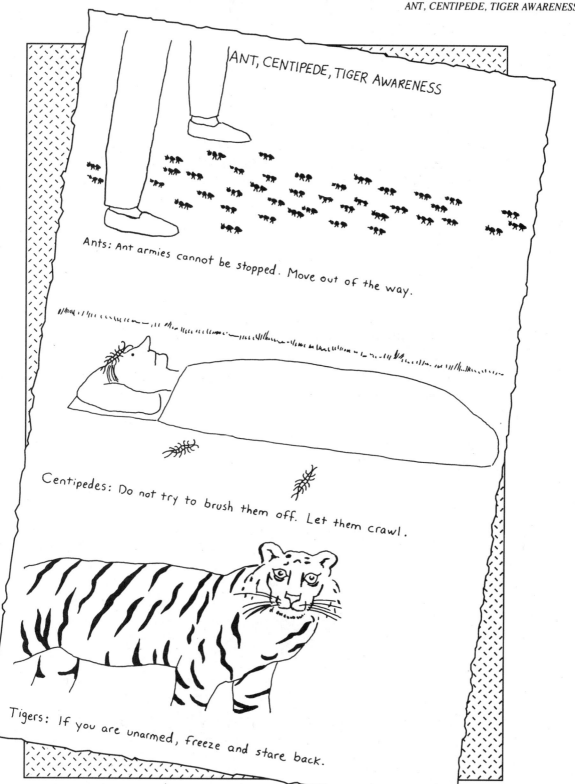

ANT, CENTIPEDE, TIGER AWARENESS

Ants: Ant armies cannot be stopped. Move out of the way.

Centipedes: Do not try to brush them off. Let them crawl.

Tigers: If you are unarmed, freeze and stare back.

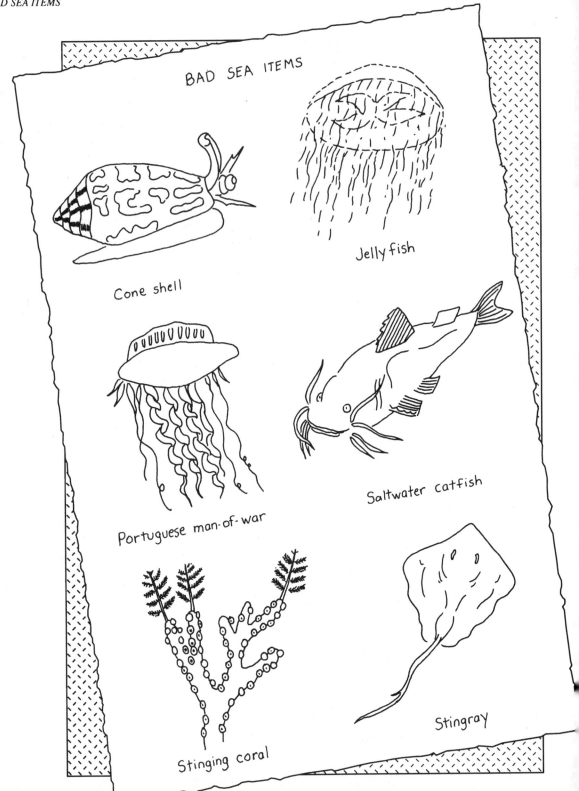

BAD SEA ITEMS

Jelly fish

Cone shell

Portuguese man-of-war

Saltwater catfish

Stinging coral

Stingray

Never camp in a dried streambed or riverbed. A storm a hundred miles away could send tons of water downstream in no time. (RL)

Camping by the sea is just lovely but make your campsite well away from it. Tides can rise fast and high. (RL)

Keep your water supply covered and in the shade. Always keep some water by the fire in case of emergencies. (DK)

Bury your trash downwind of camp but not uphill or near a water source. (RL)

Kerosene lamps are easier to work than Coleman-type lanterns, but they smell bad and are particularly dangerous. Use a small butane or propane fueled lantern. Keep the fuel supply well away from fire and food. If your car is nearby, stick the fuel in the trunk. (SD)

To keep warm at night, put as much or more under you as over you. (TF) **See under** *Emergencies,* **below.**

Pup tents are great for overnight camping. They're easy to carry and easy to pitch, but only large enough for two close friends. (RD)

Build your campfire on dirt, not on a mat of dried leaves. Rid the area of leaves, grass, needles and twigs, and site the fire well away from the tent or overhanging tree limbs.

• *Start the fire* by burning twigs, dried bark or weeds, then place tree branches or dry sticks on the fire, and soon it will be burning hot enough to place a log or two on it.

• *A good fire* depends on air flow. You should place a rock against one side of the fire so the air will come in and up. Water boils and food heats faster that way, too. (TG)

Buy a good sleeping bag. You'll never be sorry. A goosedown bag is best. Make sure it has a nylon zipper and bonded — not stitched — insulation. The bag should be made from non-allergenic, colorfast materials. (RD)

Bring your oven rack from home to place over the fire. (BNo) The easiest way to cook over an open campfire is to wrap up the food in several layers of aluminum foil and drop the bundle right into the fire. (RL)

Make an oven by digging a hole as large as the pot you'll be using. Put hot coals into the bottom of the hole, put the food into the pot (and cover it) and put the pot into the hole. Cover the pot with dirt and build a fire on top of the dirt. Leave the pot in the hole about twice the time it would take to cook something in a conventional oven. (TG)

EMERGENCIES

Emergency sleeping bags can be made from blankets, clothes or car seat covers; you can even use trash bags. The main idea is to keep two-thirds of whatever it is *under* you, one-third *over* you. Cover your head with something and tuck in your feet. Garbage bags can be stuffed with dried leaves for maximum benefit. (HL)

If you're stranded, *sleep next to a fallen tree,* under a pine tree or overhang or in a cave. Check around for snakes, skunks and rats. Once you've found the basic shelter, modify it by filling in or covering with twigs and tree branches for protection. Or, sleep against a log, facing out. Stuff all your clothes with dry leaves or weeds, put something over your head and keep your hands inside your jacket. (RD)

Any metal object rubbed sharply and vigorously against hard stone will eventually produce a spark. Collect some dry material beforehand, so when it does finally spark you'll have something to do with it. Once you get a small flame, fan it very gently and continuously until it gets going. (TL)

Ground-to-air signals are universally recognized signs that are made on the ground and can be seen from the air to alert search planes to your location and circumstance. There are only five of them and they should be memorized. (**See illustration**) Make them from mounds of dirt, leaves and twigs, strung-together logs, pieces of cloth, marks in the snow or twigs set on fire. (RL)

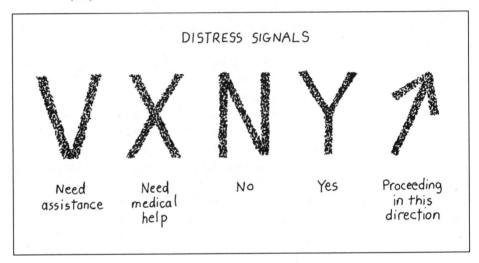

CAMP LIFE

After a camping trip, make a list of what you took but didn't use. Don't make the same mistake again. (TD)

Put dirty clothes in a covered container with soap and water, shake it back and forth for a while, rinse the clothes and hang them to dry. (HE)

Unless the campground supplies municipal water, you must purify it. You can either boil it for ten to thirty minutes, pouring the clean water into a container and discarding the sediment left in the boiling utensil or buy an over-the-counter purifying chemical to use. (TR)

Before you leave home, fill some bottle caps, jar lids or separated egg cartons with melted paraffin with a bit of string stuck into it for use as a fire starter or short-lived candles. (LR)

Use sand to scour skillets and pots. (RL)

Sprinkle salt around your campsite. This will keep away slugs and snails. If you sprinkle salt directly on a slug, it'll kill him. (PD)

Carry insect spray and use it on logs before you sit on them. (WL)

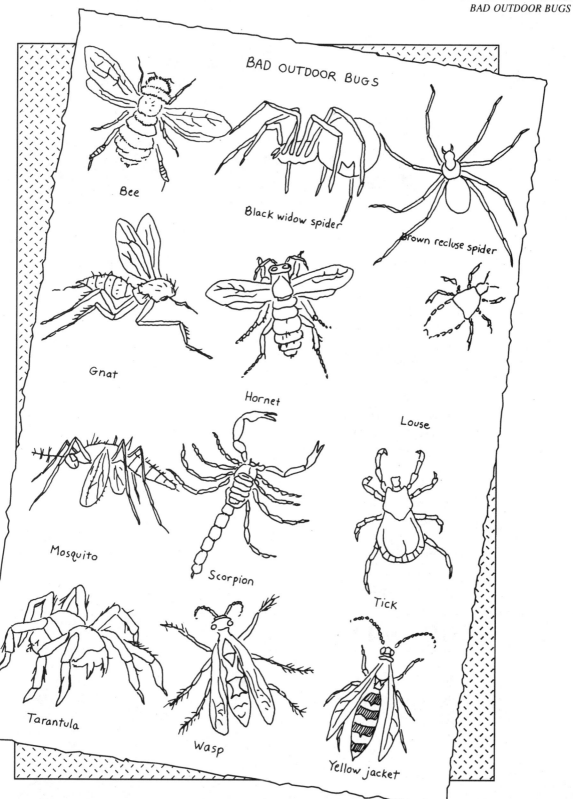

BAD OUTDOOR BUGS

Bee

Black widow spider

Brown recluse spider

Gnat

Hornet

Louse

Mosquito

Scorpion

Tick

Tarantula

Wasp

Yellow jacket

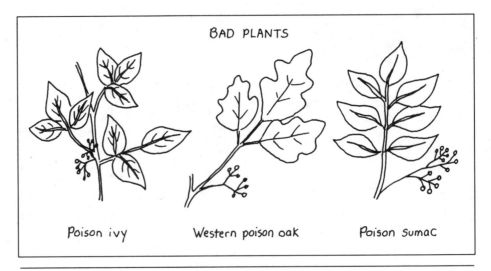

BAD PLANTS

Poison ivy   Western poison oak   Poison sumac

BASIC CAMP FIRST-AID KIT
- Antibacterial ointment
- Antibacterial soap
- Antihistamine
- Aspirin
- Bandage strips
- Elastic bandage
- Fever thermometer
- Insect repellent
- Lip balm
- Needles
- Prescription drugs
- Razor
- Safety pins
- Salt tablets
- Snakebite kit
- Sunscreen (GS)

FOOTBALL

A game that customarily has an ambulance waiting in the wings is a pretty stupid game, but since it is a national stupidity, here are the very basics.

THE OBJECT

of the game is to get the ball across the opposing team's goal line.

HOW THEY DO IT

There are two sides to every story, and this one's no different. The team that has the ball is the offense and the other team is the defense.

The offensive team gets four tries to advance the ball ten yards. These tries are called downs. If they make it, they get four more downs. The offensive team tries to advance while the defensive team tries to stop them. The offense carries the ball or throws it. The ball may be thrown if the throw is made from a point in back of where the ball was put into play. This is called the line of scrimmage. During a pass play, when a player catches the ball he runs. If he misses it, the ball is returned to the place where the play was started. On a running play, the play continues until the player with the ball is tackled or is chased out of bounds, unless there is a fumble, in which case the first player to come up with the ball may run with it.

The defensive team tries to tackle the player with the ball, pursue him across the sideline or intercept the pass. If the defensive team keeps the offensive team from gaining ten yards in four downs, then they get the ball and become offensive and try to make the ball go the other way.

Another way to take possession of the ball is by intercepting a pass or recovering a fumble. (SBl)

TOUCHDOWN

If the offensive team crosses the opposing team's goal line with the ball in their possession, it's a touchdown. A touchdown is worth six points. After a touchdown has been scored, the ball is moved a short distance in front of the goal line and the offensive team is given the opportunity to score extra points by kicking the ball through the uprights or running the ball over the goal line again. This is called a conversion.

Points may also be scored by the offense by kicking the ball through the uprights. This is called a field goal and is worth three points.

EQUAL TIME

Teams change defending goal lines each quarter so that everyone gets the sun in their eyes the same amount of time. After a touchdown, the team that scored kicks the ball to the defending team, which then takes possession.

Numbers: There may be eleven players from each team on the field at one time. (EC)

FEMME FAN HINTS

Don't go to the restroom at halftime.

If the scoreboard shows only six minutes to go, don't get excited because in football six minutes takes about thirty-five.

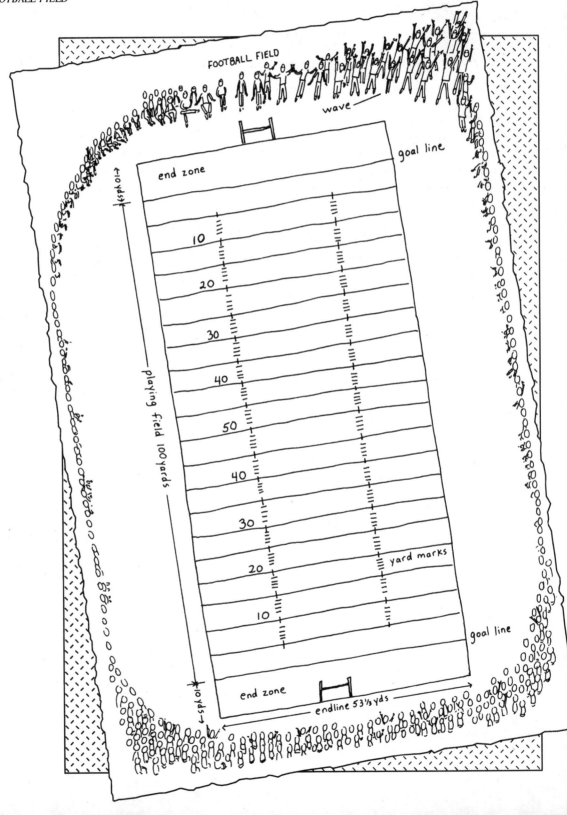

FOOTBALL FIELD

wave

end zone

goal line

←10 yds→

10

20

30

40

50

40

30

20

10

playing field 100 yards

yard marks

goal line

←10 yds→

end zone

endline 53⅓ yds

If it is winter ***take some cardboard*** to lay over the frozen ice so your feet won't freeze. Also take a blanket and a nice big thermos of coffee. (LK)

SAUCE STUPIDE

Anytime you're afraid you just aren't stupid enough, you can get a bottle of special dumb-enhancer from the local liquor shop.

Take a half-dozen glasses full before bedtime. If you don't think you're stupid before you fall asleep, you'll *know* you were stupid when you wake up.

ICE BREAKER, BREAKER

If you really want to get to know someone, go to a bar and have a few drinks too many. Believe me, you'll get to know that person much better than you probably wanted to. (SL)

BASIC LIQUOR LORE

There are two main categories of alcoholic drinks. Some, like whisky, are made by fermentation followed by *distillation*, and some, like beer and wine, are made by *fermentation* only.

Spirits are unsweetened alcoholic drinks made by distillation. There are also a number of different sweetened drinks based on spirits — called "liqueurs" or "cordials" — although the word *liqueur* is also given to aged and not sweet liquors that are fine and smooth.

Brandy, gin, rum, vodka, Scotch whisky and bourbon are other spirits.

Proof: In this country a proof number is twice the percentage of alcohol. Pure alcohol is 200 proof.

Brandy is a liquor distilled from wine or fermented fruit juices and aged before bottling. Brandy is great after dinner or with coffee.

Gin is usually made from grain. Juniper berries give gin its distinctive taste. It does not need to be aged.

Rum is distilled from fermented molasses or other sugarcane products. Pale rum is light in taste and color, golden rum is a bit heavier and darker, and dark rum is the heaviest and strongest. Rum must be aged.

Vodka is made from fermented grain. It is best if you store it in the freezer. There are no significant differences between any domestic vodkas.

Whiskies are distilled from fermented mash. *Bourbon* comes from corn. (EC, SK)

WINE

Wine is the alcoholic beverage produced from grapes by *fermentation*. Wine can smell like life must have smelled during the first week or so of creation. The smell of some wine is enough to bring back memories you never even had.

There are three principal categories of wines. ***Strong aperitifs*** are served before a meal, ***sweet wines*** are served with or after dessert, and ***table wines*** are served with food.

Wine is the only alcoholic beverage that *continues to age in the bottle,* but different wines reach their primes at different times. So a 120-year-old bottle does not necessarily mean it is going to taste like heaven itself. It may have reached its prime about 117 years ago.

Aperitif wines are fortified, which means that a small amount of brandy has been added. When a wine is fortified, fermentation stops before all the sugar in the grape has turned to alcohol. The brandy acts to preserve, prevent souring after the bottle has been opened, and add to flavor and strength. These wines keep well without refrigeration. The alcohol content of a typical aperitif is about twenty percent. Aperitifs are usually served on the rocks or with a bit of soda. Between meals, they are generally served with lots of soda and ice. Sherry is always served straight.

Champagnes should be served very cold. They are usually rather expensive because the bubble-making process takes a long time. *Natural* is the driest champagne, then *brut, sec* and *demi-sec*.

Dessert wines are sweet and usually fortified. The proper hostess serves them before, not with, coffee.

*A **dry wine*** is a table wine that has been fermented until all the sugar has turned to alcohol.

The alcohol content of ***beer*** and ***wine*** is not normally given as proof, but as a percentage. To determine the proof, double the percentage.

Store wine in a dark, cool place — 55° F. is just right. Store it on its side to keep the cork moist.

Red wines are usually dry and heavier than white wines. Serve at room temperature with meat and pasta and strong cheeses and highly seasoned foods.

Rosé wines are served cool and are perhaps too light for beef and too heavy for seafood. Yup-fern joints have started calling them "blush" instead of rosé, a particularly cloying marketing gesture.

Sparkling wines may be red, white, or pink. They can be served at any time, with or without food. Serve them chilled.

White wines are usually served with seafoood and white meats. They should be chilled.

Rules about drinking a certain wine with a certain food should be dismissed. If you discover a wine that pleases you, drink it when you please and with anything you please.

Room temperature for a wine means 60° to 65° F. Cool or cellar temperature means 55°, and chilled means about 45°.

Don't decant a sparkling wine or all those bubbles will bubble to heaven. Any other wine may be decanted. Wine is decanted so that bits of cork and sediment will not find their way into your glass. Unfortified wines should be decanted no longer than two hours before serving. Pour gently when decanting wine, and leave behind the sediment at the bottom of the bottle.

Allow red wines to breathe for about an hour before serving.

Oenobabble: People who know a great deal about wine will try to intimidate you with their wine talk, but try not to let it ruin your enjoyment of the beautiful stuff. (EC, SK) **See also under** *Wine Time* **in** *CHAPTER FOUR: MODERN P's & Q's.*

HOW TO READ A WINE LABEL

The label on the bottle tells you more than just the name of the wine. Chablis, for example, is found on a variety of wines from different regions around the world. But Chablis is the name of an individual village, as is Sauternes, Pommard, Saint-Emilion and many more. Some specific names are so well known that they become generic and are used to describe a wine that comes from somewhere else, like California Chablis or Spanish Burgundy — wines that have nothing much to do with their origin and may be only vaguely similar to each other.

Usually, *the more explicit the label, the better the wine.* Great wines may not only indicate region, but the district inside the region, and even the specific vineyard in the district. If an area or vineyard isn't particularly well known, the label may identify both the village name and the name of the grape, or even the grape name alone.

The phrase **appelation controlée** indicates that the wine is of superior quality. The more geographically specific the phrase is, the higher the quality of the wine.

Pay attention to what the label says about *the vintage of the wine.* An old wine is not necessarily a good wine, since most wines do not age terribly well, and many — most white wines and most burgundies, for example — should be drunk while quite fresh. (JS)

BOY BOOZE, GIRL BOOZE

The true and sorry fact is that most *women just can't drink as much as men can.* Maybe it's the ratio of bulk weight to alcohol, or maybe an indication of blood sugars to spirits. **See** *Hangover Therapy,* **below.**

The more a woman drinks, the sillier she gets. This silliness can run the gamut: a sudden urge to take off all her clothes or to start crying because she lost her junior high sweetheart and it wasn't her fault. In either case, the eye makeup runs and the powder disappears allowing the purple flush of drunkenness to clash with the lipstick.

The whole thing is extremely unbecoming and, unless you're with dear and lifelong friends who will always love you, don't allow yourself to go this far into the bottle. (KL)

An anecdote: I once knew a girl who was a real case. She threatened suicide, drove wildly, didn't brush her teeth. She was always involved in crummy love affairs and never wrote to her mother. Poor thing had bleeding rashes and bumps all over her hands and ankles and legs. She got very ill and had to spend two months in hospital. When she was well again and came to visit me, I was looking at a different person. Her hands were lovely, she was thin and calm. During her hospital stay, she hadn't had a drop of liquor, and it had cured her mind, soul and body. She discovered a deadly allergy that she had been unaware of, an allergy to alcohol. (AT)

And another: I started drinking when I was fifty-two years old. I had been recently divorced, had lost the house and furniture, and was forced to fend for myself. Once I had pulled things together a bit, I started dating again. Dating meant movies, dancing, eating, and drinking.

At first I was quite taken aback about the amount and to what extent people in general, and particularly in my age group, were drinking. It wasn't uncommon for my date and our friends to become quite drunk of an evening. We all had fun; no one became obnoxious or dangerous.

I'm remarried now, but still the consumption of alcohol is a social and sometimes solitary given of my life. I still feel a general sense of guilt and uneasiness about it, but I guess it's just the way things are now. Once you start in on what can be considered a habit, it's very difficult to stop. After all, it's fun, sociable and somehow exciting. (WH)

And one last one for the road: My parents divorced when I was two years old. My father would come early in the morning to my new family home and off we would go, beginning on our journey through the countryside of Pennsylvania to his farm. This was regularly an hour-and-forty-five-minute drive. My father would literally stop at every roadside tavern for a beer or two. I had a fine time, what with Shirley Temples and dancing on the bar, amusing all the old guys and especially my father. We would pull into the yard around one-thirty in the morning, to a disgruntled new wife and usually a loud argument.

But those are fond memories for me, my dad being happy, relaxed and singing, along with me. (KL)

DON'T WATER THE ANIMALS

Beware! Some men become animals, or worse, after they've been drinking. You must be aware of the signals that indicate that it's time for you to call a cab and go home, by yourself. Suddenly Billy starts talking about a girl he was really in love with; tears spring into his eyes and you can't get him off the subject. This means the evening's over. Get out of there. (FL) **See** *How to Deal With an Unruly Drunken Date* **in** *CHAPTER FIVE: MODERN MEN.*

DRUNK DRIVING GUESTS

If you're having a party and serving alcohol, you must be responsible to see that everyone gets home safely. If a cab or lift isn't possible, put the thug into a spare room, even on the floor in the laundry room. Never let a drunk out of your house unless you're absolutely sure he or she will wake up alive and well, preferably not in jail. (KK) **See** *After Dinner* **in** *CHAPTER FOUR: MODERN P's & Q's.*

In the unfortunate circumstance that you wake up somewhere, and you don't have much of an idea where it is, get out as soon as you can. (OP)

DAILY DUMB

Alcohol promotes a sort of cumulative stupidity effect. If you drink every day, pretty soon you won't be doing a good job at anything, you won't care about anything, and worse, anyone. (TH)

FIRMLY DUMB

I was sitting at the bar waiting for my table. A young, attractive couple was seated next to me. He was dashing and she a very good-looking blonde. You could tell she belonged to a gym, that kind.

The bartender asked "What will it be?"

She replied, "A Perrier, please, and a water." (KL)

STRANGE CITIES

In a new city, never frequent a bar where drinks are over $3.00. It's probably too stuffy anyway. (JI)

When in a strange city, *go to a hip-looking eatery* and ask the waiters or waitresses. They'll know the best places. (NW)

HOW TO CRASH A PARTY

Walk in backwards with a drink in your hand. (NW) **See also** *Bar Etiquette* **in** *CHAPTER FOUR: MODERN P's & Q's.*

HOW TO MAKE A GREAT MARTINI

While a martini may be made with either vodka or gin, if you ask a bartender for a martini it will be made with gin combined with vermouth. Martinis have olives in them, or tiny pearl onions, but you're dealing with an innocent if you recieve one with a pickle in it.

The recipe: Use a jigger of spirits with a quarter jigger of vermouth. Some say three parts spirit to one of vermouth, but four to one is better. A very dry martini has almost no vermouth in it.

Chill a martini glass. Pour the martini into a shaker that has ice in it. Shake it, stir it around, then strain it into the chilled glass. (LAM)

HANGOVER THERAPY

Here are ten I-told-you-so hangover cures:

1. Coke and potato chips. Four aspirins. (BNo)

2. Coke and soda crackers. Two Pepto Bismol. One Rolaid. (BDe)

3. Two large Diet Cokes, order of fries (optional), a large cheeseburger — or maybe two — and a regular Coke chaser. (DB)

4. Make some rice, mix it up with some sour cream, drink peppermint tea. (KK)

5. Six cups of coffee and six cigarettes. (TO'D)

6. Sleep as late as possible, get caffeine (coffee, tea or soda), take two aspirins, watch TV for a while. (LT)

7. A Bloody Mary with extra horseradish. (FDD) *A dissent:* A "hair of the dog" will do more harm than good. (DB)

8. Cranberry juice - gallons of it! (MK)

9. The biggest breakfast your stomach can hold, along with chocolate milk. (SNo)

10. Aspirin and vitamin C and caffeine — in Coke, coffee, tea — anyway you can get it . (SJ)

To prevent hangovers: If you know before you go under that you're going to wake up in hangover hell, here's a four-step, sure-fire preventive:

• Eat as much as you can, even if it's only a couple of slices of bread. Ideally, you'll want to get down a high-protein, high-carbohydrate meal before sleeping. A double cheeseburger is good.

• Drink some caffeine. Cola is by far the best source for this situation. Eight ounces minimum.

• The hard part: Drink one ten-ounce glass of water for every alcoholic drink you drank. Add a couple more for the ones you forgot. Drink until you leak through your skin.

• Take three aspirins.

When you wake up, you might not feel *great,* but you'll feel better than you deserve to feel. (DD)

BOREDOM

Boredom is a by-product of the modern age, something that spews out of automatic food processors, comes with every box of disposable diapers and gets tossed into the dishwasher. It's an extremely common resource. But what can you do with it?

ALIEN EXPERIENCE

Next time you're bored, pretend you just arrived on earth from another planet. Your job is to mingle with earthlings without being identified as an alien. Then go downtown and mingle. You will become more aware of social customs and etiquette. It's a good game. A variation on the same game is to pretend you are a sociologist. (FK)

BOOKED UP

Read. Don't read to elevate yourself. Read for fun. Later, when you are not bored, you can read to elevate yourself. (OT) **See** *A Dozen Ways to Pass a Lonely Night* **in** *CHAPTER THREE: SOLO ACTS.*

DOCU-ROIDS

Buy a Polaroid camera and make "Day in the Life" books for the ones you love who are far away. Take a dozen or more photos of your day from the time you wake to the time you prepare for bed — pictures of your friends at work, of the people in the supermarket, of you. Photograph your house. Your downtown. Your cat. All the dopey things of every day. Write at least one paragraph for each picture. Staple colored construction paper together and glue everything down. Mail it. The ones who love you will gobble it up. Trust me. (MO'D)
See under *PHOTOGRAPHY,* **above.**

BORED WORKING STIFF

The worst times are when you are bored at work, because you can't do anything else but be there. If it isn't possible to take a different job, then you must try hard to cultivate another life that is just as strong as your work life. Perhaps you can take classes at night in something you love, or plan weekends so that you can have at least one golden day. (RR)

TWENTY-MINUTE BURNOUT

Gin at breakfast alleviates boredom for about twenty minutes. These twenty good minutes, however, will be followed by hours of thirst, headaches, and fatigue. (CC)

BOREDOM DELUXE

Anyone bored is spoiled. Who has the time? Often boredom is confused with depression, and often depression is the result of fatigue. Next time you feel bored *or* down in the dumps, take a day off and sleep. If you're really bored, take a brisk walk. Clears the mind. (JJ)

MODERN ED

The ultimate cure for boredom: *Go back to school.*

The older student: Don't let advancing age deter you from going back to school. You've got the advantage of life experience over the young ones. No teacher or administrator could intimidate me after my having faced the meter man stark naked. *(Anon.)*

Money: Most likely, you'll need financial aid. To start this elusive quest for cash, go to the college financial aid office. The counselor will put together an aid package for you from available state and federal funds and the school's own resources. If you still find yourself short on finances, do some research. It's bad after Reagan's cuts, but it's still possible if you work hard at putting together a financial package. There are, for example, several books full of information in your public library, including the addresses of corporations, associations and organizations that have scholarship, loan and grant funds available. (DY)

HOW TO SET UP AN ART STUDIO

This is not for dilettantes. A studio is a small factory where a one-woman assembly line produces goods for sale. It's not a place where you go to find yourself or meaning in your life. It's where you go when you want to go to work.

SPACE: THE FINAL FRONTIER

Each artist has her own priorities depending on the media in which she works.

The big problem is finding the right space. Considerations may include

• Natural light
• Plumbing
• Cost
• Location

Your budget will help answer these considerations, so listen to your pocket and don't overextend yourself.

ARTIST'S STUDIO

If you want to live in a hot spot or around a hub of galleries expect a small space for lots of money. If your work is large, this is obviously untenable.

The alternative is to find a space where there aren't other artists — in other words, somewhere that hasn't yet become hip.

Be careful not to rent or buy a studio space that's too far away from a major city, because you'll never get a dealer or buyer to travel to review your work. (TO'D)

ADJUSTABLE

The first consideration about setting up a studio is your financial situation. You'll have to *adjust the space to suit you* and the type of work you do. Lights, water, storage space, working area, electrical outlets, floor treatment, wall space and rest area all need to be looked at, and all will cost you.

Make absolutely sure you can afford to customize the place and that you can afford all the materials you'll need for six months. Only then will you be able actually to work with a clear mind. (BNo)

DISTRACTION

Financial woes are a huge distraction to a working artist. Don't spend so much for a swell studio that you go in debt — then find you can't work your way out of it because you're too worried about paying the rent on the studio. (KF)

BIBLIOPHILIA

Everyone has a favorite author, and more than likely you'll have several of that author's books in your library. Why not let those books do more than just gather dust?

Book collecting, trading, and selling is an interesting hobby and if you're very lucky, one day may provide you with some extra income.

Decide which author or type of book you want to collect. If the author is living, try to establish a correspondence with him or her, see if the author is willing to sign a book or two for you. If the answer is yes, then send along your ordinary edition. Make sure the book is kept in mint condition and you've saved the dust jacket in a safe, dry place.

• You cannot resell a dog-eared book, or one without the original dust jacket. Likewise, never buy a book at an estate sale or auction if it's without the dust jacket or has a broken spine or coffee mug rings all over the pages.

• Collect everything about the author you can get your hands on — Christmas card messages written thirty years ago, movie posters listing the author as screenwriter, anything.

• A rare book is one that is desirable — say, an early first edition of a newly popular author or a first edition of a classic — and one that is *not readily available.*

• Remember, don't buy books for investment purposes only. Do it because it interests you and you have fun doing it. There's too much luck involved to make it a logical place for the average woman to invest. (RL)

HOW TO PRESERVE PAPERS

If you do get a rare document, this recipe neutralizes the acids in the paper tissue.
• Mix one tablespoon Milk of Magnesia (or one tablet) with
• One quart of water

Stir it up, cap it tightly and let it sit for twenty-four hours. Pour it into a flat bowl or deep dish and lay the clippings or papers in the solution and let them sit for two hours. Take out, pat dry and place between two paper towels until they're completely dry. The solution is only good for one time. (JGu)

Modern Women in Distress

There's a spectrum of modern mishaps out there that range from the mildly irritating to the potentially fatal.

Modern Women know that because we're all edging toward the perilous brink of a new and no doubt improved Dark Age, we have to watch every step. The short trip from the front door to the station wagon could be a journey into fear and pain, and the stroll to the corner mailbox could end in terror.

These days, there are so many assaults on good sense, we tend to get lazy about the possibility of assaults on ourselves and those we love. So Modern Women dress for the weathercloaked in diligence and ready for anything.

C O N T E N T S

Chapter Twelve: *MODERN WOMEN IN DISTRESS*

**THE LAW: Small Claims — Lawyers — RAPE: Types
— SELF-DEFENSE: Use Instincts — Use Psychology
— Use Your Feet — Use Rage — Use Surprise — Use
Your Elbow — Use Your Knee — Use Your Fist — Use
Your Foot — Use Your Head — Survival Tips from All
Over** — How to Jump Off a Cliff — **OBSCENE CALLS:
Information**

THE LAW

What a jungle the law is. Home of justice and order, it's also where bureaucrats, charlatans and bad lawyers prey on the halt and the lame. Modern Women know the landmarks and can find the trails.

SMALL CLAIMS

Small claims courts are designed to deal with problems that involve about $1000 or less (the amount varies from state to state). Be sure that your claim is within the court's dollar limit. You do not need a lawyer; in fact, in some states, lawyers aren't allowed to represent clients in small claims hearings.

When the local widget discounter rips you off, take him to small claims court. About two-thirds of the plaintiffs who file complaints in small claims court win their cases. Of course, in order to collect the money awarded to you, you may well end up back in court, but generally that won't be the case, so it's worth a try.

To find out where the small claims court is located, call the county office building or city hall. Stop by to fill out the forms and arrange the court date. You'll need to find out the procedures necessary to summon the opposing party to court. In this and other matters relating to small claims, clerks are very helpful; in fact, clerks often guide lawyers through their legal mazes.

When you get to court, the judge will ask you to explain your side of the problem. Then the other party will be asked to explain their version. It's just like "People's Court."

Be brief. Mind your manners. When you arrive in court, have with you three copies of a short summary of your case. One goes to the judge, one to the opponent, and one you keep.

If you win, give your opponent a few days to pay you. If you can't collect, return to court for help. The court can issue a warrant or find other remedies.

It only costs a few dollars to have your day in small claims court. Sometimes, if you win, your opponent will be instructed to reimburse you this expense. (LK)

LAWYERS

How to find a lawyer: The first thing to remember when you're thinking of hiring a lawyer is not to hire a lawyer if you can possibly avoid it. Many situations that look as if they require legal help may, on closer inspection, be solved quite easily by other means. **See under** *A Federal Case* **in** *CHAPTER SIX: MODERN MERCHANDISE.*

• *If you decide a lawyer is necessary,* shop around the same way you would with any other major purchase. Ask friends or call the local bar association for referrals. See who will give you a free consultation.

• *Don't feel obliged* to retain any lawyer with whom you feel uncertain or uncomfortable. Simply thank him or her and continue looking. There is an abundance of lawyers out there.

• *Watch out for lawyers with more style than substance.* Great-looking offices and impressive-sounding affiliations are not necessarily the marks of a great legal mind.

• *Ask lots of questions* at the first consultation, and ask for referrals from other clients.

• *Fees:* Make sure you understand thoroughly what the fee arrangement is.

Don't be intimidated; get the lawyer *you* want. (PC)

Take a letter: Sometimes, for a teeny amount of money, a lawyer can do wonders to improve your situation. Perhaps you need to get the attention of a landlord who refuses to respond — maybe the hot-water tap in your tub has never worked, and you have to attach a hose to the tap in the sink and stretch it across the bathroom to fill the tub, and you have been doing that for eight weeks. Why not request a lawyer to send a little note? It won't have to say anything particularly legal at all, but could just request some information regarding this matter of the bathtub. But it will be a request from a lawyer, you see. The chances are, your hot-water tap will be repaired right away. (SL)

Try a legal clinic if your problem is fairly uncomplicated. Legal clinics are law firms that try to do a whole lot of business for a fairly low rate. They might specialize in certain common problems like wills or bankruptcy, and sometimes the routine work is done by people who are not lawyers. Look in the Yellow Pages. (OT)

Understand the fees fully from the start. A contingency fee means that if you win, you will pay your lawyer a percentage of the award. If you lose, you will pay nothing. (LM)

Fair warning: Let the other party know that you are planning legal action. Hopefully, this will result in an out of court settlement. (AD)

RAPE

Do you scream? Should you fight? Should you submit?

It depends. There are several different types of rapists and there are several different ways of categorizing them. Each classification method has its adherents, and we've adopted a sort of middle-ground approach to the classification of rapists, since there's a chance you can increase your odds of survival by recognizing certain behavior patterns and varying your responses accordingly.

First, some sense of the crime itself:

Rape is almost never about sex. It's about violence. It is an act of violence that must not be seen by the victim as anything more shameful than any other assault. It must be reported to the police.

Most states have limits to testimony so that your whole prior sex life isn't put on trial. Evidence is crucial. *Don't bathe* until after the police have been called and evidence has been taken. Hair, blood, semen are all useful as evidence. **See also under** *Date Rape* **in** *CHAPTER FIVE: MODERN MEN*.

Who rapes? Almost all rapists were abused as children — and many were themselves victims of rape. All rapists are irrationally compulsive and dangerous.

TYPES

Generally speaking, there are three types of rapists. One type — the killer variety — may well include murder in his repertoire of violence. Another type commits rape as a consequence of a chronic sense of inadequacy. Still other rapists may be acting out of a psychotic, egomaniacal need to manifest power.

Killers: The angry rapist wants to hurt you because to him, women are bad people who need to be punished. He may be angry with other women in his life, and is taking out his anger toward them on you. He is the sort of rapist you see in the movies — he will strike suddenly and without warning, and he will not hesitate to injure or even kill you. He is a sadist, and your suffering will only arouse him.

• *Try to escape in any way you know how. Your life is at stake.*

• If you know any self-defense movements, use them, even the ones you've learned that might kill him. **See** *SELF-DEFENSE,* **below.**

• There are no particular strategies for dealing with this rapist. *Try anything you can to save your life.*

A rapist suffering from fear of inadequacy cannot imagine that any woman would want to have sex with him, but hopes that if he forces a woman she may realize after all that she likes it with him.

He does not wish to hurt, but to control, and he may feel sorry afterwards and apologize. He may be a well-educated person with no criminal background. And he will probably talk a great deal to the victim. He will ask about his performance, how she likes it, what she is accustomed to. He may even give her advice on how to avoid rape in the future. He may tell her what to do for him sexually and use force until she cooperates.

• *The odds for escaping* this man are fairly good.

• Dare to resist because he is unlikely to hurt you.

• Talk to him as much as you can. Let him know that you are a real person, thereby disrupting his fantasy.

• Let him think that you understand him and are even sympathetic with his situation.

• Tell him you are scared. Ask for his protection.

• If you fight back and talk a blue streak at the same time, you may avoid the rape entirely.

• *The power-rapist:* thinks he's a stud, and to him, rape is a rather minor crime. He doesn't like women. They are like any other sex toy to him, something to use for his own satisfaction. Consequently, he does not always wish to injure, but to control. He believes that the victim is asking for it and deserves what he gives her, and he does not desire affection, and will not be moved by pleas for understanding.

• *Encourage him to talk* about himself. Feed his ego and try to break through his fantasy by making him see you as a person.

Always seek the help of a crisis or rape hotline or other support group. Do not try to forget the crime ever happened. Tell somebody as soon as possible.

SELF-DEFENSE

Don't liberate yourself to death.

Some women refuse to take basic precautions to protect themselves from attack. They say, "Look, a man doesn't have to do these precautionary things. Men walk down alleys, so, if I want to walk down alleys in the dark, I will, too. No one is going to take away my right to do as I want just because I am a woman."

The murderers and rapists, however, do not realize that you are merely asserting your rights. Look, it's just a fact, you know. Men are bigger and stronger than women, and some men attack. (AJ)

USE INSTINCTS

You have a natural, instinctive awareness of what is going on around you. Use it. If something seems less than right, get out of there. When your date begins to look like rape, don't let your good, gentle manners and doubts keep you from protecting yourself until it is too late. The minute something seems less than right, go. (LK) **See** *Date Rape* **in** *CHAPTER FIVE: MODERN MEN.*

USE PSYCHOLOGY

Do a little psychological preconditioning. Act out situations in your mind. What would you do if someone grabbed you on a lonely road? How would you react if someone suddenly appeared in your bedroom in the night? You must learn to channel your fear into a counterattack, and teach your brain to turn fear into aggression. No matter how kind and gentle you usually are, the way to fight is with rage. Remember the National Geographic specials? How the great, enormous beast is worried to pieces by some tiny little rodent? That little, bitty animal wins the fight through sheer aggression and rage. That's going to be you if you train your mind correctly. (PD)

USE YOUR FEET

Always run toward help. If you are in a house and someone is chasing you do not run into an empty room. Your assailant will probably get through that door before you have a chance to lock him out. You are now cornered. Instead, run toward the door that will take you out of the house or apartment. (HLi)

USE RAGE

Remember to *use your anger and indignation.* Panic will get you nowhere. Be furious at your attacker. He is *expecting* fear. (PL)

USE SURPRISE

You're not going to win because you are the stronger one, because you are never going to be the stronger one. *You are going to win through surprise counterattack.* You are going to win because you are going to respond immediately and hard. And after you have done this, you are going to run like the wind. (KM)

USE YOUR ELBOW

If someone grabs you from behind, try slamming him with your elbow. An elbow is a good weapon, but you must slam with all your weight and force. Another way to handle this situation is to clamp your assailant's hand down with yours, grab his little finger, and pull it backwards as hard as you can. Or, try bending forward as far as you can. Reach back between your legs and grab one of his legs at a low point on the leg. Pull forward and he'll fall down backwards. Kick him in the groin on your way out. (TF)

Split. If you're sitting on a park bench and a man sits down close to you, and it seems too close, get up and leave. Don't wait around because you think perhaps you are being oversensitive or paranoid. If he touches you, don't fidget and squirm and ask in a little, frightened voice, "What are you doing? Leave me alone, please." Thrust your elbow into his nose and leave. Or you can pinch and twist the skin of his inner thigh. That will leave him speechless for a moment that will be long enough for you to make your exit. Or grab the hair on his head and pull his head down as you bring your knee up to meet it. Do these things fast and do them mean and get out of there. (TR)

USE YOUR KNEE

If someone grabs you from the front, with your hands on his shoulders draw your knee up and whack him in the groin, then run. If a flasher presents himself to you, just turn and walk away. Show no big reactions of fright or shock. Or you can point and burst into laughter first. (ED)

Flashers and other exhibitionists are *usually* not dangerous. (HYW)

USE YOUR FIST

How to make a fist: A lot of women don't know how to make a fist. When you make a fist, your thumb must be on the *outside* of the other fingers, *not* on the inside. You'll just break your thumb if it is on the inside.

How to punch: If you're going to strike someone in front of you, punch in a straight line and strike with the knuckles of the first two fingers. It is important to tense the hand. Your fist must be *rigid* to do any good. If you hold your fingers straight to strike with the side of the hand, be sure your hand is rigid. Go for the neck or the nose. (LL)

USE YOUR FOOT

Touchers are a problem in crowded places like buses and streetcars. Stamp your foot hard on the creep's foot and then slap him hard on the ear. Hurts like hell. (PH)

USE YOUR HEAD

If somebody tries to strangle you, try to turn your head to the side to free your windpipe. (WW)

SURVIVAL TIPS FROM ALL OVER

Take the long way: Avoid trouble. If the shortcut looks ominous, take the long way home. Don't take the shortcut because a man would. You are not a man. (PI)

Speed read: If you are lucky enough to be carrying something heavy like a bookbag when someone attacks you, use it immediately. Whack with all your might. Run. (RR)

Double trouble: What if two people grab you? One is behind you holding your arms, and the other is in front of you grabbing at your clothing.

• *The person to deal with first* is the man in back of you, because what you want to do is free your arms. Use your head. Smash it back into the face of the man behind you. For a moment he will let go of you.

• *Reach back to grab his genitals* and squeeze with all your might.

• *At the same time* jab the eyes of the person in front of you with the fingers of your other hand. As his hands fly to his face, knee him in the groin. Run. (LA)

What? If you can get near enough to someone's ear, scream with all your might. A scream at close range can burst an eardrum, and you will have a moment to run. (ED)

Headsets: Do you like to take walks with your little radio headset humming away? Remember that this makes you oblivious to your surroundings. Anyone can come up on you without your knowing it. (JK)

When you kick, use the instep of your foot and not your toes. (LB)

If you bite someone's adam's apple it could kill him. (FS)

Pressing hard on the windpipe can be fatal. *(Anon.)*

Nose job: If someone grabs you from the front and you can free an arm, slam the heel of your hand up into the tip of his nose. (KN)

If you shop at night, park your car right outside the entrance to the store. You don't want to have to walk through a dark parking lot. (NO)

Always look into the backseat before you enter your car. Lock your doors once you are in. If someone is following you, don't drive home. Drive to the police station. (VP)

Have your keys ready before you leave your car. You don't want to spend time fumbling about at your door looking for your keys. (GL)

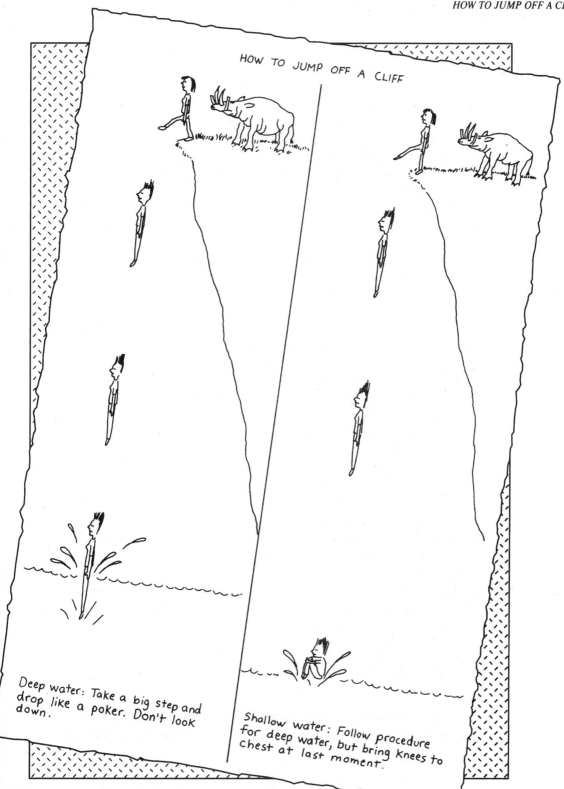

HOW TO JUMP OFF A CLIFF

Deep water: Take a big step and drop like a poker. Don't look down.

Shallow water: Follow procedure for deep water, but bring knees to chest at last moment.

When you leave someone's house at night, tell them to expect a call from you as soon as you arrive home. Or even just one ring. *(Anon.)*

Use your keys as a weapon. I have a key ring that is shaped like a small window scraper. It works beautifully on icy car windows and when held correctly can kill. Get over the fact that this sounds horrible. It is to be used in life-and-death attacks. (JC)

Keep the storm windows on year round. This helps deter burglars and will actually keep your home cooler in the hot summer months. (NM) **See also under** *HOUSE SECURITY* **in** *CHAPTER FIFTEEN: MISS, MRS., OR MS. CELANEOUS.*

Put valuables into your trunk *before* you arrive at your destination. Why park and then place your $400 camera into the trunk in full view of an entire neighborhood? Never leave packages inside the car where they can be seen. Thieves don't know that the bag contains a $9 pair of shoes until after they break your car window to find out. (GI)

If you have a convertible, never lock the doors. Thieves will slash your roof. (JS)

If the elevator arrives, and you don't like the looks of the man inside, don't get in. Don't be worried about his feelings. It's your life. (FL)

Scream "Fire!" It gets attention faster than "Help!" (BK)

Call of the wild: If someone comes to your front door asking to use the phone, tell them you will make the call for him. Don't let him into the house, no matter how sincere or "nice" he seems to be. (SL)

Don't leave your doors unlocked when you are working outside in the garden. Carry a key with you. Lots of people creep into houses while their owners are outside pulling weeds. (BC)

Look around when you leave your building. Walk with confidence and purpose. Attackers search for the timid and the unaware. Scowl. (BZ)

Carry a whistle at night in residential areas. Carrying small weapons will work against you. If your attacker is strong enough to grab you, he is strong enough to grab your weapon. (GL)

Ask your police department about programs like Block Watch or Neighborhood Watch. Neighborhoods band together in these programs to protect themselves against crime. Nosiness can be a virtue. *(Anon.)*

Direct deposit: If you're a senior citizen, your pension or compensation check can be automatically deposited into your checking account once a month. The worry of it being stolen or lost on your way to the bank to deposit it will no longer be an issue. Ask your bank what you will need to do to put this into effect. *(Anon.)*

OBSCENE CALLS

Someone calls you up on the phone. Within a few moments he has enough information to convince you that he has your mother bound, gagged, and drugged in his back room. You burst into tears. Eventually, he tells you to take off all your clothes. Hang up. It is a crank call.

Never volunteer information. Example: "Mrs. Jones?"

"No, that's my mom."

"Oh. Well, is your mom home?"

"No, she just walked over to a lecture on campus."

Now he knows that you are a daughter, that your mother has just left the house on foot, and even in which direction she is headed. Unfortunately, he already knows your address because it's in the book (it didn't *have* to be), so it is easy for him to tell you that he snatched her at the corner of Main and First.

In your frenzy, he learns that you are a college girl home on vacation, that you are at your mom's to do the laundry, and that your mom has short graying hair.

Why didn't you just say, "No, she is unavailable"?

Don't get caught in someone's cruel game. *Don't feed someone the information needed to torture you. (Anon.)*

INFORMATION

An anecdote: My father attended a Block Watch meeting on the subject of obscene phone calls. The people of the neighborhood were advised to keep a whistle next to their telephones, and, in the event of an unwanted call, to blow the whistle with all their might and hang up. At the time, my father had a silent caller. This person would call every few days and say nothing. My father couldn't bring himself to use a whistle or even to hang up on a person he felt must be terribly alone. Instead, he decided to have one-sided conversations. He would discuss the events of the day, and then he would read German poetry. He would never be the first to hang up, but would continue for up to an hour and a half before hearing the click. This continued for over two years. My father eventually moved, and the calls ceased. "You know," my dad told me, "the person could have made the effort to find my new number." (LJ)

Laugh it off: Approach an obscene call with humor. Just burst into laughter. What a letdown for the caller. (FL)

Off the hook: There are several recommended ways to deal with obscene phone calls: You can hang up, blow a whistle, threaten to call the police, and so forth. One method I haven't heard a lot about also sounds like a good idea: Simply lay the phone down quietly and walk away for a few minutes. The caller not only gets no reaction from you but also feels like a fool when he eventually discovers he's been pouring out his perversions to dead air for fifteen minutes. (ABe)

Techno-trap: The telephone company can initiate a trace on *any* calls made to your number — including calls that didn't go through because the line was engaged or because there was no reply — with a simple command to a computer. The computer will produce lists of numbers from which the calls originated, and any suspect ones can be isolated. Obscene or annoying callers, presented with such evidence by the police, almost always cease calling. The phone company is a pretty good ally in dealing with these problems, and you shouldn't hesitate calling on them for help. *(Anon.)*

CHAPTER **13**

The Medicine Cabinet

This is the chicken soup of the book, the warm broth of common sense, and it's all childproof, absolutely safe. For most ailments, our prescription is for a good dose of self-indulgence and some bed rest. If it's worse than that, look here. If it's worse than *that,* call a doctor.

By the way, the material included here is for information only. Reading this stuff is not the same as visiting your doctor — although you might want to read this while you wait *forever* in the doctor's office.

C O N T E N T S
Chapter Thirteen: *THE MEDICINE CABINET*

DOCS:When to Go to the Doctor— If the Doc Sounds Like a Duck... — Second Opinions — Eye, Eye Doc — ACCIDENTS: Some Splints **— FOLK CURES AND GENERAL PRACTICAL MEDICAL INFORMATION: REAL FIRST AID:** Circulatory Pressure Points — Tourniquet — Burns: Extent of Total Body Surface **— The Modern Woman's Medicine Cabinet** — Some Bandages — Some Reasons for Bandages **— STDs — BIRTH CONTROL: The Contraception Top of the Pops — Other Techniques — Spontaneous Miscarriages — Abortion — GYN: What You Should Expect from Your GYN — Self-Exams — Hysterectomies — Menopause — NUTRITION:** Skeleton and Internal Organs **— MODERN GRANDWOMEN: The Older Woman Is Proving — Advocacy — Age Discrimination — Government Agencies — Carrier Alert — Home Health Care — Foster Grandparents — Fooling Around — Health and Welfare — The Insults of Youth — A Dying Husband — NURSING HOMES: Nursing Home Checklist — THE END: Caring for the Terminally Ill — Treatment — Final Orders — Good-Bye — Euthanasia**

DOCS

To every thing there is a season. Cold season, flu season, hay fever season. And for every ailment, there's a well-paid doctor waiting to swap advice for cash or check.

WHEN TO GO TO THE DOCTOR

If you have a fever of 100° or more for a week and there is no explanation like a flu or a cold

If you have a pain in the chest that spreads to the left shoulder or arm or is accompanied by sweating or nausea

• *At the onset of recurrent headaches* in a person who does not ordinarily get them

• *If you have a sore throat* with severe pain and high fever

• *If you have hoarseness* for no particular reason that lasts over a week

• *If you've been coughing* for more than one to two weeks or if you're coughing up blood

• *If you have pain* in the lower right quarter of the abdomen, in the appendix district

• *If you vomit blood*

• *If you suffer from incapacitating diarrhea,* or diarrhea with blood — or any time you have blood in your stool

• *If you lose ten or more pounds* for no apparent reason

• *For infected skin wounds* — if your wound has pus, or is just hot, tender, or red, or shows red streaks.

• *If you have pain urinating* or blood in your urine

• *Any time you experience vaginal bleeding* not during menstruation

• *If you exhibit yellowing* of the skin or of the whites of your eyeballs (YJo)

IF THE DOC SOUNDS LIKE A DUCK. . .

When you're fed up with conventional doctors and have downed the pills, donned the supporters, subjected yourself to expensive and useless tests, and you still feel like a rag, you may seek an alternative method of healing.

The alternative healer, even someone who appears to be a *bona fide* physician, can sometimes be a down and dirty quack.

• Never continue seeing and paying anyone who claims to have a special formula or miracle gadget for your ailment.

• Get out of there if she announces a conviction that conventional medicine always does more harm than good.

• Avoid "doctors" who appear in sleazy print ads or on TV advertisements.

• Don't see anyone who complains that other doctors are trying to persecute her.

• And remember that AMA-listed and licensed doctors are part of a highly profitable industry that is not without its share of charlatans, incompetents and unscrupulous types. Doctors do not necessarily possess wisdom. What they do possess is a specialized technical education. Many people involved in alternate medical practices see the medical establishment as somewhat shady. (DL)

There are accepted forms of alternative medicine that are valid and that have helped millions of people. Some have been practiced for thousands of years.

• ***Acupuncture*** has been shown to be highly effective in some cases. Always get referrals from friends. Ask your doctor to help you find a good, certified acupuncturist. If the doctor demurs, ask why. Refusal to admit to other medical possibilities is not encouraging in a doctor.

Osteopaths are highly trained therapists and a valuable adjunct to the medical establishment in more medically enlightened countries. In the United Kingdom, especially, patients are often referred to qualified osteopaths by fully licensed general practitioners and specialists.

Homeopathy is an alternative system of healing based on the theory that every individual is idiosyncratic and should be treated for ailments according to that individual's specific physical, psychological and spiritual condition.

Homeopathic practitioners treat an ailment with very small quantities of natural substances that are presumably similar to the chemical imbalance that initially caused the ailment to manifest. Their choice of substance is based on an extended interview in which many questions concerning the physical, mental and emotional history of the individual are asked in order for the practitioner to gain a complete sense of the patient. (SL)

A homeopathic anecdote: I have had mild acne since I was thirteen years old. For many years, I went to many dermatologists and never found the relief I sought and for which I paid. The standard line I heard always went something like this: "Don't worry. You'll grow out of it." By the time I turned twenty-five, I still hadn't grown out of it. Finally, I made an appointment to see a doctor I had seen once before. He was considered to be the best dermatologist in my state, a man who works at one of the world's most prestigious medical institutions.

I made my appointment well in advance and arrived early. I was asked to wait for an hour and forty-five minutes before I was escorted into a smaller office, where I waited another half hour. Finally, a young woman came in, looked at my skin, told me I had acne and left.

After a while, the doctor came in, accompanied by a young man, presumably a student. The student was approximately my age, and I found his unannounced presence to be an invasion of my privacy.

"What seems to be the problem?" the doctor asked.

"Look at my face," I suggested. But without examining my skin or asking me a single question, the doctor whipped out his prescription pad and quickly scribbled two notes — one for a very large dosage of tetracycline and another for a topical skin cream he had prescribed for me before. It had irritated my skin and made my face red and sore.

When I told him I was going to London for a few months, he told me to call him when I returned. Then he left. I began to question my visit. The office call would cost me at least $50 and the medicine would set me back another $20. It would make me sick and make my face all ugly and red. The visit had also cost me two hours of my time and I saw the doctor for only a few minutes.

So I went to London, swallowing my megadoses of tetracycline every day and smearing Benzagel cream on my face every night, and my skin got worse and worse. Finally, the friend with whom I was staying told me about the homeopath she had been taking her children to see. She offered to make an appointment, and off I went.

I waited on a small bench on the bottom floor of a small, neat, clean white building near Notting Hill Gate. After a few minutes, the homeopath came, introduced himself, and escorted me into a consulting office. He sat at a plain wooden desk and I sat in a wooden chair and he asked me questions about myself for over an hour and a half. He asked what I ate, what position I slept in, whether or not I had trouble making friends. He asked about my family, my menstrual flow, what medicines I was taking, what hobbies and what fears I had. He was patient and kind and very interested and wrote down every response on a pad, and even noted any random ideas I tossed out. He volunteered that he had once had "spots" as a child, and he understood how traumatic they could be. He looked at my face very closely under a gentle light. Then he consulted a book and told me to call the next day for a prescription. The consultation cost £20 (about $38 at the time).

By this time, my skin condition had deteriorated, and I didn't hold out much hope. Certainly I didn't expect much from a batch of "natural" medicines. Nevertheless, I called for the prescription and was given a small brown envelope filled with several weeks' worth of tiny white pills and instructions to chew one each day before food. There was no charge for the medicine.

I started taking them and there was a noticeable change in my skin the very next day. Within another two days, my face was clearer than it had been at any time since I was thirteen years old. After a couple of weeks, I called the homeopath to thank him for what I considered a miracle.

He explained that the pills were a natural remedy made from a fish extract and that I need only take them another five weeks or so.

I threw the tetracycline and the Benzagel away.

But I should make it clear that homeopathy requires a willingness to consult with the practioner again and again as the condition warrants. I wouldn't advise anyone to go to a homeopath, swallow the medicine, then expect a miracle. Homeopathy treats the whole body, not just the symptoms of an ailment, and bodies are complicated pieces of equipment that require a reasonable amount of attention. *(Anon.)*

SECOND OPINIONS

When contemplating any surgical procedure recommended by your doctor, it's never a bad idea to get a second opinion. Your doctor should be glad to recommend a doctor to examine you and give his own diagnosis. If your doctor objects to your looking for another opinion, you may have the wrong doctor. (MK)

Get a second opinion. Would you buy a washing machine without looking at two or three different brands? *(Anon.)*

EYE, EYE DOC

Whom to see, if only you could:

• An *ophthalmologist* is a medical doctor who specializes in diseases of the eye. He can prescribe medication and perform eye surgery, as well as prescribe eyeglasses and contact lenses.

• An *optometrist* is not a licensed M.D. He is, however, licensed by the state in which he practices. His job is to examine eyes for vision problems and treat them with eyeglasses or lenses or with vision therapy. He also looks for signs of eye disease or systemic diseases such as diabetes or hypertension.

• An *optician* is the pharmacist of the eye-care world. He is licensed to fill a doctor's prescription for medication and to grind lenses from a prescription for eyeglasses or contact lenses. (MK)

ACCIDENTS

are the leading cause of death for all people between the ages of one and forty-four.

In an emergency, as a rule it isn't wise to rush. Try instead to work deliberately and efficiently. Here, in order of priority, is what you should do:

*1. **Evaluate the injured person*** or persons. Who needs help the most?

*2. **Is the person conscious*** or unconscious?

*3. **Check breathing.*** If the victim needs help, clear her mouth and throat, extend the victim's neck and give mouth-to-mouth resuscitation.

*4. **Check for pulse*** or heartbeat.

*5. **Place a dressing*** or use your hand to cover a sucking wound in the chest or neck. In a sucking wound, air blows or bubbles.

*6. **Apply pressure*** to control breathing.

*7. **Don't move the victim*** if her back or neck is injured.

*8. **Apply a splint*** to fractured bones. (JMcE, AKK) **See also under** *REAL FIRST AID,* **below. See illustration.**

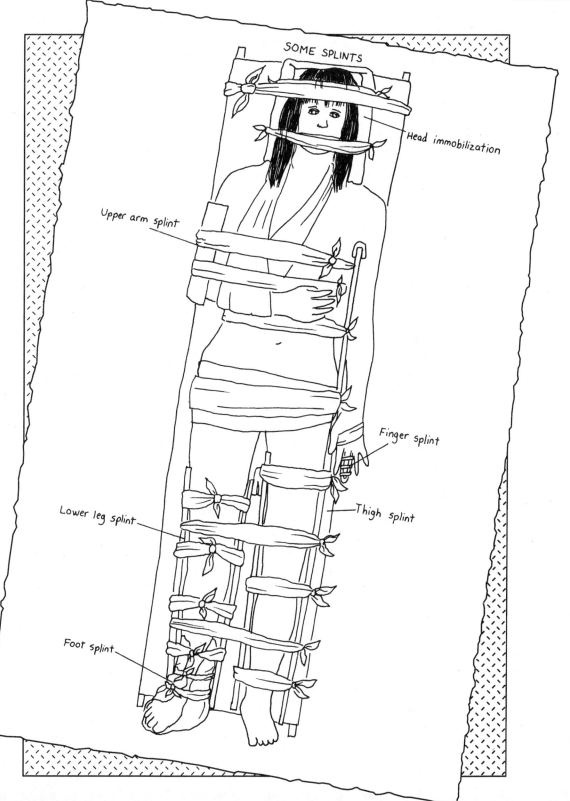

SOME SPLINTS

Head immobilization

Upper arm splint

Finger splint

Thigh splint

Lower leg splint

Foot splint

FOLK CURES AND PRACTICAL MEDICAL INFORMATION

Before you go on to look for some serious first aid, try a folk cure. If they work, they're probably better for you. In fact, if they work, they're *definitely* better for you. And if you just want to know what *might* ail you, look here.

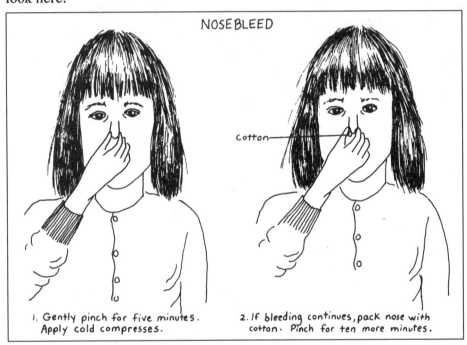

NOSEBLEED

Cotton

1. Gently pinch for five minutes. Apply cold compresses.

2. If bleeding continues, pack nose with cotton. Pinch for ten more minutes.

But remember, like everything else in this book, what is offered here is offered for information only and isn't a substitute for professional care.

Acne: Vitamin A, that's the ticket. Ask your doctor. **But see above, under** *Homeopathy.*

Alcoholism: Are you drinking too much? Here is a rough checklist to see if you need some help. Place a check mark next to the questions to which you would answer "yes."

❑ Do you occasionally drink heavily after a disappointment or quarrel?

❑ Can you handle more liquor now than when you first started drinking?

❑ When you're drinking with other people, do you ever try to have a few extra drinks behind their backs?

❑ Have you noticed that when you begin drinking you are in more of a hurry to get the first drink than you used to be?

❏ Do you get irritated when family or friends discuss your drinking?

❏ Do you often want to continue drinking after your friends say that they've had enough?

❏ Do you usually have a reason for the occasions when you drink heavily?

❏ Have you noticed an increase in the frequency of memory blackouts?

❏ Do you get terribly frightened after you've been drinking heavily?

❏ Do you sometimes feel very depressed and wonder whether life is worth living?

❏ Do you ever have the shakes in the morning and find a little drink helps?

❏ Do you sometimes stay drunk for several days at a time?

❏ Have you noticed that you can't drink as much as you once did?

❏ After periods of drinking, do you sometimes see or hear things that aren't there?

❏ Do you eat very little or irregularly when you are drinking?

❏ Do more people seem to be treating you unfairly without good reason?

❏ Do you try to avoid family or friends when you are drinking?

❏ Are you experiencing an increasing number of financial and work problems?

❏ Have you tried to control your drinking by moving to a new location or changing jobs?

❏ Have you often failed to keep the promises you've made to yourself about controlling or cutting down on your drinking?

❏ Have you tried switching brands or following different plans for controlling your drinking?

❏ When you are sober, do you often regret things you've said or done while drinking?

❏ Do you sometimes feel a little guilty about your drinking?

❏ When you are in trouble or under extra pressure, do you always drink more heavily than usual?

❏ When you wake up in the morning do you find that you can't remember part of the evening before, even though your friends tell you that you didn't pass out?

❏ Are there occasions when you feel uncomfortable if liquor is not available?

Count the number of "yes" answers to determine the stages of alcoholism: 1 to 8 indicates the early stage of alcoholism; 9 to 21 middle stage; 22 to 26 the beginning of final stage.

Alcoholism can be controlled. If you suspect that you have a drinking problem, you probably do. Get help: Ask your clergyman or doctor or contact the local Alcoholics Anonymous chapter. *You can stop* if you want to — the person typing this did. At least for today. (*Anon.*)

Bed-wetting: Don't worry about tykes under five. For five and over try getting the child to chew on toothpicks soaked in cinnamon oil. Or try a teaspoon of honey at bedtime.

Blood pressure: You can walk around for years without realizing you have high blood pressure. Your doctor can check on it for you by fitting that little cloth around the upper part of your arm and squeezing a little bulb that fills it with air. Another, less practical way is to wait until you have a heart attack, stroke, or kidney disease.

Hypertension is another word for high blood pressure. It is not necessarily connected with emotional tension, a high pressure job, or where you live. An easygoing lifestyle is not a guarantee against high blood pressure.

Blood pumps through your body when your heart beats. Your blood pressure goes up and down. But if your pressure stays up, your arteries and heart will not function to the best of their ability. Other body organs may be affected as well.

Obesity, too much salt, heredity, and body chemistry can all contribute to problems with blood pressure. However, the specific cause is unknown in 90 percent of those afflicted.

Two numbers record your blood pressure. The first is the *systolic,* or pumping pressure. The second is *diastolic* or resting pressure. If you are 120/80, that means that the column of mercury on the gauge reaches 120 before the pressure equals the pressure of your blood against your arteries while your heart is pumping. And while the heart is resting, the pressure of your blood against your arteries goes down to the amount of pressure it took to make the mercury reach 80.

There is no reading that is normal for everyone. Your blood pressure may be different at different times of the day.

High blood pressure is a problem because it means that your blood is putting too much pressure against the sides of your blood vessels. There are drugs that can control high blood pressure. If your doctor has prescribed such a drug for you, take it. **See under** *NUTRITION,* **below.**

High blood pressure cannot be cured, but it can be controlled. You may be advised to lose weight, cut down on salt, stop smoking, or increase exercise. Have your blood pressure checked once a year.

Don't stop your medicine or disregard your doctor's advice just because you feel better. There is no cure. Dust thou art, and unto dust shalt thou return. **See also** *Stroke,* **below.**

Burns: If there isn't seared skin and severe blistering, apply cool water as soon as possible. Not cold. Cool. Cooling relieves pain and prevents burns from becoming worse. The most frequent cause of burns is hot tap water, not fire. Serious burns, of course, need a doctor. **See under** *REAL FIRST AID,* **below.**

Bursitis: The Hungarian Method for the treatment of bursitis: bee stings. Capture several bees and allow them to sting you in the area of your bursitis. Don't treat the stings. The venom dissolves the crystalized fluids that cause pain in the joints of infected areas. You have to be brave to try this. You also have to be absolutely certain that you aren't allergic to bee stings.

Note: Look, you're on your own, here. We couldn't find a Modern Woman willing to try this, so maybe you shouldn't either. Remember our disclaimer? This material is for information only.

Colds: Chicken soup helps, it's really true. Or try mixing a pinch of cayenne pepper, some lemon juice, some minced garlic, and a big dose of vitamin C. Sip it slowly. Or wait it out. Colds are not terminal illnesses, but they are incurable.

Working through a cold: When you're down with that most common malady and lying around feeling miserable, exercise may seem to be either a good way to get your body's juices flowing and help it fight off the bugs, or a good way to relieve the boredom of lying around sniffling and sneezing — and necessary to keep up that hard-won muscle tone.

Sounds logical, right? Wrong! Exercising during a cold can do much more harm than good. For example, even a mild cold can irritate respiratory passages, making breathing more difficult. Your workout further strains your respiratory system, increasing fatigue and lowering your ability to resist other potential infections.

Another good reason to cool the calisthenics is body temperature. An aerobic routine can raise your body temperature by as much as 6 degrees. If you're already running a slight fever, say 3 or 4 degrees, you run the risk of heat exhaustion.

Also, exercise usually implies perspiration, and chances are you're already a bit dehydrated; the last thing your body needs is to lose *more* fluid. So relax and feel virtuous about lying around instead of increasing your health risk with nasty exercises.

Constipation: Bran.

Diaper rash: Rash occurs more often in babies wearing disposable diapers or rubber or plastic pants. Try triple cotton diapers at night with a rubber pad on the bed and no diaper cover. Or try laundering diapers in an extra rinse with diluted vinegar. Use cornstarch as a baby powder. Zinc oxide is effective in healing a rash.

Diarrhea: Bananas, but consult a doctor if symptoms persist for more than a few days. *A dissent:* Bananas *gave* me diarrhea. *(Anon.)*

Fatigue: When you're getting groggy but there's more to be done, try exercising a bit to get the blood flowing again. A short walk or some jumping jacks will help send some more oxygen to your battered brain.

Frostbite can occur very quickly at very low temperatures or over a long period of time at temperatures just under freezing. The best way to avoid frostbite is, of course, to dress properly. Even if you take all the precautionary measures, you still may find yourself in an emergency situation.

Tingling and burning of your hands, feet and nose are the first symptoms of frostbite. If this happens, wave your arms, run around and rub your face. If that doesn't work and the areas become numb, you probably have frostbite. As soon as possible, get into a shelter of some kind and put the affected area in warm, *not hot,* water for half an hour. *Never allow thawed skin to refreeze.*

To prevent frostbite from occurring, tuck your hands under your armpits, get your feet up off the freezing ground or cover your face with gloved hands. If none of these measures seems to be working, get to a hospital as soon as possible. Seriously frostbitten areas usually must be amputated. **See below under** *Cold.*

Hiccoughs: Fill a glass with water and place a metal spoon into it. Sip the water from the glass while holding the handle of the spoon against the temple. The lower part of the spoon remains in the water.

Or slowly dissolve a teaspoon of sugar in your mouth.

Or breathe into a paper bag.

Or sip water backwards. You know, slurp it from the wrong side of the cup.

Hypothermia occurs when body temperature goes below 95.6° F. because someone has become too cold or wet. A person with hypothermia demonstrates *distinct symptoms,* beginning with violent shivering and leading to difficulty with speech, erratic body movements, stiff muscles, the inability to think clearly, irrational behavior, unconsciousness and, finally, death.

A hypothermia victim must be tended to immediately. Get the person dry and warm, set him or her near a large campfire if you're in the wilderness, or into a warmed-up car, or help the victim walk around to stimulate body heat and administer warm liquids. When the victim is alert again, lay him or her down in a warm and comfortable place. **See also** *Frostbite,* **above.**

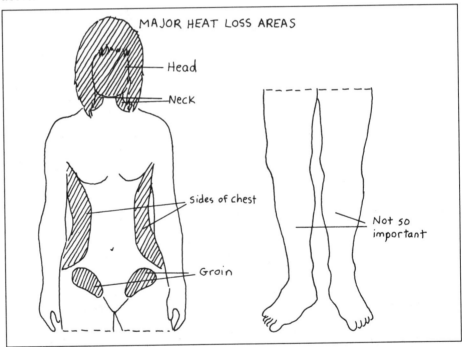

MAJOR HEAT LOSS AREAS

— Head
— Neck
Sides of chest
Groin
Not so important

Insect bites: Put baking soda and ice cold water into a container and soak the bite. When removing a honeybee stinger, scrape, don't pull. Try a slice of freshly cut onion against the sting. Or smear with honey and put an ice bag on top. A poultice of cornstarch and lemon juice is good for mosquito bites.

Bee stings are best treated by splashing on vinegar and rubbing with a slice of onion. That seems to draw out the pain and reduces swelling. It also makes you smell like a bad salad.

Campho-Phenique is the best for itchy bug bites.

Insomnia: A few suggestions on what to do when it's three in the ayem and sleep is just a memory:

• *Take a hot bath,* preferably with bubbles. If a bath is impractical, a hot shower will do almost as well.

• *Don't lie in bed tossing and turning* and feeling frustrated. Get up and do something constructive. Clean the old food out of the refrigerator or rearrange your closet. This should get your mind off whatever's worrying you.

• *Imagine yourself* in a fantastic location — in your very own beach house or mountain cabin — and design every detail to be exactly the way you want it. This will also get your mind off its treadmill and may give you very pleasant dreams.

• *Try this variation on self-hypnosis:* Focus your mind on a single image — a candle flame or the ocean surf. Keep telling yourself that your body is relaxing and falling asleep. Soon enough you will be.

Menstrual cramps: Warmth. Hot tub. Hot water bottle. Hot tea. Try medicine like Advil or Nuprin. If you have *killer* cramps, then none of this will work. So get down on your knees and put your face on the floor and your butt into the air. Looks silly, but it doesn't matter in the middle of the night. And it works.

Here's a way to deal with monthly cramps instead of taking pills. Use acupressure. Get someone to press hard on your back with the thumb approximately one inch to the right of your spine and one inch below your shoulder blade. Have the person press on the spot (a little experimentation should help you find it) for about thirty seconds and you should feel immediate relief.

Grate ginger — maybe half a teaspoonful — and boil it with a cup of water. Put a tea bag in a cup, pour the ginger broth in the cup and sip away. Cures stomach cramps in about thirty minutes.

In cases with more severe cramps, ask your doctor about the drug Anaprox. Anaprox was invented to treat arthritis and found to have the side effect of helping women with problem periods. Many women have reported drastic reduction of menstrual cramps with virtually no side effects.

For PMS: B vitamins, B_6 in particular. And cut back on sugar, salt, refined carbohydrates and dairy products.

Menopausal problems: Vitamin E is good for controlling hot flashes. Try calcium supplements and exercise for prevention of bone loss. *For sleep problems* associated with menopause, try cereal with bananas and milk. Remember good nutrition will help control the jump in cholesterol that takes place after menopause. Stop smoking.

Osteoporosis is the gradual loss and weakening of bone that comes with aging. Calcium supplements, exercise such as walking and swimming, and foods like milk, yogurt, shellfish, and sardines can stop the process.

Panic: We all get anxiety attacks and feelings of panic at times, so remember you're not alone. Still, suffering from panic or a panic attack is, shall we say, frightening. So, if you don't want to live in a Valium fog or smoke pot in the bathroom at work, you can do a few things to help yourself avoid the panic reaction.

• *Talk over your problems* with a good friend or a counselor. If you have a great relationship with your mother, you can talk to her. It's somehow very reassuring to have her tell you that you've been spun into a panic everytime you stepped into a bus since you were two — that it is not a new phenomenon.

• *You must be nice to yourself,* realize that no one is perfect and very few are even close to perfection.

• *You can look on anxiety* and panic as friends that are warning you to slow down and be realistic with your expectations.

Poisons: *Quick, an anecdote!* I know a man who after a small dinner party and too large an amount to drink went home and downed a bottle of bleach. This happened because, apart from this guy's stupidity, the bleach had been put into a spirits bottle for some reason or other.

It sounds absurd, but something like this could happen to you or a loved one, particularly if you have kids around. So the following precautionary measures, though many may seem commonplace, are worth heeding. After all, we all get stupid now and then.

• *Make sure* all potentially harmful products and medicines have child-resistant caps.

• *Keep all such items* in their original containers and well away from food products.

• *Put all products* that could be poisonous up high and out of the reach of children, or pets for that matter.

• *Clean out your medicine chest* once every six months and discard old aspirins, medications, cough syrups, prescriptions and flush them or empty into a childproof container and take it out to the dumpster.

• *Never give medicine* to anyone other than the person or illness for which it was specifically prescribed.

• *Find out and keep the local poison control center number* in an obvious place.

• *If you suspect* you or someone close to you has been poisoned, immediately call the local poison control center. If this is impossible — if, say you're camping or driving in the desert — look for the following signs of poisoning:

An open drug container

Unfamiliar or odd odor on breath

Nausea or vomiting

Convulsions

Drowsiness

Dizziness or staggering

Shallow or difficult breathing

Burns on mouth or hands

Changes in behavior, such as overexcitement

Stains on clothing **See how to get them out in** *THE PAIN OF STAINS* **in** *CHAPTER NINE: HOME EC.*

If any of these symptoms exist and you can determine how the poisoning took place, do this:

• *Inhaled poisons:* Immediately get the person to fresh air. Open all doors and windows.

If the victim is not breathing, start artificial respiration. Call the poison center as soon as possible.

• *Poison on the skin:* Remove any affected clothing and flood involved body parts with water for ten minutes minimum. Then wash gently with mild soap and water and rinse. Call the poison center as soon as possible.

Swallowed poisons: If it's medicine, do not give anything by mouth until after calling for advice. However, if the suspected poison is a commercially available product, not a medication, what to do if ingested is often stated on the label.

• *Chemical or household products:* If the person is awake and able to swallow, give milk or water immediately. Call for any professional advice before inducing vomiting. Never give salt, vinegar or citrus juices. Call the poison control center as soon as possible.

• *Poisons in the eye:* Flood the eye with lukewarm water, poured from a container two to four inches above the eye. Repeat for at least fifteen minutes. Have the victim blink as much as possible while flooding the eye. Don't force the eyelid open. Call the poison control center as soon as possible.

See also under *Ten Ways to Prevent Child Poisoning* **in** *CHAPTER SIXTEEN: THE MODERN MOM* **and also under** *REAL FIRST AID,* **below.**

Stroke: The steps to take to prevent a stroke:

1. Control your blood pressure.

2. Quit smoking.

3. Lower your cholesterol intake.

4. Aerobic exercises three times a week will help, but check with your doctor first.

5. Control your diet if you are diabetic or obese.

Teeth grinding: Chew a few calcium tablets at bedtime. (VL, JM, DD, MK, DL, YB, RLi, JGu, WG, AY, TR, *Anon*)

Yeast infections: Cranberry juice and plain yoghurt seem to be the best folk-type cure. But a yeast infection is a persistent devil and can require professional attention.

Clean yeast: To prevent yeast infection bacteria from living a happy life in your clean underwear, use garments made from cotton. After laudering, place the still damp undies in the microwave and blast them for about 30 seconds on the high setting. This will kill the bacteria that happily survived the washing machine. But don't do this with panties made from blends or synthetics. They may *explode* and you could be killed! Imagine the headline. *(Anon)*

REAL FIRST AID

You've heard it before: This material is for information only and is not intended to replace competent medical care. But in a pinch. . .

Shock is common with anyone who is badly injured. Have the person lie down. If he or she can't breathe well, elevate his or her legs, but don't raise broken bones if they haven't been splinted, and don't raise the legs if it just hurts him or her more. If an arm has been hurt but isn't broken, elevate it, too. **See under** *Bones,* **below.**

If a person is bleeding from the mouth or vomiting, put her on her side. Bend her knees and put her head on one arm.

If someone has been in a bad accident but emerges with what appears to be only minor injuries, treat her for shock anyway. People can go into shock quite suddenly, and it can kill them.

Try to keep the victim from becoming too hot or too cold.

Bleeding: A person can bleed to death from a bad cut in a minute. Press on the cut with a clean cloth. If it does not cause more pain to the person, hold the cut up. Press with your hand if you don't have a cloth. Apply a bandage only after the bleeding has stopped; then give care for shock, and call a doctor. If blood soaks through the first pad, apply another without removing the first.

If the bleeding on an arm or hand will not stop, squeeze shut the large blood vessel at the pressure point that is about halfway between the shoulder and the elbow by pressing the vessel against the bone with your fingers flat. (Reach in from behind the person to squeeze the pressure point.) With your other hand, continue holding the pad against the wound. Hold the cut up.

If a leg or foot continues to bleed, hold a pad against the cut and with the other hand squeeze the large blood vessel at the pressure point where the leg joins the body. The person should be lying down and the leg should be elevated. Push on the pressure point with the heel of your hand.

To stop a nosebleed, lean forward and pinch your nose shut. Call a doctor if it hasn't stopped after fifteen minutes. **See illustration.**

Gunshot wounds: Check both sides of the person, because there will be two wounds if the bullet passed through the body. Try not to move the victim because you cannot know what sort of internal damage has been suffered. If a bullet or knife makes a hole in a lung, you can hear air entering and leaving the wound. Stop the air by covering the hole with tape or cloth. You want the lungs to keep working.

Poison: Immediately administer water or milk because this will slow the action of the poison. Try to find out what the poison is and call a poison center. Don't try to induce vomiting, because this could injure the person more. If the person begins to vomit anyway, have her bend over very far to keep thrown-up poison from entering the lungs. Do not give any liquids if a person is having convulsions, is unconscious or appears to be in a state of exhaustion. Call an ambulance. Turn the victim onto her side.

Bones: If you must move a person with broken bones, try to keep the broken area and the joints on each side of it from moving.

To make a splint, tie one strip of cloth close on each side of the break, and others farther away above and below each joint. **See illustration.** Sometimes you can make a splint out

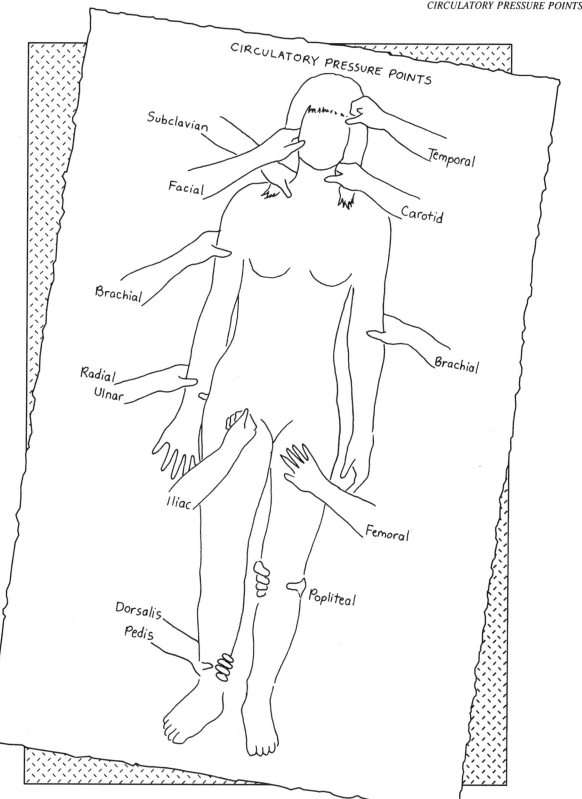

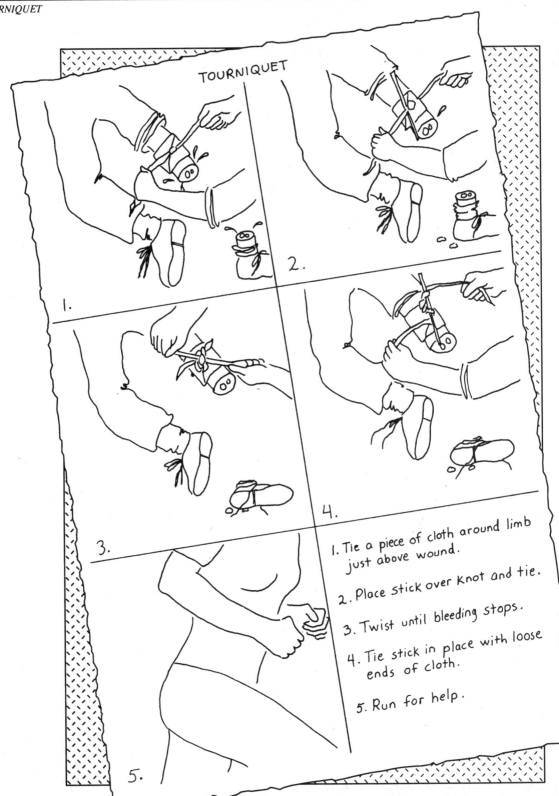

TOURNIQUET

1.

2.

3.

4.

5.

1. Tie a piece of cloth around limb just above wound.

2. Place stick over knot and tie.

3. Twist until bleeding stops.

4. Tie stick in place with loose ends of cloth.

5. Run for help.

of rolled magazines and newspapers if you do not have wood. Tree branches can work if they are quite straight. Do not make a splint too tight.

If a bone is dislocated, you might see a bump at the joint. Keep it still and go to a doctor. Do *not* yank on it to try and pop it back into place.

A *sprain* is the result of too much stretching or pulling on a joint. You may not be able to tell if it is a strain or a break, so treat it as a break.

Do not move a person with neck or back injuries.

Burns: Don't put deep burns into water. Cover with a clean bandage and find a doctor, but don't try to clean the damaged area and don't pull burned clothing away from it.

Treat a victim of a bad burn for shock.

Small burns with blisters on the face, hands, feet, or genitals can be serious. Burns on the face, nose, or mouth could mean that there may also be burns in the breathing passages. This can make the airway swell and block breathing. Get to a doctor.

If you burn your eye with grease or a spark from something, flood it with water, bandage the eye, and call a doctor. If the eye is badly burned, do not flood with water. Bandage both eyes to keep the hurt one from moving.

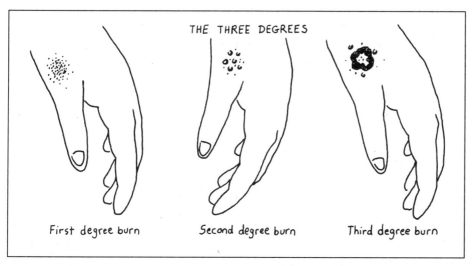

THE THREE DEGREES

First degree burn   Second degree burn   Third degree burn

Chemicals: If you splash something into your eye, flood it with water. Turn your head so that the eye with the chemical is toward the bottom so that the chemical will not wash into the good eye. Some chemicals need to be flushed for as long as fifteen minutes to prevent blindness.

Fires: Shut windows and doors on your way out of a burning building to slow the spread of the fire. Hold a thick, wet cloth over your mouth to keep your breathing passages from burning. Do not open a door if it feels hot. If it is cool, crouch down and open it slowly. If you are trapped upstairs, open the window and hang something from it so that the firefighters will know where to find you.

Head injury: Keep the victim lying on her back. Only move her if that is absolutely

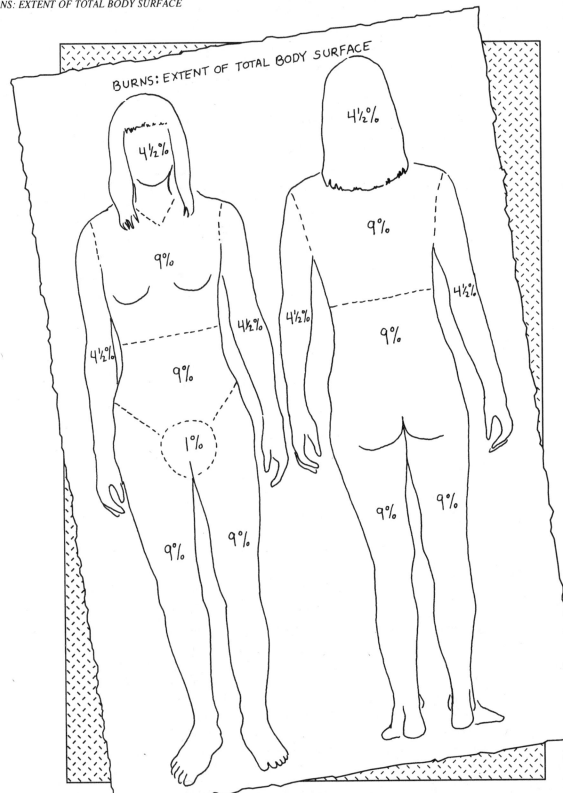

necessary. Do not give her anything to eat or drink, and if she has hurt her neck or back, do not move her at all. If the neck and back are uninjured, and the person is having difficulty breathing, elevate her head and shoulders. Do not raise her feet or legs.

Internal bleeding: The victim may feel cool and wet. Keep her lying down and still. Do not give her anything to eat or drink.

Epilepsy: Do not hold a person down, but move things out of the way. After the attack, turn her on her side and check for breathing. Loosen tight clothing. Let her sleep.

Infection: If someone has a badly infected cut and you cannot get to a doctor right away, have her lie down with the infected area elevated. Dip a cloth in warm water and squeeze it out. Lay it against the infected area. When it cools, replace it. Keep warm packs on for half an hour, then cover them with a clean, dry cloth for half an hour. Then go back to the packs. Repeat this procedure until you can get medical care. Do not move the infected area.

Snakebites: Lie down and be quiet. Keep the bite lower than the heart. Get medical care. If signs of poisoning begin to take effect, there will be swelling and pain. If the bite is on an arm or leg, tie a cloth band above the bite between the bite and the heart two to four inches above the bite. Make it tight enough so that it stops the blood near the surface of the skin, but not so tight that it stops all blood flow. Only tie a band if there are signs of poisoning. It will stop the spread. Don't tie it on a wrist, elbow, ankle, or knee. You should be able to squeeze one finger between the skin and the band.

Signs of poisoning can also be dizziness, vomiting, passing out, and stopping breathing.

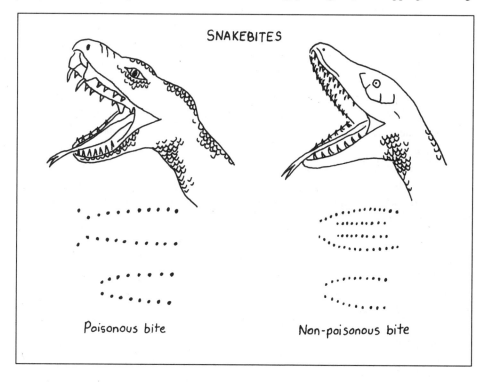

SNAKEBITES

Poisonous bite   Non-poisonous bite

Dangerous insect bites: Tie a cloth band above the bite if it is on an arm or leg. The band should be between the bite and the heart . **See above under** *Snakebites*. Put ice in a cloth on the bite. After five minutes, remove the band. Keep the arm or leg hanging down, and take the person to a doctor.

Ticks: Don't pull it out. Cover it with any kind of oil so it cannot breathe. Eventually, it will back out. Take it away with tweezers and scrub the bite with soap and water. If fever sets in, see a doctor.

Heat and sun: Give half a glass of water with a couple of pinches of salt in it to a person who has had too much sun if their skin feels cool and wet. If someone is not sweating and their skin feels hot, pour water on them to cool them down, and take them to a hospital.

Cold: A person who has been in the cold too long will get numb and sleepy and may have difficulty moving or seeing. The person needs to be warmed quickly and gently, so bring her to a warm place and remove any wet clothing.

If you can't get to a warm place, make some sort of shelter. If you have sleeping bags, get inside with the victim, or the bag will do no good. If you can, give her something hot to drink.

If a person has frostbite, the skin will turn white and then grayish yellow and may form blisters. It may be numb. Put the frozen part in warm, not *hot*, water. If there is no warm water, hold the frozen area between your own warm hands, but do not rub it. If there is warm water, keep the affected part in it for thirty minutes — even if it hurts. After it has warmed, keep it raised and bandaged. Do not use a hot water bottle or put a frostbitten part near a hot stove or fire. If you need to use the frostbitten part to get to safety, do not warm it. Keep it frozen until it can be warmed and kept warmed. **See above under** *Frostbite*.

Drowning: If you aren't trained in lifesaving, do not attempt to swim out to a drowning person, because the chances are good that you will both go down.

If the victim is near the shore, hold out something for her to grab. If she is farther out, push something to her like a lifejacket or big stick. If you row out to someone who is very tired, make her hang onto the boat while you row in. *Never underestimate the panic of a drowning person.*

Electric shock: Know where the main switch is in your house. If someone is being shocked, turn off the switch and then tend to the person. If you can't turn off the electricity, use a long, dry wooden stick to pull the plug from the wall. Do not touch the person until you have done this. (*Anon.,* DL, VL, SC, DDe)

THE MODERN WOMAN'S MEDICINE CABINET

Don't overstock. Buy medicine when you need it. It's not like stocking a bomb shelter — buy only the amount you'll need within a reasonable period of time. Some medicines get stronger with age, so don't take anything beyond the expiration date.

Basics: Here's the right stuff:
- For headaches: Aspirin or a nonaspirin substitute
- For constipation: A mild laxative like Milk of Magnesia

SOME BANDAGES

4-tail lower jaw bandage

Cravat eye bandage

Arm sling

Torso wrap

Finger bandage

Mid-section wrap

Hand wrap

Knee bandage

Lower leg wrap

Ankle wrap

SOME REASONS FOR BANDAGES

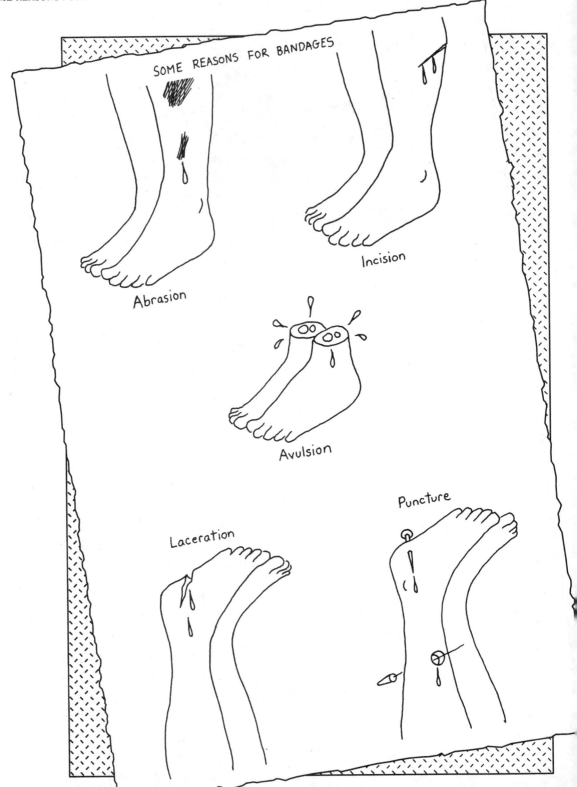

• For eye irritation: Decongestant eyedrops
• For earache: Glycerine
• For small cuts: Iodine
• For skin abrasions, sunburn, or rash: Petroleum jelly
• For muscle strain and bruises: Rubbing alcohol
• For fainting: Crushable ampules of aromatic ammonia

Ask the pharmacist for advice. A pharmacist will always tell you straight if one item is just as good but more inexpensive. (DDe)

CLASS PRESCRIPTION

Take a Red Cross First Aid course. This should be a requirement to be a mother. Employers also like the idea that at least one person in the office can respond in an emergency. *(Anon.)*

HOTLINES

The Department of Health and Human Services operates the *National Health Information Clearinghouse*, a database comprising some 1,000 health-related organizations. Most of these groups have toll-free 800 numbers for information. The *Clearinghouse's* toll-free number is 800-336-4797. (USG)

STDs

Sexually transmitted diseases are on the rise everywhere, and the only way to control their spread is to know whether you or the person you're sleeping with has one. Here are the symptoms:

Chlamydia: Symptoms include a burning discharge or painful urination; however, there may be no symptoms at all. Untreated, this can cause pelvic inflammatory disease in women (infections of the tubes or ovaries), as well as eye infections in men, women, and newborns.

This disease can be treated with antibiotics for both sexual partners.

Gonorrhea can cause oral, rectal, cervical or urethral infections. Many women and some men show no symptoms. In males, this infection is in the urethra and often causes a puslike discharge and pain during urination. Untreated, this can lead to pelvic inflammatory disease in women and a narrowing or blocking of the urethra in men. Both men and women could suffer sterility, arthritis, and heart problems. In pregnancy, this infection could cause premature labor and stillbirth.

This disease can be treated with penicillin or other antibiotics. Some strains are resistant to treatment. Both sexual partners must be checked after treatment.

Herpes: Type I affects the head and neck, causing "cold sores," and type II causes painful blister-like sores on the genitals. Both types may be found in the genital area, as well as near the mouth. If a woman contracts herpes for the first time during pregnancy, she has a higher risk of miscarriage or stillbirth, and if she has active sores at the time of delivery, a cesarean section may be done to prevent complications in the newborn. Ointments and tablets can reduce the severity of the outbreak, but the virus remains in the body and can break out following stress or illness.

There is no known cure for herpes. It can be spread by engaging in intercourse during an outbreak.

Venereal warts are caused by the condyloma virus. These are soft, cauliflower-like warts that can appear on the genital or anal areas. Some types of these warts are thought to cause cervical changes that may precede cancer.

The warts can be eradicated with topical medication, freezing, or laser treatment.

Syphilis is easily treatable in the early stages. But if left, this disease can be life-threatening in later stages. In the first stage, a painless genital lesion appears. In later stages, there can be rashes, neurological damage, and other organ damage. Untreated, syphilis can harm the fetus and cause stillbirths or birth defects. Both sexual partners must be treated at the same time.

Syphilis is treatable using penicillin or antibiotics.

Hepatitis-B: This infection is often contracted through the shared use of intravenous needles or from blood transfusions that weren't previously screened for the disease. Anyone at risk for hepatitis-B should practice safe sex. There is a vaccination that can protect those at risk of contracting the virus — including babies born to infected mothers.

AIDS: Only safe sexual practices can prevent the exchange of bodily fluids, which carry the AIDS virus and other STDs.

Safe sex means preventing one sexual partner's blood, semen, urine, vaginal secretions, or feces from entering the vagina, penis, anus, or mouth of the other sexual partner.

The AIDS virus cannot pass through a latex condom that is properly worn and used. Use water-based lubricants, rather than oils such as petroleum jelly, cold cream, or mineral oil. The spermicide nonoxynol-9 in contraceptive foams, jellies and creams kills the virus on contact and can be used in addition to condoms as added protection.

If you know for *certain* that both you and your partner have been monogamous for ten years, and that neither of you are high-risk for any other reason (for example, receiving blood products prior to 1985 or using intravenous drugs), you probably do not need to use condoms during intercourse.

Here is a list of sexual practices grouped according to relative risk of transmitting AIDS:

• *Safe:*

Massage

Hugging

Body-to-body rubbing
"Social" kissing
Masturbation
Fantasy role-playing not involving intimate contact

• *Possibly safe:*
Vaginal or anal intercourse with a condom and a spermicide containing nonoxynol-9
Fellatio *with* a condom
Cunnilingus *with* a thin latex sheet known as a "dental dam"
Hand or finger-to-genital contact with a latex glove or finger cover
"Water sports" and other external contact with urine
Open-mouthed, intimate kissing

• *Unsafe*
Vaginal or anal intercourse without a condom
Fellatio without a condom
Cunnilingus
Semen or urine in the mouth
Blood contact of any kind, including menstrual blood
Oral-anal contact
Sharing sex toys *(Anon.)*

If you are worried about whether or not your partner may be an AIDS carrier or think you may have been at risk sometime in the past, ask your doctor for a test.

If you have questions concerning AIDS, contact the U.S. AIDS hotline: 800-342-2437. You can also contact your local or state health authority.

Despite recent claims that AIDS will not spread rapidly through the heterosexual community, you must assume that it will — or it will. The media treat most stories with unnecessary immediacy. It is simply too soon to be able to chart the future of the AIDS epidemic with any certainty. Those who are claiming a containment of the epidemic in 1988 were claiming in 1987 that it would spread like wildfire. And 1989 is another year.

See also under *First Aids* **and** *Staying Alive* **in** *CHAPTER FIVE: MODERN MEN.*

BIRTH CONTROL

Think about that phrase for a sec.

THE CONTRACEPTION TOP OF THE POPS

The Pill
• It is 99 percent effective when taken correctly.
• *Risks:* Blood clots, high blood pressure, heart attacks.

• *Side effects:* Nausea, weight gain, headaches, breast soreness, fatigue.

• *Who should not take the Pill:* Women over forty; women who smoke and have high blood pressure or an elevated serum cholesterol; women with a history of blood clots, stroke, or heart disease.

Intrauterine Device (IUD)

• It is 95-99 percent effective.

• *Advantages:* Nothing to remember, low expense to maintain.

• *Disadvantages:* Fails in as many as 5 percent of women. Risk of expulsion of device in women who have not had a child. Risk of tubular infections, pelvic pain and menstrual irregularities. Risk of death through spontaneous abortion. Heavier periods, spotting. Twice as much blood lost.

Diaphragm

• It's 97 percent effective when used correctly.

• Dome-shaped cup of latex rubber that acts as a barrier between vagina and the womb. It is used with jelly or spermicidal cream. No serious side effects.

• *Disadvantages:* Can slip out of hand and bounce across the floor. Not to be used by forgetful people or people who don't like to deal with slippery things.

Foam

• Foam is 78 percent effective.

• No prescription necessary, no side effects (unless you count a 22 percent risk of pregnancy).

Suppositories

• These are 88 percent effective.

• Effectiveness rises to 98 percent if used in conjunction with a condom.

Sponges and Cervical caps

• These are 97 percent effective.

Rhythm

• The rhythm method is 80 percent effective.

• Requires refraining from intercourse during mid-cycle. Calls for restraint and good calculations. The body is not very trustworthy, and cycles can be irregular.

Condom

• Used properly, a condom is 97-98 percent effective.

• A condom is made of a soft latex rubber or lambskin.

• Latex rubber can be used to prevent the passing of AIDS and venereal diseases.

• Using a condom with spermicidal foam or jelly is an even better deal, and the nonoxynol-9 in the jelly helps in combating AIDS.

• *Disadvantages:* Partial loss of stimulation for your partner.

Coitus interruptus

• This is 75 percent effective.

• Requires withdrawal prior to ejaculation.

• *Disadvantages:* All control is left to the man. Must trust him to be rational during an irrational moment.

Sterilization

• Requires an operation to make a man incapable of fertilizing an egg (vasectomy) or a woman incapable of becoming pregnant (tubal ligation).

OTHER TECHNIQUES

Norplant: Six capsules are implanted under the skin of your upper arm. These release a synthetic hormone called progestin, which helps prevent ovulation and thickens the cervical mucus so sperm cannot make it through. These capsules last up to five years. Although it's not yet available in the United States, Norplant is being used in Finland, Sweden, Thailand, and Indonesia. It may receive FDA approval within the next few years.

Vaginal ring: A plastic ring worn around the cervix for three weeks a month and removed for menstruation. The ring prevents contraception by releasing progestin. FDA approval is expected within a few years.

RU 486: Chemically-induced abortion. RU 486 is to be taken if you miss a period. It causes the body to expel a fertilized egg by blocking an essential hormone needed in pregnancy. It is only available in Europe.

Antipregnancy vaccine: Vaccine stimulates the body to block a hormone necessary for implantation, making pregnancy impossible. Preliminary tests have been performed in Australia and India, but the vaccine probably will not be available for five to ten years.

Unisex Pill: May be available in ten years. Blocks sperm production in males and ovulation in females by introducing a higher level of the hormone inhibin.

SPONTANEOUS MISCARRIAGES

Women get pregnant constantly — as much as 70 percent of the time. Often, the pregnancy escapes notice, since there is a spontaneous miscarriage at the first period. (KK)

ABORTION

Abortion should not be confused with birth control. These are terrible times, when it is possible to even contemplate such a decision.

Dangers: During the first twelve weeks of pregnancy, the risk of death to the mother from abortion is 2.6 per 100,000.

The first step is to establish that you are pregnant through an exam by the doctor and a pregnancy test. You will have a blood and urine test, blood typing and Rh factor determination. You must not eat or drink for eight to twelve hours beforehand.

Early abortion (up to twelve weeks): Local anesthetic, dilation of cervix. The cervix may be dilated beforehand with the seaweed laminaria. With this method a small stem of laminaria is inserted into the cervix a day before the abortion. It absorbs water from the tissues, expands and produce painless dilation. A plastic cannula, which is attached to a suction machine, is inserted into the womb. Most women can go home within two hours. This signifies the end of your choice. Once this is done, there's no turning back.

After week twelve it is more complex. Labor is induced through the infusion of saline or prostaglandin into the fetal sac.

Pain: Yes.

Bleeding: Several days to a week. In exceptional cases, you may experience very heavy bleeding, in which event the clinic should be notified at once.

Follow-up: You should be examined two weeks after the abortion.

Menstrual extraction: Minisuction or menstrual regulation. This is suction abortion, but done within three weeks of a late period. No dilation of the cervix necessary.

GYN

Three little letters that ring in the ear — sort of like "TNT" and "IRS."

HOW TO GET THROUGH A GYN EXAM

Always ask questions. It is your right to know what procedures are being performed, the results of tests, and the reasons behind treatments prescribed. A good gynecologist will gladly supply you with explanations and will try to alleviate any fears you may have. Be sure to ask about anything from PMS to orgasm.

Tableside manner: It is important to go to a doctor with whom you can feel very comfortable. Some women prefer a female gynecologist for that very reason, and some women feel a female doctor is automatically more gentle during a pelvic examination. The truth is, if you are more relaxed, the exam itself becomes less tense. It is wise to consider your most personal feelings when initially choosing your gynecologist.

Never lie to your doctor about anything! In these days of life-threatening sexually transmitted diseases, your gynecologist must know the truth in order to help you. If you are in a non-monogamous relationship, no matter what the circumstances, tell your doctor. A good doctor will never judge you in these matters, but will use all the facts to better treat any symptoms you may develop.

Referral: You can usually find a good gynecologist via referral from your physician. Many women also find guidance by asking their friends or family. If you are new to a city, call the nearest medical university or teaching hospital. A reputable gynecologist would be a certified member of the American College of Obstetricians and Gynecologists.

Taking a stab at the names listed in the phone book is absolutely the worst way to find a doctor. (AAT)

WHAT YOU SHOULD EXPECT FROM YOUR GYN

• To prescribe and provide information on birth control.

• Supply AIDS testing or referrals.

• Provide a urinalysis.

• Testing of vital organs, including taking your blood pressure.

• To give you a breast exam every visit as well as provide you with monthly self-exam information.

• To give you a complete pelvic exam, including examinations of external genitals, internal reproductive organs, rectum, Pap smear and tests for sexually transmitted diseases and vaginitis.

• To make you as comfortable as possible during the pelvic exam.

• To return your phone calls.

• To explain examination procedures, diagnosis and treatment.

• Not to make you feel rushed. Your doctor should take the time to answer any questions you may have in a manner that is satisfactory to you. (AAT)

SELF-EXAMS

Know thyself: Most important to your health and welfare is your knowledge of your own body. Every woman should be able to identify the various parts of her external genitalia and internal reproductive organs. You should be able to tell the doctor the date that your last period started and if the flow and length of the period were normal. Feel your breasts every day, either upon awakening or in the shower, becoming familiar with all lumps or bumps that may be perfectly normal at different times of the month. A pattern for all these things should become apparent, so if something out of the ordinary comes up, you'll be able to speak knowingly about the change. If anything feels different your doctor should be told. (AAT)

BREAST CANCER CHECK

One in ten American women will develop breast cancer during her lifetime. The best way for a woman to protect herself is the monthly breast exam. A woman who checks herself regularly will more easily detect any changes in her tissue than her doctor, who only examines her once or twice a year.

Most doctors recommend to their patients that they examine their own breasts about one week after their period begins. Other doctors suggest that women check their breasts daily so that they become accustomed to the changes in breast tissue throughout their menstrual cycle. It is somewhat easier to remember if it becomes part of your daily routine.

How-to: The exam should take place either lying down on your back or standing up. The shower is a good place, since the water and soap facilitate the movement of the fingers over the breasts.

• Before beginning the exam, gently squeeze the nipple to see if there is any discharge.

• Next, press down gently on the nipple with the fingertips and make a small circular motion.

There are three different types of self-exams.

• *The radial-spoke method* starts at the nipple and radiates out to the edge of the breast like the spokes on a bicycle wheel.

• A better known test is one that uses *a circular pattern* starting at the nipple and gradually working around the breast, increasing the size of the circle as you go.

• A newer form of the self-exam is called the *vertical strip* method. Recent statistics show this method to have a better success rate of completely covering the breast tissue. Using the three middle fingers of the hand opposite the breast being examined, move your fingers from top to bottom, continually working your way across the breast with the same top-to-bottom action until you have covered all the breast tissue.

Self-exams should be done right after your menstrual period. After menopause, it should be done on the first day of every month.

• *Study your breasts* in the mirror first with your hands behind your head, then with your hands at your sides, then with your hands behind you while you lean forward.

• *Look for dimpling* or irregularity in the skin.

• *Lie on your back* and place a pillow under one shoulder. Use the opposite hand to feel the breast. Check your armpits as well.

• *Squeeze your nipples* to check for discharge.

• *Call your doctor* if you observe nipple discharge or a suspicious lump or mass is detected.

• *Do not panic.* As you know, early detection is the best protection against breast cancer and only 20 percent of these lumps and bumps turn out to be cancer.

Most lumps are a cystic disease or a benign tumor. (AAT, JL)

Risk factors favoring cancer:
• Age fifty-five or older
• A history of breast cancer in mother and grandmother
• Previous cancer in one breast
• Menstrual periods beginning at age eleven or under
• Menopause after 5-estrogen therapy
• Middle or upper-middle socioeconomic group
• Previous cancer of uterus or ovary
• A history of cystic disease of the breast

Factors that lower the risk of cancer:
• First pregnancy by eighteen
• Three or more pregnancies by age thirty-five
• Breast-feeding
• No history of cancer in the family (LH, JL)

HYSTERECTOMIES

*A **hysterectomy*** is the removal of the reproductive organs. It may be *partial* (just the uterus) or *total* (uterus, tubes and ovaries removed); it may be done to treat cancer of the cervix, endometrium, or ovary, or to treat severe uterine bleeding or a severe pelvic infection. It may be done when the severe bleeding or pain from fibroids or endometriosis does not respond to treatment.

For years, the ovaries were removed along with the uterus on the chance that they might later develop cancer. Do not let a doctor remove healthy ovaries. (JDP)

MENOPAUSE

Menopause results when the ovaries stop functioning and periods cease, usually between forty-five to fifty-five years of age. It is a gradual process that begins before the end of the reproductive years and stretches to five years after periods have stopped. Between 60 and 70 percent of women experience *hot flashes, fatigue, nervousness, headaches,* and *difficulty sleeping.*

Taking estrogen to relieve hot flashes and to reverse some of the menopausal changes can *increase* the risk of cancer of the uterus from five to ten times. It also increases the chance of breast cancer, gall bladder disease, and vascular disease. (JDP)

NUTRITION

You are what you eat. Nutrition is the easiest part of a preventive health care program. And if a bad day comes along, and you don't feel like stewing up the basic food groups, take a pill.

What it is	*Where it is*	*What it does*
Vitamin A	Dairy products, liver and kidney, leafy green and yellow vegetables	Necessary for proper growth in children. Important for healthy skin, eyes, hair and mucous membranes.
Vitamin D	Milk, cod liver oil, salmon, tuna, egg yolks.	Essential for strong teeth and bones. Assists in utilization of calcium and phosphorus.
Vitamin E	Vegetable oils, wheat germ, whole grain cereals, lettuce.	Vital for functioning of red blood cells. Protects key fatty acids.

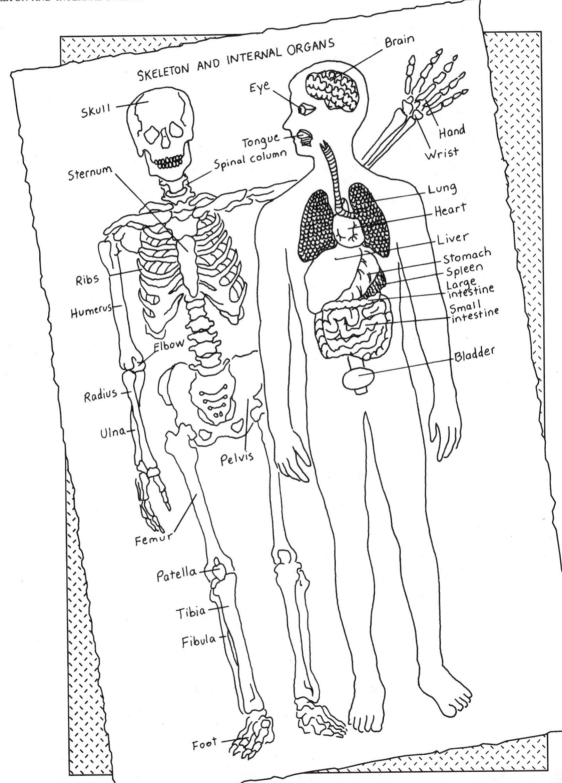

SKELETON AND INTERNAL ORGANS

Brain
Eye
Skull
Tongue
Spinal column
Sternum
Hand
Wrist
Lung
Heart
Liver
Ribs
Stomach
Spleen
Large intestine
Humerus
Small intestine
Elbow
Bladder
Radius
Ulna
Pelvis
Femur
Patella
Tibia
Fibula
Foot

Vitamin C (Ascorbic Acid)	Citrus fruits and juices, berries, tomatoes, cabbage, green vegetables and new potatoes.	Necessary for teeth, gums and bones. Builds strong body cells and blood vessels.
Vitamin B1 (Thiamine)	Fish, lean meat, liver, milk, pork, poultry, dried yeast, whole-grain cereals, enriched foods.	Essential for proper function of heart and nervous system. Signs of deficiency include loss of appetite, constipation, insomnia and irritability.
Vitamin B2 (Riboflavin)	Leafy green vege-tables, lean meats, liver, dried yeast, milk, eggs, enriched bread and cereals.	Necessary for healthy skin, helps prevent sen-sitivity of eyes to light. Essential for building and maintaining body tissues.
Vitamin B6	Whole-grain cereals, wheat germ, vege-tables, dried yeast, meat and bananas.	Important for healthy teeth and gums, the health of blood vessels, red blood cells and nervous system.
Vitamin B12	Lean meat, liver, kidney, milk, salt water fish, oysters.	Assists in preventing certain forms of anemia, contributes to health of nervous system and proper growth in children.
Folic Acid (Folacin)	Leafy green vege-tables, food yeast, meats.	Assists in preventing certain forms of anemia, important in maintaining functions of intestinal tract.
Niacin (Niacinamide)	Eggs, lean meats, liver, dried yeast, enriched cereals, enriched breads.	Necessary for converting food to energy. Aids the nervous system. Helps prevent loss of appetite.

Pantothenic Acid	Present in almost all plant and animal tissue.	Necessary for body's use of carbohydrates, fats and proteins.
Biotin	Egg yolks, green vegetables, milk, liver and kidney.	Necessary for the functioning of many body systems and use of food for energy.
Calcium	Dairy products.	Builds bone and teeth, aids in blood clotting, helps muscles and nerves react normally.
Iron	Whole grains, enriched flour, beans, red meats.	Helps make hemoglobin.
Iodine	Iodized salt.	Maintains proper function of thyroid gland.
Phosphorous	Milk and milk products, egg yolks, meat, fish fowl, nuts, whole fats, grain cereals.	Important in a number of body systems involving carbohydrates, salts and enzymes.
Protein	Meat, poultry, fish, eggs, milk and milk products, beans, soybeans, peas, grains and nuts.	Required for growth, maintenance and repair of of body tissues, helps make hemoglobin, antibodies and supply energy.
Carbohydrates	Grains and grain products.	Major source of energy, maintain body temperature. (*Anon.*)

MODERN GRANDWOMEN

You were a little younger the last time we met, weren't you?

What happened to that quarter-century, the one that was just starting yesterday, when the children moved away? Or the one that started before that, when the childen were born? Or the one before *that*, the only other one we've known?

We probably should have started here, with Modern Women older than we are, and used the contributions we received as a sort of extended dedication to women for whom much of the rest of this book will all be a flashback, anyway.

ADVICE

If you send out as many queries for advice and information as we did, you're bound to end up with a full mailbox.

And with all the strange tips on shoe care and the handy hints on latex goods, there come a few letters that sort of keep you on track. Like this:

I'm not sure I can contribute anything to add to the wisdom of "modern women." I feel like such a relic, sometimes the only survivor of an age long past, alone on my island of memories.

It was such a very different world into which I was born, in which I grew up and which I left almost fifty years ago to become an American. Surely not Ollie North's ideal as woman and patriot, but one unlikely to change.

I was so much more ignorant and sheltered than today's woman; my granddaughters are way ahead of me in worldly knowledge and experience. I really don't feel I can "tell them" anything they want to know.

But I'm very sorry for them, actually. They'll never know the security, the certainties we have known. We didn't have a fraction of the options and temptations they are growing up with, but we were a much happier, a much less driven, harassed generation. The future seemed a natural consequence growing out of adhering to the rules our parents and grandparents had adhered to. The basic decencies of life and behavior were taken for granted, and we grew up respecting authority, because we knew there was something to respect. I have a great deal of admiration for the young women of today who made their choices . . . [but] what could I possibly have to say to them of any weight or worth? (ZL)

My fear has always been that no one will hear me anymore when I am eighty and ninety years old. They'll dismiss me and cluck at me. What if I rage then, "It's just me, it's still *me* in here." And what if they just say, "Now now, dear, now now"? *(Anon.)*

I am eighty-seven years of age and don't exactly fit into your tips and techniques, advice and anecdotes for Modern Women, but I will pass along a happy birthday experience I had in 1980. My birthday was January 28, and some very dear friends asked me to a birthday dinner. Believe it or not, I had a birthday cake with *eighty* candles on it. It was a huge cake. Along with the cake was an invitation to go with them on a trip to Hawaii in July, all expenses paid. My son was there December 7, 1941, and my wish was to go there sometime. That birthday was a very happy memory.

As I said, I don't fit in with your Modern Woman, as I am eighty-seven years of age, but if I were younger I think I would. I have worked most of my life and retired at sixty-four years of age. I have experienced living in the early 1900s. I have had happy times and tragic times in my life. I still live alone and take care of myself. (WKuh)

Thank you for asking me for advice on modern life. My daughters and granddaughters would *die* before they asked me for another word of advice, so I'm happy that someone who hasn't already heard it all still is interested. I am eighty-two, and most of what I still have in my hope chest, figuratively speaking, is advice, all folded neatly — but ready to be used.

Here's my advice: Make nothing in your life more important to you than your children. Because nothing is. My husband worked his whole life. He came to this country from Ireland and got a job building tractors. When he retired, he was a senior supervisor. Just before he died, he told me what his life *at work* had meant to him — nothing. It had no significance for him whatsoever, except for the fact that it allowed him the dignity and importance of providing for me and for our children. He told me they would build tractors long after he went and no one would remember what he had put into his job. But his children would remember that he had tried his best to provide for them, and so his grandchildren would remember, and maybe they would remember him to the others that would come later. He told me that his family had given his life meaning and that I had changed the history of the world by caring for our children and doing that job — a much more important job, he thought, than any *he* ever had — so well. He had only built tractors.

So that's my advice. Love your children. If you feel nurturing children would represent a sacrifice for you, that you would miss something more important (like building tractors of one sort or another) then don't have children, please don't. *(Anon.)*

THE OLDER WOMAN IS PROVING

that she can cope at home and on the job. She has been through an era of depression and war, may have raised a family or supported elderly parents, has probably volunteered in her community, has taken courses or gone back to school when necessary before reentering the job market. Undoubtedly, she has helped family and friends through mental and physical crises and has learned to cope with illness, death and loneliness. She is dependable and caring, and gives her tasks at home and at work her best shot, even under stress.

What the older Modern Woman has going for her and does not want to lose is her deep sense of self, her true caring about *others,* her desire to pursue her personal interests creatively, her wonderful enjoyment of close relationships with family and friends, and her wish to continue taking an active part in the life of this ever-changing modern world. *(Anon.)*

ADVOCACY

The following are a few of the organizations that fight for the rights of older men and women:

- American Association of Retired Persons (AARP)
- Gray Panthers
- National Alliance for Senior Citizens (NASC)
- National Association for the Visually Handicapped (NAVH)
- National Association of Mature People (NAMP)
- National Association of Retired Federal Employees (NARFE)
- National Council of Senior Citizens (NCSC)
- Older Women's League (OWL)

By joining and supporting these organizations, you'll be able to stay informed of current issues of concern. (IM)

Be your own advocate: When something comes up, write to your representative in Congress and call your city council representative. Your letters and phone calls make a difference. (KPA)

AGE DISCRIMINATION

If you feel that you have been discriminated against on the job because of your age, file a protest with the Equal Employment Opportunity Commission. Look for the EEOC in your phone book under United States Government Offices.

Area Agencies on Aging (AAA) is the government agency concerned with helping older people. Some of the programs are senior centers, transportation aids, Meals on Wheels, legal aid, care for the housebound, etc. If you want information on Area Agencies on Aging, your reference librarian can give you help. (KGG)

Golden Age Passport: If you are over sixty-two, and carry a Golden Age Passport, you and your family or anyone who piles into your car will be admitted free to all national parks, monuments, and recreation areas. You will also receive a fifty percent discount on services such as camping and parking at parks. Look for the Forest Service under the Department of Agriculture in the phone book's U.S. Government listings. (USG)

GOVERNMENT AGENCIES

The one number: The Federal Information Center (FIC) will help you with information about any program or agency in the U.S. government. The FIC and the IRS are the only two governmental information services left in the wretched bureaucracy where you can call and speak to a live human being (be flexible here when it comes to the IRS). To find the telephone number of one of the twenty-two FIC offices close to you, look in your telephone directory's United States Government listings under "Federal Information Center." It's hard to spot — it will not be a bold-face listing and will probably be someplace between the Federal

Communications Commission and the Food and Drug Administration. If you live in a small town, you may have to go to the library to consult a directory for the nearest large city. (WG)

CARRIER ALERT

Calling for help: Some areas have implemented a system called "Carrier Alert" to keeping check on people who fear that one day they may need help and be unable to call for it. It is a method involving your mail carrier, who will pay special attention if your mail is not collected every day. Ask your post office about this service. (WG)

HOME HEALTH CARE

There are services that provide skilled help to make it possible for you to remain at home during an illness or convalescence. Ask your public health and welfare departments to help you locate them, or ask at a local group involved in medical care.

FOSTER GRANDPARENTS

Helping the handicapped: If you are in a low income bracket and sixty or over, you can volunteer to work with children who may be mentally or physically handicapped. If you work four hours a day, five days a week, you will receive a free annual physical exam, a hot meal each day you work, transportation to and from the assignment, and a small stipend. Call or write your ACTION office, a federal volunteer agency, and ask about the Foster Grandparents program. (WG)

FOOLING AROUND

It's hard sometimes to get passionate when arthritis is making my joints ache and creak, he is worrying about his heart, and I'm taking a drug that decreases sex drive. But I sure don't want to be twenty again with all the sorrows of life still to come, so I take a warm bath, we do some limbering up exercises and then we just see what we'll just see. *(Anon.)*

HEALTH AND WELFARE

After you've lived for seventy years or so, you just don't have time to care quite as much about what everyone else is thinking about you. It's such a relief. But one thing you have to worry about even more, of course, is your health. What good is a healthy mind without a healthy body? Just working on one of those things is difficult enough.

A lot of problems associated with old age are not necessarily a malfunction of aging. Your arteries don't *have* to clog, you know. Diet and smoking have a lot to do with that. Stress can be regulated, and so can diet and exercise.

As you age, your *skin becomes drier* and less elastic. Apply moisturizers to damp skin. Try to avoid hot water, and use creams that contain sunscreens.

Eyesight often begins to change dramatically after age forty. It can come as quite a shock to someone who has had perfect vision all those years. Teeth, on the other hand, are not programmed to fall apart like eyes are. If you have taken proper care of your teeth all your life, they should go with you to your grave.

Senility is not something that has to happen with old age. Sometimes other problems are mistakenly labeled as senility. Reactions to certain medications may appear as disorganization or forgetfulness. Depression may also be seen as mental deterioration. Being fed up with the company may also be labeled as senility when actually it is an indication of intelligence.

Aerobic and isotonic exercise is best for older women. Aerobic exercise improves the flow of oxygen throughout the body. Continuous activity such as brisk walking over a certain period of time is a requirement of aerobic exercise. Isotonic exercise improves strength by putting muscles through a complete range of motion. Yoga is an example of this.

Don't start any exercise program without checking with a doctor, and don't compete against the person next to you. Leave the intense competition to the yuppie studs. Let them have the ulcers and coronaries.

Normal weight leads to longer life. Being quite a bit overweight is no good, of course, but so is being quite a bit underweight. If your weight at age twenty-five was considered normal, that is what you should weigh all the days of your life.

Eat oatmeal five days a week. The old-fashioned kind. It can lower your cholesterol level up to twenty percent. And an apple a day also works wonders.

Constipation is a problem for older women. Drink at least six glasses of water a day. Not water disguised as tea or coffee or soda pop, but *water* like the kind that comes from heaven.

The three major risk factors for heart disease are high blood pressure, cigarette smoking, and high cholesterol. Skip whole milk, egg yolks, red meat, cheese, butter, shrimp, and oysters. Eat less fat and go for poultry and fish and skim milk.

Look at all those laxative ads on TV that come on around dinnertime. They want you to buy their product and use it every single day for the rest of your life so that you will be regular. Eat right and forget their sales pitches. Eat fruit, vegetables, dried beans. Roughage. Think the cavemen had to use Metamucil? But don't overdo the bran — it can cause gas and irritate the stomach and intestines.

Osteoarthritis is more likely to occur to older women than any other type of arthritis. The cartilage at the end of the bones becomes soft and worn. Joints become painful and stiff. Heredity and obesity both contribute to osteoarthritis, but a regular exercise program, maintaining a regular weight, and applying heat to the area all can help in treating the problem.

Glaucoma is the third leading cause of blindness in the United States. This is nuts, because it can be successfully treated if caught in time through regular eye exams. Eye drops for chronic glaucoma need to be taken daily — not such a hard thing to do when the alternative is blindness.

A heart attack may only feel like bad indigestion. Symptoms may include dizziness, nausea, sweating, or breathlessness. A heart attack may feel like an ache or pressure in the chest. The pain may spread to the shoulders, jaw, neck or arms. It can last for several minutes or much longer. Part of the heart muscle dies during a heart attack because the blood supply has been cut off. Usually an artery to the heart has been blocked by a blood clot.

Angina pectoris is recurrent pain caused by a decreased blood supply to the heart. This happens when fatty deposits narrow the arteries. Nitroglycerine helps treat these attacks. A person can do rather well for years and years. Finally, however, bypass surgery may be necessary.

Gender comfort: Most of the people on the coronary care floor are men.

In congestive heart failure, the heart muscle itself is too weak to pump blood to the body. Symptoms are fatigue, shortness of breath, swelling of the ankles, legs, and feet, confusion, rapid weight gain. Treatment is rest, low-salt diet, water pills, and digitalis to strengthen the heart muscle. (EC)

THE INSULTS OF YOUTH

I said to the old woman, "You haven't changed a bit in twenty years!" She said to me, "You mean I looked this old twenty years ago?" *(Anon.)*

How insulting to tell someone they must have been so beautiful when they were young. If they were beautiful then, they are beautiful now. (DBK)

Younger people mean well but they can't really understand. In fact, they're all a bit of a bore. Just as those sincere and intense eighteen-year-olds drive thirty-five-year-olds crazy, those fifty-year-olds really annoy me. *(Anon.)*

A DYING HUSBAND

It is difficult to care for a dying husband. Sometimes friends stop coming by. It is too painful for them, or stressful, or even boring. Friends reach their limits early. Grown children aren't always the best they can be, either. It is frightening for them to see their powerful father grow weaker day by day. When it is up to you to care for him, you should seek out a support group. Only those who are going through what you are going through can adequately understand. Remember to look after yourself. You will sometimes have to work hard just to remember to eat properly and get rest. Try to keep talking with your husband as long as he is able. Just because he is dying does not mean he has forgotten living. Keep in contact with the world. Reach out to your friends and other relatives whether or not they are reaching out to you. *(Anon.)* **See also** *Modern Mortals* in *CHAPTER FOUR: MODERN P's & Q's.*

NURSING HOMES

Sometime — usually right after you start worrying about your fitness club membership and the lease payment on your Bimmer — life gets real.

The decision to place an aging parent in a nursing home is perhaps one of the toughest anyone has to make. This decision-making process should be shared by you, your siblings, the doctor, and anyone else you think can offer support.

Visit. It will be time-consuming but necessary to visit a number of care facilities in your area to determine which one would best suit the needs of your parent. Look not only at health care, but at dining, recreational activities, and religious services as well. *Providing that your parent is able, let him or her be actively involved in searching for the new home.*

Understand all of the costs involved. Prices vary tremendously, so be certain of how much insurance, Medicare and Medicaid will pay and how much must come from private support.

Once you have chosen the residence, make the move as happy and enjoyable as possible. Make certain to take along familiar things: a wall clock, family pictures, special knickknacks. These small things will make the transition much easier.

Finally, remember that you are not sending your child to summer camp. This is no place for tears. It is not a good-bye. If you must cry, do so after you have reassured your parent of frequent contact and you are in your car and out of sight.

Keep your word: It is important for you to make good your promises of visits and phone calls. You aren't dumping your parent, and you shouldn't assume that the nursing home will take over all your responsibilities. (SEM)

NURSING HOME CHECKLIST

There are *three types* of nursing homes.

1. Skilled nursing facilities are for intensive care and have a resident medical director.

2. Intermediate care homes do not give intensive care but do provide help in dressing, eating and walking. There is at least one registered nurse on duty during daytimes, but the patient is under the care of her own doctor.

3. Nonskilled facilities are not usually under government inspection. They only require state licensing, which is not as tough as federal licensing. Investigate nonskilled facilities (or any nursing home, for that matter) very carefully. Get referrals, talk to the staff, look at the rooms and interview residents. (SEM, DF) (See below.)

Questions: When considering any nursing home, be sure to ask yourself a lot of questions about it before committing someone to it.

❏ Check with the state nursing home ombudsman to see if the home has had past violations of state law.

❏ Are current state licenses on display?

❏ When government or private programs of assistance are needed, does the home have certification to participate in them?

❏ What extra services like special diets or care are provided?

❏ Talk to the patients in the home. Talk to them when the staff is not around. Do they have complaints?

❏ Is there a hospital nearby?

❏ In case of fire, are there sprinklers and extinguishers? Are there plenty of exits in easy access places?

❏ Are there handrails in the halls and grip bars in the bathtubs? Are the floors nonskid? Do the bedrooms and bathrooms have call buttons?

❏ Are the rooms clean and odor free? Do they have enough space? Is there privacy in multi-bed rooms? Are there phones, radios and televisions in the rooms? Reading lamps?

❏ Is the kitchen and dining area clean?

❏ Does the home provide space for group and individual activities? Is there a recreation director?

❏ Is a medical director available who can substitute for the patient's regular doctor in case of emergency?

❏ Do the nurses and aides appear to be concerned and alert?

❏ Are the rights of the patients respected?

❏ Is the dignity of each patient maintained or diminished by institutional rules?

❏ Do most of the patients in the home appear sedated?

❏ Are you absolutely clear on financial arrangements? *(Anon.)*

THE END

Not to be depressing or anything, but after you go through all the medicine and all the hospitals and all the programs and all the insurance money, you go.

CARING FOR THE TERMINALLY ILL

If someone you love is facing death, tell that person the truth. Every person has a right to the truth and the opportunity to use the time left to best advantage. *(Anon)*

Business: If someone is terminally ill, there are things that must be faced. Wills need to be made or put in order. Finances need to be discussed. Legal problems need to be taken care of. You're not doing anyone any favors by pretending that these important things are not important because you are trying to cushion the patient from harsh reality. What is a harsher reality than death, after all? The one who is ill has the right to a voice in these things while he or she can still speak. (CB) **See** *Final Orders,* **below.**

Don't let guilt overwhelm you. You cannot change the past, and no one knows whether the future will come. Go your days one by one. (PT)

Avoid becoming a martyr when facing the death of a loved one. Treat yourself as well as you can. Remember to eat. Try to sleep. And whenever you can laugh, do it — whether it seems appropriate or not. (LL)

Do not mistake withdrawal for rejection. A person near death may put a wall between themselves and the world around them in their struggle to understand or accept their situation. (AK)

Children should be told the truth when someone they love is terminally ill. What could be crueler than promising a recovery that never happens? A child needs to be involved just like everyone else in order to come to grips with the situation. Would you just pull the whole world out from under a child's feet? (RS)

Be sensitive to feelings of stress and do what you can to alleviate them. Take a walk or soak in a tub. Eat nourishing foods. It sounds too corny to talk about nourishing foods, but it makes a difference. If you are too agitated to contemplate chewing, then drink soup. If stress is causing you to become forgetful, get a notebook and record all the important things that must be done. Check it every day to be sure you've paid the bills, kept your appointments. If you have a friend who loves you very much, unload your grief on her. If you do not have such a friend, start a journal. Alleviate stress by facing up to the practical problems that must be dealt with — the will, finances, funeral arrangements and so on. (BK)

Find a support group. Support groups exist in almost every community. People in positions similar to yours really *do* know how you feel. There is great comfort in talking. (CC)

TREATMENT

Be clear on the diagnosis and the prognosis. Know everything you can about the treatment and what to expect from it — and if there are alternative treatments. Understand the possible side effects. Find out how the doctor feels about the Living Will. If you are caring for a patient at home, be sure you know all you have to about the medications you will be administering. If a doctor uses terms you do not understand, ask what they mean. (AJ)

FINAL ORDERS

What are the important papers people always refer to when they say, "I need to get my papers in order?"

• Birth certificate or baptismal certificate. Any *three* of the following will usually be sufficient to stand in their place: school records, marriage certificate, military record, life insurance policy, citizenship papers.

• Marriage certificate.

• Social security number.

• Names and addresses of children and grandchildren, and their birth certificates if you are applying for aid.

• Names of brothers, sisters and parents, plus addresses.

• Divorce papers.

• Military discharge papers.

• State and federal tax forms for the last three years.

• Titles of ownership on house, property, etc.

• Mortgage contract.

• Insurance policies.

• Checking and savings accounts.

- Benefits received at workplace.
- Broker account number, name of firm.
- Safety deposit box number and location of key.
- Will and name and address of executor.
- Living will.
- Letter of intent.
- Power of attorney.
- Organ donor forms.
- Medicare and Medicaid forms.
- Credit cards and account numbers.
- Directions as to disposition of remains. (CD, *Anon.*) **A lawyer will be needed for some of this, so see under** *LAWYERS* **in** *CHAPTER TWELVE: MODERN WOMAN IN DISTRESS.*

GOOD-BYE

When someone you love closes his eyes and the doctor says he is in a coma now and will probably never open them again, talk to him anyhow. Hold his hand and talk about things. Maybe he cannot hear you, *but what if he can?* (AE)

EUTHANASIA

The Hemlock Society supports active and voluntary euthanasia for the terminally ill. Less controversial is passive euthanasia, which is the right to refuse life-sustaining treatment, or to give the power of life-and-death decisions to another person in the event that you are incapacitated. Check to see what the laws are in your state. (AE)

Modern Runarounds

Here's how the universe works: a Big Bang, then a lot of rough travel. You spend hours behind the wheel of a car that could turn on you at any moment just to get to an airport where your flight has been canceled. On the alternate flight, an airline flight attendant curses you for standing when the seat belt sign is on, even though she just poured tea in your lap.

This has been going on for years. And if Modern Women have learned one thing, it's this: When the going gets tough, get tough with your mechanic or find a new travel agent.

C O N T E N T S
Chapter Fourteen: *MODERN RUN-AROUNDS*

**MODERN MOTORS — HOW TO BUY A CAR:
Know Thyself — Go Shopping — Used Car Shopping
— Recycling Cars — Second-Hand Woes — The Lease
You Can Do — Hyper Mega-Options — The Modern
Woman's Car Buying Checklist — Car Insurance —
CAR TALK: Garage Chatter —** Where It Is **— CAR
REPAIRS: Car Science — What Makes an Engine Run
— Filter Frenzy — About the Electrical, Exhaust and
Transmission Systems — How a Car Steers — Whoa,
Dude — Black Gold —** Maximum Speeds **— Cooling —
Bumps and Grinds — A Final Word on Car Repairs —
WHITE-LINE SAFETY: Highway Mayday — A
Pedagogical Tale of Highway Distress — Prevention —
Seven Reasons to Stop Your Car** *Immediately* **—**
Blowout Avoidance **— What to Do If Your Car Catches
on Fire — How to Keep Your Car Yours — How to
Keep from Falling Asleep While Driving — KIDS IN
CARS: Car Seats — Traveler's Aid — OFF-ROAD
TRAVEL: —** Car Safety **— Vacations — How to Pack
—** Some Things to See and Do **— Briefly — Half a Load
— Folding — Love Handles? — Final Check —
Matched Luggage — Connections — The Bag Lady
Look — Strange Customs — Documents —** Adventures
in Travel **— Visas — THE TRAIN TRUTH: Traveling
Companions — Train Tips — Pigeonholes — HOW
TO CATCH A SLOW BOAT TO CHINA: Passage —
Life at Sea — TICKETS, PLEASE: Seal of Approval
— Paid Twice — HOME CHECKLIST — MOBILE
FOR MONEY: Dress for It — Ask the Agent — Tiny
Money — Sleepwear — BAD TRIPS: Travel Insurance
— What the State Department Can Do —** Bull
Awareness **— Medic! — That's Why They Call It**

"Sight-seeing" — Gesundheit — They Missed You,
Too — Traveler's Aid — Up in Smoke — OFF THE
BEATEN PATH: Staying Well — Your Tax Dollar —
Needles — Dressing for the Tropics — MANNERLY
MOBILE: Cultural Imperialism — Foreign Elements
— Gestures — Tipping — SAFETY FIRST: Rue,
Calle, Strasse, Straat and Via Wisdom — Hotel
Security — HOW TO SHIP A CHILD: The Peter Pan
Syndrome — Airlines — Buses — FEAR OF FLYING:
Fear Fighters — Flights to Avoid — Parachuting — But
When You Just Have to Leave. . .

MODERN MOTORS

Every now and again, do you look at that rusty, old pile of paint you're driving, pat her on the dashboard and tell her, "Thanks, Old Blue. I couldn't have made it this far without you?"

If you're a Modern Woman, you don't. Modern Women know that cars don't have cute names and have no anthropomorphic existence, no personality, no feelings, no guts — nothing. Nothing, save the *blam* of internal combustion and the wheeze of exhaust that mark the beginning of a geometrical transit from Point A to Point B via the cleaners.

Except on a grim and rainy night when you know your old car is in terrible shape because you've never changed the oil — not even *once* — and yet it keeps running through the dark storm and gets you home safely, just as it has every night, in complete defiance of the laws of car physics. Because it loves you. And you love it back.

HOW TO BUY A CAR

This is how it starts:

You wake up one Saturday morning, look at the oil-viper in the driveway, and decide to upgrade to a new car, probably one made by people who can't read the menu at McDonald's.

So you get dressed, wander down to Cal's Car City, where a man with inflatable hair and perfect teeth greets you and asks, "Well, what can I do for you?"

Such a simple question. And it's not until then that you realize you don't know how to answer it. Now what?

KNOW THYSELF

Do some homework before you go car shopping. Establish a firm definition of what your car should be — and don't allow any amount of fast talk from the salesman or your own whimsy to change it.

Never go into an ambivalent, mind-changing mode at the car showroom. You'll drive away in a headache.

Consider these four important factors:

1. Price, of course. But stick to a price once you've set it. Look in the newspapers and see what the dealers are shucking as loss-leaders for new cars. That'll suggest the upper limit of the bottom line. If you're looking for a used car, scout the prices in the classifieds to help you establish a shopping budget.

2. Options. Don't be ashamed of choosing a car because it has the nicest color combinations or the best stereo. Why not? All cars go forward and backward, after all, but not all cars have great air-conditioners or top quality, built-in cassette decks. **See below under** *Hyper Mega-Options.*

3. Dependability: Some cars just have well-deserved reputations that are better than others — especially in the universe of used cars **See** *Used Car Shopping,* **below.**

4. Warranty. If it's as good as they say it is, will they fix it if it isn't? (SV, WN)

GO SHOPPING

Car-buying isn't special. Approach buying a car the same way you would anything else. Shop around, get information, think it over. **See under** *Emergency Instructions* **in** *CHAPTER SIX: MODERN MERCHANDISE.*

Above all, don't feel compelled to drive home in a new car the first time out. A car, after all, is the second most important purchase — after a house — that most of us make. (SV, *Anon.*)

Include financing and insurance in your deliberations. If buying a convertible doubles your insurance rate, is it worth it? As for financing, as a rule the best deal is the one that has the lowest rate and the shortest term. (WN) **See** *Car Insurance,* **below.**

Never buy a car with no down payment as part of the finance package. If you do, you will *always* owe more on the car than it's worth, and the car will depreciate faster than your down payment. A $1500 down payment on a $7500 car, for example, is preferable to the $3000 or so you'll be behind after you've owned the car for a year or so. Don't let your bank or anyone else talk you into a no-money-down scam. You'll lose. (WN)

USED CAR SHOPPING

Two little words of advice: *Be careful.*

A used car can, of course, represent a substantial bargain. If you find a clean, low-mileage car at a good price, then you're a winner. The trouble is, there are a lot of losers out there, too.

Here are some tips for minimizing your risk:

• *Carefully inspect the car* — in broad daylight, never at night — before you start the engine. Crawl underneath and look for leaks. Make sure the body isn't rusting away and that the tires are evenly worn. If the body has evidence of a patch-job, ask about the collision that occasioned that kind of repair.

• *Test drive* a used car even more extensively than you would a new one. If the cooling system is weak, you won't know about it until after the car has been driven for a while.

• Make sure you *test drive the car from a cold start.* If the owner has already warmed up the engine, you're going to miss all the telltale groans and noises a cold engine makes.

Test drive a used car in the daytime and at night. Keep the radio off so you can hear all the funny little sounds. Don't just take a polite drive around the block. Stop on hills, turn on turns, apply those brakes! Try to leave the dealer back at the lot. He'll try to distract you by babbling on about the virtues of the car. If you're lucky, it will rain and you can test the car on wet roads.

• Look at the car's *maintenance records.* The history of a car will tell you lots about its future.

• During the test drive, *make sure everything works.* Give the brakes, the transmission, the gauges, even the horn, a good test.

• *Don't be too nice.* Don't worry about making the seller think you doubt his or her word. Try everything on the car out for yourself. The person selling the car would do the same to your car if the roles were reversed.

• *Buy Japanese* whenever possible. Toyotas, Hondas and Nissans are good, reliable cars, but the resale is high, since everyone wants one. Subarus can offer a good bargain, and so can Isuzu and Mazda sedans.

• But *avoid Japanese or American semi-sports cars;* chances are, they were driven by somebody who thought they really *are* sports cars. At all costs, *avoid buying used four-wheel-drive off-road vehicles* like the Suzuki Samurai. Aside from their apparent engineering and design flaws, most of them have been burned out by junior lumberjacks four-wheeling up the dangerous inclines of their suburban driveways — after a quick dash through the forest primeval. As a rule of thumb, any car marketed to younger drivers is likely to be a lousy second-hand car. (SV, WL, FDD, PAN)

RECYCLING CARS

Buy a depreciated car, drive it for a year, then sell it for what you paid for it. Net result — no expense for cost, only for operation. (LCh)

SECOND-HAND WOES

Take the risk out of used car shopping by knowing what you want before you start. Don't just head out looking for "a used car." Do some research and make sure your expectations are realistic. Choose a narrow range of auto types, then look at the classified ads to get an idea of price. Shop the used car lots by telephone — not to choose a car, but to get an idea of what advantages, if any, a dealer can offer over a private seller. After all, the dealer's price is going to be substantially higher than a private party's for the same car. (KMcF)

Understand your budget. Really understand it. Don't get mixed up by monthly payments. They always sound reasonable, but by the time you calculate the cost of the loan, they aren't necessarily reasonable at all. **See under** *Budgets* **in** *CHAPTER TWO: MODERN MOOLAH.*

If you decide to opt for financing, know what sort of loan you can get before you start out. Don't trust the math the car salesman gives you. If you can't do arithmetic, take along someone who can.

Options: Options aren't optional at all if they are a piece of equipment you absolutely need. If you have arthritis, you *must* have power steering. Do you make regular trips back and forth through Death Valley? Then you must have an air-conditioner in good condition. Options can seriously affect the price of a used car, so when you do your shopping, make sure you've included the optional equipment you require. (FC) **See** *Mega-Options,* **below.**

Read. Go to the library and find the consumer's guides. Check up on a prospective dealer by calling the Better Business Bureau. Where did the car come from? If the dealer doesn't want to tell you, it could mean that a terrible person used to own it who did terrible things to the car. Beware! (HPD)

Never buy a car that used to be a rental. Rentals are bad news. Think in your mind how a rental house looks compared to one that is owned. Have you ever rented a car? Have you ever owned a car? Compare the way you've treated them. Things that are rented age fast. (HPD)

A dissent: You can save a good chunk of money by buying a fleet car from a rental company. While the car may have been driven a large number of miles in a short period of time, it will still only have 30,000 to 40,000 miles on it — and, if you're buying from one of the large car rental companies, it will have been scrupulously maintained. (KGG)

Hot wheels: There should be an unaltered Vehicle Identification Number on the dash plate that has not been tampered with. If you buy a stolen car you are out of luck and money. (HPD)

Trust: If the dealer doesn't want to let you take the car to visit your mechanic, be mighty suspicious. And don't believe anything that isn't in writing and don't sign anything until you've read it all and all the little blanks have been filled. The dealer wants to sell you anything he can. Little last minute things. You know what Mrs. Reagan says. Just say no. (JCS)

Look at the odometer. Do one of those little numbers look sort of out of line with the other little numbers? Now, what could that mean? (BC) **For more things to check, see** *The Modern Woman's Car-Buying Checklist,* **below.**

Look at the car in broad daylight. If it glistens and shines, look under the car. The truth is often found hiding under a car. Rust, for example, is a four-letter word. If the car has been repainted, try and figure out why. Some horrible accident perhaps? Or trying to make an apple out of a lemon? Black spots are from oil. Transmission fluid spots are pink. Greenish-yellow ones are from coolant. Check the ground under the car. Know your spots. (GD)

No bluff: If you don't know anything about cars, take someone with you who does or you're a dead duck. Don't attempt to bluff your way through car talk because you can't. (ADD)

Check with your insurance agent before you buy a used car if you don't want any surprises. Insurance agents know lots of things. Certain cars, for example, are practically made to be stolen. They have thief magnets on them and the minute you park outside of your house, it will be gone. Your agent knows things like this. Never buy a car if it doesn't have a title. (LE)

Not new: Remember that a used car is a used car. It is not perfect and repairs will probably be necessary. Let your mechanic give you an estimate of what needs to be done and whether or not the deal is worth it. (CAFu) **See** *Car Insurance,* **below.**

THE LEASE YOU CAN DO

The good news about a new car lease (used cars are almost never leased) is that they're cheap to get into. As a rule, all you have to do is come up with a first month's payment and a small deposit.

The bad news is that you not only pay more for a car under a lease arrangement, but you also don't own it at the end of the lease period — unless it's an *open-end lease.*

Insurance and maintenance are all on you, and some leases specify a penalty for excess mileage.

Unless you can do *a lease as part of your business,* skip it. With a car lease, the leasing company makes money, the dealer makes money, because you lose money. (WN, PL)

HYPER MEGA-OPTIONS

There are some very expensive extras you can select for most new cars. Don't swallow the ad copy you hear on TV: Each of these options has a disadvantage, even if it's only the cost.

Turbo is short for turbocharger, an engine-mounted rotary pump. It forces a greater fuel-and-air mixture into your engine under pressure. This gives your engine more horsepower for acceleration, yet will allow highway cruising with a smaller engine for better fuel economy.

Turbocharged engines may be less durable than regular engines and may need more repairs and twice as many oil changes. You will burn more fuel because of the extra power, so you will get fewer miles to the gallon. By purchasing a turbocharged engine, you may find yourself in the high-risk car insurance group. But if you're keen on great, big Rambo-like power, it may be just the thing for you.

Valves: Four-valve-per-cylinder heads will greatly increase your car's horsepower without decreasing fuel economy. Normal engines have two valves per cylinder. With four valves you will have twice as many parts, but it will be just as reliable. It will cost a few hundred dollars more.

Fuel injection: On conventional engines, the carburetor mixes air and fuel and then a vacuum in the engine sucks the mixture into the cylinders. In contrast, electronic fuel injection is a computer-controlled device that allows the fuel mixture to be injected into the cylinders. What this amounts to is higher gas mileage, less air pollution, and better performance.

ABS, otherwise known as antiskid braking system, has a computerized sensor in each wheel. The sensor can tell when the brake is on the verge of locking. It releases the brake fluid pressure just slightly to "pump" the brakes hundreds of times per second. This has been an enormous advance for safety. You will have a shorter stopping distance and be able to stop on slick roads without losing steering control. Some makers offer this as standard equipment. As an option, it will cost about $1000. It is worth it.

Digital instrumentation: For an extra $500 or $1000, you can have an electronic dashboard and feel just like Captain Space! In some cars all you have to do is touch the perfect spot and on comes *this* and off goes *that*. These instruments can cost quite a bit to repair, but does Captain Space care about things like that? The rule of thumb here is that if a digital read-out isn't really necessary, it's just an unnecessary light, bell or whistle that could end up costing you more than just the dealer price — especially when it comes time to repair it. Almost all mechanics are analog.

Four-wheel drive: Ordinarily, the engine is connected to the rear wheels by the drive train. The rear wheels do the work and the front wheels do the steering. But with four-wheel drive, the engine is connected to all four wheels. They *all* do the work. That's why they're so good in rugged terrain and on slippery roads, because twice as many tires are pushing and pulling and working away. Most of the four-wheel drive vehicles allow you to switch back and forth, and that saves on gas expense. On the downside, four-wheeling is a great way to drain your gas tank in a hurry, and unless you're a suburban forest ranger, there is virtually no necessity for four-wheel drive. It's a fashion these days — imagine Banana Republic on wheels.

Front-wheel drive: A much more sensible option than four-wheel drive, front-wheel drive allows for increased traction in treacherous conditions without any of the dollar-sucking characteristics of four-wheelers. Front-wheel drive is an option worth taking.

Four-wheel steering: With four-wheel steering, at low speeds the front and back wheels steer in *opposite* directions. At high speeds, all the wheels go in the *same* direction. This makes for enhanced handling and control.

Air bags become a part of your life if you're driving along and your seatbelt is on (it must be on or the bags won't work), and you are in a head-on collision at speeds of approximately 12 to 30 mph. If your collision meets those qualifications and your car is equipped with air bags, a big balloon appears out of nowhere and interposes itself between your body and the hard things that are crashing in front of you, and you hurtle into a balloon instead of glass and metal. Air bags don't do much for you unless you're in a head-on. Then the $800 cost for each one of them is a bargain. (EA)

THE MODERN WOMAN'S CAR-BUYING CHECKLIST

A Note: We received a batch of contributions suggesting that one or more of the following items be checked before buying a car. Many of these items apply to new cars only; some, only to used cars. But this will give you an idea of the kind of things you will want to look into before you hand over any money:

❑ Make sure the model and style you want is the type you test drive.

❑ Get in and adjust the seat. Make sure you can get comfortable. Are the brake and acceleration pedals in a good position for you?

❏ Do the controls operate easily? Make sure all the knobs and buttons are there and not loose or broken.

❏ Does the car start up right away? How does it idle?

❏ As you drive make note of the performance — for instance, how the car handles various road conditions and how it corners.

❏ Does the optional equipment seem to pull the power from the engine?

❏ Notice the noise level at both low and high speeds.

❏ Do the ventilation, heat and air-conditioning systems work properly and are they adjustable to your needs?

❏ When checking the interior, pay attention to details like cigarette burns, frayed upholstery and stains.

❏ Do the doors, windows, hood and trunk latches open and close easily? Do they fit as they should?

❏ Are there any loose wires or hoses under the hood?

If you don't get what you want the first time, try another model or make. (AAT, *et al.*) **See under** *Hyper Mega-Options,* **above.**

CAR INSURANCE

This is the strange netherworld of transportation, where there's right and wrong, irrationality and responsibility, meanness and concern. Modern Women stand up for what's right, responsible and fair. Standing up against them are the insurance companies and the state legislatures they have purchased.

Auto policies don't vary that much, but the amount you pay does. Here's a list of factors that determine your premiums:

• *The type of car.* If you drive a little bug, your collision insurance will cost more than if you drive a big beast.

• *The age of the car.*

• *Your driving record.*

• *Where you live.* The insurance industry has divided the country into rate-making territories. Some towns are more dangerous than others, and if you live in one of them, your rates will be higher.

• *Amount of coverage* you elect to take. Every state has a minimum amount required by law, but you can have more.

• *Amount of deductible.* The higher the deductible, the lower the premium. (TR)

A standard policy covers seven areas:

1. Bodily injury liability protects you if you kill or injure another person with your car. It will pay for legal costs and liability.

2. Collision coverage pays for the damage to your car that is caused by hitting something. If it is not your fault, you will usually be paid the full amount of damages minus the deductible. If your company can collect on the other person's company, you might be reimbursed your deductible. If your car is getting on in years (five years old is considered getting on) you should consider dropping your collision coverage. The company will never pay out more than the bluebook value of your car. After about five years, this value is probably about the same as the cost of the coverage, so it's not worth paying anymore.

3. Comprehensive coverage includes all the horrible things that can happen besides running into trees and other cars. This coverage takes care of costs after your car bursts into flames and when the robbers break the windows. If your car is stolen, you will be paid its bluebook value.

4. Medical payments coverage pays for doctor and hospital bills — no matter whose fault it is. Your passengers will also be covered.

5. Property damage liability pays for your damage if it is your fault. If you wreck someone else's car, your insurance would pay the owner for it.

6. Underinsured motorists coverage takes care of you when the other person is at fault, but her insurance doesn't cover all the damage you suffer.

7. Uninsured motorists coverage protects you from irresponsible people who do not get insurance. It will also pay for damages from hit and run. (CM)

Every state requires a minimum amount of coverage. Your state may require a coverage of 10/20/5, for example. The "10" represents $10,000. This means the company will pay no more than that amount for injuries to any one person. The "20" represents $20,000 and means that the company will pay no more than $20,000 if two or more people are hurt. The "5" is $5,000. This is the amount that will be paid for property damage, which usually means the damage to the other car.

It is wise to buy more coverage than the state requires, because these minimum amounts are chicken feed. Remember, in the event of an accident, you will have to pay the balance out of your own pocket.

Consider looking into an *umbrella policy* that can insure you for a million or more dollars. This will protect you from paying high legal awards. (TN)

Discounts: Check to see what kind of discounts are offered. There are a number of different types ranging from students with a B average to nonsmokers to people over fifty years of age and so forth. (OL)

Lawyers: Your insurance will cover you if you are sued, but it will not cover your fees if you want to sue someone. (LP) **See under** *Lawyers* **in** *CHAPTER TWELVE: MODERN WOMEN IN DISTRESS*.

Book value is the present value of your car according to publicly known standards. You can find an automotive blue book listing values in your library. (TR)

Bad record: Your car insurance company can kick you out if your record gets too bad, and many will automatically boot you if you are convicted of driving under the influence. If you cannot get regular coverage, you can probably get *assigned risk coverage*. The premiums, of course, are much higher. (TR)

If you have a Corvette, nobody will insure it. Thieves love Corvettes. You'll have to get your insurance through an assigned risk pool along with the drunk drivers. (KPH)

The agent: If your agent has the letters *CPCU* after her name, she is an expert in auto insurance. You can ask her about your insurance problems and she should be able to provide you with the correct answers. (TR)

CAR TALK

The language of cars is often phallic, generally masculine and highly descriptive.

Nevertheless, there are times when a Modern Woman has to talk nuts-and-bolts. For that special, grease-filled, exhaust-breathing moment, here's a brief glossary:

GARAGE CHATTER
If you have a basic idea of how your car runs (**see below, under** *Car Repairs*), you will not have to memorize the words the mechanic tells you in order to run home and repeat them to a friend for translation. The more you know in this wicked, wicked world, the better.
- *ABS brakes:* Antilock (or antiskid) braking system.
- *Axle:* A rod around which a pair of wheels turns.
- *Cabriolet:* Virtually all automotive model names have been derived from those of horse-drawn carriages. *Cabriolet* has recently been revived as a tonier synonym for a convertible.
- *Cam:* The asymmetrical projection of a rotating *camshaft,* the shape of which opens and closes each cylinder's intake and exhaust valves sequentially.
- *Carburetor:* The part of a car's engine that mixes gasoline and air. It works on the same principle as a perfume atomizer.
- *Coupe:* Or, to be precise, *coupé.* Any two-door sedan.
- *Countershaft:* The rod that is connected by gears to the transmission shaft and the drive shaft to help send the engine's movements to the wheels.
- *Crankshaft:* The piece of metal under the engine that turns as the pistons go up and down.
- *Cylinder:* One of the round spaces in the engine that hold the pistons and gasoline and air.
- *Dieseling:* A form of autoignition in which the engine of the car continues to fire even after you've turned it off.
- *Disc brakes:* Similar to the brake on a bike, the disc brake consists of a flat rotor (the disc) that turns with the wheel, and a stationary caliper that grabs it with brake pads. They sqeal a little, and that's okay.
- *Distributor:* The part of the engine that distributes electricity to the spark plugs from either the battery or the generator (or alternator) (q.v., below).
- *DOHC:* Double overhead cam (see *Overhead cam,* below).

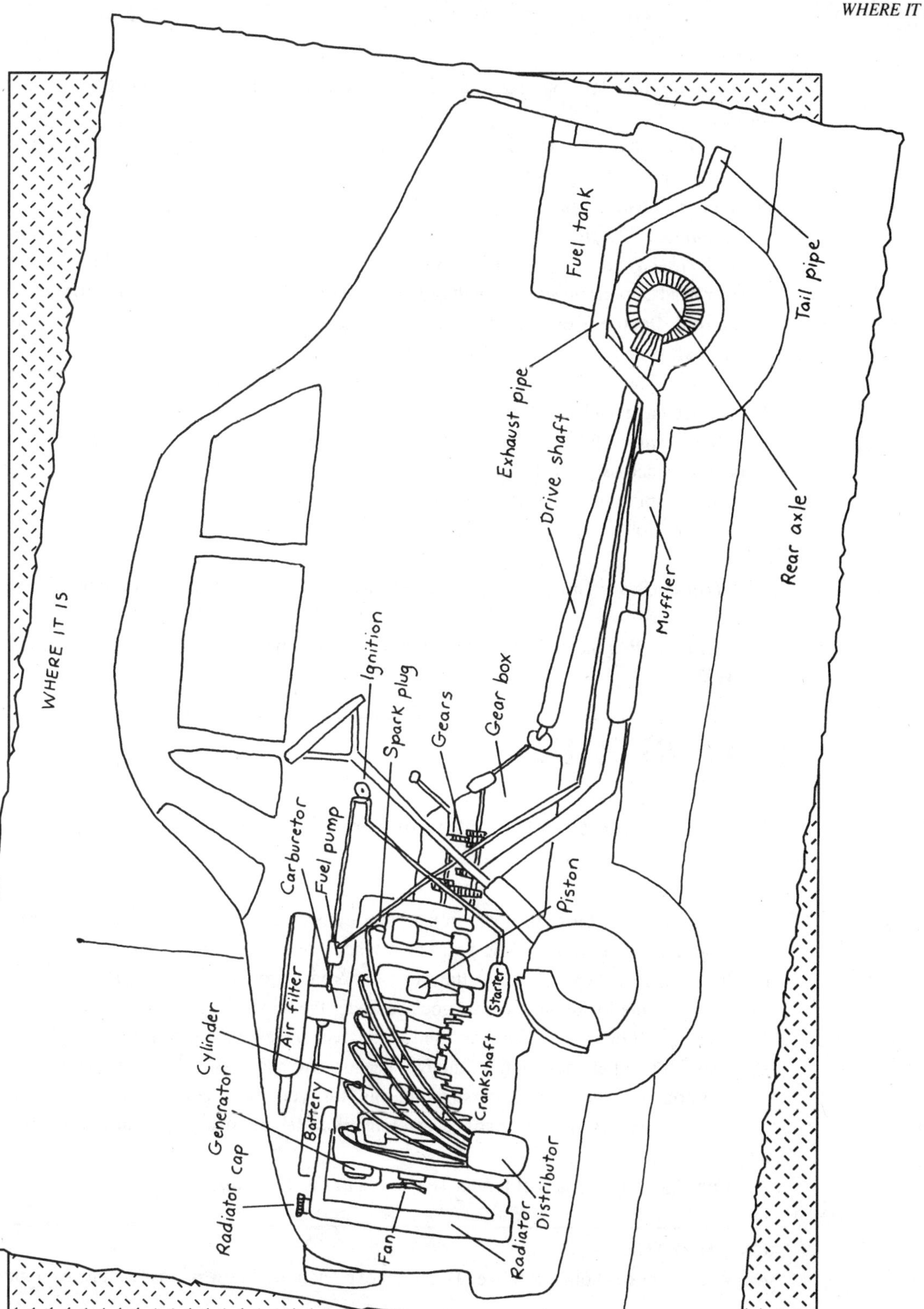
WHERE IT IS
Fuel tank
Tail pipe
Exhaust pipe
Drive shaft
Rear axle
Muffler
Ignition
Spark plug
Gears
Gear box
Carburetor
Fuel pump
Piston
Starter
Air filter
Cylinder
Crankshaft
Generator
Battery
Radiator cap
Distributor
Fan
Radiator

• *Drive shaft:* The long rod that carries movement from the crankshaft to the back wheels.

• *Four-by-four:* A four-wheel-drive vehicle — the flannel shirt of the car world — especially essential to junior execs who need that extra traction for wheeling up those shopping mall parking ramps.

• *Generator:* The motor in the engine that produces electricity. Also called an alternator.

• *Overhead cam:* A simplified system in which cams (q.v.), placed directly over cylinder heads, open and shut the valves without the use of push rods, allowing for greater engine rpm. Double overhead cams (DOHCs) use two cams per cylinder — one for the exhaust valves and one for the intake valves.

• *Piston:* The round, metal object that moves up and down in the cylinder to compress then release the gasoline and air.

• *Spark plug:* The ceramic-and-metal piece that fits into the top of the cylinder. The spark travels across the gap between the metal wires at the end of the plug. The spark explodes the mixture of gasoline and air in the cylinder.

• *Suspension:* A system made up of springs and shocks that absorbs the bumps of the road.

• *Transmission:* The system of gears and shafts that sends power from the engine to the wheels.

• *Transmission shaft:* The rod that sends power from the clutch to the countershaft. (EA, SA, WKu)

CAR REPAIRS

Maintenance and troubleshooting tips are all right if you already know what the words mean.

You can check those pistons, unbend that transmission shaft, and plug that leaking manifold, no problem, providing you know what those things are, where they are, why they're there, what they do and how they do it. Otherwise, troubleshooting is a lot of trouble.

So here's the lowdown on what goes on under the hood of a car.

And note: If this seems simplistic and somewhat condescending, you're half right. It *is* simplistic. It's not condescending, though, because we had to digest questions and notes from contributors and try to understand all this stuff ourselves. This is written so *we* can understand ourselves. If it seems condescending to you, it's because you already know about automobile repairs.

For a glossary of useful terms, see above under *Car Talk.*

CAR SCIENCE

Energy makes your car move. This is an explanation of how it gets from heaven into your wheels. After that, it's sort of like the knee bone connecting to the thigh bone:

• Turn the key in the *ignition switch.* This sends an electrical signal to the battery to send out electricity.

• Electricity travels out of the *battery* to the cranking motor, or *starter motor.*

• The starter motor connects with the *crankshaft* at the bottom of the engine. A crankshaft is a humpy, crooked piece of metal. The starter motor starts the crankshaft turning. It keeps it up until the crankshaft is turning fast enough (as a result of the engine now firing) to continue without the starter motor's assistance.

WHAT MAKES AN ENGINE RUN

Electricity is part of the action. The other part is gasoline and air.

• *Under normal circumstances, if a car engine ever stops running, it's because it's either not getting any gas or it's not getting any electricity.*

• A small tube, called a *fuel line,* runs from the gas tank to the fuel pump on the engine (**see below, under** *Filter Frenzy*). The starter motor starts the crankshaft, and the crankshaft starts the fuel pump.

• The fuel pump sucks gasoline from the gas tank and sends it to the *carburetor.* The carburetor sits on top of the engine. An air filter, which looks like a cake pan, sits on top of the carburetor. The carburetor mixes air and gas together to achieve the right richness for efficient combustion. Air comes into the carburetor through the air filter which cleans it first. The carburetor shoots the air into a tube and at the same time squirts small amounts of gasoline into the same tube. The air and the gasoline mix.

• We want an explosion to happen, and this is where *spark plugs* come in. They provide the open spark that makes the explosion that gives the engine power.

• Spark plugs are connected by wires to the *distributor.* When you turn the key in the ignition, the battery sends power to the starter motor, but at the same time it also sends electricity to the distributor. The distributor distributes this power to the spark plugs.

• There are two little pieces of metal at the bottom of spark plugs that almost touch one another. The distributor sends electricity down one side of the plug, and it makes a tiny leap across the *gap* from one piece of metal to the other. This causes a spark. The spark makes the gasoline and air explode. These little explosions happen inside the *cylinders.*

• Cylinders are long, tubular chambers within *the engine block,* which is the main part of the engine. Most automobile engines have four, six, or eight cylinders. As a rule, a car with eight cylinders is stronger than one with four or six. Each cylinder has its own spark plug in the top of it.

• There are two (and sometimes four) *valves* at the top of each cylinder which open and close. One opens to let in air and gasoline. The other opens to release fumes from the previous explosion as exhaust.

• Each cylinder has a *piston,* which fits right inside the cylinder. Pieces of metal called *connecting rods* connect the pistons to the crankshaft.

Remember how the starter motor started the crankshaft turning until it no longer needed

assistance and could turn on its own? Here's what happened:
- When the crankshaft turns, the pistons go up and down.
- Gasoline and air comes from the carburetor through the intake valve and into the cylinder where that piston is pumping away.
- The cylinder fills as the piston goes down.
- The valve closes.
- The piston comes up, compressing the air and gasoline inside the cylinder.
- A spark sparks on the spark plug and the gasoline and air inside the cylinder explode.
- The piston is driven back down by the exploding, expanding gas.
- And the crankshaft turns without using the starter motor.

FILTER FRENZY

One of the easiest things to check if your car stops running is whether or not the *fuel filter* on the fuel line is all clogged. Fuel filters are cheap and very easy to change. Just unplug the fuel line from one end, plug it into the new filter, then repeat with the other end. (DY)

ABOUT THE ELECTRICAL, EXHAUST AND TRANSMISSION SYSTEMS.

- The pistons are turning the crankshaft, so the starter motor is no longer needed. The battery, which was sending electricity to the distributor and thence to the spark plugs, is also no longer needed because its function has been taken over by the *generator* (or *alternator*), where the running engine makes its own supply of electricity. It is now the generator which will send power to the distributor, which will distribute electricity to the spark plugs. It will also recharge the battery so that it will be ready to start the car again next time.
- The exhaust *valve* opens when the *piston* comes back up. *Exhaust* is pushed out of the cylinder and through the *exhaust pipe* at the bottom of the car. It's a noisy procedure, so the exhaust passes through a *muffler* to quiet it.
- *Pistons* have *compression rings* on them to prevent the escape of exhaust, and *oil rings* to prevent the passage of oil. The rings sit in cavities around the piston and provide the sealing that is necessary to make compression possible.
- The *crankshaft* sends power to the rear wheels by turning the *drive shaft* (or output shaft), which, in rear-wheel-drive cars, is a long rod running under the car floor to the rear.
- The drive shaft turns the rear *axle,* which is a rod that connects the rear wheels. The axle, of course, makes the wheels turn.
- *A confusing aside:* The crankshaft and the drive shaft turn in one direction, and they move the axle, which turns in another direction. This works because the gears that connect them come together at right angles.
- The *transmission* is the device that sends power from the driver to the engine to the wheels by means of a series of gears and shafts. The transmission contains two shafts and is located behind the engine. One shaft is the *transmission shaft,* and the other is the *countershaft*. One gear on the countershaft connects to a gear on the drive shaft.
- Part of the transmission is the *clutch*. A *friction clutch* has three round pieces of metal.

One outside piece — the *plate* — connects to the crankshaft. The disc on the other side connects to the transmission shaft. The middle disc is rough on both sides. There is friction and pressure when the two plates of the clutch press against the disc. Pressure holds the three together, and friction makes them turn together. As these parts turn, gears on the crankshaft and transmission shaft connect to the one on the countershaft. And that shaft sends power along the drive shaft to the rear axle, and the wheels go round.

    • When the gearshift is in neutral, no gears on the transmission shaft are touching gears on the countershaft. When you shift the car into first gear, the transmission shaft moves far enough to bring one of its gears together with a gear on the countershaft. When you are in first, a little gear on the transmission shaft is turning a large gear on the countershaft. That makes for a lot of power but very little speed. But by the time you are in fourth, a large gear on the transmission shaft is connecting with a little gear on the countershaft. The big gear is not working so hard, and it is making the little gear turn very fast. You're zooming. In an automatic transmission, this whole operation takes place sequentially, usually using hydraulic power, when you put the transmision lever in the "D" position.

HOW A CAR STEERS

    A metal *steering rod* joins the *steering wheel* to a *steering box* between the front wheels. Gears inside that box join the first rod to a second rod connected with the front wheels. In conventional steering, the gears work together when you turn the wheel, to carry power along the rod to move the car wheels. In power steering, there are still gears in a box, but power to move them comes from fluid that is pumped into the box. Pressure from the fluid causes the gears, rods, and wheels to turn.

WHOA, DUDE

    • *Disc brakes* are usually used on front wheels. A disc brake is a round piece of metal on the inside of a wheel that spins with the wheel. A clamp fits around the top of the disc. The clamp holds pads that can move against the disc. Fluid is sent to the disc brake when you press the brake pedal. Because of the fluid, the clamp presses against the brake pads which press against the disc, and the wheel slows down.

    • *Drum brakes* work on rear wheels. Next to the wheels there is a piece of metal shaped like — well, shaped like a drum. There are two curved pieces of metal called brake shoes inside the drum. When you press on the brake, the brake shoes press against the drum and the wheel slows down.

BLACK GOLD

    • *Oil* helps the pistons to run smoothly and the crankshaft to turn without becoming worn out. If the engine doesn't have a sufficient supply of oil, the resulting friction causes a tremendous build-up of heat, sometimes enough to make the engine seize up, destroying it. Then you find out why it's important to keep the engine oil level up.

    • A *gasket* is just a little thin piece of steel that comes in many different shapes. Gaskets

act as seals to prevent leakage of oil, water and fuel. "Blowing a gasket" just means that one is worn out. No big deal. Not like "dropping a rod," for instance. My mother "dropped a rod" on the Bay Bridge between Oakland and San Francisco. She sold her car for $100 after that. I don't know what "dropping a rod" actually is, but it is *bad*. "Blowing a gasket" is not.

COOLING

Both *oil* and *water* help to cool the engine.

A *water pump* draws water from the radiator through passages around the cylinders where most of the heat is. The water takes heat from the engine and flows back to the radiator, where it is cooled by exposure to air from the grille and from the radiator fan. The fan belt operates the water pump, which circulates the water.

Antifreeze: Water expands when it freezes. A "cracked block" means that the water in the radiator and the block has frozen and cracked it. Antifreeze prevents this.

BUMPS AND GRINDS

The *suspension system* holds the body away from the bumps of the road. Each wheel has a suspension system. One part of that system is the *springs*, and the other is the *shock absorber.* A shock absorber is a long cylinder with a piston inside. While the spring takes some of the force of the bump, the piston will at the same time move upward in the shock and take the bump's force, too. (Material for the above sections provided by EC, JDP, WP, VS, PZ, *et al.*)

A FINAL WORD ON CAR REPAIRS

Not knowing how to fix cars can be a good thing. The skills of auto repair, in a way, resemble the skills of a typist. Many times, knowing how to type can mean that you'll wind up in a boring dead end job as secretary or typist.

Knowing how to fix cars can result in your actually fixing them, which is a messy, horrible, frustrating endeavor at best. Convincing or paying someone else to handle these issues is really far more liberating than we realize. (ARo)

WHITE-LINE SAFETY

You could just *die* out there. The highways are filled with jerks driving junk. So watch it.

HIGHWAY MAYDAY

Emergency repairs: A few things are nice to keep on hand.

• *A spare gas cap,* for example, can come in handy to replace the one that fell off the top of your car as you drove away from the gas station.

• *A spare fan belt* is a good idea because you don't want your car to catch fire.

• Make sure there is *air in your spare.*

• Keep a *can of oil* in the trunk, and a gallon of *water.*

• Have a *jack* and know how to use it.

• Keep a *flashlight* and some *flares.*

• It's a good idea to keep a small *first aid kit* in the car at all times, too.

• Keep some *tools* like screwdrivers and socket wrenches.

• Keep the *owner's manual* that came with the car in the car and not inside your house.

• Keep *battery cables* handy and know how to use them.

How to use battery cables: Connect the two positive terminals on the battery of each car, and then the two negatives. The good car can be on while you do this, but wait until everything is hooked up to turn the key in your dead car.

• *Join AAA* for peace of mind. (EA, KK, MK, VS, DT)

A PEDAGOGICAL TALE OF HIGHWAY DISTRESS

Sometimes I pretend that the little red lights on the dashboard are just malfunctioning.

The brake light, for example, is *constantly* going on and off. The other day it even exploded a little bit. How can I get insane everytime the light malfunctions? Besides, a mechanic once told me that brake lights are notorious for going on when nothing is the matter. The brake light did not come on the day all the brake fluid had fallen out of the car overnight and my foot went all the way to the floor. And it did not come on the morning that all the brakes on the left side of the car stopped working.

And there is another light called the generator light. That went on once in the middle of an endless, empty highway in Montana. But I knew what to do. You lift out the backseat (this is in a VW, of course) and there is a small, black box on the far right. You take off your shoe and you hit the box with your shoe and the light goes off. It's as easy as that!

One morning I noticed a bright light on the dash, and I went right away to the gas station in panic. It turned out that the light meant my rear window defroster was on. It was a green light. I don't even *think* anymore if I see a green light. Green lights are always good lights.

Now, this brings me to the oil light, a light to take seriously whether it comes on or not, which it never does. I know that because I once had about a tablespoon of oil left and I never saw a light. The thing to do about oil is to check it all the time. I must admit, if I ever see that light come on, I will stop immediately. Whether the bulb is malfunctioning or not, I will stop. I know that no oil means my car will explode.

But all those other lights. I can't be bothered. And there isn't any light at all for when the fan belt brakes and the engine catches fire. **See** *What to Do If Your Car Catches on Fire,* **below.** I never noticed any light at all. In fact, I didn't even notice the fire, for that matter. Thank goodness, I was in a gas station and the man next to me screamed and the attendant raced out with a fire extinguisher. Like I say, if it isn't the oil light, I don't notice a thing. That's the truth. (EA)

PREVENTION

Over half of all deaths traced to vehicle defects are because of ***worn-out tires***. Please check your tires, including the spare, regularly.

Know how to replace a tire. Instructions are in your car's owner's manual. If you don't have a manual, write to the manufacturer and ask for one. The manual will also give you other useful pieces of information, such as where your jack is. **See under** *Highway Mayday,* **above.**

• Know where to ***check the motor oil, transmission*** and ***brake fluids*** and ***coolant.***

• Know where the ***belts*** and ***hoses*** are. You don't have to know what they do. Just know where they are and what they attach to. (EA, FG)

SEVEN REASONS TO STOP YOUR CAR *IMMEDIATELY*

Here are seven car emergencies. For all of them, pull over to the slow lane, put on your emergency lights, and start looking for a safe way off the road.

1. Oil pressure warning light: Circulating oil lubricates the engine's bearings. Without oil, your engine will self-destruct. Listen for a knocking noise. If the warning light only goes on at highway speeds and goes off again at lower speeds, you are probably just low on oil. If the light goes on at idle but goes out when you accelerate, drive cautiously to a mechanic. If the light stays on even though you check the oil and it appears to be full, do not go anywhere at all. Just call a tow truck.

2. Engine temperature warning light: It may help to switch on your heater to delay a boilover, or it may help to drive at a reduced speed. Go to a service station even if the light goes out. The engine will boil over if too much coolant is lost, and a whole lot of steam will cover the engine. Pull off the road and just sit there. Sit there until things cool down. Give it about twenty minutes. Read a magazine. Nowadays, a plastic coolant-recovery tank registering empty warns of coolant loss. Before taking off the radiator cap, see if you can squeeze the top radiator hose. If it is firm and hot, do *not* touch that cap. It could blow off into your face and if you're not knocked out by the blow, you'll be burned out by the blast of steam.

In an emergency, you can use the solvent from your windshield washer to fill the radiator. Then go to a service station.

3. Brake warning light: This usually indicates a loss in brake fluid. You will probably still be able to stop, but it will take longer and the brake pedal will not feel the way it should. Add brake fluid. Go cautiously to a service station, because there could be a big hole somewhere and all your carefully added brake fluid may just be dripping out again. **See** *A Pedagogical Tale of Highway Distress,* **above.**

4. Loss of power steering: A broken fan belt or loss of power can cause great difficulty in turning the wheel. Check under the hood to see if power-steering fluid is spraying out. Don't drive if it is. Just don't do it. You could start a fire.

5. Engine stall during deceleration: Put your left foot on the brake when shifting and

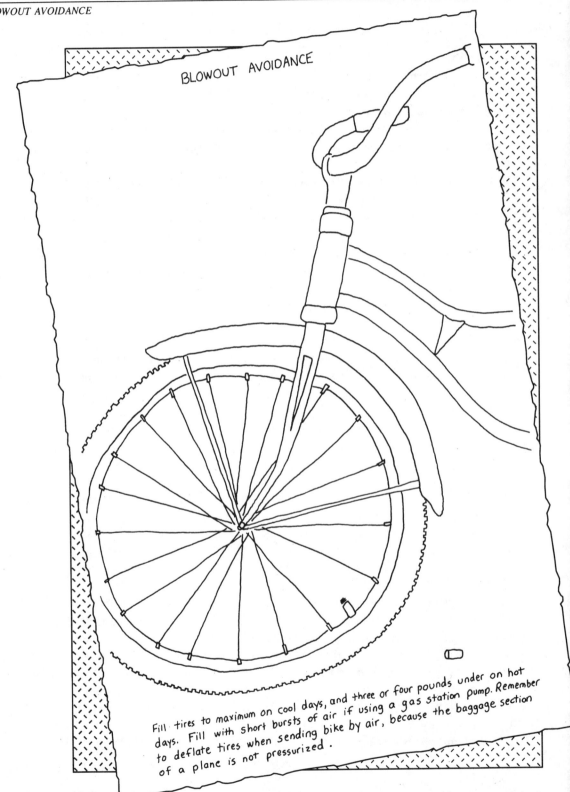

BLOWOUT AVOIDANCE

Fill tires to maximum on cool days, and three or four pounds under on hot days. Fill with short bursts of air if using a gas station pump. Remember to deflate tires when sending bike by air, because the baggage section of a plane is not pressurized.

at the same time keep your right foot on the gas to keep the engine from stalling. Once you get going, drive to a service station. It may only be that your carburetor may need adjusting. Or it could be more serious.

6. Generator (or alternator) warning light: Normally, when the car runs, the battery recharges with electrical power from the alternator. If the alternator fails, turn off air conditioning, heater, radio, and every other unnecessary thing. You can continue for almost half an hour on reserve power from the battery, so keep on rolling to help. But don't stretch it; you could easily destroy your battery.

7. Smoke: Run away fast and call the fire department. If there is no smoke, but you can smell burning wiring, disconnect the battery cables. (EA, GH)

WHAT TO DO IF YOUR CAR CATCHES ON FIRE

There are four causes of car fires:
- Gasoline
- Upholstery
- Electrical
- The emission system's catalytic converter

If the fire is small, you may be able to put it out yourself by smothering it with a blanket or extinguishing it with the fire extinguisher that you should have in your car at all times.

If the fire is under the hood, be extremely careful when opening the hood. If you're going to try and put the fire out yourself, put something between your hand and the hood latch — it may be very hot — and remember that the rush of oxygen to the fire when you open the hood will fan the flames.

If the fire is under the hood, it's likely to be *a gasoline fire.* In this case, run as fast and far as you can and take cover if possible.

Electrical fires are preceded by an acrid odor that you will definitely notice. They usually start in that mixed-up maze of wires behind the dashboard. Take a peek in there once in a while and look for any brittle or cracked wires. Have them replaced as soon as possible.

Cigarettes or matches usually cause upholstery fires. Since they can smolder for up to eight hours, you must be vigilant about making sure you and your passengers dispose of cigarettes properly. (*Never* throw them from the moving car.) You can put out upholstery fires by smothering with something like clothing or a handy cup of coffee. Foam rubber, however, can smolder for hours without any visible sign of fire. **See** *How to Break Bad Habits* **in** *CHAPTER FOUR: MODERN P's & Q's.*

Catalytic converters become very hot during the course of driving. If you've bottomed out or hit a speed bump lately, have a mechanic check to see if the converter was jammed up nearer the floor of the car. If it has moved let the mechanic fix it. Otherwise it's quite possible the converter will get so hot it will kindle the carpeting. If you feel hot spots or if there seems to be heat coming up from the floor, get it checked out.

If you ever suspect a fire of any kind, pull over right away and turn off the ignition. Close all windows and doors, then get out of there and call the fire department. (GH)

HOW TO KEEP YOUR CAR YOURS

    • Always lock your car and take the keys with you. Never hide the keys in or under the car.

    • Avoid parking in lots where you must leave the key with the attendant. If you must, leave only the ignition key.

    • Don't park on poorly lit streets or lots.

    • Put personal items like cameras and purses in the trunk when you leave the car, not on or under the seat. **See under** *Survival Tips From All Over* **in** *CHAPTER TWELVE: MODERN WOMEN IN DISTRESS.*

    • Buy a car siren alarm system or a device that renders the electrical system inoperable. (BTG)

    On the road:

    • When traveling, *keep valuables on your person,* not in your purse.

    • *Use a money belt* or pin credit cards and traveler's checks to your bra or put them down your boots.

    • *Use credit cards* and traveler's checks rather than cash whenever possible.

    • *Check valuables in at the front desk* of your hotel. There will be a small fee, but it's well worth it.

    • Keep your room *door locked* at all times. There are very inexpensive portable intruder alarms that are easy to install and don't require any tools. (BT)

HOW TO KEEP FROM FALLING ASLEEP WHILE DRIVING

    • *Have your car exhaust checked* before driving long distances. Leaking carbon monoxide can cause headaches, drowsiness and even death.

    • Set your ventilation to admit *fresh air* instead of recycling stale air, and roll down your window once in a while.

    • *Don't eat junk.* Avoid the typical fast-food belly bombs. Bring fresh fruit, cookies and boxed juices with you, or stop at a real store and buy some real stuff.

    • Stop the car and *walk around from time to time.* If you have a companion with you, change drivers every couple of hours.

    • *Limit your intake of caffeine.* Juices are better.

    • *Stay away from over-the-counter pills* designed to keep you awake. Depending on how you react to large doses of caffeine, they may only make you drowsy instead.

    • *Listen to your radio* or tape player — but don't use earphones.

    • *Pay attention* to what's happening around you. Count red cars, ponder the cows — Herefords or Guernseys?

    • *Protect your eyes* with a good set of sunglasses.

    • If all this fails and you find yourself nodding off, *pull over and go to sleep for a while.* It's better to arrive later than never. (EC, CLB)

KIDS IN CARS

Remember the way your folks used to scream at you over the front seat because you were screaming in the backseat? Well, you're in the driver's seat now.

CAR SEATS

If you have little ones, **strap them securely into their car seats**. This is a law in many states. But even where it isn't, it is absolutely nuts to drive around with a loose baby in the car. (TD) **See illustration.**

TRAVELER'S AID

Handy hints from the highway of life:

• Allow **a ten-minute break** at least every two hours. Bring a Frisbee, a ball, a jump rope. Chase the kids around the rest stop. Tell them to do cartwheels. It's good for all of you.

• **Bring books** and paper and crayons (not markers).

• **Play car games** like the famous Let's See Who Can Find the Most Out-of-State Licenses or the brilliant Let's See Who Can Be Quietest the Longest.

• Bring prepackaged **moist towlettes** by the ton.

• Bring **snacks**. Raisins and crackers. Don't bring milk.

• **Split them:** Put one child in the front seat and one in the back. No rule says children automatically sit in back, especially if they don't get along.

• Put **headsets** on their heads.

• Dress them in **comfortable clothes.**

• Bring small **pillows** and a car blanket.

• Everytime a **restroom** is available, announce it clearly and *firmly*.

• If you don't have air-conditioning and you are traveling through Death Valley, bring **squirt guns.** It sounds nutty, but it can save you all.

• Refuse to start the engine until all **seatbelts** are buckled. (AD, JK, SD, GG)

OFF-ROAD TRAVEL

As handy instruments of travel, cars are fine and good. You can take a wide variety of trips in a car — you can hop down to the store for milk, for example, or run across town for a meeting. So for hops and for runs, cars do the job.

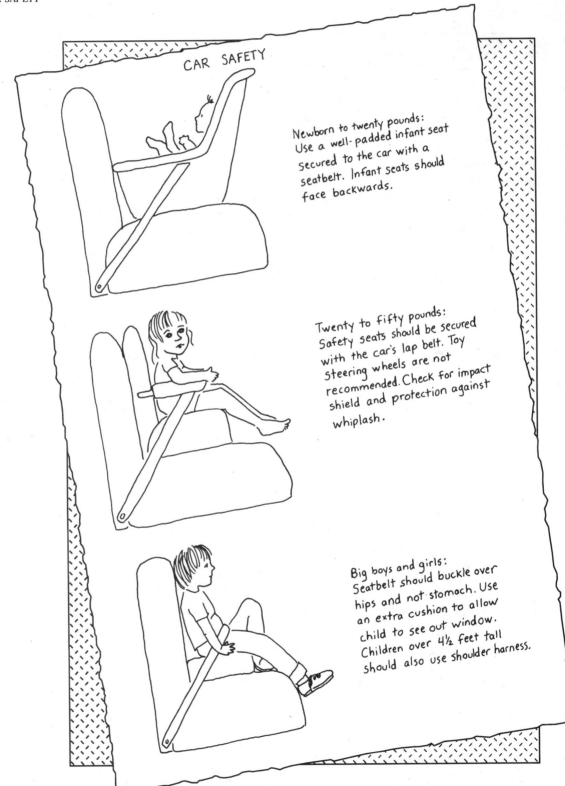

CAR SAFETY

Newborn to twenty pounds: Use a well-padded infant seat secured to the car with a seatbelt. Infant seats should face backwards.

Twenty to fifty pounds: Safety seats should be secured with the car's lap belt. Toy steering wheels are not recommended. Check for impact shield and protection against whiplash.

Big boys and girls: Seatbelt should buckle over hips and not stomach. Use an extra cushion to allow child to see out window. Children over 4½ feet tall should also use shoulder harness.

But when you think of a *journey*, well, cars just don't enter the picture. A *voyage* by car is slow, tedious and dangerous. A voyage by steamer, on the other hand, is slow, tedious and somehow altogether more enticing.

So pack your bags and have your documents ready. A Modern Woman never knows when they'll announce her departure.

VACATIONS

Camping? Hotel hopping? Trips in cars, planes or trains? Forget it — it's work! Send your kids off to camp for a couple of weeks, send your husband on a golf holiday in another city. Take it easy. (GGi)

Sometimes vacation time is best spent reacting to your internal clock. Stay at a hotel for a week, sleep all day, swim at night. Allow yourself the pleasure of living exactly as you would if you hadn't any responsibilities. (PSD)

Make vacations profitable. Look for job opportunities in different cities; browse for and buy marketable items. (JGu)

HOW TO PACK

There are two words of priceless advice here: ***Plan ahead.*** Think of your trip as a sequence of specific events that constitute one large event — like, say, a date that involves going to a sporting event in the afternoon followed by a dinner party at night — for which you have to choose appropriate outfits. (GT)

Work together: Never take an item of clothing that can only be used by itself, or one that requires taking along some other garment to make it functional. Say you have a cherished but wildly colored skirt that goes with nothing else you own save a white blouse. You're better off taking the white blouse and something more neutral.

Neutral colors: All of your outfits should be interchangeable. Take skirts for leisure and for business, and make the top decide which is for which. And pack only garments that serve at least two functions.

For a week in Paris, here's what you need:

• A dark *suit*

• Light-colored *cotton slacks*—preferably a pair that will complement the jacket of the suit

• A neutral-colored *skirt*

• Two light-colored *blouses* that will go with either the suit, the skirt or the trousers

• One dark *top* — either a sweater or a blouse

• A light *jacket* or *blazer*

• Two pairs of *shoes* — one plain and one fancy. **But see** *Work Shoes* **in** *CHAPTER EIGHT: THE MODERN MODE* **and read the bold** *italic* **type.**

• A *scarf*

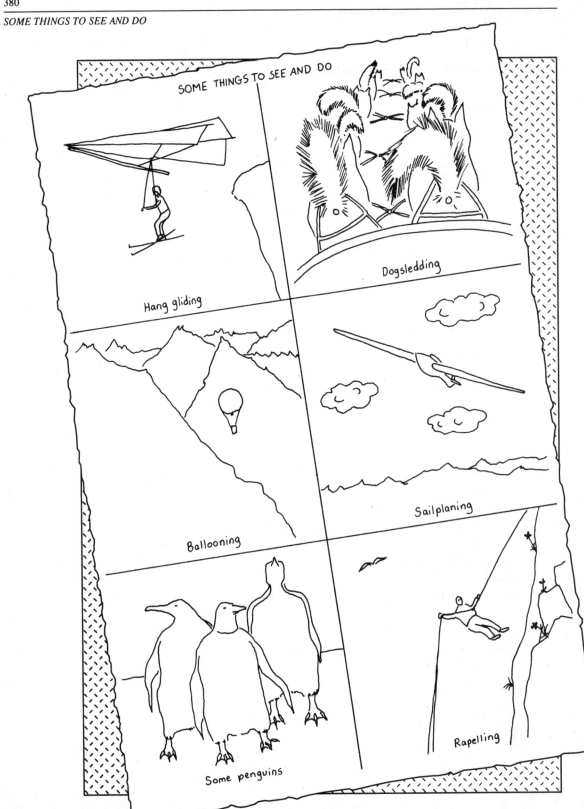

SOME THINGS TO SEE AND DO

Hang gliding

Dogsledding

Ballooning

Sailplaning

Some penguins

Rapelling

• Appropriate *accessories*. (And *appropriate* is the operative word) **See under** *ACCES-SORIES* **in** *CHAPTER EIGHT: THE MODERN MODE*.

• *Makeup* and personal things (HS, GT)

BRIEFLY

Coordinate a wardrobe that can survive in any weather. Travel light. Mix and match. (TM)

Cotton is wonderful, but if you travel in a cotton outfit you will look all crumpled up upon arrival. Tailored knits are a better idea. Look for skirts with elastic waistbands. Don't wear your highest heels. You have to run *fast* in airports. (CK)

Take an extra pair of pantyhose in your carry-on bag. Remember, nylons are created to self-destruct. (TD) **See** *Pantyhose: The Two Terrible Shades* **in** *CHAPTER EIGHT: THE MODERN MODE*.

HALF A LOAD

Assemble everything that you know you absolutely without a doubt *must* take. Then divide that in half. (LC)

FOLDING

• *A skirt:* Hold the skirt by the waistband. Fold the sides in so that you have a long, rectangular shape. Then fold up in thirds or roll it up like a sleeping bag.

• *Blouse:* Button all the buttons, then place the blouse face-down on a table. Fold the sleeves back so the shoulders overlap slightly in the middle of the back. Then fold in thirds.

• *Jacket:* Turn the jacket inside out and fold the collar up. Fold the jacket in half lengthwise and press one shoulder inside the other. Then fold in half with the lining facing out.

• *Slacks:* Flatten and fold. Watch that crease. (GT)

LOVE HANDLES?

Weight watcher: You should be able to get everything you need for a week-long trip in one medium-size suitcase. Try it. Pack the bag and carry it around the block. If the handle doesn't slice through your hand or the weight doesn't kill you, you've done a good job. *Always assume that you will have to handle all your baggage alone.* (YS) **Refer to** *THE MODERN MAN'S GUIDE TO LIFE* **under** *Types of Baggage* (illustration) **in** *CHAPTER FIVE: MODERN MOBILITY*.

FINAL CHECK

Don't check your personal items. Carry your coat with you as a carry-on item. Ditto your makeup and toiletries. If the airline loses your baggage, you'll find that nothing's worse than scurrying around putting together a temporary personal survival kit when you look and feel like hell — especially if you can't speak the language. (GT, MN)

If you can do it, *carry everything* onto the plane with you. (MH)

If possible, travel with just one suitcase, the soft kind you can stuff in the overhead compartments of trains or planes. You'll never lose your luggage, you'll get in and out of airports in a hurry, and you won't have to fuss with what to wear in the morning. (LBa)

MATCHED LUGGAGE

Often there is no one at the baggage claim area to see that the right bags go to the right people. Have your name on the inside of the luggage as well as on the outside, in case it is torn off. Don't include your address on the outside label — that could alert people to your empty house. (MH)

When traveling, *include an identification tag inside* your suitcase as well as on the outside. If the outer tag is torn off, you can prove ownership easily and quickly. If you include your destination, your bag may actually end up where you do. (AOp)

CONNECTIONS

On a long trip with connecting flights, see if you can reclaim your luggage at the connection point and then recheck it. That leaves less room for the airlines to mess up. (HH) **See under** *Airlines* **in** *HOW TO SHIP A CHILD,* **below.**

THE BAG LADY LOOK

Make your baggage as obnoxious-looking as possible so that no one else confuses it with their own. Keep a list of the contents in case you never see it again because someone with bad taste was so attracted to it. Then you can file a claim. (TT)

STRANGE CUSTOMS

Open up: Remember, there's an excellent chance some customs official someplace will want to open your suitcase. Plan for it. (GT) **See** *Eek! A Repairman!* **under** *LINGERIE* **in** *CHAPTER EIGHT: THE MODERN MODE.*

Never, ever take a parcel or suitcase for anyone else on board an airplane or through customs — even if it's for that nice guy who has just squired you through Spain and you're sure it's true love. Carry only those things that you are certain you can explain and that you're certain you own. (ES)

DOCUMENTS

Passports and visas: The off-season is supposed to be September through February. During these months it takes about two to three weeks to obtain a passport. During the busy months it could take anywhere from three to six weeks. You can apply by mail or in person.

You can renew by mail only if your passport is under eight years old. Look in the

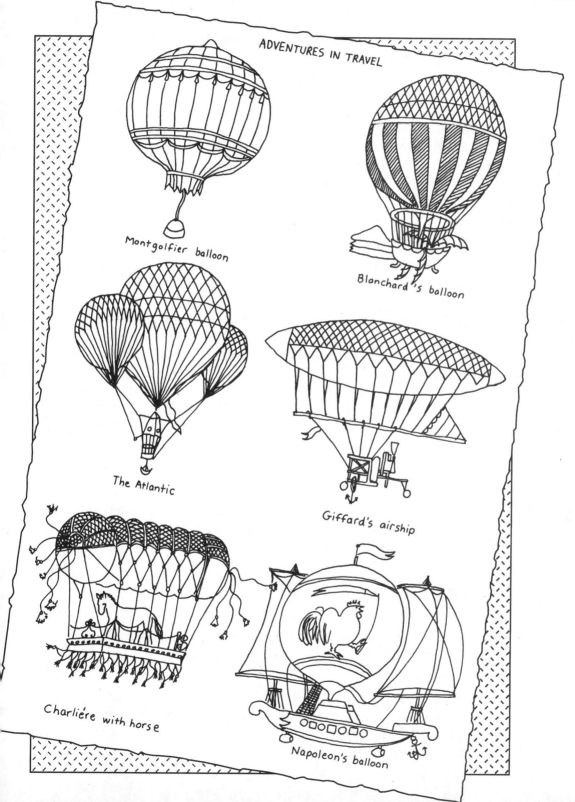

ADVENTURES IN TRAVEL

Montgolfier balloon

Blanchard's balloon

The Atlantic

Giffard's airship

Charliére with horse

Napoleon's balloon

telephone directory under "U.S. Government, Department of State," for the address of the U.S. Passport Agency nearest you. Passports cost $35, plus $7 for processing if·you apply in person. (KJ)

If you have never had a passport before, you have to stand in line in person. They have to see you in the flesh. And you must bring your birth certificate or certificate of naturalization. (JK)

You don't need a passport to travel to Canada or Mexico or to some places in Central and South America or the Caribbean, but you will need one for most other places. Note that you must have your own because there are no longer any family passports. (PO'C)

You never know: Passports are good for ten years. Have one ready at all times even if you never go anywhere. Makes a person feel hopeful. (NN)

You can update a passport years before you have to. If you are in another country when it expires, go to a U.S. consular office to get a new one. (PC)

You cannot transfer your visas from your old passport to your new one. (PC)

VISAS

A visa is a stamp inside your passport from a representative of the country you wish to visit that permits you to visit for a specific reason and length of time. The U.S. Passport Agency will send you a free copy of a brochure that lists the visa requirements of foreign governments.

Professional visa services can arrange visas for you for a small fee. This is an indispensable service if you are visiting a number of third-world countries, many of whom make obtaining visas as obtuse and difficult as the United States does for potential visitors here.

You probably do not need a visa in most of the Western Hemisphere. You will need one to visit Argentina, Brazil, Japan, most of Africa, Eastern Europe and the Soviet Union. (GD)

Never go without a visa to a country where you know they will require one. Even if the airline lets you slip through, the immigration officer at the other end won't. And unless you can talk very, very fast, you'll be put on the next flight out — at your expense. (DK)

THE TRAIN TRUTH

Here's what you get when you ride the rails: You get an up-close and personal demographic survey of the nation's more eccentric citizens, and you get low fares.

The price is right, right as rain. This is what airlines would offer if they had brains or could fly off solar energy. San Francisco to New York $238 round-trip. Los Angeles to Seattle $138. You can't beat it.

There are several essential problems, however. Each one of those trips takes two and half days. You don't get to choose who you're going to spend the night with. And you have to face about fifty people in the morning with mascara on your cheeks and hair from hell.

TRAVELING COMPANIONS

We're talking coach travel here, and there's a certain finesse to coach travel, depending on your point of departure. If you're leaving Whitefish, Montana, on a Tuesday, destination Wolf, South Dakota, chances are you'll get the whole two seats by yourself, and the car won't be full of coughing or intolerably drunk companions. On the other hand, going out of L.A. headed for Oakland, you're in deep trouble. There won't be a moment's rest, privacy, or respite from congenial State U. guys or psychic channelers. If you're in this situation, the smart thing to do is sleep a lot, invade a lounge car seat for the duration and make friends with the conductor. You're stuck, there's no way out, so you just have to do the best you can to make yourself comfortable.

If your seatmate is a real jerk, or the people in the seat in front of you are acting like idiots and you can't sleep, take your pillow into the lounge car and sleep on one of the double seats. Since you've already made friends with the conductor, he'll leave you alone and you'll get some sleep. (RK, SNo, *Anon.*) **Or, see** *JERK DEFENSE* **in** *CHAPTER FOUR: MODERN P's & Q's.*

TRAIN TIPS

• *Bring lots of magazines.* Books weigh too much and you'll score social points by passing along your magazines.

• *Bring a small Walkman* with earphones. These tiny stereos, as you know, tune out the whole world.

• *Don't get drunk.* Have a few drinks if you must, but remember, there's sleaze out there, and believe me, they follow you. It's pretty hard to sidestep someone on a train.

• *Stay aloof.* People tend to want to socialize and if you're not careful you'll end up hearing the romantic history of a slobbering drunk. **See** *Ice Breaker, Breaker* **in** *CHAPTER ELEVEN: MODERN WOMAN AT EASE.*

• *Don't ask the conductor stupid questions.* Chances are good that if you're heading north on the West Coast, the ocean will be off to your left. You'll receive a map and schedule when you board, so you can chart your own trip, ticking off the towns as you go. Wear a wristwatch, so you don't have to ask the time every hour. The railroad will seat people according to destination and tag your seat with your destination. They'll make sure to wake you and help you get ready for your departure.

• *Make friends with the conductors.* Don't seduce them or anything, but once a conductor is on your side, your chances for a great trip are much better. For instance, if you want to move your seat, or sleep in the lounge car, or spread out your papers in the diner after hours, get an extra cup of coffee from their pot or write an emergency check, you'll be able to pull it off.

• *Tipping:* You needn't tip the coach conductors, but you must tip the snack bar attendant and the dining car waiter. If you're traveling in compartments, you must tip the car attendant — five dollars is about right — upon departure. **See under** *Tipping,* **below.**

• *Redcaps:* Once you deboard, wait for the baggage cart to come along and put your bags on it. The porter will take the bags into the station, and if you palm him a buck a bag, you'll get your baggage taken to your next train, or out to the taxis. (RK)

PIGEONHOLES

A variety of private compartments are offered these days to rail passengers.

The economy sleeper sleeps one to two adults and one small child very comfortably and is equipped with a large comfortable chair that folds out into a bed, two big pillows, a closet with hangers, a sink and toilet, soap, real towels and face cloth. You also get a complimentary snack tray and nightcap, a wake-up call with coffee and juice and three huge meals a day taken either in the dining car or brought to your room. All this is included in the economy price which varies from $135 to $166 above the basic fare, depending on the season.

The deluxe compartments have about three times as much space. They include a couch and private shower and can sleep two adults and three children comfortably. As in economy, your party will receive all meals gratis for the duration of the trip. The cost, once again, varies with seasons. For example: a deluxe bedroom from Los Angeles to Seattle (two nights) will cost $346 in the high season. Deluxe compartments aren't available in all parts of the country; check with Amtrak. (RK, *Anon.*)

HOW TO CATCH A SLOW BOAT TO CHINA

Maybe you read too much Jack London, or maybe you are a true adventurer not out for the quick fix, or perhaps you have more time on your hands than cash and you want to travel.

Well, there's actually a deal for you in traveling by cargo ships. They sail out of places as diverse as Portland, Oregon, and Detroit, Michigan. Milwaukee to Tangiers? Houston to Mombasa? No problem. Freighters are carting the goods — and for a little money, they'll take you along for the ride.

PASSAGE

You can arrange a round-trip ticket, or a one-way to your point of destination. It's tricky though, because sometimes the ship will not return to the port of departure.

Book early: Cargo ships usually have a maximum passenger capacity of twelve people, so it's very important that you make your reservation by either calling the shipping line or through a travel agent as soon as possible. You can write to the freighter line and they will send brochures, rate cards and schedules. Address your inquiry to the Passenger Booking Agent of the line you're writing to.

The voyage is the thing. You must keep in mind that traveling by freighter really is an adventure. Since their job is delivering cargo, there may be sudden port changes or prolonged times in port. The ship may even bypass your destination completely. So keep in mind at the onset that flexibility is essential.

LIFE AT SEA

Once on board, you'll enjoy a private room and bath. It won't be the Ritz, but it will be quite comfortable and clean. You will dine very well, probably with the captain and officers of the ship. There's usually a bar, a game room and a passenger lounge.

Port calls: Your travel agent and the shipping company's rep can arrange tours and sight-seeing expeditions at many ports.

Health check: Be sure to ask the representative if any age restrictions are in affect on the cruise of your choice. Since there aren't physicians on board, some freighters will not take children under one year of age, pregnant women or people over sixty-five (unless they have a certificate of good health from their own physician).

You must bring your prescription drugs, antacids, aspirin, vitamins, special teas, toothpaste, shampoo and heating pads with you. Much of this stuff is not available for passengers on these ships. As a rule, most ship's stores contain a very basic inventory.

Bring sweaters and raincoats. The Pacific Ocean, even in summer is definitely not going to be like a summer eve in your backyard. Don't worry about packing lots and lots of stuff. These ships are big and allow you to bring an incredible amount of baggage with you. As a rule, there is laundry service for passengers, but check first.

While on board you won't be attending dinner dances. However, for the off onshore night out, you'll want to bring heels and a dinner dress.

You must arrange for insurance of your personal property since freighter companies cannot insure you. Leave the diamonds at home.

Tipping is iffy, but you'll most probably want to do it. Tip the steward and the waiter, same amount as in the States. **See under** *Tipping,* **below.**

Snore leave: Wave after rolling wave may get tedious. Be sure to bring along binoculars, writing materials, and books, books and more books. In other words, bring along your hobby.

Some wild destinations include Singapore, Alexandria, Fremantle, Istanbul, Trieste and Dar es Salaam.

Ask your travel agent or look in the nearest large city's Sunday paper for the ship and line in port. (KK)

TICKETS, PLEASE

A travel agent? Yeah, that's the ticket. Sometimes.

SEAL OF APPROVAL

Look for the ASTA decal, the American Society of Travel Agents. If you find it, it means that the travel agency has been in business for at least three years and that the personnel have met the society's minimum standards. (LL)

Shop around. If you and the agent are not hitting it off, go somewhere else. Having an agent who likes you can save you hundreds of dollars because she'll really search for the deals. (BNy)

Travel agents are miracles — like libraries are miracles. Free and full of wonderful information. They know the latest thing just by tapping onto their computers. You can sit down and stew and reflect and turn the pages of your calendar and a good travel agent, instead of trying to push you out the door, will tell you that it is perfectly all right and not expect you to make snap decisions. (JK)

A dissent: Travel agents are working people and to them time is money. Please help the agent do a good job for you by doing your homework before you come in to buy a ticket. A good agent will gladly supply you with enough brochures and pamphlets to take home and study so that you won't have to use the agent's office as a library. (AP)

PAID TWICE

Travel agents are not always free. Some of them are beginning to charge a booking fee, or they may ask for a nonrefundable deposit. In some of the posher towns, they won't even take you on unless somebody has recommended you. Cancel them. *Walk out of any travel agency that tries to charge you any fee of any kind.* Travel agents receive very handsome commissions from airlines, hotels, steamship companies and everyone else who has a service for them to sell. To try to charge *you* money for helping *them* make money is ridiculous. (CS)

HOME CHECKLIST

Here's a list of the things you should take care of around the house before you go:

• Ask a friend to *pick up your mail and newspaper* every single day, or ask the post office and newspaper office to hold your papers and mail for you.
• *Stop all home deliveries* of milk, diapers, whatever.

• *Install automatic light timers* all over the place. Some timers can even vary their own setting from day to day. There are some new devices on the market now that even make shadows move around against your curtains.

• *Stow away the valuables.* Leave your brand new computer with a trusted friend. If your priceless jewels aren't already in a safety deposit box, put them there now.

• *Give a trustworthy neighbor a key.* Let her come in to water the plants and watch TV and maybe have a little peaceful time away from her own hectic household.

• *Pet check:* If there is a kitty to feed, make sure your volunteer feeder loves your cat. Otherwise, consider a cat kennel. Cats can stand the lonely life for a while with just one visit a day. But not dogs. Dogs do not use litter boxes, either. **See also under** *PET DIETS* **in** *CHAPTER FIFTEEN: MISS, MRS. OR MS. CELLANEOUS.*

• *Call the cops:* In some communities, the police will drive by your house every now and then while you're away. In any case, you should notify the local precinct of any prolonged absence.

• *Let your family know* where you will be.

An anecdote: We once left for just one week without telling anyone. There were no emergencies, but my poor father really agonized when we didn't answer his long-distance calls day after day. He knew we couldn't still be out at the movies after about the third day, and he really began to fret. Worry about those who worry about you. (EC)

• Have a trusted *house sitter* sit your house, and then you won't have to worry about the cat, the mail, the lights, your papa, or anything else. (EC, YL)

Also, see under *HOUSE SECURITY* **in** *CHAPTER FIFTEEN: MISS, MRS. OR MS. CELLANEOUS.*

MOBILE FOR MONEY

Travel isn't always for pleasure (and even when it is, the travel part isn't always very pleasurable). When business calls you away from home, here's some carry-on advice:

DRESS FOR IT
If you are a business traveler, dress like one. You will be treated in a more deferential and professional manner. (JC)

ASK THE AGENT
Use an experienced travel agent to recommend *places where women usually stay.* Many hotels, for example, have promotional programs aimed at traveling women executives. Don't be reluctant to inform the hotel of your safety concerns. (TM) **See under** *TICKETS, PLEASE,* **below.**

TINY MONEY

Have some money available in small bills. Carry a cash card and a phone credit card. (TM) Do what they tell you: Record the numbers of your traveler's checks, and leave those numbers in a safe place *away* from your purse. (KH)

SLEEPWEAR

If it's an *overnight flight*, go ahead and wear pants. We're professionals, not idiots. (LW)

BAD TRIPS

Once you crawl out of bed, you start running the risk of something going just terribly *wrong*. And the farther you get from home, the more risks you run.

On the other hand, these days staying in bed can be pretty dangerous — unless, of course, you're alone.

Everything has a dark side, and to everything there is a proper premium.

TRAVEL INSURANCE

It's not a bad idea when preparing for your next trip, particularly if it's overseas, to give some thought to travel insurance.

A good travel agent can give you information on policies that cover as little as lost luggage or everything, including trip cancellation.

If you carry *homeowner's insurance,* check your policy carefully. You may find you've got all the protection you need against the possibility of lost or stolen items.

It's also a good idea to *check your health insurance* to see if it covers treatment abroad. If not, consider a policy that covers medical expenses. (SA) **See also under** *Homeowner's Insurance* **and** *Health Insurance* **in** *CHAPTER TWO: MODERN MOOLAH*.

WHAT THE STATE DEPARTMENT CAN DO

American consular officers can

- Issue you a *new passport* if yours has been lost.
- If you are robbed, they can help you to get *emergency money from home.*
- *If you are sick,* they can direct you to an English-speaking physician. (PLl)
- *If you are arrested* in a foreign country, an American consular officer can notify your relatives and friends, provide a list of lawyers, and pay for emergency medical care — as long as it's reimbursed later. They *cannot* provide bail or get you out or act as interpreters or arrange for free legal or medical service. (GF)

• *Miscellaneous:* They can tell you how to replace your traveler's checks, cancel stolen credit cards, and report a robbery to the police. (PF)

MEDIC!

Before you leave for faraway places, have a complete physical check-up even if you feel wonderful. Ask your doctor for a prescription for high altitudes, and consult him about any intestinal disorders you might be in danger of contracting. Get the prescriptions filled while you are still at home and carry them with you. (YT)

Carry any medicine in the original containers with a letter from your prescribing physician with his phone number and address in case customs inspectors give you any trouble. (BB)

THAT'S WHY THEY CALL IT "SIGHT-SEEING"

Take *extra eyeglasses,* contacts or prescriptions for lenses. (LL)

GESUNDHEIT

Carry *a card on you listing any allergies* or conditions that you have. You can write to Medic Alert Foundation International, P.O. Box 1009, Turlock, CA 95381-1009, for a bracelet or necklace with these things inscribed on them, plus a card for your wallet. (MN)

THEY MISSED YOU, TOO

Be calm when negotiating air travel difficulties.

In case you have missed your plane, never panic. Discuss your plight serenely with the personnel at the check-in desk and be quiet while they work on your situation for you. Trust them. They will really try to do their utmost to get you — and your luggage — on another flight. (JJ)

In case you lose your ticket, life is much simpler if you have a record of the ticket number. If you paid with a card, it is right there on the receipt. That's one reason why it's nice *not* to pay with cash. Keep identification on you that proves without a shadow of a doubt that you are who you say you are. (BA)

TRAVELER'S AID

If you're in *travel trouble in the United States,* look for a Traveler's Aid booth. They are often difficult to locate. Check in the phone book if you can't find one in your particular bus station, airport, or train station. The railroad station may have a passenger service manager. (JS)

UP IN SMOKE

If you are traveling by air and you have a *cute little cigarette lighter* in the shape of a cute little gun you will be in big trouble, trust me. (PM)

OFF THE BEATEN PATH

Much of the third world is out of order much of the time. When the army or the government manages to behave itself, however, the ends of the earth are great places to start an adventure.

STAYING WELL

Water quality and sanitation practices vary tremendously from country to country. In some countries, using tap water to brush your teeth or taking even one bite of salad can infect you so badly it may take weeks to get well. But with proper precautions, your chances of getting through unscathed are good. **But see** *What the State Department Can Do For You,* **above, just in case.**

Fruits and vegetables: Although everyone cautions against eating salads and unpeeled fruit, you can — if you know how to kill the bugs that can get you.

• *Get ordinary iodine,* available in any pharmacy and pronounced *ee-o-deen* in most countries.

• *Clean any soil off* fruits and vegetables and tear apart lettuce or cabbage leaves.

• *Fill a sink or bowl* with tap water and add iodine until the water looks like weak tea.

• *Soak the edibles* in the iodine water for at least a half hour. Then dry them — but *do not* rinse. You can then chomp away to your heart's content. The iodine kills the parasites, and the small amount of iodine won't hurt you at all.

To purify drinking water, you can boil it for at least half an hour — but that obviously is not a possibility for hotel-based travelers.

• *If you're touring, use bottled water,* beer or soft drinks, but make sure the bottle is factory sealed.

• *If you travel to parts where bottled water is unavailable,* you should take a supply of water purification tablets, like Halazone, available over the counter from most pharmacies.

Remember, no ice cubes when you suspect the water is unsafe. A room-temperature gin and tonic tastes wonderful after a long day in a difficult place. (LBa)

YOUR TAX DOLLAR

Write to the Superintendent of Documents, Government Printing Office, Washington D.C., 20402, for Health Information for International Travel. This document will *list all the vaccinations required for travel* to each country, the risks of malaria in each country, and information on medicines, diseases, and ways to stay healthy while you are there. (HH)

NEEDLES

If you fall sick in a developing country, consult the American Embassy for the doctors they use. It's not a bad idea to take along two or three syringes (hypodermic needles) of different sizes. It is better to supply your own completely safe, throwaway syringes. Theirs may be dull from many uses and not thoroughly sterilized. (LBa)

DRESSING FOR THE TROPICS

Do not take man-made fabrics to hot, tropical countries. They have virtually no absorbency. A polyester dress is a portable sauna. Take cotton that can be rinsed and worn without ironing.

When traveling to tropical countries, *check the temperature range* of the cities you plan to visit. Mile-high equatorial cities like Nairobi and Quito can get colder than their situation on the map would suggest. (LBa)

MANNERLY MOBILITY

You can do a lot to ruin the reputation of your native country all by yourself, so mind your manners when you travel.

CULTURAL IMPERIALISM

Don't assume that your cultural orientation has universal appeal. Believe it or not, many women in other places don't share your zeal for discussing the latest feminist fashion. In fact, in many countries — and especially in the third world — Western women are seen as being self-indulgent and self-obsessed. At a recent U.N. Women's Conference in Nairobi, many of the European and American delegates were ridiculed by women from underdeveloped countries, who considered the problems they encountered — often questions of life and death — somehow more pressing than questions of sexism in pronoun usage. Don't expect the world to be liberated. Follow the customs of the country you are visiting, and complain about it to people who will be able to sympathize with you — after you return home. (KK)

FOREIGN ELEMENTS

Err on the side of formality. Learn the names of the people with whom you are dealing. If you have any questions as to what they wish to be called, ask them. If you forget, ask again. Get it right. (DJ) **See under** *CIVILITY* in *CHAPTER FOUR: MODERN P's & Q's.*

Say "Ah." If you are offered something to eat which you consider absolutely horrible, you must eat it anyway with enthusiasm. (DJ)

Understand the rules regarding clothing.

An anecdote: My mother purchased a shirt she thought particularly beautiful but mildly shocked everyone when she wore it, because it was a man's shirt. (EC) What if you were to wear as an outergarment an item of clothing meant as an undergarment?

Be aware of the boundaries of the country you are visiting. Don't confuse one nation with another just because they are both tiny and far, far away from California. How would you feel if you were born and raised in Montana and had a guest who insisted upon referring to your state as Idaho then, after you had finally convinced him of the difference between the two, he shrugged and said something like, "Whatever"? (EC, DJ)

GESTURES

Body language can be as important or more important than verbal language. Remember this before you begin wiggling your fingers and waving your arms. If all conversation in the room abruptly ceases, you have probably committed an error. **See** *Silent Language* **in** *CHAPTER FOUR: MODERN P's & Q's.*

In the United States we are taught that strong eye contact is honest, direct, and an indication of interest, but don't do it in Japan.

When in *Europe*, thumb your nose to signify mockery. Tap it to signify drunkeness.

If someone in *Italy* flicks their chin at you, you are probably annoying them.

If you want to make the *victory sign,* be sure your palm faces away from you, and never give the O.K. sign in Brazil, Greece, or the U.S.S.R.

Don't point with your finger in the Middle and Far East.

If somebody *makes a fist* and then slaps it with the other hand, be very insulted. If somebody jerks their forearm upward and at the same time slaps the upper part of that arm, be *very* insulted. **But, see** *JERK DEFENSE* **in** *CHAPTER FIVE: MODERN MEN.*

Don't wave your hands in Greece.

To *wave good-bye* in Europe, wag the fingers together with the palm outward. Don't wave the arm back and forth. (EC, DJ, AOp, *Anon.*)

TIPPING

Restaurants: In the *United States,* for waiters and waitresses 15 percent is still the deal. Ten percent is simply stingy, and 20 percent should be reserved for extraordinary service. Leave nothing at all if you receive poor service. Before you leave the bar for your table, give the bartender 15 percent of the bar bill. When the parking attendant brings you your car, give him 50 cents. When paying with a credit card, you can enter the tip on the slip, or leave it in cash.

In Europe, especially outside Britain and Ireland, a service charge is automatically added to your bill. It should be clearly noted — *service compris,* in French — both on the check and on the menu.

Hotels: It may drive you nuts, especially when you wanted to carry your bags yourself, but here are the rules for tipping the *bellman* — $1 per bag plus a buck for opening the door.

Tip the *maid* a few dollars a week. You can leave it in an envelope marked "maid" if you cannot give it directly to her.

If you order *room service,* give the room waiter 15 percent.

Trains: Give 15 percent to dining car waiters, 15 percent to waiters and stewards in the bar car, and $2 per night to the sleeping car porter for each person.

Taxis: At least 25 cents for a fare up to $1.50, and after that about 15 percent.

Cruise Ships: Take 10 to 15 percent of the total fare, then take half of that amount and split *that* half between the *cabin steward* and the *dining room steward.* Divide the rest between the *head steward* and the *deck steward.*

Lounge and bar stewards receive 15 percent at the time of the service.

If you have to reserve your bath time, give a dollar to the *bath steward.* And give the *cabin boy* a small tip for each errand he runs.

If the *porter* carries your suitcases, tip $1 for each bag. If one of the bags is huge and has your complete library in it, shell out $5.

Airplanes: A dollar per bag for the person who lugs your luggage from your car to the counter, or $3 for a full cart.

U.S. letter carrier: It's *theoretically* illegal to tip the letter carrier. Postal employees *hate* theoretical work rules.

Paperboy: Tip $5 at Christmas time for good service.

Grocery baggers: Fifty cents a bag — but only if they load it into your car for you.

Parking Attendants: Tip $1.

Hospital: For Pete's sake, *don't tip.* ("Doc, here's a few dollars for saving my Papa's life ...") What a wild and horrible idea.

SAFETY FIRST

Let's just be careful out there.

RUE, CALLE, STRASSE, STRAAT AND VIA WISDOM
• Carry only enough *cash* for one day. **See** *Mobile for Money,* **above.**

• Never carry valuable items in a *camera case* — maybe not even the camera.

• *If you are in a crowd,* and somebody pushes you, turn around and look at that person straight in the eye. You'll know you have just been robbed if he turns and starts to run. (MB)

• Walk a few feet *away from the curb* with your purse on the side of you away from the street. (CC)

HOTEL SECURITY
Carry around a little *wedge of wood* to jam under your hotel door in case there is no chain. (HH)

HOW TO SHIP A CHILD

No stamps on the forehead, no cramming junior down a mail box. Just a little planning.

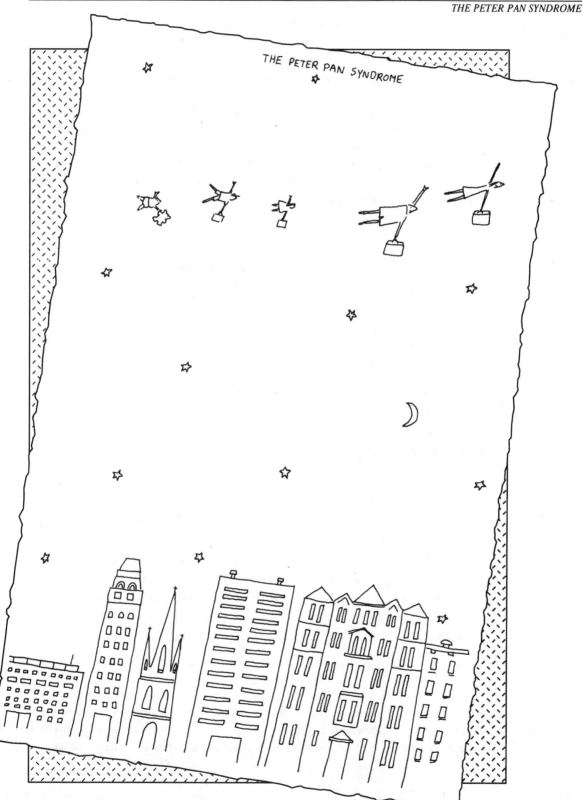

AIRLINES

Don't stop: It's a good idea to book a nonstop flight if you're taking the kiddies along. The idea of frantically finding the gate for your next flight while coordinating children, diaper bags, toys, blankets, coats and your purse and tickets is just horrifying. Also, try to stay out of an airline's hub city — hubs are always twice as crowded and confused. Remember, children under the age of two fly free, but only if they sit on your lap. For a long flight or in a crowded cabin, cough up the extra dough. Everyone will be happier. (KL)

You can be fairly confident that *the airlines will look after a child* under twelve who is traveling alone. Once they are twelve, though, children are pretty much on their own. (RR)

Most airlines will not carry *unaccompanied children under five.* Children from five to seven traveling alone are permitted if there is going to be no transfer of planes involved. Eight- to eleven-year-olds are allowed to make connections.

Be sure to tell the airline when a child will be alone, because there are forms to fill out and promises to make. (LK)

BUSES

Buses will accept kids under five if the driver feels they are capable of going it alone. Children five to eleven may travel alone only if the trip is five hours or less in length. Hopefully, the driver will tend to the child's welfare if no adult is there to meet him. (LK)

A dissent: As for buses, they'll dump your baby out as soon as the destination is reached. No one there to collect him? Not their problem. (RR)

FEAR OF FLYING

Look. Everybody knows that flying is the safest way to travel, right? You want terror? Try the San Diego Freeway at rush hour. *That's* terror. Or the New Jersey Turnpike. Or Main Street, U.S.A.

Statistically speaking, bikes, cars and trains are deathtraps compared to riding in a high-speed, multi-ton metal monster five miles above the surface of the earth, supported aloft by invisible forces you can only dimly comprehend. You're safe up there, way up there, like an angel close to God.

FEAR FIGHTERS

One in ten Americans are afraid to fly and 15,000,000 don't fly at all. Even thinking of flying can produce, in many people, ringing ears, dizziness, nausea, dry mouth and wild erratic heartbeats, nightmares and bleak, dark daydreams. Some say drinking only fruit juice, eating oranges or placing a pillow on your stomach and strapping it tightly next to you

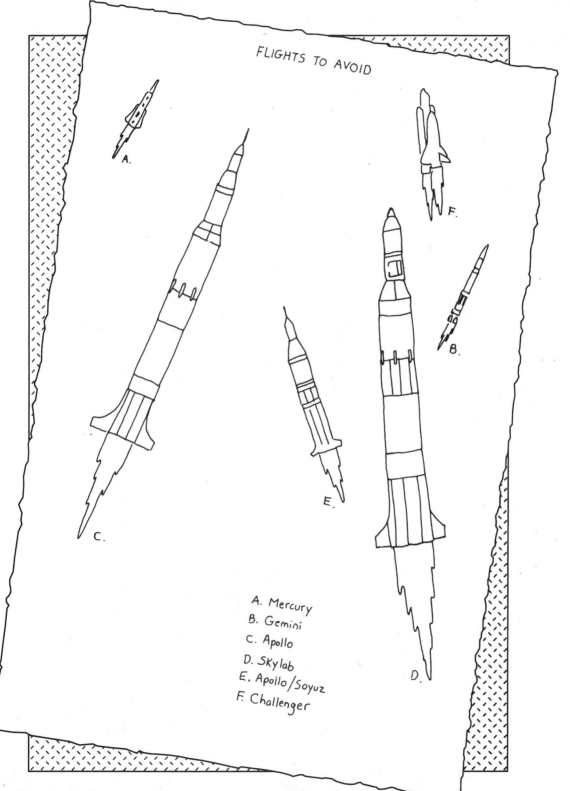

FLIGHTS TO AVOID

A.

F.

B.

E.

C.

D.

A. Mercury
B. Gemini
C. Apollo
D. Skylab
E. Apollo/Soyuz
F. Challenger

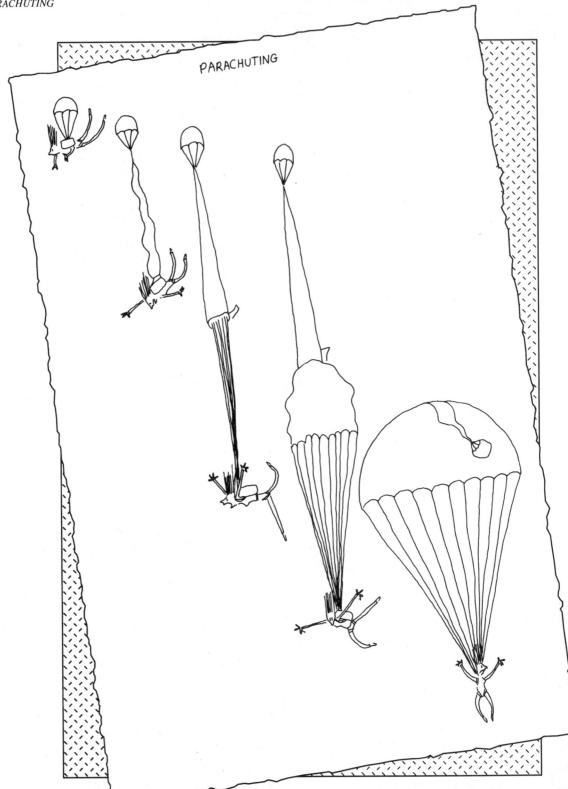

PARACHUTING

will help to assuage these symtoms and permit you to at least tolerate the trip. Others need nothing less than three Valiums and a couple vodkas to muddle through it.

Flying lessons: Assuming you want to help yourself to rise above your fear, you can try hypnosis, or better yet, enroll in a seminar specifically designed for working folks through their fear. Be sure the seminar contract stipulates a complete refund if, by the end of the last class, you still can't set foot inside a plane. (LK)

Sometimes *talking to a pilot,* studying aerodynamics or hanging around airports can allow one to feel a bit more comfortable about flying. (CL)

Sit as far from the window as possible. During takeoffs and landings, focus on something emotionally compelling — a photo of a loved one, maybe — or on something distracting, like a romance novel or magazine article. Wait as long as necessary for the sensation of motion to go away. For the duration of the flight, keep your attention on things close at hand — reading is ideal. Don't look around the cabin; you'll be more comfortable if you stare at the seatback in front of you instead of at your fellow passengers. Under no circumstances should you look out the windows. (VS)

BUT WHEN YOU JUST *HAVE* TO LEAVE . . .

Note: It's probably best to look this information over *before* you actually need it, since it's hard turning pages when you're free-falling at the rate of 128 feet per second.

Strap on the parachute as soon as the engines stop running, or when the pilot tells you to prepare for an emergency jump.

Remember, there are very specific rules to follow, the essences of which are *time and panic.* You're pretty well committed the moment you step out into thin air, and you don't have a lot of time to conceptualize and solve interesting problems, so you can't panic, and you must use the time wisely.

• *When you exit the plane,* obviously, hurl yourself away from the aircraft and assume the spread-eagled position. Then count the seconds — one thousand, two thousand, three thousand. After three seconds, pull the main ripcord handle.

• *If the main chute fails* or does not fill completely with air, use the reserve parachute immediately! Hold the reserve handle with your right hand, and wrap your left hand around the front of the reserve container. Put your feet together, then pull the handle and throw it away. Then grab the reserve parachute out of the container and throw it hard, *down and away from you.*

• *On landing,* keep your arms up, hold onto the straps and keep your elbows tucked in and forward. Bend your head forward, as close to your chest as possible. Round your back and bend your knees slightly, keeping your knees and feet tightly pressed together, with the bottom of your feet parallel to the ground.

• *As you hit the ground,* come down with both feet then lean with knees slightly to the left or right, allowing your body to follow through into a natural roll. Unhitch yourself from the chute.

• *If you come down in trees,* make your body straight, close your eyes and fold your arms across each other and over your head so that the inside of your elbows are covering your face.

People do this sort of thing for fun. If you want to get into parachuting, contact a club or commercial parachuting school. (HJS)

CHAPTER **15**

Miss, Mrs. or Ms. Cellaneous

Call it what you want. We call it a mess of stuff that
didn't quite fit in anyplace else.

C O N T E N T S

Chapter Fifteen: *MISS, MRS. OR MS. CELLANEOUS*

**DREAMS: Lifesaving — Dream Drop — Step Right
This Way — Waking Dream — Nightmares —
HOUSE SECURITY:** Locks **— Home Security Package
— Fire — Lightning Protection — Twist Again —**
Lightning Awareness **— POKER: Know Your Hands
— Know the Rules — Know the Lingo —** Poker **—
Bluffing — Wager Warning — DROPPING FOOD
FROM THE AIR — PETS: Pet Diets —** Cat Anatomy
**— How to Stuff and Mount a Cat or Small Dog —
About Tropical Fish**

DREAMS

We'll spend five to six years of our lives dreaming, when our sleeping eyes dash back and forth beneath their lids. If you interrupt a remming person's REMs (rapid eye movements) for a night, you'll have *two* miserable people the next morning.

Dreams can restore us. They can help us cope and clue us into the great universe. And they're chock full of science. For example, here's some news for you pregnant moms: If you've been dreaming lately of giving birth to a monster, you'll probably have a shorter labor. And no monster.

A dreamy anecdote: I have found all aspects of my life enhanced by writing down my dreams when I remember them and sharing them with the people I care most about. I've even joined a dream group that meets every week, and I've grown to care very much about everyone in the group. We use these suggestions for how to work:

• Remember that all dreams — even the nasty, scary ones — come in order to help us be more whole and healthy.

• Only the person who has the dream can say with any certainty what it may mean.

• There is no such thing as a dream with only one meaning.

• Whenever we speculate about someone else's dream, we always start off by saying, "Well, if it were *my* dream ..."

We have agreed not to gossip about what happens in the dream group, but we've agreed that we can tell about what we learn about our dreams. This work and play with my dreams has helped me to be much happier and more conscious and creative in all areas of my life. (JS)

LIFESAVING

If I couldn't remember my dreams, I would jump off a cliff, because dreams are my only entrée into a larger place. In the daytime I am stupid and clumsy. In the night time I am in the universe. It saves my life. (AD)

DREAM DROP

*Twelve years ag*o I had a best friend who all of a sudden and without explanation dropped me like a hot rock. Every week for the next ten years I had almost the same dream — that I went to her and begged to know what had happened between us. In the dream I would always tell her that a recurring dream had been eating at me, and to please explain her actions to me, and she would finally tell me why she had left, and we would talk.

Every time I would end the dream by saying, "Thank God, this is finally not a dream. Thank God, it is finally straightened out." I would wake with a feeling of enormous relief before realizing that it was yet another dream. The feeling of frustration would hang on me all day.

Two years ago I was passing through her town, and I called her. I said, "I know you have refused to see me for ten years, but here I am again. Can I come over?" and she said *yes*.

After we had chatted a while about this and that, I said, "This is going to sound a little odd, but I have to tell you about a recurring dream." And then I did in real life what I had been doing in my dreams every week for ten years.

And she did what she had done in my dreams every week for ten years. She explained.

And when it was over, I said, "Thank God, this is *finally* not a dream. Thank God, it is straightened out." It was such a huge moment. I was frightened that I might wake up.

I haven't ever dreamed the dream since, so it's over — the friendship and the dream. *(Anon.)*

STEP RIGHT THIS WAY

When I was fifty, I began to volunteer my time at a halfway house where men and women were in transition from a state mental institution. I taught art as therapy.

I became more and more involved in the lives of the patients, and it began to take up more and more of my time. The staff at the house asked if I could add additional hours. Then I had a dream.

I dreamed I walked up a flight of stairs with our old family dog. When we reached the top there was only a black void. The dog stumbled on the top step. I grabbed her just in time.

When I woke up I called the halfway house. I told them I could no longer work there.

There are many ways to see a dream, and that is how I saw mine. I believe our dreams will guide us, if we will try to listen. (JAO'N)

WAKING DREAM

I think paying attention to dreams is terribly important to mental health, but whenever I try to keep a dream journal I spend the whole night waking and writing and waking and writing. I dream a million dreams, and I can't get a bit of sleep when I try to record them. So I guess I'll just have to forget about my mental health. (AG)

I really count on dreams. Sometimes, when life seems bad or empty, I decide that this is the night I will have a remarkable dream, one with insight and heart, a dream that will fill my life with hope, give me answers. I put a pad and pen by the bed. Then I dream the stupidest dreams of my life. But I keep trying. (SY)

First Methodist Sleep: I wish to comment on that private place within every woman where she may go for comfort, peace, strength, renewal and joy. I refer to that inner world of dream and image making, both waking and sleeping, where hopes and wishes come true, where angels guide and guard you, where visions of beauty surround you, where love enfolds you, and where you may talk with the Divine, expanding your horizons and enriching all facets of your life. (AW) **See also** *In Brief* **under** *LINGERIE* **in** *CHAPTER EIGHT: MODERN MERCHANDISE.*

Hi, I'm God: Do you think God's going to come up on the street and say, "Howdy do?" I don't think so, either, so that's why I try to remember dreams. It makes more sense He might decide to greet me in a dream rather than on the corner of Hawthorne and 20th. (DL)

NIGHTMARES

This is when it turns ugly. Buildings are crumbling, bricks are falling. All the dogs are turning rabid and huge. People are murdering. Cars are crashing. The sky is dark. All the laws are gone. There are tidal waves. I am running through the falling bricks and bursting fires, and crazy dogs and killers are everywhere.

I am ten. My father walks down the stairs in the middle of the dark night. I stand at the top step. I hear him scream an insane dying scream, and then there is silence. There is nothing outside the room but black. The neighborhood is gone. My family is gone. The universe is gone. There is nothing but the box of my room, and in the closet there is a man and he is going to come with a knife and cut off my legs. The knife is cutting me. I think, "This is only a dream," but I feel the pain.

My father calls me on the phone. He cries out, "Oh my God, help me, I'm dying." I turn to my mother in a frenzy. I tell her Dad is dying. If I hang up to call an ambulance, he'll die all alone. If I don't hang up, he'll die because I didn't call for help. My mother falls to the floor. I scream, "Daddy!" and there is no answer. There is a broken down house as tall as the sky. There are thousands of rooms. The ceilings are tall. In every room there is a terror reaching for me. I walk down the wide halls. My death is everywhere. It is yawning for me. Every time my foot takes a step there is a thud and there is nothing in the world but terror. The house is going to murder me. *(Anon.)*

HOUSE SECURITY

Keeping out the creeps can be a killer.

When leaving your home unoccupied for a weekend or a long vacation, protect your home and belongings by doing all those commonsense things you always intend to do, but never do. Let's refresh your memory.

• First, and you know this, discontinue paper deliveries or have a neighbor pick them up daily.

• Notify the post office to hold your mail until you return.

• Have the grass mowed weekly or the snow shoveled from your walk and steps.

• Set your thermostats according to the weather, and leave blinds and drapes open.

• Install a timer that will turn on and off lights in different rooms at different times. Simple. (SL) **See also** *HOME CHECKLIST* **in** *CHAPTER FOURTEEN: MODERN RUN-AROUNDS*.

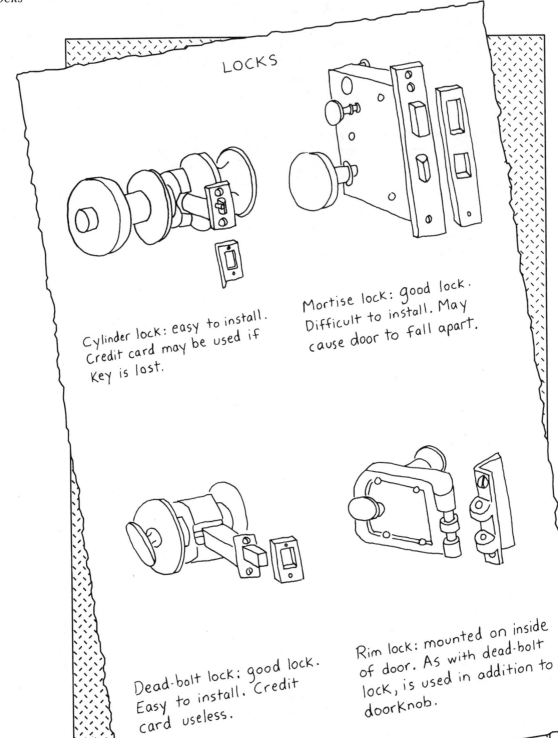

LOCKS

Cylinder lock: easy to install. Credit card may be used if Key is lost.

Mortise lock: good lock. Difficult to install. May cause door to fall apart.

Dead-bolt lock: good lock. Easy to install. Credit card useless.

Rim lock: mounted on inside of door. As with dead-bolt lock, is used in addition to doorKnob.

Install a dead bolt lock to all your doors. This is complicated and needs tools that you probably don't have lying around the house. Buy the locks at a hardware store and pay a locksmith to install them. On sliding windows and doors, place a wooden or metal dowel between the wall and sliding side of the door to make entry impossible. On double-hung windows, pound a nail through the wood where the bottom and top sashes meet. There are also special locks you can purchase for double-sash windows, so you can open the windows whenever you want. (OBL)

Get an electric engraver and mark valuables like cameras, bicycles, golf clubs, musical instruments, power tools, stereos and televisions. Use any sequence of numbers or letters, but you must make a list of what you numbered or lettered and where you did it, and include on the list the manufacturer's number. Don't mark the item on a removable part. Store your checklist in a safe place. (RHW)

HOME SECURITY PACKAGE

Here's what it takes to keep misfortune from taking what you've got:

• A couple of *smoke detectors.* Read package carefully as to where to attach the device.

• A *gas detector* to monitor dangerous concentrations of gas in your furnace and kitchen.

• A *power failure detector* to let you know immediately if power is lost to freezer, refrigerator or furnace.

• A *motion detector,* along with all the window stickers. If you can spend the extra money, wire it directly to the police or a private security firm. Otherwise, rely on the siren alarm. (DDS)

Household security alarms range in price from $75 to $2000. Basically, there are *four kinds* of systems to choose from, depending on your need.

• *The Switch sensor* is installed at all entry points accessible from the ground. If a door or window is opened, the alarm is triggered.

• *Pressure mats* are designed to protect specific areas of the home. They can be placed under carpets. When pressure is exerted on the mat, the alarm sounds.

• *Ultrasonic motion detectors* fill a room with sound waves and any movement in the room will disturb the wave pattern, triggering the alarm. You must buy an expensive model or your dog will hate you and run away. Demand an in-home demonstration to see if you can stand the sound.

• *Infrared photoelectric sensor:* With this system, an infrared light is projected between two points. Anything interrupting the beam will sound the alarm.

Now you must decide if you want *a local or a remote system.*

The local system detects an intruder and the alarm is sounded just in your home. This probably will scare away the intruder and give you time to call the cops.

The remote system transmits the alarm to a location away from your home. You can transmit to a neighbor's house, the police department or a private security company. The local and remote systems can be combined. (RLL)

FIRE

• Equip your home with fire extinguishers, several smoke alarms and some kind of escape ladder.

• Make sure everyone in the family knows how to get out of the house in case of fire.

• Remember always to dispose of cigarettes and matches carefully.

• Never empty ashtrays at night. Place ashtrays in the sink at night and empty them the next morning.

• Keep matches and lighters away from heat sources and children.

• Keep all your appliance and lamp cords in good condition. Replace a cord if it becomes frayed or if the interior wires are visible. **See under** *ELECTRICITY* **in** *CHAPTER NINE: HOME EC*.

• Purchase only UL-listed products.

• Use nonflammable cleaning fluids, and keep closets, basements and attics free of stacks of papers and piles of rags. (JH, GGi)

LIGHTNING PROTECTION

Outside: Take cover in a building or some sort of ditch. Stay away from trees, open grassy places, open boats, telephone poles or any overhead wires. Cars offer good protection, but don't park under a tree or power lines.

Inside: Avoid metal objects, sinks, stoves and radiators. Stay away from fireplaces, open doors and windows. Don't use telephones or appliances. If the storm gets very severe, camp out in a closet or your basement till it blows over. (FC) **See illustration.**

TWIST AGAIN

In preparation for tornadoes or major storms, here's a checklist of what you should have ready:

❏ A battery-powered radio with plenty of batteries
❏ Flashlights
❏ Clothing and bedding
❏ Nonperishable foods and juices
❏ Eating utensils and a can and bottle opener
❏ A first-aid kit
❏ Candles
❏ Matches
❏ Plastic bags
❏ Toilet paper and paper towels
❏ Lots of reading material, puzzles or other diversions
❏ *It's very important* to have large, covered containers for human waste.
❏ Store many containers for *fresh water*
❏ Remember to shut off all utilities at the main switch (FC)

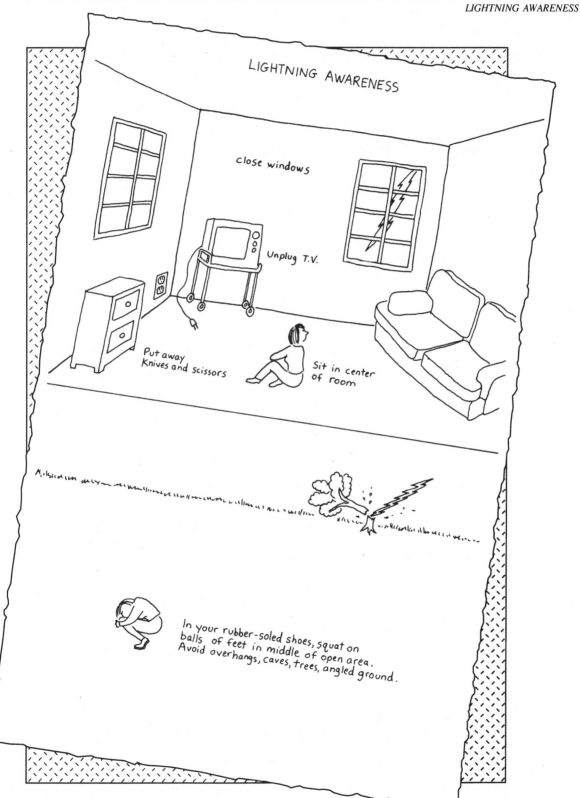

POKER

Poker is traditionally a man's game, which is probably why so many women are good at it. Men don't expect women to know how to fold, raise and call. And they *never* expect a woman to bluff.

KNOW YOUR HAND

Look at the illustration here. It shows the order of poker hands, from a simple high-card hand to a royal flush. If you're going to play poker with the boys, memorize the order of the hands.

Never ask whether one hand will beat another; you will be revealing information about your hand (**see below**). (DB)

KNOW THE RULES

Poker comes in two sizes, one with five cards and one with seven cards. Beyond that, there are two basic versions of the game — draw and stud poker. There are no wild cards in poker.

Draw poker: Draw is a five-card game in which each player receives five cards face down. There is a betting round, then a draw round, in which up to three (or four, depending on house rules) cards may be used to replace cards in your hand. Another betting round follows.

Stud poker: Stud requires some cards to be dealt faceup and others facedown.

• In *five-card stud,* the first card is dealt down and all others are dealt faceup. There is a betting round after the first two cards, and after each subsequent card is dealt. High card showing bets first.

• In *seven-card stud,* the classic stud game, the first two cards and the last card are dealt down. Betting rounds follow the dealing of the first three cards and after each subsequent card. High card showing bets first. The best five cards constitute the hand. (KL)

KNOW THE LINGO

Here's a poker glossary:

• *Jacks or better:* In draw poker, you must have a pair of jacks or a better hand to open the betting. You cannot bluff your opening, since if you open the betting, you must reveal your openers at the end of the hand. **See illustration.**

• *Bet:* The amount wagered by the first player in any betting round.

• *Call:* A wager equal to the amount bet by the last player in a betting round. If a call is made during the final betting round, it's called a *see* bet.

• *Raise:* A wager higher than the last amount bet during a betting round.

POKER

Royal Flush - Highest

Straight Flush

Four of a Kind

Full House

Flush

Straight

Three of a Kind

Two Pairs

One Pair

High Card · Lowest

• *Fold:* When a player no longer wishes to play a hand, she *folds* her hand and places it facedown in front of her. (KL)

BLUFFING

Never act excited or disappointed when you look at the cards you were dealt. In order to play poker properly, you must remain inscrutable. Remember: *Any* information you reveal will be used against you.

The principal of bluffing is simple: You need to lie so convincingly that a man will back down from betting his hand. Your lie must be based on two things: The probability of having the hand you pretend to have, and the appearance of credibility. If you bluff every hand, you'll lose every hand except, perhaps, the first one. (DB, KL)

WAGER WARNING

Never, ever, bet more than you can actually afford to lose. Poker players don't look kindly on promises of payment and, as with most other things, it's a point of honor to pay up on the spot. (KL)

DROPPING FOOD FROM THE AIR

Every now and then you open the mail and something so odd, so incredibly *miscellaneous* falls out that it makes your eyes roll.

Hence, the following instructions for parachute-dropping bundles of food from small, slow-flying aircraft. If Domino's Pizza gets hold of this info, you'll have pepperoni-and-cheese pies coming down your fireplace.

• *What you need:* A small aircraft with a high wing, say a Piper Super Cub or a Cessna 172, a parachute with static line (see below) attached, a bundle of food, some hungry people in a remote area and a willing passenger. The passenger will be well-advised to wear a seat belt.

• *Not too low:* The aircraft must be more than 500 feet above the ground for the parachute to function.

• *Allow for wind.* Strong surface winds combined with the aircraft's forward motion can contrive to make your food delivery somewhat wide of the mark.

• *Bundle the static line* concertina-style, so it wraps back and forth. Don't coil the line, as it can easily foul during the drop. Use a large rubber band or a piece of elastic to keep the static line in order.

• *Tie one end of the static line* to a handy part of the airplane. The passenger seat frame will do nicely.

• *The passenger* should hold the bundle carefully in her lap until the target site is reached.

• *Hold the bundle* at arm's length out of the airplane.

• At a signal, the passenger should *drop the load* and at the same time *pull in the static line.*

If the static line fouls, cut it immediately and keep it clear of the aircraft. (TCo) *And if you have to throw yourself from the air,* **see under** *FEAR OF FLYING* **in** *CHAPTER FOURTEEN: MODERN RUNAROUNDS.*

PETS

People feel perfectly free to make the rudest remarks concerning another's pet.

My brother says my cat looks like an ottoman. "Tell me, just how do you go about fattening a cat like that?" he asked.

Someone else said, "How does your cat get around corners without tipping over? She's a perfect oval."

I've heard them all. Do I look at my friend's children and say, "Wow, is that child a tub of lard or what?" "What a little beach ball. Does he float?" Get the picture? So let's have a little consideration for those of us who adore our pets.

PET DIETS

Cry kitties: A veterinarian once told me to slim my cat on cottage cheese and yogurt and maybe some lettuce, too. My cat cried all day and I couldn't take it and so that diet didn't work at all. Maybe some cats like lettuce, though. (EC)

Purina Lite: There is always a recommended amount on the side of the food bag. Don't believe it, though. After all, the food people are in the business to sell more food. Give your animal less and you'll save money and also have a very alert pet. (CD)

Walkin' the dog: Exercise! Take your dog on lots of walks and you'll both feel better. If you have a house cat, get down on your hands and knees and chase it down the halls for fifteen minutes a day. If you have bad knees, do a sort of Frankenstein walk while emitting low growls. Puts the cat into a real aerobic frenzy and is fun at parties. (EF)

Kennel rations: Face it, there are plenty of people who would turn down an all-expense-paid, two-week holiday in Tahiti because they couldn't bear the thought of putting their pet into a doggy or pussy kennel. Trauma. You know, the psychological damage of a kennel on Fido or Snowball is simply more than the owner can bear.

There's money to be made here: Pet sitting — perfect part-time work for the young or old Modern Woman. There is definitely a growing demand for responsible pet sitting, which,

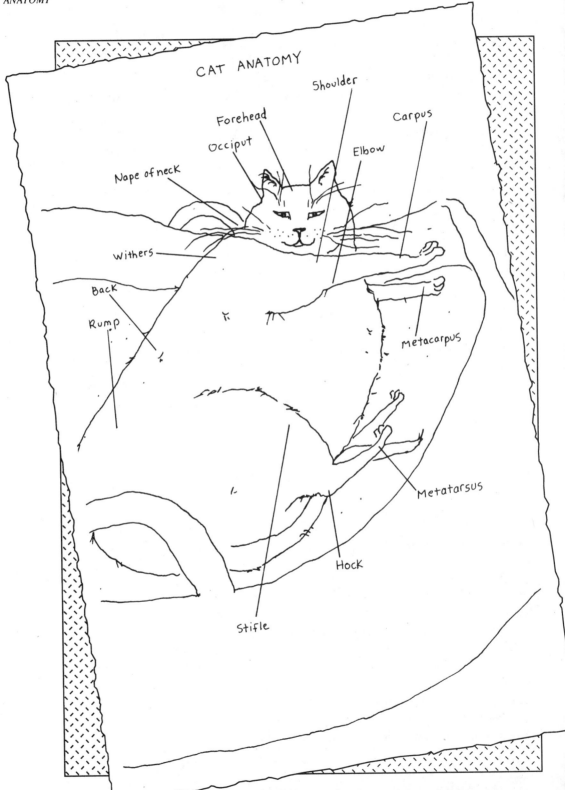

CAT ANATOMY

if properly advertised in the local paper, bulletin boards or vet clinics, can provide a lucrative and gratifying sideline. I have watched several ladies handle this type of work either by "renting themselves out" as pet or house sitters or just by properly checking on or feeding temporarily left-behind dogs, cats, chickens, horses, birds — you name it. (GM)

Monkeys are a horse of another color. Monkeys really *are* extra-sensitive little beings, and really can't be left with just anyone. (GM) Especially Russian space scientists.

HOW TO STUFF AND MOUNT A CAT OR SMALL DOG

If you just can't *stand* the thought of parting with little Fluffy, you can always stuff and mount her and put her up on top of the TV.

Get ready. If you want a few days to mourn the passing of old Fluff, you can always toss her in the freezer until you're ready to get to work. When you're feeling better, let Fluffy thaw overnight.

Cutting the pelt: Spread-eagle the animal on its back so the paws are out to the side. With a surgical knife, cut in a straight line from the chin to the tip of the tail. Next, cut up the center of the legs. Start at the paws and work toward the center cut; if you start at the center, you'll end up with a sloppy sort of spiral cut. Pull the pelt off, cutting away the subcutaneous membrane as you go. Do the head last.

The head: When you get to the ears, cut the cartilage loose from the skull, making sure the cartilage in the ear is still in place. Cut around *inside* the lip and near the gum and teeth; do the nose last, carefully removing the cartilage.

Make a pattern: Spread out the skinned carcass on a piece of heavy cardboard and carefully trace around the legs and body.

Tanning: With dogs, tanning the pelt is essential. Otherwise, you get a bad odor surrounding the stuffed pet. With cats, it's optional. Tanning kits are available from any leather shop or craft supply shop.

Make a dummy: Use the measurements you made with the carcass on the cardboard to make a properly fitted dummy. Using a stiff wire — about coat hanger gauge — make a spine with a doubled-over length of wire exactly as long as the body. Attach wire legs, according to the length and position indicated on your tracing. Don't forget the tail.

Use Bondo brand resin — the stuff they use on car bodies — to reinforce any part of the pelt that will come in contact with the wire ends. Otherwise, the wire will puncture the skin. Again, don't forget the tail.

Use large cotton wads — not little cotton balls — and start wrapping the wire with lengths of the cotton fiber. Attach the cotton to the wire with string. Apply one layer after another until you achieve the proper dimensions. Carfeully consult your pattern tracing to ensure the proper proportion. Work from the tail to the head.

Buy cat's eyes at a craft store or a medical supply company.

To make a skull dummy, use clay or plaster. You more or less have to sculpt the skull bone. Use Bondo inside the skull and attach it to the wire. Use clay to hold the eyes in place in the scupted skull.

Wrap the hide around the cotton carcass and sew up all the stitches with thick thread. You can use dental floss on a white-skinned animal. Be careful of bulges — on a short-haired animal, they'll really show. If the cotton is lumpy, smooth it out before you sew up the hide.

Finally, bend the wire form to achieve the posture you desire.

It's easier to work with a slightly flattened animal, so — unless your sense of propriety would be offended — it might be best to drive the Chevy over Fluff a few times before getting underway with this project.

A taxidermist would charge as much as $250 for something like this, so you'll have saved enough to go out and get yourself that nice purebred you saw down at Pet Central. (KRe)

ABOUT FISH

Modern Man, our companion volume, has *nothing* about tropical fish. Apparently, Modern Women felt a responsibility to take up the slack, even though we personally have no feelings in this matter.

If you really feel that fish are important , then for heaven's sake don't be casual about it. You don't just throw any old things into a tank and assume they'll be friends just because they all live in water. If you have recently introduced a congenial little crab into your aquarium and then one morning discover that the angel fish (the big, lovely one) is *not there any more,* well, use your noggin. Did it just evaporate? Don't wait until the catfish, the tetras, and half the neons have evaporated. Get that crab out of there! I don't mean kill it outright. Do like we did. Put it into an attractive bowl with a rock in the middle and in a week it will die of boredom.

Tank placement: Put your aquarium anywhere except near a radiator or in direct sunlight. Light causes algae to grow. Don't use soap to rinse the aquarium. Use warm water.

Rinse the gravel well by putting it into a bucket and running plain water through until it runs clear. You need about two pounds of gravel per gallon of water.

Downhill: Place gravel into tank so that it slopes downward from back to front.

Use dechlorinating drops or allow water to stand for twenty-four hours. Pour dechlorinated water into a saucer in the center of the tank until the aquarium is two-thirds full.

Tiny bubbles: Set up the air system. Your aquarium will have instructions.

Make it pretty. Add plants and rocks and little plastic reindeer if you want.

Plastic plants are fine. Your fish will feel protected and happy and they will not complain that the plants are artificial. They honestly don't care. Check with your pet store about what you do put in the tank, though. Some items can cause unhealthy conditions.

Install the heater according to package instructions. Attach a background with tape to the back wall of the tank. This will cover wires and air lines and make it look sea-ish. Or you can have an outer space scene or any other thing at all. Makes the fish secure.

Light: Place the cover with the reflector light over the tank. There are specific bulbs to use. Ask your fish person. The proper pH is 6.8 to 7.2. The proper temperature is 70° to 80° F. (GG, NLW)

The Modern Mom

You can skip this chapter if you want. You can go straight back to the chapter on work, ease into the chapter on leisure — especially the part about boredom — then right on to terminal illnesses in the medicine cabinet of this book.

Or you can follow orders from headquarters: Quick-step right this way and onto the next page, where reality starts to settle in.

This is the chapter of last resort, the place you go when all else fails. Because when all else fails, you should always ask Mom.

C O N T E N T S

Chapter Sixteen: *THE MODERN MOM*

**FIRST STEPS: The Test Child — The Instinct —
Pregnancy — Prenatal Care — The Most Common
Indications for Prenatal Counseling —Five Indications
of Possible Birth Defects — Prenatal Testing — Tubal
Pregnancy — Delivery Techniques — Do-It-Yourself
and Save — Swap for Sleep — After the Trauma —
Night Cry — Breast-Feeding — The New Kid —
ADOPTION — BABY HEALTH: Signs of Serious
Illness in a Child — Immunizations — Ten Ways to
Prevent Child Poisoning — FACTS OF LIFE: Child
Abuse — Sex Abuse — Nuke Fears — Sex Education
— CHILD CARE: Baby-sitters — Day Care — Family
Day Care — The Other Side — The Government and
Day Care — Warning Signs of Poor Child Care — Day
Care With Dad — TOYS 4 TOTS: The First and
Foremost Rule —** Places Not to Leave a Baby **— Present
Sense — DISCIPLINE: For Their Own Good, Right?
— Food Torture — Kid Kash — Minor Manners —
MODERN MOVES: Junior Partner — New Circles —
MOTHER LODE: Sally in the Alley —Trust Funds —
Documents — Tow Heads — Take a Meeting — Little
Mistakes — The Age of Discovery — Women and
Children First — Brighter Lights — A Little Advice**

FIRST STEPS

Let's say, just for the sake of argument, that you're thinking seriously, *very seriously,* of getting pregnant. Let's just say, okay? Try this first:

THE TEST CHILD

When you are considering having a child, ask a friend with kids if you can baby-sit for a week, *day and night.* She'll love you for it. You'll learn a lot from it. (SL)

This is, after all, the ultimate lifelong hobby, the full-time job, the launch site for two score years of worry and emotional terror. Get *into* it, mama.

THE INSTINCT

If you're waiting for maternal instinct to come knocking on your door, forget it. For many, many women — most of whom will *swear* they have no maternal instinct — it comes in a hurry the moment the baby arrives. It will amuse your friends and surprise you and will be the strongest emotional bond you've ever felt. (KK) **See under** *BIRTH CONTROL* **in** *CHAPTER THIRTEEN: THE MEDICINE CABINET.*

PREGNANCY

For a first pregnancy, an exam every two or three weeks after the first missed period is advisable.

Subsequent pregnancies: Get the first exam after two missed periods.

Three things — among many others, of course — to consider: What method of childbirth will I use? Where will I have my baby? What physician will follow my condition?

Prepared childbirth is the traditional method of delivery. Painkillers are administered during labor, and you may be put to sleep or have a spinal or local injection of anesthetic. The baby will be taken to a nursery and brought to you at prescribed times.

Natural childbirth: Prenatal education and breathing exercises are prescribed to reduce labor pains. Drugs are not used or are used sparingly. Often the father remains in the delivery room. Your pubic hair is not shaved and the baby stays with you at all times.

Home delivery: Natural childbirth with the aid of a midwife. Arrangements should be made beforehand for transportation to a hospital should it become necessary.

PRENATAL CARE

On your first visit to your doctor she will work up a history, conduct a physical exam, take a Pap smear and blood count, do a blood type, make an Rh factor determination, conduct a urinalysis and tests for syphilis, German measles antibodies, and, these days, AIDS, although sometimes only by request. **See** *What You Should Expect From Your GYN* **in** *CHAPTER THIRTEEN: THE MEDICINE CABINET.*

You should expect to see your doctor once a month until the seventh month, then every two weeks until weekly visits during the ninth month.

Eat a well-balanced diet from the four food groups: meats, fruits and vegetables, breads and cereals, and milk and milk products. **See** *NUTRITION* **in** *CHAPTER THIRTEEN: THE MEDICINE CABINET* **and** *Duck Fat* **in** *CHAPTER NINE: HOME EC.*

Do not take any drug at any time during pregnancy without consulting a doctor — *especially* not marijuana, alcohol, or hallucinogens. Not even aspirin.

Stop smoking. A pack-a-day smoker will have a baby weighing on the average twelve ounces less than a baby born to a nonsmoker. **See** *Bad Habits* **in** *CHAPTER FOUR: MODERN P's & Q's.*

A program of exercise is important. Swimming is good, and walking is a marvelous exercise.

Cunnilingus is not safe during the last three months of pregnancy. You could die from it. You could also die from douching.

To combat swelling in the hands and feet, elevate your feet when resting. Walk several blocks twice a day and reduce your intake of table salt.

To combat morning sickness, eat a light breakfast of juice and toast. Avoid grease. Eat four small meals a day rather than three large ones. The doctor can prescribe something should vomiting become a problem.

To combat constipation, eat high-fiber foods and drink lots of liquids. Prune juice, apple juice, peaches, pears, bananas, figs, and apricots are all good.

Don't have X-rays. Tell the dentist if you are pregnant not to give you X-rays. (Consider telling the dentist not to give you X-rays even if you aren't pregnant.)

VD can be treated during pregnancy. The penicillin will cure the baby, too. Herpes cannot be cured this way, and an active herpes infection is an indication for cesarean section. **See also under** *STD's* **in** *CHAPTER THIRTEEN: THE MEDICINE CABINET. (Anon.)*

THE MOST COMMON INDICATIONS FOR PRENATAL COUNSELING

There are a variety of reasons why prospective parents should explore prenatal or genetic counseling during pregnancy.

• If the *mother is over thirty-three* years of age

• If the parents have *a history of chromosomal abnormality* or genetic disorders in the immediate or extended family — which extends, in most cases, as far as first cousins

• For couples who are *known carriers of genetic disorders* such as cystic fibrosis, sickle-cell anemia or Tay-Sachs disease

• If *the mother has used drugs* during the pregnancy, especially without consultation with her obstetrician — and especially any street or illegal drugs

• For *women who have been exposed to radiation,* a single X-ray will not expose you to a high enough level of radiation to endanger the fetus

• For *couples with multiple miscarriages*

• For those who simply have a *parental concern* (JH)

FIVE INDICATIONS OF POSSIBLE BIRTH DEFECTS
• Family history of inherited disease
• Previous pregnancy resulting in a child with a defect
• Pregnancy complicated during the first few months by German measles or a generalized viral infection
• Exposure to harmful drugs, chemicals or high radiation during pregnancy
• A mother who is over forty years of age *(Anon.)*

PRENATAL TESTING
Amniocentesis involves the insertion of a needle into the womb to remove a small amount of the liquid surrounding the fetus. It is used to discover chromosomal or biochemical abnormalities and done between the fourteenth and sixteenth week. The sex of the fetus can be determined at this time.

Ultrasound scanning is done in conjunction with amniocentesis so that an appropriate place for withdrawing fluids can be found. Hydrocephalus, microcephaly, anencephaly may be detected.

Fetoscopy: The doctor can visualize individual parts of the fetus through a tiny telescope.

The incidence of miscarriage following amniocentesis is one out of every 300 or 400 studies. (FO)

There is a 15 to 20 percent risk of *spontaneous miscarriage* in the first trimester. Well over half of all spontaneous miscarriages involve chromosomal abnormalities, placental insufficiencies, hormonal imbalances or other factors and are the result of the body's own selection process. *(Anon.)*

TUBAL PREGNANCY
In a tubal pregnancy, the fertilized egg never reaches the uterus, but instead begins to grow in the tube. The phenomenon is often caused by partial scarring of the tubes through infection or by exposure to gonorrhea.

Between the sixth and twelfth week of pregnancy, the placenta ruptures through the tube — a life-threatening emergency. The woman must be hospitalized immediately. (LN)

DELIVERY TECHNIQUES
Generally, there are *two types of delivery:*
A vaginal delivery, in which there are no exceptional problems
A cesarean section, in which the baby is removed surgically
Indications for a cesarean section:
• The fetus is in distress.
• The fetus is in a breach position.
• The mother's pelvis is too small to allow for passage of the baby's head.

424

FIRST STEPS

There are three major delivery methods used in most hospitals — although not every hospital uses all three methods. Each hospital has one or two favorite methods and as a rule will not advise parents of the other methods. For details, call the parent education group at any large hospital.

• *The LaMaze method* involves displacing anxiety and stressing breathing techniques.

• *The Bradley method* also stresses breathing techniques and encourages the father's participation as a "coach."

• *The Dick-Read method* emphasizes various approaches to relaxation.

Additionally, there is the *LeBoyer method,* which can be used in conjunction with any of the above delivery methods. The LeBoyer method is built around providing the fetus with a nontraumatic delivery. The delivery room is dimly lit and the baby is provided with a warm bath. Warmth and softness are everywhere in a LeBoyer delivery room.

Select a delivery method far enough in advance to ensure you receive proper training. (CBE, GF)

DO-IT-YOURSELF AND SAVE

It is possible to deliver your own baby, but not very modern and certainly not very advisable. Nevertheless, if you're determined, then here we go into the breach:

Try to remain calm, because fear of pain produces pain.

• *Don't lie down.* Lean your back against a wall and squat on a pillow or folded clothes with your knees pulled up.

• When the first urges to push arrive, *hold your breath and don't push.* When you can no longer stand it, push, but not too severely.

• *Take deep breaths during contractions.*

• *Stay in the squatting position* as baby begins to emerge. Do not be upset by burning feelings as the body begins to bulge outward because of the baby's head pushing against it.

• At this point, *do not bear down* any longer. Breathe little breaths and keep your abdominal muscles as relaxed as possible.

• *Now lean back* halfway between sitting and lying. Keep your knees up and out. The baby will arrive face down. Lean over to catch her in your hand.

• Babies twist before they shout. Yours will rotate to the side in order for the shoulders to pop out. *Don't pull the child straight out* or you may tear yourself, but help it upward toward you.

• *Bring the baby slowly toward you* without pulling the cord.

• *Wipe the baby's mouth and nose and eyes immediately* with a clean cloth or lay the baby over your thighs, face down, and press down gently on her back to expel any fluids that may be in her throat, mouth or nasal passages. (This is a variation on the old turn 'em upside down and whack 'em on the butt approach for dislodging mucus.)

• *Let the baby drink.*

• Shortly after the delivery, *the placenta will be expelled.* If it doesn't come out on its own, press your abdomen and cough.

• *Wrap the afterbirth with the baby* and the uncut cord in the cleanest thing available.

There are a lot of people in the world (and now there's one more). Stand up with your new baby and go find one to drive you to a doctor.

If there isn't the immediate possibility of finding someone to help within an hour or so, you must cut the umbilical yourself. Find something strong, like twine or shoelaces, and tie the cord in two places. The tie nearest the baby should be about six inches from her navel. Now you must cut the cord somewhere in the middle of the two ties. Try to sanitize whatever cutting instrument you have the best you can — even if it's only heating it with a lighter. Don't pull the cord from the baby, just wrap the baby up in the cleanest thing available. Hold her close, talk to her, get to know each other. And get to a hospital. (SMcP)

SWAP FOR SLEEP

When awaiting the birth of your child, let it be known to your friends and relatives that you will gladly forego the flowers, sleepers, and receiving blankets for two hours of uninterrupted rest during the day or for meals brought over to your house for a week or so after the birth of your baby.

Also, ***have your husband arrange for a week off work*** . (KL)

AFTER THE TRAUMA

of having an infant and you're feeling pretty comfortable with the whole situation, expose your child to as many experiences and people as possible.

Not that you should take your baby to Coney Island at eleven at night in October or treat it to the experience of busing it to your girlfriend's house 400 miles away. But office situations, dinner parties (**but see under** *Good Form* **in** *CHAPTER FOUR: MODERN P's & Q's*), grocery markets, shows, libraries, baseball games, lots of good friends hanging around — if you're lucky enough to have them — all of this expands your child's experiences, allowing her to broaden herself without even realizing it. Allow her to poke around in dirt and leaves, safe drawers, and cupboards, to roll around in clean laundry, and to bang pots and pans. Doesn't hurt a thing and helps everyone a lot. (KL).

NIGHT CRY

Shhh: If your baby or toddler seems to wake up nights without an apparent reason, try feeding her a bit of complex carbohydrate — say, some bread. It will keep her blood sugar level up through the night and make those little eyes sleepy. (ARL)

Tryptophan, the sleep-inducing natural amino acid found in most dairy products — especially milk and cottage cheese — is a great cure for your baby's sleepless nights — and for yours. *(Anon.)*

BREAST-FEEDING

Like everything in this life, there's an upside and a downside (except for the baby; to her it all looks upside down) to breast-feeding:

Advantages: Breast-feeding is natural, close and warm. Mother's milk is available, sterile, and easier for baby to digest — and far less likely to cause an allergic reaction. Mom's antibodies will pass naturally to her infant. Breast-feeding also results in a lower incidence of diarrhea and ear infection.

Disadvantages: Some women have a poor milk supply. Breast-feeding is difficult for working mothers, and some infants do not nurse well. The cosmetic disadvantages — that breast-feeding causes the breasts to droop and all the rest — don't merit much discussion. Breasts exist for reasons other than to be pleasing to the eye of a man — or other women.

Breast size has nothing to do with milk supply. *(Anon.)*

THE NEW KID

The arrival of a new sibling is as traumatic for one kid as it is for the other. If the age difference is more than five years, it becomes especially stressful.

Don't send the big brother or sister to relatives while you're in the hospital. It is more comforting to remain at home in familiar surroundings. If you are going to the hospital, make sure the child knows how long you will be gone. Phone frequently. Talk to the child at length about the arrival of a new sibling. (BC)

Let the older child help with the new baby. Be sure to give the older child your total attention when you can. (KJ)

Sibling etiquette: If you are visiting a new baby, bring a gift to the big brother or sister in celebration of big brother- or sisterhood. Spend plenty of time talking to the older child — and not just about subjects related to the infant. Compliment the child on her appearance, because you have undoubtedly gone on with the parents about the cuteness of the new baby. (TD) **See under** *Gifts* in *CHAPTER SIX: MODERN MERCHANDISE.*

ADOPTION

is an ancient tradition, long institutionalized, in which every single participant benefits. If you can't have children of your own, by all means give your love to a child who needs a good mom.

If you tell a child about her adoption from as early an age as the first year, it will never be traumatic. Even before she can talk you can tell her how much you love her and how lucky you are to have adopted her. (ARL)

When a child reaches the age of three, she may begin to ask you where babies come from. During this conversation you can tell her more about adoption. Stress that there was nothing wrong with her but that her mother felt that she could not take good enough care of her, and that she loved her so much she gave her to someone who could give good care and would love her. (NNR)

Be matter-of-fact when explaining adoption. If you are anxious, your child will be anxious. Tell your child what she wants to know and refrain from going on and on. Be sure you stress your love and the foreverness of your relationship. *Never in your life tell a child in anger that you're going to send her back* or that you wish you'd never adopted her. (NN)

If you've chosen to give your child up for adoption, look for an *open adoption situation.* You can interview and choose the parents for your child, write letters, make inquiries as to the health and well-being of the child and exchange videotaped messages for your baby to keep. (RK)

BABY HEALTH

Omigod, the baby's got a cold!

Easy, now. It's just a sniffle. With a runny nose. And a little cough. And a *fever.* At least it *feels* like a fever.

Relax, okay? If it's *really* serious, it's here:

SIGNS OF SERIOUS ILLNESS IN A CHILD
- Breathing difficulty
- Loss of consciousness or extreme lethargy
- Convulsions
- A fever of 103° or more
- Chest pain, wheezing, rapid breathing
- Persistent headache or stiff neck
- Severe abdominal pain or persistent abdominal pain
- Persistent vomiting, diarrhea, lack of appetite
- Bloody urine, very dark urine, blood in stool
- Severe pain in testicles

Don't panic. Especially if it's your first child, overreaction is normal. Your job is to *call the doctor.* If your doctor cannot be reached, an emergency room physician can treat your child. (NNR)

IMMUNIZATIONS
If only there were shots for all the things moms worry about. Antiboy shots, nonsmoking boosters, antidate doses — that kind of thing. Where is science when you need it?
The Basic Series:
- Two months: diphtheria, pertussis (whooping cough), tetanus (lockjaw) and oral polio
- Four months: diphtheria, pertussis (whooping cough), tetanus (lockjaw) and oral polio
- Six months: diphtheria, pertussis (whooping cough), tetanus (lockjaw) and oral polio

• Fifteen months: measles, German measles, mumps (triple vaccine)

• Eighteen months: diphtheria, pertussis (whooping cough), tetanus (lockjaw) and oral polio

Boosters

• Four to six years: diphtheria, pertussis (whooping cough), tetanus (lockjaw) and oral polio

• Ten to twelve years: German measles vaccine for a girl whose rubella titer is negative or less than 1:16

• Fourteen to sixteen years: tetanus (lockjaw), adult diphtheria

• Every ten years: tetanus (lockjaw), adult diphtheria

See under *Documents,* **above.**

TEN WAYS TO PREVENT CHILD POISONING

Making your home childproof is essential. With drugs and medicines, special care must be taken. A bottle of pills looks mighty tasty to a tyke.

1. Don't leave medicine within reach of children. Doing this one thing will go miles toward making your home safer for your child.

2. Don't let your child watch you take medicine.

3. Don't compare medicine to candy.

4. Don't store medicine, chemicals or poisons in food containers or near food.

5. Don't leave gasoline, charcoal lighter or paint thinner in a cup or glass.

6. Go through the house and make sure you know where all poisonous substances are.

7. Put Mr. Yuk labels on all unsafe substances.

8. Use safety caps.

9. Keep chemicals, cleaning agents and insecticides on a high shelf and well out of sight.

10. Make your bathroom safe. Kids often meet disaster when left alone in a bathroom. (NNR)

See also under *FOLK CURES AND GENERAL PRACTICAL MEDICAL INFORMATION* **in** *CHAPTER THIRTEEN: THE MEDICINE CABINET.*

HOSPITALS

The horrors of hospitalization for a child include not only the trauma of the injury or illness, but also separation from the parents, fear of the unknown, the intimidating medical procedures, and loss of control.

If a child must be hospitalized for an illness, be sure to prepare the child for it.

• Give an older child about a week to get accustomed to the idea, and a day or two for a little child.

• Tell the child what is going to happen while she is in the hospital and what day she can expect to return home.

• If some of the hospital procedures are going to be painful, be straight about it.

• A small child might benefit from picture books about hospitals. (BA)

If you can stay with the child during hospitalization, by all means do. If you must leave, be *absolutely* clear about when you will return. Remember that even tiny children may hear and understand the things you say. When you are discussing their condition with other adults in front of them, even crib babies will understand and remember your words loud and clear. (LL)

FACTS OF LIFE

For much of this century, this planet hasn't been a fit place for children.

In fact, it hasn't been much of a place for children to fit in. They're in the way when it comes to our careers, and they're a source of exhaustion for us when we're at home. Try as we will, we can't seem to make their fathers into mothers and we curse the government for failing to provide day — and, presumably night — care, although the thought of producing a generation of governmentally-raised kids may cause some of us alarm.

The business at hand for women — and men — is to provide a secure and safe place for the kids to play. The modern world is a wilderness for babies and it's going to take a lot of work for a Modern Woman to civilize the place.

CHILD ABUSE

There are a wide variety of reasons why mothers — and fathers — abuse their children. Proper counseling can help you understand why you feel rage toward your child. *The important thing, however, is to get help for you and your child immediately.* If you (or your spouse) are abusing your child, you must protect the child any way you can — even if it means protecting the child from yourself. Call for help immediately.

Since one of the principal messages of this book is the importance of competent mothering for children, we could go on at great length on the subject. In the end, though, it would all come out the same. If you abuse your child, *you must get help*.

SEX ABUSE

Listen to your child. If he or she tries to describe a sexual assault, don't dismiss it. You must take all such reports seriously. Although a strong reaction is normal, try to remain calm. Be careful not to react hysterically. It will frighten your child, who has already been through a traumatic and frightening experience. (DJ) *Believe what your child says.* Maybe it is not true. Maybe it is. Begin with total belief and proceed from there. (DS)

Give clear instructions. Telling a child to keep away from strangers will not do the trick if Uncle Dan is the one doing the molesting. (KJ)

Touching: Make sure your child knows the difference between good touching and bad touching. Play "what if" games with your children to help teach them good responses to bad situations. (SS) **See also** *Sex Education,* **below.**

Have a secret code to use when you must send someone other than yourself to pick up your child. If the adult cannot give the child the secret word, then the child will know that you did not really send this person. (PT)

Do not worry that you are going to foster paranoia in your children. Discuss the problem of abuse in a matter-of-fact way. Bring it up while you are discussing other safety matters, such as crossing streets and avoiding poisons. If you don't get all bent out of shape, neither will they. They'll simply accept it as yet another in a number of survival skills. (CB)

Start educating your children way before they even get to kindergarten. Why wait until age nine or ten? Molesters start at two weeks. (JA)

Let the children talk about it. Don't ever tell them to try and forget all about it. They never will. (SD)

Tell your children that you are proud of them for reporting an incident to you. Be very clear that you in no way blame them for whatever happened. Keep your feelings of horror and rage to yourself when you are with the child. Release your emotions to another adult. (AF)

In this day and age, safety precautions need to be hammered into our children's little heads. For your peace of mind and, more importantly, for your kids' safety, you must take care to teach them safeguards.

The following suggestions are not meant to produce a bunch of uptight paranoids — although these days a certain amount of paranoia is not a bad thing — but to allow the children to feel in control and a bit streetwise. It's never too early to start. These rules — and any others you come up with yourself — should be laid down firmly, with no exceptions permitted:

• *Never alone:* Since we know that molesters usually pick on a single person, teach your child to walk or ride the bus with a friend whenever possible.

• *Walk with your kid* to the places she goes most often and point out what you consider danger zones.

• *Figure out which route* to and from school seems safest and make your child walk that agreed-upon path. That way, if she's late from school, you can check out that route first.

• *Tell her never to take anything* from a stranger, including a lift.

• *Tell her to avoid strangers* like the plague and never to tell them where she lives or to give out a phone number or address. **See also under** *OBSCENE CALLS* **in** *CHAPTER TWELVE: MODERN WOMEN IN DISTRESS.*

• *Tell her to scream* like crazy and run if a stranger approaches. Rehearse it and make sure she can do it. (LK)

Develop and maintain a friendship with your day-care person. After all, she's with your child more than you are. (DT) **See under** *CHILD CARE,* **below.**

Archive: It's wise to keep current photographs, videos and fingerprints of your child on hand. (DT)

Phone home: Train your child to call home or a close friend when she's away from the home. In case anything should go wrong or out of the ordinary, the child will naturally seek out a telephone. (VS)

NUKE FEARS

Once aware of the possibility of nuclear war, your child may ask you to explain it. Since the issue is inexplicable to a small child (or anyone with sense), the best advice is to talk about it openly, sharing truthfully your feelings and knowledge. Try not to express your deepest fears and anxieties, though; you'll just scare the child even more. (MH)

SEX EDUCATION

Use the correct words. Practice them when you are alone so that you can get them out of your mouth without cringing. (LK)

Little kids are more apt to ask questions about sex than bigger kids. Bigger kids are dying to know, but they are probably too embarrassed to ask. Don't let it get you if you bring up the subject and they greet it with groans and rolling eyes. Don't even let it get to you if they say, "Oh, Mom, I've known that stuff for *years*." Maybe they have. Maybe they haven't. So give it your best shot. (EW)

If you answer all their questions beginning when they are three, by the time they are thirteen you will have it made in the shade. (EC)

CHILD CARE

Of course you want to take care of your own child. It's only natural, after all.

But economics and the realities of daily life often conspire to defeat Mother Nature. It's an ongoing battle, but while you're fighting it, you'll want to make sure the baby's in good hands.

BABY-SITTERS

While still pregnant, begin to seek and interview potential baby-sitters and child care centers. Sign up with a day care center once you've found one you really like — the waiting periods are often six months or longer. (KK)

After you've interviewed and chosen a few baby-sitters, pay them to come to your home a couple times to spend the evening with your family. The person, you, and the child will get to know each other and the way things work in your house. (FSR)

Live-in sitters are great. If you have to go out of town, a lot of in-home sitters will stay with your child overnight. Some sitters keep their job for years and become a real part of the child's life. (LK)

Some sitters are hired to do housework, too, which is wonderful. Most Europeans are familiar with the au pair system, in which a student comes to live with a family and in exchange for a small salary and room and board helps with the children and with housework. The program is catching on in the United States, but very slowly. Check the classified directory of the largest city near you to find an agency that will arrange the appointment. (PY, VEW)

Baby-sitters know the whole story on your house and life. If you have any skeletons in your closet, better watch out. They'll be in the living room before you can blink your eyes. (CAS)

Get a nanny if you want a top-notch person to care for your children. Of course, you have to have the money to pay them. Most sitters are not trained, and you can't really know what goes on every day between the sitter and your child — especially if your child can barely talk. (ST)

A lot of sitters sit while waiting for the next segment of their lives to begin, especially if they are young. Your child may adore the sitter, and then suddenly the sitter goes off to boarding school. It's hard. (NB)

Children can sometimes be left with relatives — a great solution because the child is loved and cared for by a person who is a real part of her life. If you're lucky, you don't have to pay as much to a relative — or maybe you can exchange services as a way of payment. (BG)

A dissent: Have you ever tried to tell your mother that she is not caring for your child properly? Have you ever had to listen when your mother tells you that you are not raising your child properly? I wouldn't leave my child with a relative for all the tea in China. (CAS)

And from the other corner: Grandparents love their grandkids but can resent terribly the fact that the children are always getting dumped on them. *(Anon.)*

DAY CARE

Finding the best possible day care center for your child is difficult and sometimes fraught with anxiety and uncertainty for you *and* the child. If you must go to work and leave your child in the care of others for all or part of the day, you can look, research and feel out specific criteria so that you feel satisfied your child will be safe, happy and content about the choice of facility.

Following is a bare-bones list of things that *must* be addressed before signing up anywhere, whether it's family day care or a day care center.

Plan to visit each home or facility a few times for at least an hour during different times of the day.

Before your initial visit, plan to sit down and have a talk with the care-giver. Ask about anything that concerns you — no inquiry is too silly or stupid.

• Ask to see the sleeping area, cribs or mats.

• Look inside the refrigerator to check for cleanliness.

• See if the toys are sticky or kept reasonably clean.

The overall attitude and feeling of the place is very important, too; if everyone appears to be interacting, the care-giver appears competent and pleasant, and the children look busy and content, then you can ease up somewhat.

At the first visit, you must ask to see certification of licensing either by the state or another appropriate governmental agency.

The facility should ask for a complete medical history of your child and insist on having your pediatrician sign a paper proving the good health of your child. They should also insist on having your doctor's name and number for future reference should an emergency arrive or to check prescriptions and dosages they may have to administer.

The operating policies covering fees, illness, vacations, hours and meals or snacks should be given to you in writing.

There should be an open door policy for parents. You must never put your child in a place that isn't available to you without an appointment or agreed upon specific time. You must be able to pick up or check on your child any time of day *without advance warning.*

The number of children assigned to one care-giver should be small enough to give each child special attention. In a family day care arrangement, the care-giver should have no more than five children, and not more than two under the age of one. In a day care center, there should be one adult for every three or four infants or toddlers, one adult for every four or six two-year-olds, one adult for every seven or eight three-year-olds, and one adult for eight or nine four-year-olds.

The indoor area must be large enough to accommodate the total group.

• There should be room to play alone if the child chooses to do so.

• There should be soft pieces of furniture so children can relax if they want to.

• The indoor area should be well organized, with different activities taking place in specific areas.

• The toys should be safe, easily available, varied and plentiful.

There should be basic routines — specific snack times, nap times, story telling, singing and free play times. The children should always have an alternative activity if they do not feel like participating in the group activity.

Discipline should be maintained through careful supervision, clear limits, age-appropriate explanations and the use of "time-outs" as a disciplinary measure. No harsh discipline — such as spanking, shouting, shaming or withholding of food — should *ever* be used. The care-giver should use praise and attention to promote cooperation and helpfulness, and there should be a general feeling of warmth and affection.

If you feel your child has a special problem, the care-giver should be willing to sit down with you and discuss the problem and possible solutions.

Children's artwork or other projects should be displayed where the children can see it. Art materials should be safe and easily available. Some kind of music should be available for listening, singing or dancing, and singing should be a part of the everyday organized activity.

Safety precautions to look for:

• All toxic materials or chemicals should be stored and kept well up and out of the way.

• The electrical outlets should be covered and there should be gates on every stairway.

• There should be a completely fenced outdoor area, free of any debris including trash, animal contamination or poisonous plants.

• There should be an adequate number of smoke detectors and fire extinguishers and more than one exit out of the building.

• Car seats or safety restraints should be available for each child if they go anywhere in a vehicle.

Any accident a child has should be immediately reported to a parent. The care-giver should have both parents' telephone numbers and a backup person willing to take responsibility in case of an emergency.

If you feel uneasy at all, if you lack confidence in the care-givers, or if you find yourself worrying about your child, it's time to take action. Take an entire afternoon to stay at the home or center, and if this doesn't reassure you, find another place for your child. *(Anon.)*

Day care centers are wonderful. Children are exposed to so much more than they would be exposed to at home. They learn how to get along with other children. And the center has a large staff. If one adult calls in sick, the whole place doesn't shut down. (LL) The personnel are often trained in child development. They can help a child in a lot of ways that a plain baby-sitter cannot. (ED)

Low-income families can often get government help in placing their children in day care. Children from disadvantaged families often do better in school after they have attended day care. (DT) *Day care can cost a bundle.* Many people earn too much money for government aid, but not enough money to pay the full amount of child care. (KM) **See under** *Compromising* **in** *CHAPTER ONE: MODERN MOOLAH.*

Day care centers have definite hours that simply do not work for many people who must leave at dawn or return by six or seven in the evening. Children in this situation need additional care in those early or late hours, and it all gets complicated — a lot of shuffling and dashing around town. (EAJ)

Tiny children are usually not accepted in day care centers. A lot of centers insist on potty-trained kids only. And sick children, of course, must be cared for elsewhere. (PC)

FAMILY DAY CARE

It's great for a child to be able to stay at a home near her own. There will be a lot of other children from the neighborhood, and their ages will vary. It's like a family. (DT)

You can trust the person in charge of a family day care location. You know her. She lives right there in your neighborhood. The hours are pretty flexible, so a parent can breathe easy when the car stalls on the way home, or a late meeting is suddenly called. (CF)

Family day care costs much less than group care. *(Anon.)*

THE OTHER SIDE

Note: We received a number of contributions that didn't express as much enthusiasm about day care as the above contributors. This note summarized the feelings of many:

I made a mistake putting my child in day care so I could go back to work. I should have eaten beans every night so I could stay home with him. It was something I'll regret forever. *(Anon.)*

There were others, too. Here's a sampler:

Some children are shy. A day care environment is just too much for them. Some children have a greater need to be alone, just like some adults do. It seems unfair to push them into a situation just because they are powerless. (RE) **And see below under** *Warning Signs of Poor Child Care.*

Family day care: In a family day care setting, you can't be sure what kind of care your child is getting. The adult in charge probably hasn't had any training in what she is doing. She's playing it by ear. (ML)

The person who runs a family day care location may be tempted to take on more children than she can handle in order to make more money. How can she give all the children the proper amount of supervision? (CO'N)

You might come to pick up your child and find that she has been watching television all day long. Wouldn't you do the same if you had eight kids in your house? (DS)

If the care-giver in a family day care gets the flu, no day care that week. Then what? (SD)

THE GOVERNMENT AND DAY CARE

Ask parents if they think the federal government ought to ensure day care for everyone who needs it, and they'll all say, "You bet." Then ask them if they think the federal government should get into the business of taking over the rearing and nurturing of infants. (DB) **See under** *Day Care, above.*

WARNING SIGNS OF POOR CHILD CARE

• *If after a reasonable period of time your child still seems unhappy* or too upset to go to the home or center, or if she suddenly becomes so, you must assume something is wrong and attend to it. This is particularly true if your child talks of being afraid, or even seems afraid to be left, or seems quiet and shy in the care-giver's presence.

• *If the care seems indifferent* and you notice children being left unattended for long periods of time outdoors *or* indoors.

• *If your child seems to have an inordinate number of bruises,* cuts or scrapes that cannot be explained comprehensively by the care-giver.

• *If the care-giver seems harried,* rude, shouts or seems indifferent to the child or job in general, or if, when you express any concern about your child, the care-giver seems defensive or claims not to know about any problems.

• Again, *if you're not permitted to drop by* any time you choose or are not allowed into the play, sleep or eating areas. (KM, LL, ED)

DAY CARE WITH DAD

A dad's duty is to help with parenting however he can. However,

Men aren't made to be mothers. Women are. Confusing the two roles may make it easier for you, but it won't do baby or Dad or — in the long run — you any good at all. (AD) **See under** *FACTS OF LIFE,* **above.**

TOYS 4 TOTS

From the sensible to the expensive, toys are musts if you have children. You'll get them from grandparents, aunts and friends, you'll even feel compelled to buy a bunch of them yourself.

THE FIRST AND FOREMOST RULE

is to buy safe toys. Every parent's main concern is that all the parts will stay intact and that nothing is swallowable. Of course, all parents also want their kids to be special, intelligent and above average. So do the grandparents.

A report from the front counter: In my five years of retail toy sales experience, I've heard, at least three times a day, "My grandchild is so advanced for her age." All grandparents believe this, and, when we have children of our own, we do, too. The truth is, the suggested ages printed on puzzles, books and most toys are there for a reason. Buying a child a toy beyond his or her age will cause frustration and often tears.

Sometimes the issue is financial. Here you have two choices. Either let the grandparents buy that particularly fancy item or, what the hell, buy it yourself and lie to your husband about the price. Both are dangerous choices. We should at least buy one "spendy" item for our children so that we can use this against them as teenagers.

Two items in particular come to mind that I have purchased that were indeed out of my price range. When I first discovered that I was going to have a child, I was so overwhelmed with joy that I bought an expensive plush animal of very fine quality. I have seen my daughter play with this toy twice. Once, when we were baby-sitting a puppy, she gave it to the dog to play with, and the second time she dressed it in training pants and stuck it in the toilet.

The other expensive toy I purchased for my daughter was an antique wooden rocking horse, which was a "bargain" at half price. My daughter does occasionally sit on the horse, but only when my husband and I promise to lie between the rockers. My daughter says she saw this on television. What she was watching is anybody's guess.

My point is, of course, that you *let the grandparents buy the expensive toys.* They enjoy

buying what they could never afford for you, and it keeps them from buying ugly clothes. **See** *TOYS-R-THEM* **in** *CHAPTER SIX: MODERN MERCHANDISE.*

Be aware of the revenge of the grandparents. This is when they purchase musical toys like poppers for the baby and then later, for the preschooler, they buy toy vacuums, lawn mowers, drums, horns and other obnoxious toys.

They will present these items to your child with the utmost glee and with a special twinkle in their eye. This will make the child think this is a "special" toy, to be played with often — much more often than you would like.

So remember, shop carefully, ask for assistance, and always read the boxes for pertinent information for ages, safety standards. Different magazines offer advice on toy shopping, especially at the gift-giving seasons. (KR)

PRESENT SENSE

For a newborn, choose a colorful, lightweight toy of smooth material. Avoid anything that might break, including stuffed animals that have potentially removable eyes or noses. Don't give crib toys, like mobiles, that have any cords, loops or strings that will hang down into the crib.

When babies get to the crawling around stage is when one must purchase safe toys. Kids can find a way to poke an eye on a stuffed teddy bear, it seems, so buy wisely, always remembering to purchase a toy according to age and skill level.

Giving a child a toy that's too simple is boring, while one that is too complicated or too heavy is frustrating and dangerous.

For two-year-olds, simple toys that can be taken apart and put back together again are best. Watch out for sharp edges or small parts that could be swallowed. Books start to be appreciated now — elementary picture books with numbers and letters that go with the picture.

For three-year-olds, things start to pick up. Action toys are good — cars, wagons, things to fill up, push and pull around. Remember, as with two-year-olds, watch out for parts that could be stuck up a nose, into an ear or down a throat. Books can now prove exciting — simple stories understood and mimicked. Crayons and coloring books or tablets of plain paper are fun, but buy nontoxic crayons. A tricycle can be mastered without difficulty.

Four-year-olds want to be grown-ups, silly things, and want trucks, tractors, and dollies. Some children can be trusted to play with electric products like tape recorders and video machines — but play it by ear, it's a big investment. Watercolor sets, pastels, blunt scissors and reams of construction paper are fulfilling and fun. Sports equipment also comes into play at this stage — footballs, bats and balls. *Five-year-olds* will tell you what they want, thanks to TV, and you must use your own discretion and common sense. Some children aren't ready for scissors, for instance, until they're about twelve, so be careful, you could get hurt. (KK)

DISCIPLINE

Easy, now. You know how kids are — standing around the playground telling tales of restriction atrocities and homework hell. To kids, parents are personal Stalins.

FOR THEIR OWN GOOD, RIGHT?

Your child needs discipline to develop self-confidence, self-respect and dignity.

Discipline consists of teaching and limiting, not screaming and spanking. Children learn to develop inner controls by your example, your respect, acknowledgment and encouragement of their achievements; your guidance and insistence on cooperation; and by the limits you set on their compulsive behavior.

This is a process by which you gradually pass along your values and your sense of meaning and purpose of living. (KK) **See** *Teach Your Children Well* **in** *CHAPTER FOUR: MODERN P's & Q's.*

Not one more step: You must set limits even though they — and you — will be met with resentment. Remember to change the limits and expectations you want to enforce as your child grows. Never feel guilty about insisting that these rules be met, as they represent your value system. (LC)

If you can say no to your child without exploding or feeling guilty, consider yourself a successful parent. (KK)

Don't confuse love with indulgence. If you really love your child, you must say *no* when necessary. *(Anon.)*

FOOD TORTURE

The green bean dilemma: After listening to my children complain about squash for dinner on Monday and green beans on Tuesday, on the third night I offered both leftover squash and green beans and told them they could choose whichever they wanted. Because they felt they were getting off easy, they each ate one vegetable without further complaints. (NJLo)

When I was a little girl of ten or less, I used to thumb through my mother's *Baby and Child Care* book by Dr. Spock. My memory is a little shaky all these decades later, but I believe I remember something about bananas. Something like if your child wants to eat nothing but bananas and apple juice for three weeks, let him. His body knows what it wants, and after a few weeks, your child will get back on track on his own. Doesn't that sound smart? Keep offering all the good foods, and right will triumph. Would you holler at a dinner guest over a pile of peas? Of course not. Respect your baby. (AA)

I have seen children as old as nine weep over unfamiliar food. Don't force it. Offer it. And then be *polite* about it. Put a well-balanced meal in front of your children. If they don't want to eat it, say, "Gosh, I'm sorry, but that's dinner. That's all there is until breakfast." If they don't eat dinner, perhaps they will approach their breakfast with a greater gusto. And they'll survive the night, really. (CWC)

KID KASH

Allowances are a form of positive discipline. If you would give your child discipline, make her a capitalist. *(Anon.)*

When my preschooler receives holiday or birthday money we keep it in a special place of his choosing. On trips to the store, he decides how much to take along and what to buy. He completes his "business transaction," receives his change, and off we go.(OF)

When your children receive gifts of money, you may want to use this cash as a nest egg, for college perhaps. Put the money in a bank savings account or invest it in savings bonds or mutual funds in the child's name. You will not have to pay taxes on the first $500 of interest that the child's money earns; you don't even have to file a tax return on the money. The child will need to have a personal social security number and will need two pieces of original identification to get it. (EJo)

MINOR MANNERS

Screamers: A lot of people only yell at their children. Nag and bitch and scold. Would they do that to a friend? Would they do that to someone they work with? Would they do that to someone they love? Why would parents do it to their babies? (EC) **See under** *CIVILITY* **in** *CHAPTER FOUR: MODERN P's & Q's*.

Explain the rules that you make, and stick to them. If you say "no," mean it. But don't spank a child in front of others. It is too embarrassing for them. Why mortify a child — or anybody else for that matter? (EJo)

MODERN MOVES

Moving from one place to another is hard enough for grown-ups. For children, it's hell on wheels.

JUNIOR PARTNER

Include your children in the search for a new home. If you are house hunting, take them with you. Reduce their feelings of powerlessness. If you buy a house that is far away, have pictures to show your children of the house, the neighborhood, and the school. (EKF) **See** *Docu-Roids* **in** *CHAPTER ELEVEN: MODERN WOMAN AT EASE* **for an idea.**

Let the children help arrange the furnishings in their new room. It may comfort them to have the new room in a similar arrangement. Give a child every opportunity to say good-bye to her old home and friends. Let her help pack her own things and carry them out of the house. (MO'B)

NEW CIRCLES

If your child has a favorite activity, try to sign her up for a similar program in the new community before you even get there. This way she can begin to find a new circle of friends immediately, and in a familiar and enjoyable context. (WH)

If you can move late in the school year, try to do so. New teachers will have well-established classes by then and will have more time to devote to your child. Also, a child will have a summer to look forward to and new friends by the time summer comes. (ME)

MOTHER LODE

The accumulated lore of Momdom: Motherly messages from our far-flung correspondents.

SALLY IN THE ALLEY

Take your toddler to a bowling alley or a roller rink. It's fun for you and the child is totally occupied. Children *can* skate and they *can* push a ball down the alley. It's cheap and it sure beats sitting home watching cartoons. (KL)

TRUST FUNDS

Set up a trust fund for your child's future. Look for an income-producing mutual fund or a custodian account along with a mutual fund.

Mutual fund possibilities include corporate bond funds, government-secured funds, a taxable income fund, or a Treasury fund. You must get a child a social security number to obtain any of these. See the trust officer at your bank. (KK)

DOCUMENTS

Keep your child's birth certificate, medical records, social security number, passport and any bond or fund certificates in a locked metal box, along with the dated envelope containing the curls from his first haircut. (KK)

Keep an accurate and up-to-date health record of your children, including all immunizations. Often nursery schools require this information before accepting a child, and if you move you'll need all the information to give to the new pediatrician. It's a good idea to keep a photocopy of it all for your own.

Before your child can be accepted to public or most private schools, she will need immunizations against diphtheria, tetanus, pertussis, polio, measles, rubella and mumps.(KL)
See *Immunizations,* **above.**

TOW HEADS

If at all possible, buy a bike trailer to cart your children around in. They love it. It's something you can use to improve your health, slow down the day, and it's safer than a bike seat attached to your bike. Remember to get the kids their own helmets, though. (PMu)

TAKE A MEETING

Just because you're a Modern Woman doesn't mean your Modern Kids have to be neglected because of your busy schedule. Instead of watching two hours of sitcoms with your children, use the time to discuss school, their friends, and other aspects of their lives.   An hour of family reading time in the evening will be far more rewarding to you and your children than reruns of "Family Ties." (SJH)

LITTLE MISTAKES

Kids are people, too. They make mistakes. It's all too easy for you to do a chore they were supposed to do and "do it right the first time." Resist this temptation and allow your children to learn as they work through a project. This will teach your child responsibility and self-respect. (SNo) **See under** *Oops!* **in** *Executive Actions* **in** *CHAPTER ONE: WOMEN AT WORK.*

THE AGE OF DISCOVERY

While putting clean socks in your daughter's third dresser drawer between the clean underwear and her concert ticket stubs, you find birth control pills. What should you do?
   Don't:
   • Scream at anybody
   • Fall into a hysterical heap blaming yourself as a failure
   • Run to your husband or anybody else until you've had a chance to collect your thoughts
   Instead, try one of these:
   • Discuss the matter with your husband. Decide if the confrontation should be a team effort. If so, organize your game plan fully before talking to your daughter. If you both agree that you should do the talking, solicit his help anyway in planning your next move.
   • Remember what you were doing at her age and consider the societal difference today.
   Also see under *STDs* **in** *CHAPTER THIRTEEN: THE MEDICINE CABINET* **and have your child read it.**
   • Approach your daughter in a friendly but serious way and talk about it.
   • Tell her that you know what's going on and encourage an open discussion.
   • Let her know that although you may not approve, you know you can do nothing to stop her. Also you trust her enough to make the right decision.
   • Tell her that you are pleased that she is mature enough to arrange for birth control — but do not miss the opportunity to tell her that she could wind up with something much worse than a baby unless she uses condoms in addition to her pills.

Lastly, you must remember that you do have the ability to take away her driver's license, but also that you do not have the ability to keep her from driving.

These points should also be kept in mind on the day you find a package of condoms in your son's drawers. (If you'll pardon the play on words.) (AKa)

WOMEN AND CHILDREN FIRST

Don't be afraid to put your children's needs first. It's very fashionable to be self-this and that, but children cannot speak up for themselves. Don't be *Big Chill* sellouts when it comes to your children. (PMu)

BRIGHTER LIGHTS

Is there any way to encourage a bright child? Yes! Spend time with her. In the school classroom, volunteer your time (the teachers will love it); by doing this you demonstrate that you believe in education and the importance of the way your child is spending the major part of the day. A special interest may show up in the classroom that you can further facilitate at home. (JA)

Read to your child every night at bedtime for the first eight or nine years. Then forever after the smell of books and the feel of the paper and the sound of turning pages will be ingrained so deeply in your offspring that she will always be drawn to books. It's not hard to recognize people with this sort of childhood memory. When they pick up a book they open it up first thing and breathe in the smell. When people look like they are going to eat a book, it means they were read to as children, and they are lucky. (PJ)

A music lesson: Children become involved in school and after-school activities and do not want to give up time for music lessons. What worked with my daughter was success in finding teachers for lessons *before* school. Even the teachers appreciated having a child fresh and relaxed and not anxious to be at play. Sometimes lessons before school enable the parent to be in attendance — something especially good for five- and six-year-olds. (HT)

Art: When she was eighteen months old, I bought my daughter her first set of Crayolas and hoped for the best; either she would eat them and later become a computer analyst, or she would learn to draw and become a "starving artist" who would live at home until she was at least thirty.

Actually, she took to them quite well, and in turn my refrigerator became an artist's gallery. At first, I would leave up as many pictures as there were magnets. Then I began to trade new pictures for old ones, but as a proud mother of an "only child" I had not the heart to throw out any of these masterpieces. My solution: I took an ordinary notebook and began punching holes in the sides of each page. I could then put them away for the day when she would be old enough to appreciate my efforts.

She already enjoys the fact that Mom keeps her pictures and that she has her own book. The grandparents also enjoy this when visiting, because they can see her artful endeavors and her progress.

I categorize the drawings by using notebook dividers and placing them by age. One could even put them into intricate categories by whether they are colors, paintings, or pencil drawings. (KR)

The question is ... Remember how the teacher went on and on and somebody would interrupt with something and the teacher would say, "That's a very interesting point that we will be sure and get back to," but no one *ever* got back to it?

When your child asks a question, *that's* the time to reply. (RS)

A LITTLE ADVICE

Giving advice to a child? Know what you're talking about, and if you don't, admit it. Give advice in small dosages. Get to the point and shut up. Don't preach. And don't be angry if your advice is not followed. (KK)

A NOTE ON CONTRIBUTORS

We only know a few of the people listed here, and we know that some of the people listed here used phony names because they wouldn't be caught *dead* talking about sex or something else. Not only that, but we awarded anonymity on request.

We figured anybody nice enough to write this book for us ought to be left alone.

But we didn't extend that courtesy to their copy. We rewrote and edited everything we received, and when we received duplicate contributions, we either credited all contributors or the best one.

ACKNOWLEDGEMENTS

We thank our mothers and fathers for all the obvious things, and we thank the men in our lives for their support, tolerance and patience during the compilation and writing of *The Modern Woman's Guide to Life*.

We also owe thanks to our editor at Harper & Row, Craig D. Nelson, who was there when we needed him and wasn't when we didn't. Natalie Ross at Harper & Row gave us good advice, and so did our agent, Meredith Bernstein, while Jenna Hull at Harper & Row gave the manuscript the final push it needed. April Reinking read the chapters on shopping and wardrobe and not only made valuable editorial suggestions, but also contributed much useful information. The chapter dealing with make-up was read with care by Ellen Sara Popiel, whose expertise and generous advice was incorporated into the text. Both women, incidentally, didn't agree with everything in those chapters, and any errors which exist are ours, not theirs. Denis Boyles, Alan Rose and Alan Wellikoff, the authors of *The Modern Man's Guide to Life* broke the trail for us and thereby made our professional lives a little easier. All three were very helpful with their advice and suggestions.

Spence Waugh provided the kind of support only a good friend can provide, while Morton's Gourmet Deli in Baltimore, Maryland, provided a wide range of liquid refreshment. The Shirley-Madison Inn in Baltimore — and especially the manager, Ellen Steininger Roberts, and her assistant, Monica Gesue — gave us extremely comfortable shelter during the final, busy stage of manuscript completion.

The Modern Woman's Guide to Life was produced by Smith Graphics in Spokane, Washington, whose talented proprietor, John Smith, worked far harder than he had to in order to insure the visual quality of the book. The design of the book was the work of Alan Rose, who also designed *The Modern Man's Guide to Life*. The wonderful illustrations are by our colleague, Elizabeth Chapman.

Finally, we thank those people whose names appear below. In every sense, this book would have been impossible without them. (EC, MK, KK)

The contributors listed below appear alphabetically according to the first initial. We thank them all.

AA	Abby Almquist
AAD	Audrey Ann Dwinnell
AB	Alicia Baeder
ABe	Andrea Becker
ABo	Amy Bookman
AC	Arlene Carroll
AD	Alice Derocher
ADe	Alexis Dellar
ADu	Amelia Dunlop
AE	Amy Eakins
AF	Alicia Fennen
AG	Ann Gooden
AJ	April Jordan
AK	Alison Kaler
AKa	Annette Kallestad
AKK	Alice Kelly-Klundt
AL	Adele Langley
ALu	Alicia Lund
ALy	Agnes Lyman
AM	Amy Montgomery
ANP	Alexandria N. Phelan
AO	Arla Oberst
AOp	Andy Opland
AP	Aileen Platter
AR	April Reinking
ARo	Alan Rose
ARL	Anne Rene Lundquist
AS	Anne Scitovsky
ASt	Angie Strom
AT	Annie Taggart
ATT	Amy Anne Todd
AW	Audrey Waters
AY	Amanda York
AZ	Avi Zijonc
BA	Beryl Ashby
BB	Barbara Balocco
BC	Becky Capehart
BD	Billy Dane
BDe	Beverly Deforrest
BG	Bonnie Golden
BH	Betsy Hood
BK	Bett Kellogg
BL	Bridget Lawton
BLo	Brenda Loring
BM	Becky Moynihan
BN	Beth Neville
BNN	Bonnie N. Negretti
BNo	Barbara Noonan
BNy	Barbara Nylander
BP	Bob Peterson
BPr	Bobbie Price
BR	Bea Ramona
BS	Bonnie Strandberg
BT	Brenda Traynor
BV	Bev Vance
BZ	Bev Zamora
CAF	Carole A. Freeland
CAFu	Cathy A. Fugitt
CB	Cecilia Bates
CBe	Charlotte Beals
CBC	Casey B. Comstock
CC	Cheryl Cannon
CD	Cammie Dearmore
CDe	Cindy Deife
CF	Cecile Fouche
CFo	Cherie Fournier
CFu	Carol Fujmura
CG	Cynthia Graham
CGr	Connie Grove
CH	Chris Hedsstrom
CK	Cheryl Kimsey
CLC	Connie Lee-Compogno
CL	Celia Lydig
CLB	Claire Lyn Berezay
CM	Colleen Mitchell
CMu	Carol Murakami
CMF	Connie Marie Fulsaas
CNC	Claudia N. Comer
CO'N	Carol O'Neill
CP	Cristine Paquette
CR	Consuelo Ruiz
CS	Connie Strindberg
CWC	Cory W. Churchwell
DB	Denis Boyles
DBe	Deane Bertrand
DBG	Dana Benetti-Grimm
DBK	Dee Beresford Kalke
DC	Dicki Connors
DD	Denise Delgado
DDy	Dierdre Dyson
DE	Duffy Eves
DF	Dora Franson
DFS	Donna Fink-Selkirk
DJ	Deborah Justice
DK	David Kenney
DKu	Deanna Kurtz
DL	Donna Lesker
DLe	Diane Lewiston
DML	Darlene May Lubinsk
DRD	Dawn R. Duffner
DRW	Daphane R. Washington
DS	Diane Smithson
DT	Debra Tomlin
DW	Daphne Ware
DWi	Donna Winkler
DY	Daniel Yourde
EA	Elizabeth Allen
EAn	Eliza Andrews
EAJ	Edith Anne Jenkins
EC	Elizabeth Chapman
ED	Estelle Dullanty
EE	Erica Edington
EF	Evelyn Flack
EH	Ellyn Huether
EJ	Elena Jahan
EJo	Evie Johnson
EK	Emma Kinchen
EKF	Eva Konrad-Fogel
EL	Eileen Lee
ELe	Emily Lepagnol
EP	Ellen Payne
ER	Elisabeth Riddle
ES	Edward Sedley

ESP	Ellen Sara Popiel	HT	Helen Tombropoulos	KL	Kim Lorenzo
ESR	Ellen Steininger Roberts	HYW	Holly Yerkes-Whitney	KLi	Kathy Linderman
FC	Felicia Cummings	ID	Irene Dashiell	KM	Kit Menscher
FDD	Faith Dark-Drinnen	IJ	Ingrid Juvonen	KN	Kerry Neidiger
FG	Francine Granger	IM	Ilene Morgan	KO	Karen Oldershaw
FL	Florida Lee	IR	Irene Rue	KPH	Karla Pierce-Hampton
FLi	Frannie Lizotte	IS	Ila Skoko	KR	Kristal Rogers
FM	France Metcalf	ITG	Irene T. Gibbs	KRe	Kathy Reese
FR	Fran Robinson	JA	Janeen Ash	KRT	Karel Reid-Tuveson
FS	Fern Squires	JAO'N	June Anne O'Neill	KT	Katherine Tibbet
FSR	Fay S. Reardon	JC	Joanne Catlyn	KY	Kit Young
FU	Freddie Uryga	JCS	John C. Smith	LA	Laurel Aponte
FW	Flo Wong	JDP	Jerri D. Payne	LAM	Lisa A. Morrison
GB	Gayle Bonander	JG	Julia Gauthier	LB	Linda Blackburn
GC	Georgia Cattaneo	JGr	Julie Graham	LBa	Libby Bassett
GD	Gerry Dobson	JGu	Joe Guarisco	LBo	Laurie Bourke
GF	Geneva Franstead	JH	James Hackett	LBY	Linda Barnes Yendwine
GG	Gregory Gaynor	JJ	Jo Jefferson	LC	Laura Canipe
GGi	Glenda Giles	JJe	JoBeth Jensen	LCh	Landy Chapman
GH	George Hauser	JK	Jennie Keane	LDB	Lisa Davis-Burnes
GI	Gail Isemann	JL	Jane Lassel	LDC	Lorna Dinsmore-Connerly
GJ	Georgie Jooreas	JLo	Joanne Lotte	LD	Leona Dremma
GL	Gayle Langford	JLH	Jamie Lynn Hardy	LE	Lee Enman
GM	Gina Mayer	JM	Joan Manners	LEv	Lyn Evans
GMH	Ginny Matte-Higgs	JMcC	Judi McClure	LFD	Laura Francine Deterding
GN	George Norisada	JMcE	Jerry McEvoy	LG	Leah Glastre
GS	Grace Stanley	JN	Jean Nakata	LH	Lacey Hanks
GSt	Gregg Stebbins	JNY	Jessica Neal-Taylor	LHi	Lois Hiderman
GT	Ginnie Thirson	JS	Judi Steinauer	LHo	Laurie Howard
GTB	Gloria Tan-Bennett	JW	Jonathan Wendell	LJ	Lorraine Jenners
GY	Gabrielle Young	JWa	James Walsh	LK	Liza Kellerman
HC	Helen Campo	JWe	Jan Wells	LKe	Lucinda Kelway
HE	Hope Egland	KAL	Kimberly Ann Larson	LL	Lou Leiberman
HG	Heather Grier	KB	Kathy Beninger	LLW	Linda Lynne Wilks
HH	Hattie Hempel	KD	Katherine Dodd	LM	Lynn Maughm
HJS	Heidi James-Smythe	KDa	Karen Davis	LN	Linda Neilson
HK	Harriet Kellman	KF	Katie French	LOP	Leslie Ontiveros-Price
HKa	Helen Karagiozis	KGG	Kristine Grier-Griswold	LP	Lori Plovanic
HL	Hannah Lewis			LPo	Leslie Poole
HLi	Hope Lyons	KH	Kirsta Hake	LPu	Linda Purcell
HN	Heather Noel	KHe	Karla Helzer	LS	Leslie Skeens
HPD	Helen P. Day	KJ	Kathleen Jagoditsch		
HS	Hope Sholon	KK	Karen Kriberney		

LStJ	Linda St. James	NW	Neil Wolfson	RM	Rene Massett
LT	Lettie Tabor	OAH	O. Arielle Hannon	RN	Rena Nedved
LV	Lawrence Vaughn	OBL	Octavia Benneto-Lepard	RO	Rhonda Ocampo
LW	Linda Wagonner			RP	Rita Paulsen
MA	Marianne Ainsley	OL	Olivia Lorenzi	RR	Robyn Repp
MB	Molly Berstein	OT	Odette Tanas	RS	Roslyn Smith
MC	Mary Cullaway	PA	Pamela Ableman	RT	Rosemary Tinn
MD	Matthew Donally	PAG	Patti Ann Greene	SA	Sally Appleton
ME	Michelle Evers	PAN	Pam A. Northhart	SB	Sylvia Ballock
MEv	Meagan Everett	PC	Patty Crell	SBB	Sami. B. Bliss
MF	Misty Fromin	PD	Peg Dipaula	SBl	Steve Blewett
MG	Molly Gonwick	PG	Pam Galloway	SC	Sally Campbell
MGe	Monica Gesue	PH	Pat Harsh	SD	Sharon Drader
MGr	Muriel Greyerbieh	PI	Phoebe Irsfield	SEM	Sue Ellen Mishler
MH	Madeline Holyoak	PJ	Penny Jahns	SF	Sandy Flannery
MHi	Mary Hildago	PK	Pamela Konrad	SG	Sally Gower
MHL	Mary Helen Leinwall	PL	Pauline Leduc	SH	Shirley Hayes
		PLi	Pearl Lloyd	SI	Shelley Iseminger
MK	Maggie Kassner	PM	P. Mosgar	SJ	Shirley Jackson
MKa	Marcia Kay	PMu	Pamela Mull	SJo	Sheri Johnston
ML	Maude Lelevier	PN	Pat Norgata	SK	Sydney Kaiserman
MM	Max Mandyke	PO'C	Peggy O'Clair	SKo	Suzanna Kotkie
MN	Maureen Ness	PPK	Pauline P. Keefer	SL	Susan Lackley
MO'D	Madeleine O'Day	PR	Paul Reese	SLa	Stephanie Larner
MO'R	Mary O'Reilly	PS	Pamela Scott	SLo	Shirley Loew
MP	Monica Perlman	PSA	Peggy Smith Anderson	SM	Sue Morganstern
MPN	Marlene Patricia North	PSD	Patti Seibert-Donaldson	SMcP	Sandi McPhee
MS	Miriam Scheffe			SN	Steven Naccarato
MT	Michael Tyrrell	PT	Pam Talbot	SNo	Sommer Noonan
MWH	Maxine W. Hood	PZ	Paul Zehring	SS	Sue Smith
NA	Nicole Aden	RD	Ramona Descheemarker	ST	Sheila Tenyon
NAR	Nancy Anne Romoff			SV	Susan Voss
NC	Nathan Cohen	RE	Ruth Estrop	SW	Stephanie Wallings
NCo	Natalie Conway	RF	Ronnie Fecht	SWa	Spence Waugh
NF	Natalie Falkner	RFF	Renee F. Felice	SY	Selma York
NJL	N.J. Lukenbil	RGR	Rebecca Graffe-Rosen	SZ	Sandra Zorne
NJLo	Nancy Jarratt Loring	RHW	Rebecca Hahn Winters	TB	Tanya Boydson
NLW	Noreen Linda Walder			TC	Terri Christilow
NM	Nadine Magneson	RK	Rachel Kriesel	TCo	Timothy Corfield
NNR	Naomi Norcan-Rice	RL	Rene Leitheiser	TD	Trudi Daumer
NO	Nina Oliphant	RLe	Riva Leviten	TE	Toni Elavan
NS	Nora Sell	RLi	Robert Littrell	TEs	Tina Eskelson
NSc	Nancy Schwartz	RLL	Robyn Lynne Laird	TF	Theresa Folk
				TG	Teresa Graedel

TH	Timothy Hershey	TS	"Toots" Schillinger	WKu	Wally Kubitsch
THMc	Tina Holmes-McPherson	TT	Torrie Tarkington	WKuh	Winifred Kuhn
		TU	Timi Ulijohn	WL	Willy Lengyel
TL	Tink Libelman	TY	Tina Yokoyama	WN	Win Nunes
TM	Theresa Moldenhauer	UJ	Ursula Jessen	WP	William Pincannon
TMK	Teena M. Kantner	USG	United States Government	WW	Willie Wendell
TN	Tooly Novus			YB	Yvonne Bruckner
TO'C	Tammie O'Connor	VB	Valerie Bills	YJ	Yvonne Jewell
TO'D	Thomas O'Day	VL	Vanessa Lussier	YJo	Yvette Johnson
TP	Terry Partlow	VP	Vicki Poole	YL	Yves Lacroix
TR	T. Ravell	VS	Vivian Schierman	YML	Y.M. Lacey
TRe	Terri Reese	WG	Wanda Gwinn	YO'B	Yardy O'Banion
TRS	Tara Ruthern-Sutherland	WH	Wendi Hathaway	YT	Yvette Taladoy
		WK	Winnie Kent	ZL	Zsuzska Lanyi

WHAT DO YOU KNOW?

If you know something you think other Modern Women ought to know, or if there's some subject you think we forgot, make a note of it here (or on another sheet of paper) and send it to:

The Modern Woman
P.O. Box 4709
Hampden Station
Baltimore, MD 21211

The material you submit will be edited and quite possibly rewritten to conform to style and to length limitations. And all you'll get for it is your name stuck in the back of the next book, if there is one, and a hearty handshake if ever we met.

But really, it's worth it.

You're name and address are required. (If you want your name withheld, we'll do it. But we have to have something for our records.)

NAME: _____

ADDRESS: _____

_____

May we credit you by name? _____

SUBJECT: _____

_____
_____
_____
_____
_____
_____
_____
_____
_____
_____

Index

Page numbers in italic type denote illustrations

A

Abortion, 335
Abuse,
    battering, 105
    kids and sexual, 429
see also child abuse
Accidents,
    emergency tips, 312
    some splints, *313*
Acne,
    help for, 128
    folk cure for, 314
Acupuncture, 310
Adoption, 426
Adventures in travel, *383*
AIDS,
    concerns, 333
    hotline, 333
    prevention, 332
see also sexually transmitted
    disease
Airplane Travel, 398-402
    fear of, 398
Alcoholism, 314
Amtrak Reservation Number,
    1-800-USA-RAIL, 386
Answering Machines, 268
Apartment Farming,
    planters, *251*
    what to plant, 250
Applaud,
    when to, 61
Appliance Repairs, 186
Appliances, 187, 193
Art,
    buying, 113
    decorating with, 169
    kids and, 443
Art Studio,
    setting up an, 292

Assets, 33
Auctions, 116, 171

B

Babies,
    alternatives, 432
    breast feeding, 425
    crying at night, 425
    delivering your own, 424
    immunizations, 427
    signs of illness, 427
    theirs, 52
Baby-sitters,
    alternatives, 432
    choosing, 431
    day care, 432
see also child care
Bad Habits,
    how to break, 72
Bathing Suits, 150
Beauty,
    homemade, 131
Bed-wetting,
    folk cure for, 315
Behavior,
    on the job, 7, 9, 10
see also Etiquette
Birth Control, 333-336
    alternative, 335
Birth Defects,
    indications of, 423
Bleeding,
    circulatory pressure
        points, *323*
    first aid for, 322
Blood Pressure, 315
Blowout Avoidance, *374*
Bluffing,
    in poker, 414
    orgasms, 94
Boat Travel, 386-387

Boat Travel *(cont.)*
    booking passage, 387
    preparation, 387
    tipping, 387
Body Camouflage, 126
Bones,
    broken,
        first aid for, 322
    osteoporosis, 319
    skeleton and internal
        organs, *340*
Book Collecting, 293
Boredom, 290-291
    at work, 291
    coping with, 290
    relief from, 291
Boss,
    being the, 19, 21, 23
    being your own, 24-28
Boyfriends,
    platonic, 54
    wrong one, 53
Breakfast,
    crepes, 218
    eggs Benedict, 218
Breaking Up, 97-99
Breasts,
    men and, 83, 426
Breast Cancer,
    risk factors, 338
    self-exam for, 337
Breast-feeding, 425
Budgets,
    one that works, 34
Bull awareness, *391*
Burns,
    extent of total body
        surface, *326*
    first aid for, 325
    folk cure for, 316
Bursitis,

Bursitis *(cont.)*
  folk cure for, 316
Business Cards, 28
Buying,
  a business, 27
  a camera, 270
  a computer, 272
  a house, 38
  a mirror, 171
  a telephone, 268
  a television, 263
  a used car, 357
  à VCR, 264
  an answering machine,
    268
  art, 113
  bathing suits, 150
  books, 293
  carpets, 158
  condoms, 93
  fur coats, 150
  furniture, 168
  furniture from thrift stores,
    169
  gifts, 112
  impulse, 112
  makeup, 122
  rugs, 158
  seafood, 225
  shoes, 146
  sleeping bags, 279
  toys, 113

C

Cameras,
  pinhole, 270
  some cameras, *271*
  types, 269
see also photography
Campfire,
  building a, 279

Camping, 275-282
  ant, centipede, tiger
    awareness, *277*
  avoiding accidents, 276
  bad outdoor bugs, *281*
  bad sea items, *278*
  building a campfire, 279
  emergencies, 279
  ground-to-air signals, 280
  sleeping bags, 279
  tips, 276
Canning, 232
Car,
  buying, 356-362
  insurance, 362
  terminology, 364
Car Repair, 366-371
Cars,
  battery cables, 372
  brakes, 369
  car-buying checklist, 361
  cooling, 371
  driving safety, 376
  electrical, exhaust and
    tranmission systems, 368
    emergency repairs, 371
  fires, 375
  fuel filters, 368
  insurance, 362
  leasing, 360
  oil, 369
  options, 360
  security, 376
  seven car emergencies,
    373
  steering, 369
  suspension, 371
  what makes them run, 367
  where it is, *365*
Carpets, 158
  carpet burns, *159*
Child Abuse, 429

Child Care, 431-435
  danger signs, 435
  day care, 432
  places not to leave a
    baby, *437*
  safety precautions, 434
Child poisoning,
  preventing, 428
Childbirth,
  different methods, 421
Chlamydia, 331
Civility, 57-71
Cleaning, 171-175, 179
  clothes, 175
  kit, 172
  schedule, 173, 175
  tips, 173
Clothes,
  antique, 149
  bargain, 149
  core wardrobe, 142
  Eurosize conversion, 142
  for travel, 381
  sexy, 151
  the skirt issue, *143*
  tropical, 394
  washing, 175
see also Wardrobe
Cocktail Parties,
  crashing, 289
  how to host a, 70
Colds,
  folk cures for, 316
Color Analysis,
  choosing your colors, 139
Computers, 272-275
  Apple vs. IBM, 273
  buying a, 272
  hardware, 272
  protection, 275
  second-hand, 274
  software, 273

Computers *(cont.)*
  terminology, 274
Compliments,
  on the job, 10
Compost Heap,
  how to make a, 240
Condoms,
  buying, 93
  facts, 334
Condominiums, 40
Constipation,
  folk cure for, 317
Contact lenses, 133
Contraception,
  See birth control
Conversation,
  dinner, 68
  in bars, 67
  simple rules for, 74
  sex talk, 96
  small talk, 75
  starting a, 82
  tips, 75
Cooking, 210-236
  calorie count, 222
  fatty foods, 222
  freezing, 234
  kitchen ditchenary, 216
  measurement conversion,
    234
  methods, 236
  pasta, 221
  seafood, 225
  turkey, 221
Court,
  small claims, 297
Courtship, 83
Cowboy Bars, 50
Criticism,
  giving, 22
Crying,
  at work 9, 21

D

Date Rape, 86
Dating, 79-91
  blind, 79
  co-workers, 14
  dealing with a drunken
  date, 88
  don'ts, 87
  dressing for, 84
  good, 84
  impress your date, *85*
  who not to, 87
  who to, 87
Day Care, 432
  cons, 435
  discipline, 433
  facility, 432
  family, 434
  finding, 432
  investigating, 432
  pros, 434
  the government and, 435
see also child care
Decorating, 166-171
  basics, 168
  do it yourself tips, 169
  interior decorators, 168
  with art, 169
  with mirrors, 171
  with paint, 166
Diaper Rash,
  folk cure for, 317
Diarrhea,
  folk cure for, 317
Discipline,
  at home, 439
  day care centers, 433
see also Child Care
Divorce, 105-106
  kids and, 106
  preventing, 103

Doctors, 309-312
  eye, 312
  gynecologists, 336
  ophthalmologists, 312
  opticians, 312
  optometrist, 312
  osteopaths, 310
  quacks, 309
  when to go, 309
see also Health
Dreams, 405-407
  as therapy, 406
  escapism, 406
  friends in, 405
  journals, 405
  meeting God in, 407
  ugly and scary, 407
Drinking,
  alone, 50
  hangovers, 289
  liquor lore, 285
  martinis, 289
  what to wear, 50
Drip, *204*
Dying,
  caring for the, 350
  euthanasia, 352
  final orders, 351
  saying goodbye, 352

E

Electric Shock,
  first aid for, 328
Electrical Repairs, 193
Electricity, 193-196
  conservation, 196
  fuses and circuit breakers,
    193
  knots,loops,splices, *195*
  plug repair, *194*
Emergencies,

Emergencies (cont.)
    car fires, 375
    highway, 371
    tubal pregnancies, 423
Entertaining,
    as a single, 67
    cocktail parties, 70
    picnics, 71
    pool parties, 70
    weekend guests, 71
    with booze, 210
Etiquette,
    bar, 66
    bathroom, 64
    business, 60
    dining, 65, 67
    engagement, 62
    funeral, 65
    sibling, 426
    taxi, 61
    traveling, 394
    wedding, 63
    writing, 76
see also manners
Euthanasia, 352
Exhibitionism, 95
Eyeglasses, 134

F

Facials, 126-127
    homemade, 127
Factory Outlets, 118
False Advertising, 116
Fashion,
    building a wardrobe, 142
    color glossary, 140
    self-analysis, 141
Fat Sucking, 136
Fatigue,
    folk cure for, 317
Fences, *249*

Fire prevention, 410
Fires,
    basic tips, 325
    car, 375
First Aid, 328, 331
    camp kit, 282
    some bandages, *329*
    some reasons for
    bandages, *330*
Fish,
    buying, 225
    tanks, 418
    tropical, 418
Fish facts, *226*
Fishy business, *227*
Fitness Centers, 49
see also health
Flea Markets, 118
Flights to avoid, *399*
Flower Gardens,
    planting, 247
Flirting,
    how to, 81
    partners, 82
    silent signals, 82
Floors,
    carpets, 158
    painting, 158
    protection, 158
    refinishing wood, 156
    sanding wood floors, *157*
Flowers,
    easy-to-grow, 250
Food,
    dropping from the air, 414
    for cats, 415
    for crabs, 418
    for people, 210-236
    for thought, 343
    kids, 439
Food Torture, 439
Football, 282

Free-falling, 401
Friends,
    and their kids, 52
    defining, 54
    fighting with, 52
    losing, 53
    soul mates, 52
    vs. acquaintances, 54
Frostbite,
    first aid for, 328
    folk cure for, 317
Fruits,
    buying, 228
    determining freshness, 235
    storing, 228
Frying Pans,
    preserving, 212
    seasoning, 212
Fur Coats, 150
Furnace,
    repair, 198
Furniture,
    auctions, 171
    fixing scratches, 196
    thrift store, 117
    yard sale, 171

G

Garden,
    apartment, 250
    flower, 247
    pests, 245
    planters, *251*
    tools, 242
    vegetable, 242
Gardening,
    available area for, 239
    determining sunlight for,
    240
    garden tools, *243*
    soil, 240

Gardening (cont.)
  some more garden tools,
    244
Gazebo city, *248*
Getting rid of a jerk, *73*
Gifts,
  appropriate, 112
  for children, 438
  for weddings, 63
  horrible, 64
Glasses,
  types of, 205
Gonorrhea, 331
Grandwomen, 343-348
  advice, 343
  advocacy, 345
  attributes, 344
  discrimination, 345
  health and welfare, 346
  the government and, 345
Guest,
  how to be a, 71
Gunshot Wounds,
  first aid for, 322
Gynecologists,
  the exam, 336
  what to expect, 336

H

Hair, 131-133
  care, 131
  cuts, 131
Hangovers, 289
Head Injuries,
  first aid for, 325
Health,
  baby 427-429
  foods, 219
  hotlines, 331
  when traveling, 393
Hepatitis-B, 332

Herbs,
  how to plant, 252
  how to use, 223
Herpes, 332
Hiccoughs,
  folk cure for, 317
Home Movies, 267
Homeopathy, 310
House Security, 407-410
  complete security package,
    409
  electric engravers, 409
  fire prevention, 410
  locks, *408*
  security alarms, 409
  tips and fake-outs, 407
Houseplants,
  bulb basics, *254*
  bulbs, 253
  deserting, 255
  easiest to maintain, 256
  easy plants, *257*
  maintaining, 255
  propagation, 259
How ants get in, *170*
How to jump off a cliff, *303*
Humility,
  on the job, 11
Humor,
  on the job, 9
Husbands,
  best friend's, 53
  shopping with, 110
Hypertension, 316
Hypothermia,
  folk cure for, 318
Hysterectomy, 338

I

Immunizations,
  babies and, 427

Immunizations *(cont.)*
  travel, 393
Impulse Buying, 109
Infection,
  first aid for, 327
Insect Bites,
  first aid for, 328
  folk cure for, 318
Insomnia,
  folk cure for, 318
Insurance, 42-46
  car, 362
  disability, 45
  health, 45
  homeowner's, 42
  life, 45
  terminology, 43
  travel, 390
Internal Bleeding,
  first aid for, 327
Investments, 35-42
  for children, 441
Investment Property,
  how and when to buy, 41
IRA (Individual Retirement
  Account), 35

J

Jerk Defense, 72
Jewelry, 148
Jobs,
  getting fired, 21
  how to resign, 20
  interviewing for, 4
  looking for, 4
  promotions, 15
see also work

K

Kerosene lamps, 279

Kids,
  air travel and, 398
  art and, 443
  bed-wetting, 315
  bright, 443
  bus travel, 398
  car safety, 378
  clothes and, 145, 113
  discipling, 439
  divorce and, 106
  fun with, 441
  food and, 439
  giving advice to, 444
  in hospitals, 428
  manners, 60, 440
  mistakes and, 442
  money and, 440
  moving with, 440
  music and, 443
  parties and, 68, 70
  poisons and, 428
  sex and, 442
  sexual abuse and, 429
  sex education, 431
  shipping, 396
  toys for, 113, 436
  trust funds for, 441
Kitchen,
  basic inventory, 212
Kitchen Ditchenary, 216
Kitchen Gardens, 240
Knives,
  kinds of blades, *208*
  kitchen, 207
  sharpening, 207
  types of, 207

L

Lawyers,
  clinics, 298
  fees, 298

Lawyers *(cont.)*
  finding, 297
Leasing,
  a car, 360
Lightning Protection,
  inside, 410
  lightning awareness, *411*
  outside, 410
Lingerie, 147
Liposurgery, 136
Liquor Lore, 285
Living Alone,
  coping, 51
  eating, 50
  lonely nights, 49
  pleasures of, 51
Lover,
  best friend's, 53
  how to meet a, 79
  leaving a, 97
Luggage,
  ID tags, 382
  security, 382
  the right bag, 381
Lust,
  five sure signs of, 92

M

Makeup, 121-126
  application, 124-126
  buying, 122
  definitions, 121
  kit, 122
  the right conditions, 121
Manners, 57-71
  abroad, 394-396
  carpool, 65
  everyday rules, 58
  kids and, 60
  men and, 59
  table, 65

Manners *(cont.)*
  women and, 60
see also etiquette
Marketing Surveys, 25
Martini,
  making a, 289
Mates,
  care for a dying, 348
  screening a, 101
Matrimony, 99-105
Maximum speeds, *370*
Meat,
  grades, 228
Meat slicing techniques, *230*
Medicine,
  alternative, 310
  cabinet basics, 328
  first aid, 321-328
  folk cures, 314-321
  homeopathy, 310
see also first aid
Men,
  booze and, 288
  competing with, 9
  cooking and, 216
  fooling around clues, 99
  getting rid of, 86
  manipulating by guilt, 90
  manners and, 59
  older, 90
  sandwiches and, 228
  sexual inadequacies, 93
  things you can say to drive
    them crazy, 89
  younger, 90
Menopausal Problems,
  folk cure for, 319
Menopause, 339
Menstrual Cramps,
  folk cure for, 319
Minerals
  see also nutrition

Money,
    getting more, 16
    keeping, 34
    kids', 440
    saving at home, 196
    ways to save, 34
Money, *37*
More meat slicing
    techniques, *231*

N

Net Worth,
    figuring your own, 33
Networking, 23
Nightmares, 407
Nursing Homes, 348-350
    checklist, 349
    decisions concerning, 349
Nutrition, 339-342

O

Obscene Telephone Calls, 304
Office Politics, 16
Ophthalmologist, 312
Optician, 312
Optometrist, 312
Osteopaths, 310
Osteoporosis,
    folk cure for, 319

P

Packing,
    folding, 381
    how to, 379
    what to take, 381
Paint,
    exterior, 162
    interior, 160
    removal, 164

Painting,
    floors, 158
    tips, 164
    tools, 164
    walls, 160
Panic,
    folk cure for, 319
Papers,
    preserving, 294
Parachuting, *400,* 401
Passports,
    applying for, 382
    renewing, 382
Pasta,
    how to cook, 221
Perfumes, 134
Pests,
    bad outdoor bugs, *281*
    garden, 245
    houseplant, 260
    worm begone, *246*
Pets, 415-418
    cat anatomy, *416*
    growing grass for, 253
    fish, 418
    how to stuff and mount,
        417
    monkeys, 417
    pet sitting, 415
pH balance, 135
Photography, 269-272
Pinhole Camera,
    making a, 270
Place settings, *69*
Pickling, 233
Plant Lights, 252
Planters, *251*
Plants,
    easiest to maintain, 259
    see also houseplants
Plastic Surgery, 136
Plumbing,

Plumbing (cont.)
    faucets, 203-205
    finding leaks, 200
    fixing leaks, 205
    leaky toilets, 202
    tools, 201
Poisoning,
    first aid for, 322
Poisons, 320
Poker,
    bets, 414
    lingo, 412
    poker hands, *413*
    rules, 412
Poultry,
    chicken cutups, *224*
    thawing, 223
Prenatal care, 421
Prenatal testing, 423
Pregnancy,
    delivery techniques, 423
    prenatal care, 421
    prenatal counseling, 422
    prenatal testing, 423
    tubal, 423
Prenuptial Agreements, 102

R

Rape, 298-300
    date, 86
    types of rapists, 299
Recipes,
    breakfast, 218
    chicken breasts, 220
    coleslaw, 221
    dips, 218
    marinated lamb, 221
    meat loaf, 219
    nutty lentil salad, 211
    stew, 220
    tuna casserole, 220

Recipes *(cont.)*
turkey, 221
western chili, 211
Recognizing,
a come-on, 83
a good deal, 169
a married man, 84
Refrigerator Maintenance, 191
Relationships,
ending peacefully, 97
sharing in, 102
when to end, 98
with friends, 52
Repairs,
appliance, 186
car, 366
electric plug repair, *194*
electrical, 193
emergency car, 371
furnace, 197
furniture scratches, 196
knots,loops,splices, *195*
some basic tools, *183*
water heaters, 187
windowpane, 182
wobbly chair, 196
Retirement Planning, 35
Résumés, 4
Rugs,
quality of, 158

S

Safety,
car safety, *378*
highway, 371-376
personal, 300
sexual, 331
when traveling, 396
Scissors,
scissor anatomy, *209*
sharpening, 210

Security,
hotels, 396
travel checklist, 388
Seeds, 242
Self-defense, 300-304
instincts, 300
methods of, 301
on the job, 15
psychology, 300
survival tips, 302
Sex, 92-97
condoms, 93
disease and, 331
disease inquiries, 92
excuses for not having, 96
in public, 94
kinky, 94
oral, 95
possibly safe, 333
safe, 332
talk, 96
unsafe, 333
see also sexually transmitted
diseases
Sexual Abuse,
prevention tips, 429
Sex Education, 431, 442
Sexual Harrassement, 13
Sexual Inadequacies,
men's, 93
your own, 94
Shock,
first aid for, 322
Sick,
calling in, 11
see also first aid
Singing,
public, 64
Shoes, 145-147
alternating, 145
athletic, 146
buying, 146

Shoes *(cont.)*
high heels, 146
protecting, 146
returning, 110
tips, 147
trees, 145
work, 146
Shopping,
auctions, 116
by mail, 110
complaints, 114-116
factory outlets, 118
flea markets, 118
for a car, 357
for a used car, 357
for trouble, 86
home, 114
out of season, 113
spree planning, 109
thrift, 117
tips, 110-114
what to wear, 109
with your husband, 110
Skeleton and internal organs,
340
Skin,
cleansing, 129
conditioning, 130
dry and oily, 128
exfoliating, 130
moisturizing, 130
Skin Ailments, 128
Small Claims Court, 297
Smoking,
in carpools, 65
rules for, 61
Snakebites,
first aid for, 327
Some things to see and do, *380*
Spices,
how to use, 223
rule of thumb, 216

Splint,
    making a, 322
Squeaks, sticks, drags, rattles,
    167
State Department, the,
    emergencies, 390
    passports, 390
Stains, 176-179
    greasy or nongreasy, 177
    removal guide, 177
    the three rules, 176
    water, 174
Sexually Transmitted
    Diseases, 331-333
Striptease,
    how to do a, 151
Stroke,
    prevention of, 321
Sunglasses, 133
Syphilis, 332

T

Talking,
    job interviews, 6
    tips, 18
Telephones, 268
Televisions,
    how to buy, 263
    in bedrooms, 263
Terminally Ill,
    caring for the, 350
The Peter Pan syndrome, *397*
Thrift Stores, 117
Timing,
    business meetings, 17
Tipping,
    abroad, 395
    at home, 395
    at sea, 387
    in bars, 66
    on the rails, 386

Toilets,
    fixing leaky, 202
    tampons in, 200
Tools,
    appliance repair, 187
    basic, 182-186
    garden, 242
    painting, 164
    painting supplies, *163*
    plumbing, 201
    some basic tools, *183*
    some more basic tools,
        184
Tornadoes,
    preparing for, 410
Toys,
    safe, 436
    the right ages, 438
Train Travel, 384-386
    accommodations, 386
    companions, 385
    tipping, 386
    tips, 385
Travel,
    business, 389
    by bus, 398
    by cargo ship, 386
    by plane, 398, 402
    by train, 384-386
    dressing for, 381
    etiquette, 394
    foreign gestures, 395
    health tips, 393
    immunizations, 393
    insurance, 390
    luggage, 382
    medical tips, 392
    packing for, 379
    securing your home, 388
    traveler's aid, 392
    vacations, 379
    with kids, 377

Travel Agents, 388
Tripping, *5*
Turkey,
    choosing one, 223

U

Used Cars,
    buying, 357
    test driving, 357
    tips for buying, 358-359
Utensils,
    basic kitchen, 212
    frying pans, 212
    kitchen equipment must-
        haves, *214*
    knives, 207
    silverware must-haves,
        215
VCR,
    buying, 264
    programming, 267
    recording, 266
VCR tip, *265*
Vegetable Garden,
    arranging, 242
Vegetable Gardening, 245
    easy-to-grow, 242
Vegetables,
    basic, 219
    buying, 229
    determining freshness, 235
    storing, 229
Venereal Warts, 332
Visas,
    applying for, 384
    transfers, 384
Vitamins, 339

W

Walls,

Walls *(cont.)*
  patching, 164
  wallpaper tips, *161*
  wallpapering, 160
  washing, 166
Wardrobe,
  for Paris, 379
  vacation, 381
Washer and Dryer
  Troubleshooting, 191
Washer/gas dryer, *192*
Water Heaters,
  electric water heater, *189*
  gas water heater, *188*
  maintaining, 199
  repairing, 187

Wedding,
  planning a small, 63
Where to meet people, *80*
Windows,
  cleaning, 179
  screen repair, *181*
  sticky windows, *180*
  windowpane replacement, *178*
Wine,
  babble, 287
  decanting, 286
  etiquette, 68
  glasses, 206
  how to read a label, 287
  storage, 286

  varieties, 285
Work,
  adversaries at, 15
  at home, 26
  dressing for, 16
  kids and, 3
  taking meetings at, 17
Work Injuries, *12*
Working, 28
  for yourself, 24
Wrong moves *8*

Y

Yeast Infections,
  folk cure for, 321